CULTURAL CAPITALS

Re-materialising Cultural Geography

Dr Mark Boyle, Department of Geography, University of Strathclyde, UK and
Professor Donald Mitchell, Maxwell School, Syracuse University, USA

Nearly 25 years have elapsed since Peter Jackson's seminal call to integrate
cultural geography back into the heart of social geography. During this time, a
wealth of research has been published which has improved our understanding of
how culture both plays a part in, and in turn, is shaped by social relations based
on class, gender, race, ethnicity, nationality, disability, age, sexuality and so on. In
spite of the achievements of this mountain of scholarship, the task of grounding
culture in its proper social contexts remains in its infancy. This series therefore
seeks to promote the continued significance of exploring the dialectical relations
which exist between culture, social relations and space and place. Its overall aim
is to make a contribution to the consolidation, development and promotion of the
ongoing project of re-materialising cultural geography.

Other titles in the series

Cultural Landscapes of Post-Socialist Cities
Representation of Powers and Needs
Mariusz Czepczynski
ISBN 978 0 7546 7022 3

Towards Safe City Centres?
Remaking the Spaces of an Old-Industrial City
Gesa Helms
ISBN 978 0 7546 4804 8

Fear: Critical Geopolitics and Everyday Life
Edited by Rachel Pain and Susan J. Smith
ISBN 978 0 7546 4966 3

Geographies of Muslim Identities
Diaspora, Gender and Belonging
Edited by Cara Aitchison, Peter Hopkins and Mei-Po Kwan
ISBN 978 0 7546 4888 8

Cultural Capitals
Revaluing the Arts, Remaking Urban Spaces

LOUISE C. JOHNSON
Deakin University, Australia

ASHGATE

Published by
Ashgate Publishing Limited
Wey Court East
Union Road
Farnham
Surrey, GU9 7PT
England

Ashgate Publishing Company
Suite 420
101 Cherry Street
Burlington
VT 05401–4405
USA

www.ashgate.com

British Library Cataloguing in Publication Data
Johnson, Louise C., 1953–
  Cultural capitals : revaluing the arts, remaking urban
  spaces. -- (Re-materialising cultural geography)
  1. Urban renewal. 2. Arts and society. 3. Cultural policy.
  4. Culture and tourism. 5. Cultural industries. 6. Urban
  renewal--Case studies. 7. Arts and society--Case studies.
  8. Cultural policy--Case studies. 9. Culture and
  tourism--Case studies.
  I. Title II. Series
  307.3'416–dc22

Library of Congress Cataloging-in-Publication Data
Johnson, Louise C., 1953–
  Cultural capitals : revaluing the arts, remaking urban spaces / by Louise C. Johnson.
    p. cm. -- (Re-materialising cultural geography)
  Includes bibliographical references and index.
  ISBN 978-0-7546-4977-9 (hardback) -- ISBN 978-0-7546-8917-1 (e-book) 1. Urban re-
newal. 2. Arts and society. I. Title.

HT170.J64 2009
307.3'416—dc22

2009002112

ISBN 978-0-7546-4977-9 (hardback)
ISBN 978-0-7546-8917-1 (ebook)

Mixed Sources
Product group from well-managed
forests and other controlled sources
www.fsc.org Cert no. SGS-COC-2482
© 1996 Forest Stewardship Council
FSC

Printed and bound in Great Britain by
TJ International Ltd, Padstow, Cornwall

Contents

List of Figures   *vii*
List of Tables   *ix*

1   Creating Value, Valuing Creativity   3

2   Conceptualising the Cultural Industries/Cultural Capitals   23

3   The Emergence of Cultural Capitals   55

4   Glasgow: Cultural Tourism and Design   85

5   Bilbao: The Guggenheim and Post-modern City of Spectacle   123

6   Singapore: Post-colonial City of Cultural Heritage and Performance   155

7   Geelong as a Cultural Capital? Down Under Echoes   193

8   Cultural Capitals:
     Re-valuing the Arts and Re-making Sustainable City Spaces   235

References   *253*
Index   *275*

List of Figures

1.1   Mapping Cultural Capitals 1985–2005   10

4.1   Gordon Cullen's plan for Glasgow City Centre and
       a 2005 Tourist Map   99

4.2   Mackintosh re-discovered – The Lighthouse and Mackintosh Festival   113

5.1   August Festival in the City of Spectacle 2005   146

6.1   New Asian landscapes in Singapore   168

7.1   Battle of the spectacles – Pako and Waterfront   217

List of Tables

1.1	Cultural (Goods) Trade for Australia, Canada, Singapore, Spain, the United Kingdom and the United States of America, 1980–1997	13
2.1	A framework for analysing c/Cultural Capitals	54
3.1	Economic Structures of Australia, Canada, Singapore, Spain, UK and US 1970–2000 (Gross Domestic Product Composition by Sector)	61
3.2	Embodied, Objectified and Institutional Cultural Capitals in Bilbao, Glasgow, Singapore and Geelong 1980–2008 (Selected/Published Examples)	80
5.1	Guggenheim Bilbao, Impacts (2003)	131
5.2	Embodied, Objective and Institutional Cultural Capital in Bilbao, Spain	142
5.3	Bilbao – A Post-Fordist Economy? 1975–1996	150
6.1	Ethnic composition of Singapore 1850–2000	160
6.2	The Institutional Framework for the Arts, 1820–2006	172
7.1	Economic structure of the City of Greater Geelong, 1991–2006	228
7.2	Some Dimension of Cultural Capitals in Geelong, Victoria 2008	229
8.1	Economic structure and tourist numbers in Bilbao, Glasgow, Singapore and Geelong 1980–2000	242
8.2	Numbers and proportions employed directly in the Creative Industries – Glasgow, Bilbao, Singapore and Geelong 2001	243
8.3	Bilbao-Glasgow-Singapore-Geelong as Cultural Capitals – Similarities and Differences	249

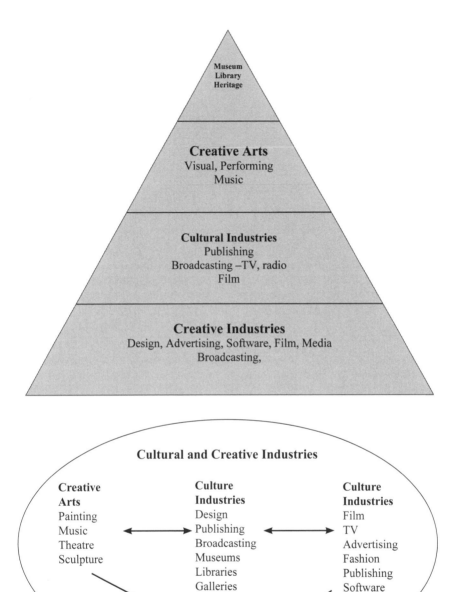

Creative industries and the creative arts – nested, separate, connected?

Chapter 1
Creating Value, Valuing Creativity

Introduction

In 1973, in pursuit of a more efficient and globalised economy, the Australian government cut tariffs on manufactured goods and de-regulated the financial system. The resulting flood of cheap textile, clothing and footwear devastated the industry of many regions and cities, including that of Geelong, the second city of Victoria. Ten years later, another round of trade liberalisation and corporate restructuring saw the closure of a major truck making plant and the downsizing of car manufacturing. Ten years after that, a local building society, into which most of the population stored their retirement savings, collapsed. With a neo-liberal state government committed to winding back the public sector, this decline in manufacturing employment was now accompanied by a reduction in service sector employment. Already struggling with its reputation as a "sleepy hollow", Geelong was now lumbered with a new label – that of a "rust bucket" city. Into this economically depressed, socially polarised and physically degraded urban landscape came the idea that the New York based Guggenheim Foundation could locate a major new gallery there. Inspired by the example of Bilbao in Spain and the words of creative city apologists Charles Landry and Richard Florida, a number of city luminaries seriously courted the idea that Geelong, industrial city of 120,000, could become a world famous Cultural Capital. Ten years on, there is no Guggenheim, but there is a refurbished waterfront, arts policies, public art and well developed plans to develop an arts precinct. The story of Geelong is a particular one, anchored in its own history, social geography and political economy. But it is also one that has remarkable parallels around the world, as cities that were once centres of industry, move to reinvent themselves as attractive centres of service sector employment, spectacle and culture. Just how an idea of renovating cities in this way emerged, and the physical, social and cultural consequences of this agenda, is worthy of closer examination, to offer lessons to others and to highlight the process by which the creative arts have been revalued in particular locations around the world over the last thirty years.

This then is a book about creating value and valuing creativity. It is a story of hope which involves an optimistic assessment of how the arts have activated individuals, rebuilt communities, enlivened the polity, guided the physical regeneration of derelict spaces and re-oriented economies. It is also a story of the contradictions and conflicts which often surround the creation and appropriation of artistic value. It is a narrative which ranges across scales – from the localised creation of art works, to city authorities marketing a new image, to companies franchising "art" across the globe – and which critically engages with academic discourses on globalisation, post-modernity and restructuring, to analyse the process of making Cultural Capitals.

Cultural Capitals are those cities that have deliberately set out to become centres of art and culture. This study will not be concerned with the global centres of culture – such as New York, Los Angeles, Paris and London – but rather with those second order cities that have attempted to remake their economies, urban spaces and societies through mobilising some aspect of "culture". Ranging across the world, from Helsinki to Singapore, from Boston to Brisbane, the move to create a Cultural Capital involves deliberately cultivating artistic activity in a place. But making a Cultural Capital has also involved the physical regeneration of abandoned industrial and port sites, a re-imagined image for a city, the creation of iconic cultural artefacts, and an economy oriented to consumption rather than production, services rather than manufacturing, the arts and knowledge industries rather than other activities. The transformation of a city into a Cultural Capital therefore involves social, economic and spatial change. Such cities often have similar histories and strategies and, because of their origin, tend to be confined to the Developed world. Beyond planned outcomes however, mobilising culture can also have unintended effects; as the arts are often uneconomic rather than profitable, may well be critical rather than politically benign, social and communal as much as individualised, and produce social and cultural rather than economic or physical transformations. This book is concerned with the intended as well as unintended effects of creating Cultural Capitals, with the contested nature of the cultures that are mobilised and place-specific examples of iconic buildings, public art works, performances, heritage precincts and community festivals – with artistic statements that have a recognised and ongoing impact on a city. This chapter will focus on what exactly is meant by Cultural Capitals and where they have been designated across the globe, Chapter 2 on their conceptualisation.

Drawing on a range of examples and academic literatures, the book will also examine why Cultural Capitals have emerged since the 1980s and how they have been theorised. As Chapter 3 will detail, for many academics, communities and governments, what has been fundamental in reshaping societies and cultures across the industrialised world has been the shift away from manufacturing for the bulk of employment and profitability towards services, and a growth in the role of culture in defining commodities, identities and economic activity. Such *restructuring* has been variously impelled by the internal dynamics of capitalism, by a reformed international division of labour and new computer-mediated technologies. Along with such changes has been an alteration in the nature of goods and services, as aesthetics, symbols and experiences replace narrow notions of utility. Governments have facilitated but also engaged with the social and spatial consequences of these changes, including high levels of unemployment and abandoned industrial, city centre and port areas. One inspired response has been to mobilise the arts to enliven these urban and social environments. Such a mobilisation has necessarily involved a re-valuing of the creative arts – as civic container, as social saviour and as economic driver. While this strategy has been criticised for seeing the arts as an instrumental vehicle for economic transformation or community development, I will argue that it is a positive response, one that also re-values creative endeavour, difference and communities.

The remainder of this chapter will offer some preliminary definitions of Cultural Capitals and offer a framework by which they can be evaluated. It will also give some indication of the global scale of this development and introduce the case study countries – Australia, Singapore, Spain and the United Kingdom. Chapter 2 will consider how cultural capital has been conceptualised by a number of disciplinary-based scholars before offering my own hybrid definition which will guide the analysis of the case studies. Chapter 3 will address the questions of why and how Cultural Capitals have emerged over the last thirty years. Subsequent chapters will focus on particular sites and forms of cultural capital: Chapter 4 will examine the post-modern city of style, consumption, celebrity and spectacle through the example of the iconic arts building – the Guggenheim in Bilbao, Spain; Chapter 5 will consider the focus within Cultural Capitals on identity-making and articulating the colonial/post colonial subject in performance and heritage precincts in Singapore; Chapter 6 on the tourist gaze as it constitutes culture, design and heritage in Glasgow; and Chapter 7 will focus on how these various elements of Cultural Capitals – the iconic arts building, performance and festivals, heritage and cultural precincts – have been emulated in a post-industrial regional city in Geelong, Australia. The final chapter looks at the ways in which international trends, exemplars and consultants have taken the discourse of Cultural Capitals across the world generating models, simulacra but also unique and ultimately valuable spaces and artistic outcomes. The remainder of this chapter will examine how the Cultural Capital – as a place and notion of value – has been defined, and present a framework by which its various dimensions can be discussed and evaluated. It will also establish the geographical spread of centres which have defined themselves as Cultural Capitals in the last 30 years and sketch their national contexts.

Questions of Definition and Evaluation

Before considering how Cultural Capitals can be delimited, it is first necessary to define some key terms. As with any attempt to fix a referent, there will be variability across space and time, a divergence of opinion, and disparities between academic and official definitions (Weedon 1987; Madden 2004). Despite these problems, a preliminary fixing of terms can and should occur. The eminent sociologist and wordsmith Raymond Williams traces three interconnected meanings of the word "culture": as describing the general process of intellectual, spiritual and aesthetic development; as a particular way of life of a people, period, group or humanity; and also the works and practices of intellectuals, especially artists (Williams 1983: 90). Drawing these dimensions together here will involve seeing *culture* as: *objects or events which are produced by those defining themselves as artists which in turn encapsulate and give meaning to the particular way of life of a people.* Within the discussion that follows, what is and who defines a "culture" on which an urban economy can be refashioned into a Cultural Capital is a key political decision, one which infuses and shapes the form, location and "value" of the outcome.

A *Cultural Capital* is a city which has recently and consciously made the arts (and often related Cultural Industries) central to its society, economy, urban form and place identity. For this book, I am not concerned with those global centres that are readily identified as centres of culture. There are a number of obvious contenders – such as London and New York for the English-speaking world or Mecca for the Islamic world– as well as cities which are recognised vortices for particular dimensions of contemporary culture, such as Paris and Milan for fashion, Los Angeles, Hong Kong and Mumbai for film. Then there are cities whose international reputation rests on their custodianship of historical cultures; such as Florence, Rome and Venice in Italy; Kyoto in Japan; Cairo in Egypt; Athens in Greece; Beijing in China and so on. All of these centres are in most senses Cultural Capitals and many have vibrant Cultural Industries (Hall 1998; Scott 2000). Their place in the pantheon of recognition is uncontested and of very long standing, but their urban economies are not in any sense under threat. There are also those cities that have been designated by various international agencies as Creative Cities. Thus, since 1990 the European Union has had a program of delimiting one or, in some years, twenty Cultural Capitals while since 1995 the United Nations through UNESCO (its Educational, Scientific and Cultural Organisation) has designated cities as members of its Creative Cities Network. These include Aswan, Egypt the first UNESCO City of Crafts and Folk Art, Popayan, Columbia designated the first UNESCO City of Gastronomy as well as cities such as Edinburgh, UK and Melbourne, Australia (Literature), Buenos Aires, Argentina, Montreal, Canada and Berlin, Germany (Design), Seville, Spain and Bologna, Italy both Cities of Music (http://portal0.unesco.org/culture/admin/ev.php?URL_ID=2780...24/8/07).

In contrast, I am interested in those cities which have been in decline; which have been industrial centres and are dealing with the agonies of spatial and economic restructuring by attempting to rebuild their economies and societies through the mobilisation of the arts. It is an ambitious and potentially progressive social and economic agenda which has and continues to offer a model to others. Such a delimitation necessarily precludes large numbers of cities, many of which are in the Developing World. By definition but also as a result of the political economy of the Cultural Industries, Cultural Capitals tend to be but are not confined to Developed economies.

The Cultural Capital agenda may or not be successful. How success is measured is itself a difficult question; but the answer needs to offer clear criteria and be an ethical guide to any appraisal. For a number of commentators on the role of the arts in urban regeneration – such as Sharon Zukin (1995) or Rosalyn Deutsche (1996) – the process is primarily exploitative or misdirected. Coming from progressive and leftist positions which critically engage with those projects which entrench conservative values as well as boost corporate profits, my argument here is that such a conclusion is unnecessarily pessimistic. Subsequent pages will demonstrate that, while many art projects can indeed boost corporate profitability and benefit a narrow range of already privileged individuals, they may not do so and may also add a great deal to a place. The assessment needs to be an open one and range across a number of dimensions. Thus, emanating from a similarly progressive politics, the evaluation here of any cultural object or activity will be in terms of their contribution to social equity, citizenship, economic well being and the enhancement of cultural identity and diversity. Therefore, a public art work, the redevelopment of an urban precinct, or a city image will be assessed in terms of its social, cultural, political and economic *sustainability*. In general, despite some problems in different localities, I will be arguing that the arts contribute in various ways to the sustainable regeneration of their cities.

The notion of *sustainability* is fundamental to many discussions of urban and "natural" environments. Central to the sustainability movement is action to ensure that current generations do not use the environment in a way as to compromise that available to future generations (Brundtland 1987; Low, Gleeson and Radovic 2005; McManus 2005). An early and ongoing ecological emphasis of the concept has been usefully extended to human populations, generating notions of social, cultural and economic sustainability. Such a broadening is often associated with the idea of "sustainable development" This idea connects the ideal of economic development with ecological preservation and enhancement (Throsby 2003a: 183). In these terms, any city and its arts agenda should ensure that:

Economically, growth can be facilitated and ongoing without damaging the physical or social environment while ensuring a wide distribution of benefits;

Socially, the city is a place of justice and care in which opportunities, services and risks are shared fairly; while action is taken to ameliorate current inequalities and benefit all;

Culturally a city should ensure the maintenance and expression of its diverse and interconnected social identities, inter and intra generational equity and protect the quality of its built environment (Throsby 2003a: 184–185);

Any Cultural Capital must also arise from and ensure meaningful political participation in decisions that effect people's lives and environments, and;

Not compromise its ecological sustainability so that a city should function so that the needs of the present will be met without sacrificing the ability of future generations to meet theirs. It should have adequate open space, bio-diversity, clean air and water.

This broad notion of sustainability will form the basis of assessing the efficacy of Cultural Capitals; to offer an ethic as well as a framework for their evaluation.

The Global Cultural Industry – Quantifying its Value

Any appraisal of the arts in urban redevelopment is confronted with the tendency to widen the definition of what is included as a creative or cultural activity. Most of this book will be concerned with specific art and cultural projects in particular places, but the broader context of such activity needs to be acknowledged – within international trends, expansive definitions of the arts within the Cultural/Creative Industries and national policy frameworks. To assess the global significance of the arts, it is necessary to locate the discussion in what has become known as the Cultural Industries – the traded, commodity form of the arts and latterly the media economy. Consistent with a broad ranging notion of "culture" but one which encompasses its commercial form, the United Nations through UNESCO, defines "Cultural Goods" as those consumer goods that convey ideas, symbols and ways of life. Such Goods inform or entertain, contribute to building collective identity and influence cultural practices. The result of individual or collective creativity – but also copyright based – those Cultural Goods recognised by UNESCO are reproduced and boosted by industrial processes and worldwide distribution (UNESCO 2000a:13). For the United Nations, the value of Cultural Goods lies with their role as expressive creative objects which are copyrighted, mass produced, traded and distributed across the globe. This definition goes well beyond a craft view of the arts to embrace industrial processes, international trade and the legal protection of intellectual property rights. It is the arts positioned within an industrial, commodified and globalised economy.

In recognition of the growth in the importance of such Cultural Goods, UNESCO's Institute for Statistics documented their global trade over the 1970s, 80s and 90s. These items "which are the result of individual and collective creativity, include printed matter and literature, music, visual arts, cinema and photography, radio and television, games and sporting goods" (UNESCO 2000b: 2). Despite this broad ranging definition, when the statistics are presented, the focus is less with the *content* of Cultural Goods than the artefacts which underpin their presentation. The notion of Cultural Goods also merges the arts with sport and leisure activities more generally. Thus while "Printed Matter and Literature" includes books, newspapers and periodicals and "Visual Arts" paintings, drawings, prints, sculptures, collectables and antiques; "Music" covers phonographic equipment and musical instruments as well as sound recordings, "Games and Sporting Goods" includes sports equipment as well as computer games; "Cinema and Photography", photographic and cinematic equipment and supplies but not films; "Radio and Television" involves receivers but not content (UNESCO 2000b). Within these categories, UNESCO notes an exponential expansion in the trade of Cultural Goods from 2.5% of global trade in 1980 (with $US47.7 billion in imports or $12 per capita) to 2.8% in 1997 (US$213.7 billion or US$44.7 per capita). Over this period, annual world trade of printed matter, literature, music, visual art, cinema, photography, radio, television sets and programs, games and sporting goods surged from $US 95,340 to US$387, 927 million (UNESCO 2000a: 15–16).

Such a trade is highly regionalised; with the countries of the Asian Pacific Economic Co-Operation group (including Australia, China, Japan, Singapore, the United States of America [US]) and the European Union (including France, Germany, Ireland, Spain and the United Kingdom [UK]) accounting for 91% of all imports and 94% of all the exports of cultural goods (up from 79% in 1970 and 85% in 1980) (UNESCO 2000b: 4). In 1998, thirteen countries were responsible for more than 80% of imports and exports (UNESCO 2000b: 8). By 1998 China had become the third most important exporter and the new "Big Five" (US, UK, China, Germany and France) were the source of 53% of cultural exports and 57% of imports (UNESCO 2000a: 15–16). The balance of trade was relatively modest for most countries, though in 1998 the most significant trade surpluses were those of Japan (US$14.5 billion), China (US$13.3 billion), Malaysia (US$5.7 billion), Mexico (US$5 billion), Ireland and the Republic of Korea. Conversely, the main consumers of imported cultural goods were the US (US$38.2billion), Hong Kong (US$38.2 billion), Canada (US$6 billion) and Australia (US$3.1 billion) (UNESCO 2000b: 5–6).

This trade reflects the global shift in manufacturing production (Dicken 2003) as much as the dominance of a few countries in the production of Cultural Goods which, to reiterate, includes the industrially produced equipment that delivers TV, radio, film and music as well as their creative content. Thus, while the United States is the largest single market for all categories of goods, Canada and the United Kingdom are prominent importers of printed matter, Hong Kong of games and sporting goods, and the UK and Switzerland for visual arts. Such import patterns have been relatively stable, though exports have reflected the decline of Japan – especially for music goods, radios and televisions – and the growth of Ireland (second only to the US as the main exporter of sound recordings) and China (especially for games and sporting goods); while the UK has become the world's leading exporter of visual arts and Mexico the major supplier into the US of radios and TVs (UNESCO 2000b: 9). In 1996 cultural products (film, music, TV programs, books, journals and computer software) became the largest US export, surpassing, for the first time, all other traditional industries, including cars, agriculture, defence and aerospace (UNESCO 2000a: 17).

In spite of a ten fold increase in the contribution of "Developing" countries to the trade in Cultural Goods, the production, trade and consumption of them is very much dominated by a few Developed countries within Western Europe, North America and South East Asia. Commenting on these statistics, Leo Goldstone (2003) observes how they record those aspects of world culture that are readily measurable and reflect the material means of communication, not the cultural content that is being communicated. Further, he notes that poorer people will pursue their cultural

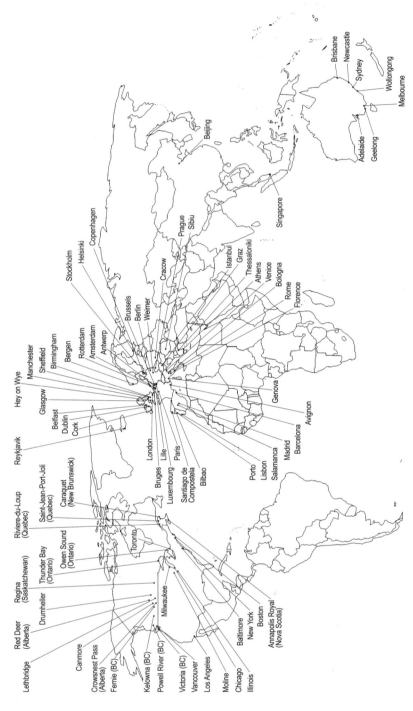

Figure 1.1   Mapping Cultural Capitals 1985–2005

Australia

Adelaide, Brisbane, Melbourne, Sydney, Newcastle, Wollongong, Geelong

Asia

Singapore, Beijing, Shanghai, Shenzen (Guangdong), Guangzhou (Guangdong), Hongkang, Xi'an (Shaanxi), Hangzhous (Zhejing), Lijiang (Yunnan), Istanbul

Canada

Vancouver, Red Deer (Alberta), Thunder Bay (Ontario), Caraquet (New Brunswick), Riviere-du-Loup (Quebec), Regina (Saskatchewan), Kelowna, (BC), Owen Sound (Ontario), Powell River (BC), Lethbridge, Canmore, Drumheller, Crowsnest Pass (Alberta), Fernie (BC), Toronto, Victoria (BC), Annapolis Royal (Nova Scotia), Saint-Jean-Port-Joli (Quebec), Edmonton (Alberta), Como Valley (BC), Moose Jaw (Saskatchewan), Baie-Saint-Paul (Quebec), Wendahe (Quebec), Surrey (BC), Nanaimo (BC), Morden (Manitoba), Sackville (New Brunswick), Trois-Rivieres (Quebec), Fredericton (New Brunswick), Carquet (New Brunswick)

Europe

Athens, Florence, Amsterdam, Berlin, Paris, Glasgow, Dublin, Madrid, Antwerp, Lisbon, Luxembourg, Copenhagen, Thessaloniki, Stockholm, Weimer, Avignon, Bergen, Bologna, Brussels, Helsinki, Cracow, Reykjavik, Prague, Santiago de Compostela, Porto and Rotterdam, Bruges, Salamanca, Cork, Sibiu, Graz, Genova, Lille, Rome, Venice, Florence, Barcelona, Bilbao

Britain/UK

Belfast, Birmingham, Sheffield, Manchester, London, Hey on Wye, Glasgow

United States

New York, Los Angeles, Chicago, Boston, Baltimore, Moline, Illinois, Milwaukee.

South and Central America

Merida (Mexico), Iquique (Chile), Maceio (Brazil), Panama City, Curitiba (Brazil), Santiago (Chile), Guadalajara (Mexico), Cordoba (Argentina), Cuzco (Peru), Brasilia (Brazil), Asuncion (Paraguay)

Arab Cultural Capitals

Cairo (Egypt), Tunis (Tunisia), Sharjah (UAE), Beirut (Lebanon), Riyadh (Saudi Arabia), Kuwait City (Kuwait), Amman (Jordan), Rabat (Morocco), Sana'a (Yemen), Khartoum (Sudan), Muscat (Oman), Algiers (Algeria), Damascus (Syria), Jerusalem (Israel), Doha (Qatar)

activities via non market cultural practices like festivals, rituals, music and storey telling. Referring to the UNESCO definition of the Cultural Industries – which includes only those items which are industrially produced and sold onto the world market – Goldstone concludes that market culture is essentially what the rich practice. As a consequence he notes of the UNESCO statistics: "This results in a self-perpetuating, value-laden, exclusive definition of culture, which is the culture of the comparatively rich expressed through the market place" (2003: 181).

Industrial and commodity based cultural production is therefore a limited indicator of the cultural capital present in any place. Such an observation does not preclude the examination of the process of producing cultural capital in Developed economies, for issues around whose culture, how it is accessed, freedom of cultural expression and the relation of culture to community identities are ever present, while the very question of how such expressions become heard or dominant needs to be addressed. Because of my own position within such an economy, my definition of a Cultural Capital, and as an exercise in understanding this dominance, this book will focus on those countries and cities which have moved to commodify their culture in UNESCO terms, creating a cultural industry which is visible beyond individual regions and borders, commercial, internationally exchanged and consumed in a market place.

Within the world in which Cultural Capitals are defined and operate, the global cultural economy has an international geography which privileges some countries and regions over others. Such an economy does not operate without engaging the rest of the world, and subsequent chapters will illustrate the ways in which particular forms of cultural capital in specific locations – such as performance art in Singapore, urban festivals in Geelong or art galleries in Bilbao – have relations to times and places far removed from the country in which they are located. For as Doreen Massey points out (Massey 2005), space is co-terminus and simultaneous, with notions such as "globalisation" – and the Statistics Division of UNESCO – giving a somewhat misleading view of the homogeneity, autonomy and linearity of a country's cultural production, trade and consumption.

Recognising the interconnections between countries and regions in the production, circulation and consumption of cultural goods does not detract from the dominance of a few countries and regions in the Cultural Industries. It also follows that it is these same countries where these industries are economically as well as socially and politically important and which have the most comprehensive measures and debates on the value of this sector. Thus in the OECD, the Cultural Industries account for 4% of GDP while it accounts for 1–3% (and declining) in Developing countries. (UNESCO 2000a: 22). When the term "Cultural Capital" is typed into that great global product of the cultural (and defence) industries – the internet – what is presented is all of those countries and regions which have used this designation as a public policy tool to enliven the arts or engender a certain form of development. Such designations from the mid-1980s can be connected to local efforts and to academic studies of them to create a map of the global extent of Cultural Capitals. Figure 1.1 illustrates the pattern.

The map of Cultural Capitals suggests four groupings:

1. The readily recognised centres of global culture and the Cultural Industries– New York, London, Paris, Los Angeles, Athens, Florence, Amsterdam – cities which are large (over 5 million) and concentrated in Europe and the United States.
2. Cities which in another discourse are labelled World or Global Cities (Hall 1966; Friedman and Wolff 1982; Sassen 1991, 2000); centres of corporate command and control which may also be national capitals – New York,

London, Beijing, Shanghai and Paris are global centres of multinational capital but so too is Singapore, Madrid, Amsterdam, Copenhagen, Brussels, Sydney, Brasilia, Vancouver and Toronto which are regional centres. These regional centres are somewhat smaller than those in Group 1 – with around 3–5 million people.

3. A set of other cities which are distinguished primarily by being older, 19th and early 20th century centres of industry – Glasgow, Belfast, Sheffield, Birmingham, Baltimore, Barcelona, Manchester, Bilbao, Adelaide, Melbourne. They also tend to be smaller again – in the realm of 1–3 million people.

4. A final unremarkable clutch of relatively small cities which are little known outside of their own regions and located beyond major metropoles and axes of corporate or political power. Such centres are also relatively small – less than one million people. They include: Newcastle, Wollongong, Geelong (which are also industrial cities in Australia), Red Deer (Alberta), Thunder Bay (Ontario), Caraquet (New Brunswick), Riviere-du-Loup (Quebec), Regina (Saskatchewan), Kelowna, (BC), Owen Sound (Ontario), Powell River (BC), Lethbridge, Canmore, Drumheller, Crowsnest Pass (Alberta), Fernie (BC), Annapolis Royal (Nova Scotia), Saint-Jean-Port-Joli (Quebec) in Canada; Cairo (Egypt), Tunis (Tunisia), Beirut (Lebanon), Riyadh (Saudi Arabia) and Rabbat (Morocco), Antwerp, Luxembourg, Thessaloniki, Stockholm, Weimer, Avignon, Bergen, Bologna, Brussels, Helsinki, Cracow, Reykjavik, Prague, Santiago de Compostela, Porto, Rotterdam, Bruges, Salamanca, Cork, Sibiu, Graz, Genova, Lille, Hey on Wye in Europe, Cuzco, Curitiba and Santiago in South America; Shenzhen, Xian and Lijang in China; Milwaukee and Moines in the United States.

Table 1.1 Cultural (Goods) Trade for Australia, Canada, Singapore, Spain, the United Kingdom and the United States of America, 1980–1997

Country	1980 US $Millions	1997 US $Millions	% Capita 1980	% Capita 1987	% of GNP 1980	% of GNP 1997
Australia	1,042	10,442	72	564	0.9	2.7
Singapore	1,968	72,322	815	20,633	17.9	24.4
Spain	1,323	14,912	35	377	0.7	2.7
United Kingdom	6,392	77,906	113	1,329	1.4	6.2
United States of America	11,290	177,474	49	648	0.4	2.2

(*Source*: UNESCO World Culture 2000c)

Within the bounds already set for this book, I am not going to focus on the readily recognised, successful and well researched centres of global culture (Groups 1 and 2). Rather, what invites further study and understanding are those industrial and resource-based cities which have sought for various reasons to mobilise art and culture. While often within a policy framework which offers finance and status to such a quest – as with the European and Canadian Cities of Culture programs – this policy frame as well as the other cases where the arts are deliberately activated as part of an urban regeneration project, have arisen at particular times and involve some cities and not others. Within a socio-economic and political environment which extols the virtue and viability of such a strategy, its uneven geography demands an explanation as well as an evaluation.

To keep such a quest manageable and focused, case studies will be drawn from a limited number of countries and regions. Four countries have been chosen on the basis of personal familiarity, their relative significance in Groups 3 and 4 and to ensure a geographical spread of case studies. They have also, in particular ways, been either early innovators in the development of the Cultural Capital idea (Glasgow in Scotland), archetypical in their pursuit of the agenda (Bilbao in Spain), or idiosyncratic in their own instructive ways (Geelong, Australia and Singapore). As the case studies will be drawn primarily from these countries, subsequent discussion will focus on them. Despite the many problems of finding and utilising comparative international data (see Madden 2004), Table 1 gives an insight into their respective Cultural Industries, with data on international cultural trade with the United States added for comparative purposes.

Table 1.1 follows the advice offered by Madden (2004) in drawing such internationally comparative data from one source, using standardised, relatively simple measures and offering trend rather than one off indicators. While limited measures, what is readily evident is the rapid growth of the Cultural Goods trade for all five countries, but especially for Singapore and the United States; the vastness of the sector per capita and as a contributor to GNP for Singapore and the UK as well as its relative importance to all countries by 1997. Looking more closely at each country, data will necessarily be confined to that valued by governments and their economists – not only trade but also employment, output, turnover and growth rates. What will also be evident in such an overview are other dimensions that each nation regards as vital – tourism to the United Kingdom; attendance and participation in Australia; relationship to other productive sectors for Singapore; to image for Spain and role as a global cultural producer for the US – and the relative locations of their cultural industries.

Case Study Countries – Australia, Singapore, Spain and the United Kingdom

The move in a number of countries to broaden what was counted within "the [creative] arts" (usually visual arts, performance and media arts [film, video, photography]) and to morph artistic activity into something called the Cultural Industries (including the creative arts as well as publishing and the electronic media and sometimes museums and libraries) and then into the Creative Industries (which often excludes the creative arts while including fashion, design, computer games and architecture, depending on the time and place) has occurred across these countries over the last twenty years. It has been impelled by technological changes – which has meant that computer-based creativity was recognised as an art form – by a political challenge in some countries (Britain and Australia) – to State subsidies for the arts – and a more general shift towards valuing the symbolic, experiential and aesthetic in goods and services along with the rise in the economic importance of media and leisure companies (see Chapter 2). Changes in categorising cultural as economic activity has also been political and strategic, occurring in different places for particular reasons. Such shifts make an accurate comparison over time and between nations of the economic contribution of the arts very difficult if not impossible; while in turn highlighting the intensely political nature of such definitions. Each country will therefore be considered individually to sketch general trends of definition as well as the extent and location of their Cultural Industries. As later chapters will focus on particular cities, artefacts and policies within these countries, only a general overview will be given here.

United Kingdom

As the United Kingdom moved to define itself as "Cool Britannia" in the 1980s and to justify public investment in the arts, John Myerscough was commissioned to tabulate and evaluate their economic importance. (Myerscough 1988). In this exercise, completed before the conceptualisation of the Cultural Industries, his subject was delimited narrowly to cover museums and galleries, theatres and concerts, creative artists, community arts, the crafts, screen industries, broadcasting, the art trade, publishing and the music industries. Fashion, architecture, software and the leisure industries were excluded along with arts education (Myerscough 1988:5). As an economist, Myerscough was primarily interested in the arts as a form of productive activity, in terms of employment, income generation and in patterns of economic organisation. Within such a definition, he noted how the arts employed half a million people in 1986 or 2.1% of the total employed population, including 35,000 in craft-based industries and 23,000 practising artists, with a further 175,000 jobs indirectly supported in the national economy. With a turnover of 10 billion pounds, he estimated that the sector grew by 23% between 1981 and 1986 and was a strong exporter (Myerscough 1988: 61). In addition to the measurable economic impact of the arts, Myerscough also noted how they contributed to the image and business climate of a region, had strong spin off effects into other industries and stimulated tourism and urban renewal. He therefore presented the arts as a part of the economy which had a broad range of economic but also social impacts, following the lead offered by studies in Australia and Canada (Myerscough 1988: 5).

A decade later, the British Department of Culture, Media and Sport (DCMS 1998) commissioned The Creative Industries Task Force to once again survey the industry, but this time it was far more than the creative arts. This report gives a total of one million employees in the Creative Industries and an output of 57 billion pounds. The report notes a further 450,000 creative people were employed in other, related industries, raising the total (UK) to 1.4 million or 5% of the entire workforce. What was included in the Creative Industries in 1998 was: advertising, architecture, arts and antique market, crafts, design, designer fashion, film, interactive leisure software, music, performing arts, publishing, software, TV and radio production and receivers. What therefore had been added to the notion of a Creative Industry – compared to the arts – was architecture, advertising, computer software and designer fashion; those activities that had at their core the commercial and industrial – if workshop based – production and distribution of symbolic values. The expanded boundaries of the industry were impelled by the notion that individual creativity was at the core of each activity and that such activity could generate wealth and employment. Such a definition was an extension of the romantic notion of the artist to embrace computer related activity, corporate forms of organisation and industrial production as well as whole new economic activities. By 2001 these Creative Industries accounted for 8.2% of Gross Value Added, employed 1.9 million people and, after growing at 8% per annum from 1997, contributed 4.3% of all British exports (DCMS www.culture. gov.uk/creative_industries, 2005). Such a shift in definition and emphasis has, over time, led to far more interest being focused on the high technology, corporate end of the Creative Industry in official policy and in academic discussion. There has also been a growing recognition of the interconnections between different parts of the industry, between, for example, design, computer software and advertising. There is therefore deepening interconnections between at least some elements of the new Creative Industries, though not necessarily between the older arts and new cultural industries, a point explored in a series of comparative studies by Andrew Pratt from the London School of Economics.

Pratt begins his analysis with the products of the Cultural Industries and their interconnections – performance, fine art and literature, their reproduction as books, journals, magazines, newspapers, film, radio, TV, recordings on disc or tape and advertising – focusing on the many ways in which value is added (Pratt quoted in Hall 2000). He thereby delimits a Cultural Industries Production System including the production, distribution and display processes of printing and broadcasting as well as museums, libraries, theatres, night clubs and galleries, but excludes sport, tourism and entertainment (Pratt 2000: 3). Pratt subsequently divides the industry into four sectors – Original Production, Infrastructure, Reproduction and Exchange – and charts their patterns over time and space in Britain.

In this he highlights London as the biggest centre of activity with 59% of all urban and 24% of all British cultural employment. By his definition, the Cultural Industry sector employed 972,000 or 4.5% of all employees in Britain in 1991. Significantly only 1/6 were creative artists, with 1/3 in distribution or sales (Pratt, quoted by Hall 2002). By 1996 the number had grown to 1.4 million people, a further increase of 14% (compared to a 3% increase in employment generally) to involve 6.4% of total employment. The concentration in London and the South East had increased over these five years (Pratt 2000: 11) though he also notes an overall decline in employment related to sub-contracting out and the digitisation of media as well as the physical dispersal of media production. Pratt's production chain approach, which recognises the interconnection of elements in the Creative Industries as well as the importance of infrastructure and what Caves calls "humdrum" activities and people (such as critics or agents, essential to the Creative Industries realising their value but not involved in the creation of value, Caves 2000), offers a useful way to conceptualise the field which will be developed further later. However, his approach also highlights the relatively limited role creative artists play in the newer Creative Industries, as artists and software makers, work in very different worlds, though both contribute to the creative economy.

Western Europe and Spain

Pratt's definition engages with a broad view of the Cultural Industry in motion, as a set of interconnected relationships of production, exchange and consumption. His use of the internationally comparable Standard Industrial Classification system has allowed others to utilise his approach in their own countries. Thus, Dominic Power defines the Cultural Industries as: economic actors involved in the production of goods and services whose value is primarily or largely determined by their aesthetic, semiotic, sensory, or experiential content (Power 2000: 106). Operationalising this notion, she draws on Pratt's schema to survey Sweden's industry which employed 9% of people in 1999 or around 350,000 people in 91,000 firms. As in the UK, the Swedish industry grew rapidly: from 1994–1999 there was an increase of 24% in employment and an even greater increase of 41% in firms (which she relates to 'cultural entrepreneurialism' and fragmentation); especially in design (124%), software and new media (112%) and fine arts (71%), with lesser but still notable expansions for advertising, furniture, music, libraries, museums and heritage. There was also some declines – in jewellery, print and broadcast media, the latter related to concentration and rationalisation of operations (Power 2000: 111–12). In addition, as with Britain, Power notes a strong association of the Cultural Industries with the urban hierarchy of the country; confirming other experiences of metropolitan concentration (34% of employment was in Stockholm) and agglomeration.

In charting cultural policy across Western Europe, Franco Bianchini notes how a shift occurred from the consideration of arts access in the 1970s to the arts as a key to economic development and urban regeneration in the 1980s. He notes how across Europe, official strategies from the 80s emphasised political consensus, partnerships between business and public sector agencies, the value of "flagship" cultural projects and the contribution of culture to economic development (Bianchini 1993: 2).

Translated into Spain, these general policy moves were realised in efforts to gain major events – the Olympics and Expo for Barcelona – and artistic icons – such as the Guggenheim in Bilbao – but also to address local concerns for linguistic distinctiveness, regional fiestas and the urban fabric (Garcia 2003). In assessing the economic contribution of the arts and cultural industries to the Spanish economy, discussion is difficult as these activities are included within the leisure, recreation and culture sector. Indeed, there is no explicit definition for the cultural sector itself in the available sources on economic sectors (Prieto 2005). Within this broader categorisation then, the contribution of leisure, recreation and culture to GDP in Spain rose from 3.1% in 1992 to 4.5% in 1997. Employment in culture and recreational activities increased by more than 35% between 1982 and 1997 compared to an expansion of only 6.9% in the rest of the economy. Cultural employment rose 24% between 1987 and 1994 (Hesmondhalgh 2002: 90) Far more can be said at a regional level, where political and economic autonomy ensures that there is much well documented activity. The experience of the Basque region and of Bilbao within it will therefore be taken up in Chapters 3 and 5.

Australia

The primary government funded body supporting the arts in Australia – the Australia Council – since its inception in 1969 has focused on supporting the creative arts – performance, music and the visual arts (Throsby and Withers 1984). From the late 1970s and into the 1980s however, the focus of the Council and various Federal and State arts bureaucracies became "the arts industry" – a set of activities which contributed to Gross National Product, employed workers and produced commodities for sale – suggesting a way of thinking about the arts which drew direct parallels with other economic sectors. In more recent discourse, dating from the 1994 *Creative Nation* policy of the Keating Federal Government, the emphasis became the Cultural Industries. This term refers to that sector of the economy organised around the production and consumption of cultural goods and services, ones which include but go well beyond the creative arts (Gibson, Murphy and Freestone 2002).

The Australian Bureau of Statistics (ABS) from the mid-1980s defined the Cultural Industries as comprising:

> Printing and publishing (including newspapers, books, periodicals);
> Film, video, radio and television;
> Libraries and museums (including zoos, parks and gardens);
> Music and theatre production; and
> The retail and support services to these activities (such as recording studios, book and magazine wholesaling, recorded music retailing, video hire outlets and photographic studios).

In Census tabulations, the ABS identifies "Artists and Related Professionals" (ABS 1997) as: artists, designers, craftspeople, photographers, film makers, dancers, directors, presenters and writers as well as those working in museums, libraries and technical staff in film, video and television. All are thereby workers in the Cultural Industries. Such a conception is boosted further when broadened to include the Creative Industries – all of those above, plus fashion, advertising, architecture and interactive leisure software. Following the British definition of the Creative Industries, these are activities which have their origin in individual creativity, skill and talent and which have the potential for wealth and job creation through the generation and exploitation of intellectual property (CITF 2001; Gibson, Murphy and Freestone 2002).

What then is the value of such activity? Since the designation and broadening of the arts as a Cultural Industry, the economic contribution of the sector has been systematically measured by the Statistics Working Group of the Australian Cultural Minister's Council. It is this group that regularly collects and publishes information on the employment, turnover, visitation patterns, multiplier effects and export performance of the cultural sector. Thus in 1993–94, the Cultural Industries produced \$19.3 billion worth of goods and services and contributed 2.5% of Australia's Gross Domestic Product. In comparison, the road transport industry contributed \$15.14 billion, residential building construction industry \$24.8 billion and education \$23.6 billion (ABS 1997: 33). In 2000–01 Australia exported \$478 million worth of cultural goods (though there was also \$3.1 billion of imports!); primarily books, magazines, radio and television receivers and exposed photographic and cinematographic media and artistic works (ABS 2003).

Within Australia, these industries have been growing rapidly over the last 20 years – with paid employment rising from 112,300 in 1986 to 202,500 in 2001 (ABS 1986, 2001). From 1991 this growth in employment was over 20% – compared to 7.4% in all industries (Cultural Ministers Council, No 7). Though these workers constitute only 1% of the national workforce, their contribution to the social as well as to the economic life of the nation is far more than these statistics suggest. As Gibson, Murphy and Freestone note, those working in the Cultural Industries are grossly under-enumerated. They quote an ABS national survey of 26,000 households as yielding a figure of 2.5 million in paid or unpaid work in the cultural industries in 2000–01 (2002: 178). As well as the significant numbers involved in paid and unpaid work, attendance at cultural venues and activities is vast – 85% of the Australian population over 15 – 12.6 million people – attended at least one cultural activity when surveyed by the ABS in April 1999, spending \$10 billion or \$27 per week on culture (SWG No. 9, 2002 and 2004). Further, during 2000 there were 2.5 million people – or 16.8% of the population over fifteen – who did some paid or unpaid work in culture and leisure activities. Therefore, as an economic sector, the arts and cultural industry is significant – generating employment, exports, mass participation and expenditure. In addition, there is a huge contribution through unpaid labour.

As with Britain, Spain and Sweden, the location of the cultural industries is strongly related to the pattern of urbanisation in Australia. With a long history of State-level primacy and a more recent tendency towards Sydney being the major, global city of the nation; Gibson, Murphy and Freestone document high levels of metropolitan concentration of the cultural industries. Thus they note Location Quotients above 1.0 for Sydney (1.4), Melbourne (1.1), Canberra (1.4) and Hobart (1.1) with even higher levels of metropolitan primacy (comparing the capital cities to the next order cities) for all of the capitals. Further, Sydney has over 30% of all cultural industry employment, with high rates of concentration in pursuits such as music, publishing, film and television (Gibson, Murphy and Freestone 2002: 180–181). In turn they document locational concentrations for the different sub-sectors of the industry within the city. This issue of metropolitan location, the role of second order cities and the place or the arts in urban regeneration will become the main focus of later discussions.

Singapore

The idea of valuing the arts and cultural activity in Singapore arose in the context of slowing economic growth and conscious efforts and incentives to shift the economy from an industrial to a post-industrial structure in the 1980s. While always dependent on trade and the activity of importing some form of product/raw material and transforming it with skilled labour and technology into something else (eg petrochemicals, micro-electronics), the necessity after the1985 recession was to move more into services, especially those with an export orientation – health, education and tourism. There was an official recognition that to capture and keep international workers in these industries, an attractive culturally-rich environment had to be offered. There was also a recognition that the city-State needed to offer a culturally-rich tourist experience if it was to grow significantly. Subsequent State investigations into economic restructuring suggested the need to develop the Creative Industries as a "key pillar and strategic enabler for the Singaporean economy" (MITA 2003). A central government planning agency – the Ministry of Information, Technology and the Arts (MITA) is now empowered to oversee a Cultural Industries Development Strategy, to identify and ease local gaps in creative manpower (sic), infrastructure and institutional frameworks as part of integrating the Cultural Industries into the overall economic and social agenda of the Singapore State.

Official interest in the arts and Cultural Industries has therefore been growing in Singapore, especially since the 1980s. Such interest is refracted through other planning agendas, especially for social integration and economic development. Up until very recently, employment in the sub-sector was difficult to quantify – as official statistics emphasised manufacturing and did not break down "Other Service Industries" (Economic Survey 2005). Other published data emphasised infrastructure and attendance figures as key indicators of success – related to the overall policy emphasis on the arts providing an attractive climate for investment and underpinning tourist interest rather than an expansive Cultural Industry sector (Renaissance City Report 2000).

A dedicated survey on the Economic Contribution of Singapore's Creative Industries finally appeared in 2003 and it adopted a Canadian model to present the direct, indirect as well as intangible contribution of the Cultural Industries to Singapore's national economy. Delimiting the industry into upstream (or traditional arts activities such as performance, literary and visual arts) and downstream activities (which involves the "applied arts" of advertising, design, publishing, the media and computer software), the industry is seen as emerging from the creative confluence of art, business and technology. As such the Creative Industries – defined via the UK Creative Industries Task Force – employed 79,000 or 3.8% of the workforce in 2000. It contributed S$2.98 billion or about 2% of GDP and was growing rapidly at 17.2% per annum from 1986 to 2000 (compared to the average for all sectors of 14%) (MITA 2003).

Having sketched a range of definitions of the Cultural Industries across the globe, a number of common time lines, conceptualisations and dimensions emerge. Thus, since the mid-1980s in Europe, Australasia and North America, there has been a political imperative to assess and boost the contribution of the arts to national, regional and urban economies. Along with such demands has been an expansion of what the arts embrace, to go beyond traditional emphases on visual, performing and to some extent media arts (film, TV, broadcasting) to now include an array of activities and products which have broader symbolic, semiotic and entertainment value. There has subsequently been a rethinking of the arts as a creative enterprise towards the arts as an economic activity – concerned with the allocation of scarce resources to create commodities for the market place. What has become the focus of economic assessment and political intervention then is the "Cultural Industries" – a combination of the traditional arts (visual arts, performance and media arts) and an array of other commodified creative endeavours. In this shift the influence of thinking in the United Kingdom – via its Creative Industries Task Force – has been critical, emulated in a number of countries, including Singapore. So too has been the entry and importance of economic measures in tracking and evaluating the "success" of the arts and Cultural/Creative Industries, though social agendas – of participation and access as well as of social integration – are also evident. The implementation of these national policies will be considered in each case study chapter while the question of why such policies have emerged *now* and in particular locations will be addressed in Chapter 3.

Chapter 2
Conceptualising the Cultural Industries/ Cultural Capitals

In the previous chapter, an overview of the Cultural Industries and Cultural Capitals across the globe and in a sample of countries highlighted three key dimensions – their economic contribution to income generation, their sociological import in terms of employment but also participation and consumption, and location in relation to urban settlement patterns. From such well documented dimensions, it follows that the main disciplines offering systematic analyses of the Cultural Industries and to a lesser extent Cultural Capitals are economics, sociology, tourism studies and human geography. What follows is an overview of some key contributions to the interrogation of the arts in urban space by these disciplines; to trace their various conceptualisations and debates as a prelude to drawing out each discipline's take on Cultural Capitals. Coming from very different starting points and assumptions, what emerges is a convergence of approaches, paralleling the shift from modernity to post-modernity in the nature, experience and study of culture in place. While the trajectory is different for each discipline, each offers useful tools, insights and abstractions that can be connected to Pierre Bourdieu's formulation of cultural capital. This chapter will map these various trajectories, focusing on each discipline's formulation of cultural capital, before sketching the composite framework that will structure the case studies presented in the remainder of this book.

Economics has long considered the Cultural Industries like any other – as a product of scarcity and individuals seeking to maximise utility – but also as special, in that it is the victim of ongoing market failure and deserving of particular support. From such a conceptualisation and with a relatively unexamined commitment to the value of the creative arts, economists have argued that public subsidy should occur for what is ultimately a welfare good, necessary for society but basically an economic drain upon it. Such a view dominated arts policy over the latter part of the 20th century in Europe, North America and Australasia, so that the main aim of such policy was the survival and popular engagement with a non-viable but culturally valuable economic sector. With the 1980s emergence of the Cultural and Creative Industries as a productive sector, however, this view was replaced by one which saw the arts as a key driver of economic growth and innovation. Cultural Economics has therefore shifted in its concerns and arrived at a formulation of Cultural Capitals best represented by the work of David Throsby; a view that is broadly based but still ultimately concerned with economic value. Cultural Economics thereby continues to be limited by neo-classical views; the most serious being truncated assumptions of human motivation, an unyielding focus on the economic value of culture, the absence of an ethical concern for power and social justice, and a view of the State as a facilitator of the market and capital accumulation. While offering useful evaluations and tools for appraising the economic impact of the arts, Cultural Economics also tends to focus on the production rather than consumption side of the arts. Ultimately, it does not offer an approach that is socially or politically sustainable, though the cultural economics of Cultural Capitals remains an ongoing consideration.

Taking much from economics, including an active engagement in government policy-making, many in Tourism Studies have also been pre-occupied by the financial impacts of the arts and cultural activities – such as major events, attractions and festivals. Generating useful tools for the quantification of such activity, studies of the tourist, the tourist experience and the tourist product have also admitted the importance of the cultural artefact to travel and tourism. If the economics of cultural tourism remains an ongoing and central component of tourism studies, more recent work has been influenced by post-modern thinking on the nature of place making and marketing, representation, identity construction, "Othering" and the symbolic economy. Drawing on disciplines such as Anthropology, Sociology and Cultural Studies, many tourism studies are now concerned with the multi-faceted ways in which the tourist gaze is constructed, the changing nature of the tourist experience and the rising importance of cultural tourism. From such developments, studies of public art, heritage sites, galleries and museums have assumed a multi-faceted perspective – engaging with the economics but also the politics, social structuration and representational complexity of such activities. In such work Tourism Studies has borrowed heavily from Sociology and Human Geography.

In contrast to cultural economists and many in tourism studies, sociologists have tended to focus on the nature and reception of cultural products as well as on the structured social relations of cultural production. In doing so, their analyses have theoretical rigour and political import; but they also tend to underplay the role of textuality, space and the local. Unlike Tourism Studies, Sociology tends to ignore the issue of location and space in the arts and Cultural Industries. In contrast human geography has as its main concern the creation and nature of places, while cultural geography has a particular interest in the role of culture (if not the arts) to this process and, along with studies in cultural tourism, examines the ways in which places and cultures are made and projected into the public domain. Drawing heavily on literary and cultural studies as they have engaged with the post-modern turn, cultural geographers have been critical in bringing the role of texts and meaning in the construction of landscapes to the fore, while also engaging with the economics, sociology, tourist and cultural dimensions of place-making.

The following discussion will interrogate these various disciplinary takes on the Cultural Industries and cultural capital, drawing from each conceptual tools useful to the analysis of the arts and sustainable place making. I will argue that these disciplines together offer real insights but on their own they do not produce analyses of Cultural Capitals that adequately capture or ensure their economic, social or political sustainability. An alternative lies in melding elements of a progressive cultural economics, tourism studies and cultural geography with the work of sociologist Pierre Bourdieu. The final part of this Chapter will therefore mount a case for reconsidering Bourdieu's notion of "cultural capital", relating it to processes of cultural production, class constitution and product realisation as well as to the values of social, economic and political sustainability. The resulting framework emphases the interconnection of three dimensions of cultural capital – the embodied, objectified and institutional – across various scales – from the highly localised to the social group, the region and nation, within an ethics of evaluation which will structure the subsequent interrogation of various Cultural Capitals.

Cultural Economics and the Cultural Industries

Chapter 1 briefly outlined the policy contexts in which the arts and cultural industries in a few developed economies were codified and quantified. In these accounts, the economic contribution of the sector became, by the 1980s, the most important for governments, who subsequently ensured that national and international agencies collected data on employment, turnover, value adding, international trade and the overall contribution of the cultural industries to gross national product. The ascendancy of economic discourses in political and popular imaginations has been analysed as an integral part of neo-liberal state formations which assumed dominance in many countries across the 1980s (see Kearns and Philo 1993; Hall and Hubbard 1998; Hesmondhalgh 2002). Chapter 3 will consider the form and timing of such a development which has been vital to the official support and widespread policy agenda of revaluing the arts: mobilising cultural capital to progress inner city regeneration, urban re-imaging and social integration. Here the concern is with how such developments were conceptualised as the arts joined many other activities in becoming subjected to economics.

The changing place of the artist in Western societies – from the artisan and independent contractor of the Renaissance to individual professionals in the 20th century – was accompanied by growing interest from the emergent field of economics. As Jason Potts notes, by the second half of the 20th century, the arts were widely understood to produce both private and public goods and though these markets were subject to endemic failure, they were given a social and political imperative to succeed (Potts 2007: 9). The arts were therefore labelled as economic mendicants but socially vital in various countries, so that governments came to have a particular role in supporting them. In this they were assisted by the new sub-field of cultural economics. Along with arts policy advice, cultural economists conducted micro-analyses of particular market failures in the arts and macro analyses of the value of public goods expenditure. The language and techniques of such analyses carried a set of neo-classical assumptions about what was important and how "value" was defined. Cultural economics unashamedly drew on its neo-classical tradition to quantify, assess and derive insights into the arts. In its focus on the market, quest for limited state intervention, a-spatiality and concern for economic efficiency rather than social or political sustainability, the sub-discipline has limited use in this study of Cultural Capitals. However, neo-classical cultural economics does offer some insights which can assist in the theorisation and examination of Cultural Capitals, specifically delimiting how the arts and cultural industries operate within a capitalist marketplace and offering one working definition of cultural capital.

For the cultural economist Ruth Towse, the arts can and do benefit from the application of economic principles to them. For her, once this is done, it becomes clear that art is subject to scarcity, its production and consumption is the result of individual behaviour and therefore, as with all other commodities, demand and supply matters (Trowse 1997a, also Frey and Pommerehne 1990). For Trowse, cultural goods have in common with all others the utilization of land, labour and capital in their creation. Artistic artefacts have high fixed costs in the production of an original product, though they also have very low marginal costs in creating copies. She argues that it is these characteristics which lead to price regulation and copyright protection for artistic products (as well as, for example, pharmaceuticals). Unlike other goods though, cultural products also have some of the characteristics of "public" and "merit" goods and therefore they will not necessarily be supplied by the market. They are therefore often supported by governments who recognise this market failure and have a commitment to a cultured and critical society (Trowse 1997b, 2003). In addition, cultural products are risky and subject to radically uncertain reception by consumers. An artist never knows if their work will be accepted and appreciated by an audience. There are rarely guarantees and market research offers limited insights into what might sell. Coupled with high entry costs (at least for some cultural activities), this leads to a high risk environment. These characteristics of artistic commodities also produce barriers to entry, including the copyright of intellectual property. For Trowse, such characteristics of the productive and regulatory environment as well as the qualities of art works themselves within an uncertain market place, explains the tendency towards mergers and the concentration of ownership and control in the Cultural Industries (Trowse 2003).

Richard Caves (2000) builds on these ideas in delimiting what makes the producers and products of the Creative Industries – visual and creative arts as well as film, publishing and the media, special – as a prelude to discussing what organisational and contractual arrangements have emerged to meet industry needs. Along with the insights offered by Trowse, his analysis provides some building blocks for a working model of cultural capital.

Caves too draws on neoclassical principles to reaffirm the importance of uncertain demand and incomplete information, such that nobody knows if a creative product will be purchased or successful. The result of the *nobody knows principle*, Caves argues, is flexible specialisation and unique option contracts designed to spread the associated risks, especially in those parts of the Creative Industry – such as film – where there are very large sunk costs (2000: 2–3). He also notes how *creative workers care about their product* more than pay or conditions, producing *art for art's sake*. While often dismissed as a quaint Romantic notion, this particular character of art results in the making of works often without regard or even in defiance of those who might pay for them. Art works may indeed be made for totally different reasons, such as for a political or social objective as well as an artistic one. This is most clearly seen in some public and performance art (to be examined in Chapter 6 for English language theatre in Singapore). The result of the focus on producing art is that artists will produce more creative output than if they valued only the incomes they received, and on average earn lower incomes than their general skills, ability and education would otherwise command (2000: 4). They also produce *an infinite variety* of *differentiated art* products, some of which may be readily realisable if not sold (such as paintings) others not (such as a performance of Wagner's Ring Cycle) (2000: 4–5). Art is therefore by definition always new and often produced regardless of a market. Artists also have *vertically differentiated skills* which results in the market producing rankings of artists – such as A-list actors, singers or screen writers – so that the superior artist or celebrity can command a higher rent or wage because of that position (2000: 7, 183–184). The notion of celebrity is a key element in differentiating artists and this notion will be taken up in Chapter 5 in relation to the architect Frank Gehry's Guggenheim Museum in Bilbao.

To realise their work, Caves argues that artists usually have to collaborate with "humdrum workers" – such as agents, distributors and marketers – who are like those in other sectors in having a pecuniary focus and who also demand comparable wages (2000: 3–4). Caves suggests that this relationship and the different values which drive it, lead to much tension and potential conflict within the Cultural Industries between, for example, actors, producers and distributors. Further, many artistic products arise from the collaboration between a number of creative people. Film and theatre production involve people with skills that are irreplaceable by others. The result is what Caves calls the *motley crew quality of art,* whereby each team member is unique and their co-operation is required for the realisation of an artistic vision. Collective art production is thereby even more risky than the solo effort, because of the dependence on a large number of creative as well as "humdrum" individuals. In their collective production, *time is of the essence* as co-ordination is essential to ensure that a performance or a film happens on schedule. The reliance of creative activities for economic profitability on close temporal coordination of production and the prompt realisation of revenues, Caves calls the *time flies* property (2000: 8). Finally, as creative products are durable but can also be readily copied – detailed copyright provisions – the *arts longa property* (2000: 8–10) are central to defining and regulating artistic work in a commercial economy (see also Howkins 2001).

A number of economic logics therefore, according to cultural economists such as Trowse and Caves, distinguish the arts and Cultural Industries. Such logics mean that artists create work without a strong regard for the market, earn relatively low incomes (unless they are propelled into the ranks of the celebrity), struggle to produce a unique, often high cost, enduring product often in collaboration with others (artists and non-artists) which in turn can be reproduced at low cost. They also work with others – a motley crew – who can be numerous, with a range of skills and income levels, who in turn are vital to the realisation of the art work. Such a work may or not have an audience and a market but it does have a unique value which thereby supports a whole sub-class of creative producers. These economic logics would ultimately lead to the creation of very few art works were it not for regulatory and supportive structures and institutions. Thus Caves and Trowse both recognise that the arts have a social value which in turn is often recognised by governments. Governments across the world intervene to safeguard the value of creative endeavour – through the copyright protection of intellectual property amongst other measures – and to support the very production as well as the circulation of artistic artefacts through direct and indirect subsidisation. These logics also impel the agglomeration of Cultural Industries, to spread risks, bring together related workers in place and facilitate the interconnection so important to the making of many cultural products – such as film, computer games and television production – as well as access urban markets.

The economic geographer Allan Scott picks up on these economic logics and empirically verifies their implications for the Cultural Industries across the United States and around Los Angeles in particular. He argues that the "cultural products industries" are epitomised by five organisational elements:

1. Technologies and a labour process that involve a great deal of direct human involvement and advanced flexible computer technology
2. The organisation of production in dense networks of small to medium sized firms strongly dependent on one another for specialised inputs and services
3. These multifaceted industrial complexes exert huge demands on local labour markets which require an enormous variety of skills and attributes
4. External economies lead to mutual learnings and creativity from thesse interactions
5. Institutional infrastructure facilitates information flows.

In short the economic logic associated with the Cultural Industries produces a specific geography of agglomeration seen especially in the film industry of Los Angeles (Scott 1999, 2000: 11–12, 2001).

In his subsequent evaluation of the Creative Industries, Caves notes how economists, with very few exceptions, have focused on the production side of the capital circuit. He observes how economic analysis of consumption, when it occurs, is focused on "deriving the decision rules that utility-maximizing persons should follow in determining what to consume" (Caves 2000: 175). The role of pleasure, taste, sociability, class, gender, power relations and meaning in such consumption is what sociologists, geographers and those in cultural studies rather than economics have focused upon. Caves diverges from this tendency with his consideration of the role of values, sociability, critics, fashion and celebrity in the constitution of demand for cultural goods though he still reduces such impulses to a "rational addiction model" (Caves 2000: 177) and ultimately concentrates on the organisation and contractual relations governing production relations. There is therefore a recognition by at least some cultural economists of the need to broaden the analysis from production to consumption and from rationality to the constitution of tastes and values. While Caves does not fully achieve this shift, significant progress in this direction is achieved by David Throsby in his formulation of "cultural capital".

The cultural economist David Throsby has been a major figure in developing the sub-discipline and in promoting the rigorous economic evaluation of the arts in Australia. Drawing on neo-classical concepts and techniques, he has developed instruments for assessing the economic impacts of cultural institutions (Throsby and O'Shea 1980); argued for cultural policy in Australia (Throsby 2005), defined the relationship of economic to cultural policy (Throsby 1997, 2001) and overseen surveys on how artists earn their incomes and how the arts are perceived by the Australian population. (Throsby and Withers 1979, 1984; Throsby 1986; Throsby and Thompson 1994). Throsby is not alone amongst economists in devising and applying frameworks for the assessment of the economic role of the arts – be it an organisation or event impacting on a locality, city, region or country. Indeed such work has become a key contribution of economics to the discussion of the arts and Cultural Industries across the globe, with many studies confirming the various income, employment, participatory and other monetary effects on places. The techniques devised by cultural economists such as Throsby have been utilised by local, city, state and national governments to assess the role and impact of cultural activities on their communities. Such techniques – which involve quantifying the economic costs and benefits of an object, event or activity, their contribution to employment, turnover and income as well as the impacts on unrelated businesses within a city or region – have to be utilised when assessing the economic sustainability of case study works and places. The mass replication of such studies confirms their utility as well as the official and now popular conception of the arts as increasingly and primarily an economic good. This remains one of the most widely recognised contributions of the arts and Cultural Industries to urban regeneration and sustainable economic development.

In addition, Throsby has been involved in developing concepts to evaluate and support the arts. These go well beyond the narrow conception of the arts as an economic good, though ultimately they are still constrained by his neo-classical assumptions. In developing his particular version of *cultural capital*, Throsby begins by defining capital as goods which, when combined with other inputs (such as labour) give rise to further goods. He notes how over the years, different dimensions of capital have been formulated – physical or manufactured capital (plant, equipment, buildings), human capital (skills, education, experience) and natural capital (water, air), before focusing on cultural capital. Recognising that such a concept has been developed to incorporate the distinctive features of art works and other cultural goods, he also grounds this concept on the longer history of capital, seeing cultural capital as a capital asset which can contribute to the production of further capital goods and services (Throsby 2001, 2003a and b).

For Throsby, *cultural capital* is *embodied* in cultural goods. These goods involve human creativity in their making, convey symbolic meaning (or multiple meanings) and have some intellectual property which may or may not be formally recognised. The *value* of the resulting cultural capital goes well beyond a simple monetary measure; for cultural value also involves attitudes, beliefs, mores, customs and practices. His aim is to bring together the economic (or price) and cultural value of an artistic object through the concept of cultural capital (Throsby 2001). Cultural value may give rise to economic value, though cultural values need not always translate into economic ones (Throsby 1999). Thus he gives the example of a church, which has a price but also a religious and architectural value and may well also be a symbol of identity for a place. All of these things constitute its "cultural value", the multidimensional representation of the building's cultural worth assessed in quantitative and qualitative terms against a variety of attributes such as aesthetics, spiritual meaning, social function, symbolic significance, historical importance and uniqueness. It is a process involving different agents and time. Many of these dimensions will influence the economic value of the building but there is no one to one correspondence. Cultural capital for Throsby is an asset that embodies, stores or gives rise to cultural value in addition to whatever economic value it may possess. It can be tangible – such as artworks, buildings or sites of cultural significance – or intangible, encapsulating a broader public good; such as music, literature and the stock of inherited traditions, values and beliefs which constitute the "culture" of a group. Cultural capital also exists in the cultural networks and relationships that support human activity and in the diversity of cultural products within communities (Throsby 2003b).

True to his disciplinary foundations, Throsby notes how an economist can talk about the stock of cultural capital assets and their growth or subtraction over time. This stock gives rise to a flow of capital services which might enter final consumption directly or might be combined with other inputs to produce further capital goods and services. For example, the operation of a museum restoration project will generate longer term economic and cultural benefits. While describing these various dimensions with great eloquence, Throsby also suggests that the appraisal of any one cultural artefact can be reduced to a formula and quantified, such that the many dimensions of an art work express linear and causal relations within a neo-classical logic driven by the market (Throsby 1999).

In Throsby's formulation, cultural capital remains primarily an economic term with a lineage direct to other forms of productive capital. In contrast, Pierre Bourdieu's notion of cultural capital is more akin to human capital as it relates to "an individual's competence in high status culture" (Throsby 2003b: 168) and hence their sociological position rather than command of economic resources.

Throsby is careful to distinguish his version of cultural capital from Bourdieu's, though I will argue, the two can usefully be integrated as part of a re-formulation of the concept, one that can adequately capture the two major dimensions of value in the arts and Creative Industries – the economic and the social – as well as straddle the production and consumption side of the equation.

What can be taken from Cultural Economics into this analysis is:

- A definition of the Cultural Industries which can be quantified and mobilised internationally. Such a formulation – present in studies by UNESCO and others – confirms the growth and importance of the Cultural Industries as an employer and generator of wealth in a number of countries as well as significant levels of trade between them. It also highlights the global and regional geography of the industry which privileges certain Developed over Non-developed countries and metropoles over smaller cities (see Chapter 1).
- Codification of what makes the cultural industries special as a set of activities and economic sector which thereby impels particular organisational forms and contractual arrangements, including intellectual property arrangements. At least in some parts of the Cultural Industries, such as film, television and new media, these in turn often generate a particular agglomeration geography.
- Techniques which structure the documentation and evaluation of the economic value of the arts to cities, regions and nations.
- A definition of cultural capital which is not only practical but conceptually engaging, in that creativity is at its core across a number of cultural practices as is the process by which these practices are enacted to produce content, events and structures as valuable commodities. However, the focus on the production and quantifiable side of a causal equation limits the utility of this formulation and suggests the need to broaden it through an engagement with cultural, sociological and geographical discourses focused on circulation and consumption.

Cultural Economics therefore remains constrained by its neo-classical origins, with certain limiting assumptions – about rational human behaviour, the operation of markets, the role of the State, the causal power of "the economic" – and techniques – of quantification, a reduction of human behaviour to models and equations – as well as a focus on production at the expense of circulation and demand. There is also a neglect by cultural economists of the role of space and place in the creation and realisation of cultural value. In addition, the role of values, meanings and tastes in driving the desire for and consumption of art and cultural goods (as well as their production) is not readily incorporated into a cultural economic analysis, along with the critical, somewhat transcendental function of art works in society. It is these aspects that have been addressed more successfully by other disciplines.

Cultural Tourism and Cultural Capitals

One of those disciplines is Tourism Studies which draws heavily on Economics for documenting the impact of travel but also goes beyond it to understand why and how cultural tourism has emerged in particular places and amongst particular social groups.

As an activity, travelling for pleasure, relaxation and education has a very long history, dating to at least the Medieval "Grand Tour" of ancient monuments, the health spa or the sublime landscape by the European aristocracy. A more widespread engagement with travel had to await the industrial revolution, mass forms of motorised transport, decent wages and the creation of leisure time (Urry 2000). It was not until WWI that the demand for paid holidays slowly entered the negotiating agenda of some unions and employers and not till after WWII that such demands were widely accepted. So for example, in 1940 only 25% of American workers enjoyed paid holidays; by 1957, this number had risen to 90%. Made possible by the creation of the concept and opportunity of leisure time, the 20th century growth of tourism was supported by a host of related industries – hotels, cruise liners, travel agents, guide books and air travel – who packaged and marketed increasingly distant and differentiated destinations.

As a consequence of growing affluence, education and leisure time in developed countries, and the construction of a desire to experience other places, tourism became one of the world's biggest industries. It was projected to be the world's largest employer by the year 2000 (Lord 1999: 1), growing at more than 6% pa from 1995, 23% faster than the world economy. The result was that 1 in 15 workers worldwide was employed in the industry in the early 1990s. Despite set backs in the 21st century – including downturns associated with terrorism and epidemics – tourism continues to be a massive industry and popular activity. The rise in the economic, social and cultural importance of tourism over the latter part of the 20th century, spurred the creation of a whole new academic discipline. Thus the study of tourism emerged as a distinct sociological sub-field in the 1970s.

Concerned initially with documenting the extent and impact of tourism, the academic field was soon dominated by a debate as to the value of tourism as a social and political phenomena. On one side were those who saw tourism as social decadence, with the modern tourist experience a trivial and superficial quest for contrived experiences (Barthes 1972; Boorstin 1964; Turner and Ash 1975; Eco 1986). On the other side were those who saw the tourist experience as a meaningful modern ritual which involved a quest for the authentic "other" – people and places different from the mundane (MacCannell 1973, 1976). Still others documented in great quantitative detail the costs and benefits of mass and later niche tourism, establishing the notion of "carrying capacity" for tourist places and guiding policy makers in the promotion and management of events and sites (such as Glasson et al. 1995; Butler et al. 1999). Much theoretical heat within tourist studies was devoted to establishing the value and processes associated with constituting tourists and tourist sites.

A key theorist within the broader debate on the origins and value of tourism, Dean MacCannell (1976) observed in the mid-1970s how cultures of the world had been radically displaced and altered by the movement of peoples, as migrants as well as tourists, such that there were few unique cultures remaining. For him, this produced a broader displacement, so that signs and artefacts of cultural difference were used imaginatively in a continuous process of positive reformulation and hybridisation. Consumers of culture, especially the tourist, for him therefore create and are presented with a mythical construction of traditions uprooted by globalisation. In this encounter tourists locate the "other" as more whole, structured and authentic than their every day lives (see also Selwyn 1996).

For MacCannell, the quest for and experience of the hybridised culture was relatively benign with a relationship best captured by notions of host and guest. For others, the desire for a unique experience built on or required unequal social relations. This process of "othering" in turn could be related to specific colonial histories which meant that, for example, tourists from Europe would seek out and consume "Asia" or Africa in particular ways, continuing the process of appropriation begun by colonial exploitation. Such othering was also the result of widespread desires by the wealthy and time rich for the exotic, the natural and, increasingly, for the culturally different, unrelated to colonial histories. As Jennifer Craik argues, tourism is increasingly a unique post-colonial experience – arising from guilt about forms of European settlement and expansion – but it is also as a celebration of national, ethnic and indigenous cultures and can itself involve critiques of consumer products and relations. For Craik, post-colonial tourism involves exoticism and voyeurism, spectacle and the commodification of all culture, though she also notes how tourism is not experienced in the same way in all ex-colonies and exploitative relations do exist without the colonial heritage and have considerable variety – with for example some First Nation peoples in the US achieving financial security through tourist and gambling ventures (Craik 1994). So too June Nash describes how tourism provides the cash flow that makes the exercise of traditional arts feasible for Mayan groups in Guatemala (Nash 2000) and others question the whole notion of pristine cultures which are either constituted or consumed by tourism as a fiction (Crick 1988).

Such debates not only highlight the importance of colonial and other power relations in the tourist experience, but also how tourism had moved from being about relaxation and escape to being more about the consumption of cultural difference. This quest for recreational, natural, monumental, ancient and health-related tourist experiences was increasingly commodified and differentiated from the 1980s – to create eco-tourism, adventure tourism and the like – and came to be dominated by the desire to consume cultural artefacts and culturally "different" peoples (Lord 1999). A whole new sub-field – of cultural tourism – emerged, to be consciously developed by cities and regions. Studies across Europe and North America documented the trend. Thus a 1998 survey conducted by the Travel Association of America reported that 46% of the almost 200 million travellers surveyed included a cultural, arts, heritage or historic activity while on a trip during the past year (Lord 1999: 2). So too in the 1980s, less that a third of people surveyed in Wisconsin indicated that "visiting cultural, historical and archaeological treasures" was a key motivator. In the 90s, it was important to a full half of respondents. Those travelling to "understand culture" was important to just less than half in the 1980s, in the 1990s an overwhelming 88%.

The most popular cultural activities were – any cultural event (46%), historic site or community (31%), museum (24%), art gallery (15%), live theatre (14%) and heritage/ethnic festival (13%) (Lord 1999: 6). Such trends were paralleled in Europe (see Richards 1996a). Thus during the 1990s, cultural tourism was identified as one of the major future growth areas in Europe, with the World Trade Organisation estimating that 37% of all international trips would have a cultural element and this figure would increase by 15% per annum to the end of the 20th century (cited by Smith 2003: 31). While subject to some contestation and refinement – with cultural tourists differentiated by the degree to which they were motivated by and sought out cultural attractions (Bywater 1993) – such figures were interpreted by many in the tourism sector as a shift from escape to enrichment. (Lord 1999: 1). Explained in the industry by growing affluence, the greater economic power of women, an ageing and better educated population (Lord 1999; Brown 2000), others saw the rise of cultural tourism as part of a more general shift to a post-modern sensibility (see Chapter 3).

In place of the modern notion of cultural provision being driven by the development of the productive base, post modernity is marked by consumption driven cultural production (Richards 1996b: 262). This has been particularly concentrated in the major but also minor industrial cities of developed countries. As the geographer David Harvey observed in the late 1980s: "the grim history of de-industrialization and restructuring … left most major cities in the advanced capitalist world with few options except to compete with each other, mainly as financial, consumption, and entertainment centres" (1989a: 92).

Such a socio-economic plight and inter-urban competition led to cities re-imagining themselves and projecting these images to tourists as well as to prospective investors. Imageability and its sale to tourists became a key strategy for city revival in the 1980s and 1990s (Rowe and Stevenson 1994: 179). This strategy was particularly appealing to provincial cities which, lacking the size, density, accessibility, diversity and international prominence of metropoles, sought to siphon off tourism from established centres. So, for example the Boston festival marketplace re-development of the 1950s became a model for other depressed cities (Rowe and Stevenson 1994: 181). More modest schemes were also developed for creating cultural precincts, emphasising local culture (Roodhouse 2006), as was implemented by Glasgow in the 1980s (see Chapter 4). For Rowe and Stevenson, such a development illustrates the success of using cultural planning to re-imagine the city (Rowe and Stevenson 1994: 182).

The consumption of culture is increasingly used as a vehicle to promote economic regeneration and to differentiate cities from each other in their heightened competitive battle for survival and growth (Bianchini 1993). As a consequence, the relationship between cultural experience and the city has been turned on its head, as cultural expression is thought of less as a socioeconomic practice that follows urban life, but is regarded and becomes the motor of the urban economy. As such, modes of cultural experience have been identified as the quality of the city that allows it to compete within the global economy (Newman and Smith 2000). Following on from such observations, David Harvey (1989b) concludes that cultural capital becomes an attribute of place. In order to attract investment capital and the spending power of the middle class, regions and cities now differentiate themselves by emphasising the aesthetic qualities of their material commodities and services which in turn represent symbolic capital. The cultural thereby translates into the economic through major events, exhibition centres and waterfront redevelopments which are designed to attract further investment and tourists.

Much contemporary tourism, then, and urban cultural tourism in particular, can be seen as the expression and outcome of competition between places, indicative of the growing economic power of culture and the relation between centres and peripheries, with a power dynamic ever-present in their production and consumption. How exactly such a relationship works became the subject of extensive theorisation, with John Urry formulating the notion of *the tourist gaze* as a powerful way to conceptualise the activation and consumption of tourist sites. For Urry, tourism is a leisure activity which presupposes its opposite, namely regulated and organised work. The tourist gaze arises from a movement of people to, and their stay in, various other destinations. The places gazed upon are for purposes which are not directly connected with paid work and offer some contrast with work. Viewing them involves different forms of social patterning, often utilising more visual elements, which are also captured and endlessly reproduced via photos, postcards, video, films and so on. The gaze is constructed through signs, and tourism involves the collection of such signs, such as images that capture "timeless romantic Paris", "true England" or "typically Italian". As a substantial proportion of the modern population engages in tourism, for Urry, new forms of provision cater for the mass tourist gaze. Places are chosen to be gazed upon as a result of their construction by non-tourist practices, including films, magazines and television in an endless cycle of self-referential image-making. An array of tourist professionals develop ever-new objects for the tourist gaze. For Urry, these objects are located in a complex and changing hierarchy, which depends on the interplay between different state and capitalist interests providing these objects, and changing class, gender, and generational distinctions of taste, which drives their consumption (Urry 1990: 26–7, 2000). Significantly, Urry as a sociologist moves the analysis from tourist places and localities to those who produce and consume them.

Focusing on the key dimensions of taste and distinction in the creation and consumption of the tourist experience led Urry to explore the work of fellow sociologist Pierre Bourdieu. Others too in Tourist Studies interested in the manufacturing and circulation of sites and artefacts also draw on the French sociologist. In particular Greg Richards utilised Bourdieu's notion of "distinction" to analyse the class dimensions of contemporary cultural tourism. Thus Bourdieu (1984) argues that to understand or appreciate cultural products, people must attain the cultural competence, or acquire the requisite cultural capital. This is generated through education, upbringing and other forms of socialisation. Such a position and cultural capital is demonstrated through consumption which becomes a form of distinction for the individual and allows membership of a specific social group. A form of class struggle ensures for control of scarce cultural economic and social resources. Class fractions seek to distinguish themselves from each other in all areas of life, especially education, occupation and location as well as through the consumption of commodities, not only cultural products but also tourism experiences. These different elements of distinction are combined to create a certain culture or milieu, a *habitus*, which forms the basis for the reproduction and differentiation of classes (Richards 1996c: 48). Significantly, empirical research indicates that it is the "new bourgeoisie" who are the main consumers of cultural tourism. It is they who are firmly located in the service sector – with finance, marketing and purchasing as occupational exemplars – a class fraction high on both economic and cultural capital. In addition there are the "new cultural intermediaries" young, self employed and working in occupations related to culture. High in cultural capital they are also relatively low in economic capital. According to Richards, it is they who also pursue cultural capital and actively engage in cultural tourism (Richards 1996b).

The work of Harvey amongst others has highlighted the importance of place in cultural tourism while that of Urry has focused on the class dimensions of its production and consumption. Both dimensions need, however, to be systematically brought together and in this Greg Richards progresses the task utilising both Bourdieu but also the work of Sharon Zukin. Zukin (1991: 28) regards culture as "both the property of cultured people and a general way of life" and while culture is a mark of class distinction, it is also "an inalienable product of place". For Zukin the cultural products of place are a physical form of cultural capital, what she calls "real cultural capital" which for Zukin is just as important as symbolic forms. On the supply side, cultural consumption creates employment for a self-conscious critical group of people and lower level service personnel, who in turn create these places by their labour. Cultural consumption further contributes to capital accumulation, by enhancing profits on entrepreneurial investment in the production and distribution of places, artefacts and experiences. Cultural consumption thereby has a positive effect on capital accumulation in real estate development. Cultural goods and services therefore constitute real cultural capital for individuals, groups, investors and developers – so long as they are integrated as commodities in the market based circulation of capital (Zukin 1991: 260). Through cultural tourism then, cultural capital is integrated into the real urban economy in a host of ways.

Cultural tourists are the fractions of the new middle class who are distinguished – after Bourdieu – by high levels of cultural capital and specific forms of symbolic consumption. Through their cultural tourist activities they add to their own store of cultural capital. They are Bourdieu's "new cultural intermediaries" and are major consumers of cultural tourism. Through their direct involvement in the production process and their class positions they also directly influence the taste and behaviour of others (Richards 1996d: 315). Even more significant is that a large proportion of these cultural consumers are also cultural producers who are connected in some way with the cultural industries (Richards 1996a: 314–5). Richards therefore moves to use real cultural capital as a vial link between explanations of cultural consumption (via Bourdieu) and the production of cultural tourism attractions. This leads to an analysis of the social conditions which determine the consumption of cultural tourism (such as education, socio-economic status, occupation [especially cultural industry employees who constitute 30% of cultural tourists], leisure time availability, the economic position of women and the ageing of western populations) and the economic processes that govern its production (including the long historical investment in medieval and Renaissance cities of Europe, but also more recent efforts to create cultural attractions and Cultural Capitals). Analysis is therefore directed to both the class fractions involved in the production and consumption of cultural capital and the places that arise from such a process, which, necessarily are unevenly distributed across space, and which therefore have a particular geography. As Richards concludes, just as cultural capital is unequally distributed among individuals so "real cultural capital" is unequally distributed in space (Richards 1996a). From tourism studies, then, analysis is directed to cultural tourism and its relationship to the cultural capital of individuals, class fractions, events and localities.

Tourism Studies therefore offers to this study a set of approaches and theorisations of great utility. In particular,

- Tourism Studies points to the need to document the economic, social and cultural creation of the traveller and the impact of travellers on particular localities
- Tourism Studies has directed attention to the constitution of places, objects and events as commodities to be engaged with and variously consumed
- Tourism Studies has defined the tourist gaze as an active, constitutive element in the creation and consumption of places, events and objects. The focus on sight to the exclusion of other senses and non-representational elements is limiting though the emphasis on the constitutive, social and power relations of the gaze is enormously important in any theorisation of cultural capital
- Cultural tourism recognises, legitimates and builds on the interconnection between the cultural and the economic, confirming the materiality of the cultural
- Cultural tourism as a set of practices, class positions and sites directs analysis to the emergence of these places and the class fractions who staff and consume them

- Cultural tourism further directs attention to particular phenomena which are vital to it – especially the festival, the heritage precinct, galleries and museums – as newly commodified sites which successfully combine the cultural and the economic
- Such sites and the cities or regions in which they are located become known indirectly through various forms of representation, in particular tourist and city marketing agencies but also through films, videos, post cards and guidebooks. Such images become part of the anticipated and actual experience of these places
- The meaning of such sites has been variously described as oppressive, ersatz but also as legitimate and vital – judgements made without necessarily being tied to an explicit ethical position
- John Urry's use of Bourdieu's distinction and cultural capital ideas directs attention to the social process whereby Cultural Capitals are created, linking this to the emergence of new fractions of the middle class – service and cultural workers who may well be in tension but who have various degrees of cultural capital to bestow and utilise in the process of valuing/creating sites and enhancing their own cultural capital
- David Harvey and Sharon Zukin's focus on how places are constituted to be consumed by tourists can be connected to the class analysis of Bourdieu and Urry by Richards. This conceptualisation offers a powerful set of tools for the analysis of how Cultural Capitals are made, circulated and experienced.

What has also emerged from Tourism Studies is the interconnection between those who produce and consume artefacts and places. This sensitivity to place has long been the preserve of geographers who also offer insights into its systematic study.

Cultural Geography and Urban Cultures

Cultural Geography has gone through a revival in the last twenty years, a development related to the renewed importance of culture in contemporary social-spatial relations, the demand by "sub-cultures" (women, blacks, gays) to be heard, and a general crisis in the legitimacy of western knowledges with a related ascendancy of post-structuralism as a way of defining, valuing and analysing texts in the humanities and social sciences (see Chapter 3). In a break from the 1920s Berkeley School of Carl Sauer – with its use of material artefacts and homogeneous ways of life to identify and reconstruct cultural regions – the "new cultural geography" is concerned with how landscapes and dominant meanings are produced through the interplay of social relations and texts (Cosgrove 1989, 1990; Jackson 1989; McDowell 1994; Jacobs 1999; Stratford 1999). Now a vast subfield covering everything from urban images and agricultural landscapes to marginalised social groups, only those studies which focus on dimensions relevant to Cultural Capitals will be introduced here, to be considered in greater detail where relevant to the case studies.

In summarising what the new cultural geography comprised in the 1980s, Duncan and Duncan argued in a special edition of *Society and Space* that literary concepts and techniques were now central to the interpretation and analysis of landscapes. These landscapes and artefacts within them are to be approached as texts; material statements of dominant, if contested, ideologies (Duncan and Duncan 1988). They cite Kay Anderson's work on Vancouver's Chinatown as a classical example of such an approach. In this study Anderson problematises the very notion of "race" along with the idea of "Chinatown" to track their mutual constitution over time by various agents of the Canadian state within a changing set of labour relations (1988, 1991). Deconstructing printed material and buildings as texts broadens the application of the tools of Cultural Geography, and such a technique has been replicated in studies of suburbia and city marketing campaigns (such as Watson 1991; Mee 1994; Silverstone 1997).

Textual studies have since abounded in cultural geography and can provide both a useful methodology and set of case studies relevant to the study of the urban image, festivals and art works within Cultural Capitals. The approach will be utilised when city images are considered in later chapters, while the possibility of reading buildings and art works as texts located within a network of discursively produced power relations will inform my readings of the Guggenheim in Bilbao (Chapter 5), "heritage" landscapes in Singapore and Glasgow (Chapters 4 and 6) and the cultural precinct development of Geelong (Chapter 7).

If geographers like David Harvey highlighted the importance of imageability for tourists and investors, other geographers detailed the ways in which city images were constructed and circulated. So, for example, Sophie Watson traced the ways in which a de-industrialised part of inner Sydney was re-imagined and sold to potential developers as prime real estate during the 1980s (Watson 1991) thereby "gilding the smokestacks" of South Sydney. Crucial to the re-imagining of this place in the eyes of investors was the production and circulation of glossy brochures, which Watson "read" using deconstructive methods. So too, C.A. Mills examined the gentrifying landscapes of 1980s Vancouver through readings of promotional material as well as of houses, to relate stories of different landscape meanings for those moving into and leaving these older areas of the city (Mills 1993). Gentrification was and continues to be seen as a key process by which many western cities replaced industrial spaces with residential ones around port and inner urban areas (Ley 1993; Zukin 1991). Associated with this process is a re-imagining of previously blighted areas of the city.

The discussion and theorisation of gentrification mirrors not only significant spatial changes but also the major trends in geographical thinking on the urban environment over the last thirty years. First defined by the Chicago School of Urban Ecologists in the 1920s, the area immediately adjacent to the central business district of industrial and commercial cities had been singled out for its physical, economic and social diversity but also for being primarily a working class precinct. Labelled the Zone in Transition by Ernest Burgess (1925), this was an area that in 1964 Ruth Glass observed for London:

> One by one, many of the working class quarters of London have been invaded by the middle classes...Once this process of "gentrification" starts in a district it goes on rapidly until all or most of the original working class occupiers are displaced and the whole social character of the district is changed (Glass 1964: xviii).

This area of working class concentration, new migrant ghettoisation and of bohemian and artistic ferment, thereby became one not of invasion and succession by the central business district – though this certainly happened in some cities over the 1960s and 70s – but also one of class displacement and revalorisation. Gentrification thereby became a process primarily associated with a process of class-based colonisation of cheaper residential neighbourhoods and a reinvestment in the physical housing stock (Atkinson 2003: 2343–4). Basically it was a process of middle class resettlement and urban renewal which Marxist Geographers such as David Harvey and Neil Smith explained primarily in class and economic terms. Thus Smith (Smith 1979, 1996) argued that the main driver of gentrification was the gap between property values and land values in the inner city – related to declining physical stock and the flight of the middle class to the suburbs – in a highly accessible location. The resulting *rent-gap* eventually became so wide that it was exploited by property-based capital, real estate agents and developers who purchased cheap housing, rehabilitated it and sold it at inflated prices to those who could afford to pay – the new middle class of service workers. Such a development was facilitated by what he called a "revanchist state", government primarily concerned with capital, informed by neo-liberal principles and working to advance the interests of both. For Smith, gentrification is a back to the city movement by capital first not a movement driven by key groups of overseas born, female professionals or artists. In contrast feminist geographers such as Damaris Rose (2004) and Liz Bondi (1999) highlighted the importance of this precinct for low income single women and latterly those women who were increasingly being incorporated into the business and other service sector industries of the central business core, generating a very different set of aesthetic and service demands in these inner city residential precincts. David Ley (1996) concurred, highlighting the intersection of desire, social reproduction, cultural preferences and the gendered new middle class in the newly gentrifying areas of Toronto and Vancouver.

Thus for economic and cultural geographers, the revaluation and re-population of the inner urban areas of major North American and European cities arose from their changing economic base and related class structuring, in particular the move from manufacturing to a service class which saw the decline in numbers of working class residents and their inner city activities and a rise in a new professional, educated and wealthy middle class. Critical to this shift were single, professional women who valued heritage aesthetics, life style, consumption, social diversity, the arts and accessibility, above all. The economic thereby intersected with the social and the cultural, to create very different valuations and spaces within the city, producing gentrified neighbourhoods which also valued and housed the arts and cultural activity. It was also an area now occupied by those classes who were the biggest fraction supporting the cultural industries and cultural tourism. The resulting urban regeneration and class displacement associated with such a process remains a key issue amongst those seeing this part of the city as critical to the definition and making of Cultural Capitals.

The inner city and its associated economic and cultural activities became the focus of a wave of theorisations on the post-modern city of spectacle (Harvey 1989a) and the creative class. To be considered in more detail later (Chapter 3), Richard Florida (2002) argued for a new class of creative workers involved in the knowledge industries – IT, education, bio-tech, the arts – as emerging in the new century. He observed how they valued social diversity and high quality physical environments. They also consume the arts and culture in cities of technology, talent and tolerance and want to live close to the city centre, ensuring both the gentrification of certain precincts and the growth of new urban economies. In the latest cultural geographies of the inner city, economic and cultural drivers interconnect (Atkinson 2003) so that gentrification arises from changes in economic and class structures as well as from new cultural economies. Whether such a process is uniformly positive, generating social equality, tasteful and sensitive renewal along with broad based economic development, is debatable. For much research confirms that gentrification usually involves working class or lower income displacement, conflict over land use and rights of occupancy and debates over who "owns" the right to access the city/public spaces and urban renewal within a middle class aesthetic and economy of conspicuous consumption. How exactly such debates and realities play out in different locations will be considered in subsequent chapters.

Cultural geographers have not only considered urban buildings, neighbourhoods and city marketing campaigns as texts, but also events and artefacts within them. Thus Ley and Olds (1988) have studied World Fairs (in particular Expo 88 in Vancouver), Rachel Fensham the Sydney Olympics (1994) while Peter Jackson has examined the Notting Hill Carnival as cases where "spectacle" was being mobilised by city authorities to achieve certain political, economic and social objectives. In the case of the Notting Hill Carnival in London, Jackson argues that ethnic difference was activated and presented as a spectacle within a set of historically derived but also geographically dispersed meanings. He thereby details the change in the meanings of carnival from medieval times to pre-colonial and post-colonial Trinidad before documenting the ways in which the festival has been represented by the British media, participants and spectators (Jackson 1988). His argument is that such activities are performances that have particular histories and geographies which can and should be interrogated. Such textual analyses also need to be put alongside the experience of those who participate in the festivals (Jacobs

1999). Such an approach and examples will inform my own study of spectacles and pageants as part of the constitution of Cultural Capitals (in Chapter 7).

The approaches adopted by cultural geographers have focused on texts and meanings, with the built environment, activities, festivals and artefacts considered in these terms. Such studies have brought a vital new perspective to the study of cultures in and through space. Cultural geographers have also brought into the discipline a range of methods – such as close readings and hermeneutics – and perspectives – on the importance of the colonial experience for most parts of the world – which will inform this work. However, the emphasis on texts can and has occurred at the expense of considering power relations and questions of social justice (Nash 2002), while the prioritising of the cultural over other dimensions has limited the disciplinary impact of the approach. The theoretical question of how the material is related to the cultural has bedevilled much of this work (see Gregson, Simonsen and Vaiou 2001). As a result some recent cultural geographies have more explicitly engaged with the issue of relating the cultural to the material, the social to the economic. For example, Kay Anderson has reworked her Chinatown study and applied this refined perspective to other sites to highlight the material as well as cultural permutations of her textual analyses.

Thus Anderson interrogates official discourses and resident interviews to unpack the role of government agencies, the media, police, local black and white activists and indigenous residents in the creation of a negative image for Redfern, a small parcel of land in inner city Sydney, Australia. Here images of blight, crime, poverty, substance abuse, truancy, vandalism, youth disaffection, and despair have become associated with an Aboriginal population which constituted less than 5% of this local government area in 1991. In examining such images and localised efforts to create health, housing and legal alternatives to it, Anderson is careful not to buy into what she calls "resistance readings of the ghetto" or an equally heroic notion of "trans-culturation" but rather prefers "to turn a conceptual spotlight to *sites* of racialised poverty, discursively and spatially located in what (Teresa) de Lauretis …calls those "in-between spaces", minoritised spaces carved in the interstices of discursive regimes (of) capital, race, gentrification, and redevelopment (Anderson 1998: 216). In so doing discursive readings of documents, actions and interview texts are strongly connected to images, policies and practices which shape this place and the identities of those who live and work there.

In a similar way Jane Jacobs analyses a set of community art works completed by one Aboriginal and one non-Aboriginal artist in the centre of Melbourne, Australia in the 1980s. These works were designed to offer "Another View Walking Trail", an urban geography of Aboriginality "that challenged the conventional understanding of the city" (1998: 269). Jacobs' analysis tracks their creation, censoring and mixed reception by the media, the commissioning local government and, to a lesser extent "the public" and Aborigines in Melbourne. A set of confronting art works variously dramatise the violence of colonisation. They are placed on a route that also includes alternate readings of some well known monuments to the European version of settlement. Arranged around the central business district of Melbourne, the works were to be "read" with the assistance of a tourist brochure. In her analysis of this work as well as other urban development projects in Australia and Britain, Jacobs argues that the post-colonial context is essential to understanding their meaning and significance (see Jacobs 1996), a theme I will revisit in Chapter 6 in relation to Singapore. Her study demonstrates that debate over such art works, mobilises and crystallises much longer colonial histories. When played out in the media, in courts and on the streets, such a history and its contested representation has material effects – be it a stalled brewery redevelopment in Perth or the withdrawal of five sculptures from a heritage walk in Melbourne.

Jacobs also locates her discussion of the Walking Trail within what she calls the "aestheticization of the city" in post-modern discourse. Arguing that commentators such as David Harvey, Frederic Jameson and Edward Soja (see Chapter 3) posit art works and the mobilisation of spectacles as vehicles primarily for the expansion of capital and middle class power, Jacobs concludes her analysis by pointing to the power of art to unsettle, trouble and challenge dominant views (see also Gelder and Jacobs 1998 and Chapter 6). She writes of the "Another View Walking Trail":

> It sought to create a legitimate space in which difference could be articulated. This was not simply in terms of traditionalized constructs of Aboriginality … It also provided space for artworks with more troubled (and more clearly political) messages of Aboriginal suffering under colonialism. This example unsettles many of the assumptions that are associated with the process of urban aestheticization. This spectacle served a nationally endorsed political agenda (of reconciliation between Black and White Australians) rather than the honed needs of profit makers. Here the spectacle did not work as a "veil" but as a mechanism in the unveiling of a nation's past (Jacobs 1998: 271–2).

Such a view of the potency of art works is one that will inform the discussion in subsequent chapters. Following Jacobs, I will argue that the activation of creativity in the form of cultural capital can and does have material effects on cities which may trouble dominant views of that city, express something of the marginalised people in them and offer alternative representations. Such a critical and alternative set of spaces are crucial to effective social and cultural sustainability. The arts and urban regeneration can therefore be about social mobilisation and cultural expression as well as capital accumulation. In such a view Jacobs offers a way to value creativity as well as a methodology by which to analyse the creation of cultural value.

Cultural Geography therefore foregrounds the importance of text and textuality in any reading and understanding of the city. Particular studies have focused attention on specific groups, activities and artefacts in the mutual constitution of space and these social groups. Useful techniques of deconstructive analysis have been trialled while an initial focus on texts has been broadened to connect the discursive to power relations and the material in the constitution of particular spaces in the city. Cultural Geographers such as Jane Jacobs have also signalled how cultural artefacts and the aestheticisation of the urban environment need not be politically reactionary and solely about profit, but can involve profound challenges to the ways in which spectacle or public art are constructed and viewed as well as offering broader challenges to political ideologues.

Surprisingly, few cultural geographers have actually focused on the Cultural Industries – with the exception of Chris Gibson (Gibson 2003; Connell and Gibson 2003) and Louise Crewe on fashion design and retailing (Crewe and Forster 1993; Crewe 1996). In his work on music production and performance in Australia, Gibson argues for the mutual constitution of the cultural and the economic; to uncover assumptions and meanings which define the cultural industries as cultural which in turn impact on the meaning of work and labour relations within it (Gibson 2003). Subsequent work has considered the notion of the Creative Class and the Cultural Industries as travelling discourses that may or may not translate across the globe and may or may not facilitate economic and cultural development or allow minority voices expression. Thus in a study of the planned application of the Creative City idea to Darwin, Australia, Gibson joins with Susan Luckman, Tess Lea and Chris Brennan-Horley to critically assess the notion as one which has both blinded city authorities from appreciating the extant cultural industries and limited their appreciation of its socially and racially regressive effects but also potential (Luckman et al. 2007).

In other geographical studies on the Cultural Industries – such as that completed by Allan Scott on *The Cultural Economy of Cities* (2000) – the analysis is driven primarily by the economics rather than the cultural aspects of the industry. Therefore there remains a need for an approach that adequately meshes the cultural and discursive with the material and social; one which recognises the socio-cultural complexity but also groundedness of art, precincts and the city. Assistance in such a quest is provided by those working within the discipline of sociology and others concerned with the social relations of the Cultural/Creative Industries.

Sociology of the Cultural Industries

One of the earliest uses of the term "Cultural Industry" was by two members of the Frankfurt School of Critical Theory – Theodore Adorno and Max Hokkheimer – as they bemoaned the corruption wrought by the mass production and commodification of the creative arts. For these two key founders of sociology, culture had lost its capacity to offer critique and utopian alternatives because it had become part of the market place (Hesmondhalgh 2002: 15). In an essay on the "Culture Industry Reconsidered" Adorno noted how the commodification of art "impedes the development of autonomous, independent individuals who judge and decide for themselves" (1991a: 92). Further he noted how:

> The concoctions of the culture industry are neither guides for a blissful life, nor
> a new art of moral responsibility, but rather exhortations to toe the line, behind
> which stand the most powerful interests. The consensus that it propagates
> strengthens blind, opaque authority (Adorno 1991a: 91).

This is a pessimistic view of corporate culture invading the creation and circulation of
all forms of commodified culture. For Adorno this was a development which not only
lessened the creative autonomy of the individual artist, but destroyed the distinction
between low and high art, industrialised cultural production and undermined the
critical aspects of both its production and consumption (Adorno 1991b).

While not invoking Adorno's work as a precursor, Sharon Zukin has seemingly
inherited his pessimism when she writes of the many costs and problems associated
with the "symbolic economy" (1995), an intertwining of cultural symbols with
entrepreneurial capital (1995: 3). In elaborating this term, she writes of the ways
in which public space has been given over to private entrepreneurs and security
officers in the streets, parks and shopping centres of New York; of the restrictive
labour relations which underpin the city's economy; as well as the fantasylands
that the Disney Corporation creates across the world. In this exercise she connects
the creation of cultural symbols to urban transformations, materialising the arts
into a political economy which is enriched as a consequence. Consistent with her
location within a Marxist tradition, though, instead of seeing aestheticisation as
permitting some measure of creative expression and critical questioning, Zukin's
narratives tell only of artistic co-option, corporate greed and the limited social
and cultural success associated with galleries, museums and artistic activity.
For her the "symbolic economy" in action is corrupting; as the association with
entrepreneurial capital devalues the artistic product, compromises creative people
and imposes exploitative social relations on all those involved. Examining such
activities at various locations shows how these oppressive social relations are
translated into parks, theme parks and gallery spaces which are private rather
than public, exclusive rather than inclusive and inhibiting rather than liberating.
Pleasure is thereby reserved for the duped, pain for the many and riches for the
few in this new economy.

Despite her grinding pessimism, Zukin's emphasis on the social and spatial
relations involved in the "symbolic economy" offers a useful approach and some
great case studies. Overall, in her studies of the Massuchetts Museum of Modern
Art (MassMoMA) and on the plight of New York artists, there is a sense that the
cultural dice are loaded from the start, that her approach to the intersection of
corporate capital with the arts demonises the former as it ripped off by the latter.
While hard lessons in the cost of pursuing iconic galleries to revive local economies
must be acknowledged, I will be arguing that such negative experiences do not
apply in all such cases. Further, as later pages will illustrate, even where there are
local conflicts and corporate profits to be made, these do not necessarily preclude
the creation of well designed parks, provocative performances and enlivened
heritage precincts. Introducing meaning, power, space and social relations into the

analysis of Cultural Capitals is to be commended, but there is also a need to allow space for the critical role of the arts, and for the reading of works, projects and communities to be contested and celebratory as well as oppressive. Any notion of a "symbolic economy" also needs far more theorisation than is possible through a series of case studies united by their connection of art to corporate capital. Just how that capital operates to create oppressive social relations also needs further analysis. Such an analysis as well as a related but different view of the symbolic economy is provided by David Hesmondhalgh (2002) in his sociological study of the Cultural Industries.

For Hesmondhalgh the Cultural Industries are distinguished by the creation and circulation of texts. Focusing primarily on what he describes as the "Core Cultural Industries" of advertising and marketing, broadcasting, film, music, print and electronic publishing, video and computer games as well as the internet industry, Hesmondhalgh draws heavily on the insights of cultural economists to delimit the main imperatives, contradictions and solutions within the industry. Endorsing Zukin's approach, he sees the main driver as the pursuit of profit by the companies involved. While acknowledging that this may well be detrimental to the interests of people as citizens, he concentrates on the problems in the industry for its participants. Drawing heavily on the logics of cultural economics, his analysis is primarily concerned with the risks associated with the Cultural Industry: especially with high production but low reproduction costs in its creation of semi public goods. For him, such economic imperatives necessitate a large repertoire, corporate concentration, integration and co-opting strategies, the creation of artificial scarcity as well as a range of formats – such as stars, genres and serials – and the loose control of symbol creators along with tight control of distribution and marketing (2002: 17).

Ignoring the creative arts, Hesmondhalgh concentrates on what he regards as those activities that are most powerful in the contemporary economy and society – the film, publishing, music and electronic media industries. Focusing on their social and power relations, he concludes that while there has been significant growth, internationalisation, vertical and horizontal integration of the companies involved, the fundamental autonomy of the creative individual remains, albeit with tighter control over the reproduction and circulation of their work and a larger role for market research in its creation (Hesmondhalgh 2002). These developments, along with the growth in what he describes as "diasporic television" and the media industries of Hong Kong, India and Latin America, have failed to dent the overall dominance of US companies in the Cultural Industries he considers. He thereby analyses why and how the United States has come to dominate key elements of the industry while also admitting counterveiling developments in other parts of the globe. For him US dominance has a very long history and is related to the progressive de-regulation of its media, film and computer corporations, alongside a tightening of controls over intellectual property, huge defence industry investment in computer technologies and the strength of the consumption economy. Hesmondhalgh does not accept that there is a high and inevitable level of convergence via digital technologies in the industry or a significant shift towards a knowledge economy either in the United States or globally. For, in recognising the regionalisation of the industry across the world, he notes how levels of ownership and access to digital technology are profoundly limited across the world as well as within Developed countries, while the degree of interconnection between segments of the industry also remain limited. He therefore concludes: "There may have been a partial shift towards economies based on culture, information and symbols. But none of us yet live in a 'knowledge economy' or an 'information age'" (2002: 261).

Hesmondhalgh has particularly insightful discussions of the changing role of the state in a number of countries as well as the various technical and other imperatives that drove the expansion of the Cultural Industries over the 1980s and 1990s (see Chapter 3). He charts the rise of neo-liberal policies in Australia, the UK, the US and Europe such that a neo-classical economic view of the industry came to prevail – along with limited state support and regulation and the triumph of marketisation. "The result was the privatisation of public telecommunications organisations and some public broadcasting institutions; the opening up of television systems to other broadcasters operating cable, satellite and other means of delivery; the tearing down of regulatory walls between different industries; plus significant changes in laws and rules on content, media ownership and subsidies" (2002: 257). In his consideration of the role of governments in setting the regulatory context, the power of corporations and also of creative individuals within them, Hesmondhalgh gives a nuanced analysis of the sociology and power dynamics operating in key parts of the Cultural Industries.

Seeing the Cultural Industries as those which produce and circulate texts, it is intriguing that Hesmondhalgh concentrates on the social relations of their production and circulation and so little on their reception. Indeed, in his conclusion he argues for an "open-minded attitude towards the kinds of uses and pleasures that people might take from texts" and a need to "focus on symbol creators". However, he offers no tools or examples by which this might proceed, though a whole tradition within sociology and cultural studies exists which allows such individuals, their artistic products and audiences to become the focus of study (such as Bennett, Emmison and Frow 1999). As noted earlier, cultural geographers have also provided the tools and exemplars for such an analysis.

Both Zukin and Hesmondhalgh have focused on the social relations which constitute the Cultural Industries; one at the level of companies operating across the globe and the other looking at the way such organisations operate in small parts of New York. Inheriting the tradition extending back to Adorno, both writers view the Cultural Industries as limited by their profit orientation, technology and concern with creating and selling texts/images/environments. While seeing the industry as a vital part of the future, the view of both is somewhat pessimistic. In contrast, another analyst of the social relations underpinning the Cultural Industries sees only a buoyant future, one where there is a different geography and sociology underpinned by a more expansive definition of "the creative class".

Thus in an enormously influential book – *The Rise of the Creative Class* (2002) – Richard Florida argues that the various economic, technological and social transformations which have made the media and communications industries vitally important have also engendered other changes. Beginning with the geography of regional buoyancy across the United States, Florida isolates a number of common characteristics which for him explain the emergence of cities like Washington DC, Boston, Austin, Chicago and San Francisco as centres of rapid population growth. He argues that their growth did not arise from firms moving into these areas or the mobilisation of their social capital, but rather arises from creative people seeking out and making these urban environments their own. These cities in turn become centres of innovation and high technology industry. What they have in common Florida argues is "technology, talent and tolerance" (2003:10). Technology involves mobilising capital and innovation in the creation of new things, processes and industries. The two most important and recent are software and bio technology which, Florida argues, have benefited from the availability of venture capital and the capacity of universities to connect with their communities to form centres of productive enterprises. Another key is talent, collections of highly educated creative people, who come together to be innovative and productive in particular places. They in turn, Florida argues, are attracted to places which have a social milieu which fosters and supports their creativity and associated work and life style. One vital indicator of the openness of these places to new ideas, creativity and innovation is their "tolerance" and this in turn Florida measures with a Gay and Bohemian index. Of great importance to later case studies – especially in Singapore but also Australia – the number and proportion of gay people as well as those involved in the creative arts – writers, dancers, musicians, actors, photographers, painters and sculptors – is seen as crucial to the future economic and social success of a city (Florida 2002). All three dimensions – of technology, talent and tolerance – are necessary to ensure the convergence in any one place of the creative class and the related buzz to ensure the ongoing growth of that city or region (Florida 2002, 2003).

The creative class is a broad category of workers who "engage in work whose function it is to create meaningful new forms" (2003: 8). The "super creative core" includes scientists and engineers, university professors, poets and novelists, artists, entertainers, actors, designers and architects as well as thought leaders – non-fiction writers, editors, researchers, analysts and other opinion makers. Beyond this group are "creative professionals" who work in a range of knowledge-based occupations; in high tech sectors, financial services, the legal and health-care professions, and in business management. The creative class is therefore an expansive social grouping, one which includes creative artists but also many others from what would have been labelled previously the middle class of managers, innovators and upper level white collar workers. Collectively these groups comprise 30% of the US workforce. Florida demonstrates how these groups are in far higher concentrations in those cities and regions which are booming. These groups staff the core industries of the creative economy – publishing, software, TV and radio, design, music, film, advertising, performing arts, crafts, video games, art, fashion and research – a list comparable to that devised by UNESCO and in Britain, Singapore, Australia and Spain when quantifying their Cultural or Creative Industries.

Florida's analysis in this and in a subsequent book on *Cities and the Creative Class* (2003, 2005) has proliferated across the globe – a point to be considered again in Chapter 8 – and has inspired major policy shifts towards the arts and political tolerance in a range of places (Singapore being the most noteworthy). While criticised for being somewhat tautological (i.e. if you have a broad definition of a growth class you will necessarily get growth regions), somewhat instrumental, neglectful of social divides, empirically flawed and overly optimistic (see Malanga 2004; Peck 2005). Florida's work has catapulted the notion of a Cultural Capital to the fore of many urban political agendas. His model has legitimised a focus on the arts and creativity as vital for sustainable urban social and economic development. His focus on the actual individuals and social groups that create cultural capital as well as on the social environment that they make and are attracted to, offers guidance as well as inspiration to the analysis that follows. Beyond noting the demographic and creative class profile of a place, however, I would argue that it is necessary to isolate just how the arts are valued in a locality and how the mobilisation of creative arts engenders social, economic and physical changes in a place. Florida points to these developments after they have occurred and works backwards to distil commonalities. If indeed his analysis and suggestions for growth are correct, then it should be possible to track the impact of particular artistic or creative activities on one place as it unfolds. Such is one of the many objectives of the case studies which follow.

A comprehensive engagement with Cultural Capitals therefore should involve a systematic consideration of their cultural economics, the social relations associated with the production and consumption of creative works as well as a cultural geography of the meanings associated with the objects and environments which arise. While inspired and guided by Florida's notion of the creative class, such a model can emerge from a reworking of cultural capital as a concept drawn from Sociology, Tourism Studies and Cultural Economics.

Cultural Capital in Cultural Capitals – A Framework for Analysis

In approaching the theoretical issue of defining what is cultural capital, I am drawn past the model offered by David Throsby and Cultural Economics to the work of that great critic of capitalist society – Karl Marx – his dialectical historical materialism and theory of human nature. However, it is necessary to go beyond Marx's labour theory of value to focus on the particular case of artistic creation. In this I am assisted by the work of Throsby, Richards and the French sociologist Pierre Bourdieu. The concept of *cultural capital* which Bourdieu developed connects values to artefacts within a specific array of class and institutional settings. When linked to the work of Throsby, Richards, Richard Florida and the

New Zealand economist Anne De Bruin, the production of cultural commodities can be thought of and researched in a way that recognises creative labour and the socio-political dynamics of creating, circulating and institutionalising its symbolic as well as economic value at particular locations. Such a production regime needs to be connected to a social economy of consumption, one which also acknowledges the vital class, gender and place-based processes involved. Doing this as a cultural geographer foregrounds and rightly recognises the importance of *place* in this process and offers tools for analysing the cultural artefacts; as the various networks and biographies which produce cultural objects and activity as valuable are place specific and have spatially localised impacts .

My reading of Marx and those who then applied his framework, lead me to conclude that he approached nineteenth century European capitalism with a particular theory of human nature on which he then constructed the labour theory of value. In Marx's formulation, human beings have objective and necessary powers and needs. In his schema it was human labour power that then acted on nature to create goods which satisfied these needs. Further, it was these powers and needs that were corrupted and alienated by capitalist social relations. Conceptualised as abstract and outside of history, human powers and needs could only be described when they assumed concrete forms in particular times and social situations. In a similar way, his notion of value was formulated with an abstract and then a socially located set of meanings (Horvath and Gibson 1984).

In his three volume *Critical Analysis of Capitalist Production*, labour power is the ultimate source of value and its alienation one of the great tensions within the system. Actual value is derived when labour power is applied to raw materials within a production process with particular class relations. Such a production system in turn creates goods whose value can only be realised through exchange and consumption (Marx 1954, 1956). It is a cycle with each stage related to and dependent on the other. The value of a factory-produced shoe, for example, derives from the raw materials and labour power expended to produce it. However, this value and shoe is useless unless it has some utility to others who are willing to exchange something – usually money – for it. In the process of realising the value of the shoe, an exchange has to occur. While profit is siphoned off, along with an amount for the necessary labour involved in producing the shoe, its value is only realised once it has been consumed and the spoils re-invested. It is an upward cycle of accumulation where every stage is dependent on the other.

Marx's notion of value was inextricably linked to powers and needs registered in the labour process and systems of production and circulation in historically specific social situations. His concept of value – like all others in his schema – was *relational;* in that the meaning and activity of creating value emerged from a complex set of interconnected social relations (Ollman 1976). Any study of value therefore has to focus on the process by which value is created and ascribed. In a way not dissimilar to that offered by David Throsby when he was delimiting an economic view of cultural capital and Richards in his understanding of class-based tourist activity, David Harvey suggests that a fixed notion of value has to be replaced with an understanding of the social processes of valuation (Harvey 1996: 10-11). Such a system of creating value is both social and economic; as what is valuable is profoundly cultural. How to move beyond such an abstract approach to the actual study of value systems in the art world is assisted by the work of Pierre Bourdieu and his formulation of *cultural capital.*

As noted earlier, Pierre Bourdieu developed the notion of cultural capital to describe the possession of knowledge, accomplishments, formal and informal qualifications *embodied* by individuals and used by them to negotiate their social position. Though not necessarily matching the distribution of economic and social capital, in Bourdieu's analysis, cultural capital tended to reinforce the unequal class order of late twentieth century France (Brooker 1999). Bourdieu subsequently used his formulation to analyse and explain the high failure rate of working class children in the French school system as well as to detail and socially situate the tastes of the bourgeoisie. From this he argued that the notion of "culture" had the effect of reinforcing and legitimising middle-class power as its members worked to gain more of it and to act as models to others (Bourdieu 1984, 1994).

If cultural capital is held (or *embodied*) by individuals as a consequence of their family background, education and placement in the class system creating a form of class distinction, the cultural object – or *objectified cultural capital* – intersects with the schema to attain its value through its position in a *field of cultural production.* Within each field for Bourdieu, there are objective qualities which govern success, and these include price, awards or grants. These fields are comparable to the particular qualities of artistic activity delimited by cultural economists such as Throsby – and they include aesthetic, symbolic and historical value as well as values ascribed by the market place. Each field is the consequence of forces and struggles between key arbiters of taste, institutionalised interests, those who gaze upon, value and purchase the artistic products and the political context in which such transactions occur. As a result, changes in literary or artistic possibilities result from alterations in the power relations which constitute the positions and dispositions by those involved in defining art and its value – bureaucrats, patrons, critics, producers, arts managers, viewers, tourists and consumers (Bourdieu 1994). It is the intersection of embodied and objectified output with artistic institutions which thereby give any art object or activity its value.

Such an analysis by Bourdieu relativises taste, artistic production and valuing within specific social and spatial orders while also recognising that such systems obtain a real potency in their operation which reinforces particular class orders. For Bourdieu such a framework allowed the delimitation of cultural matrices on axes of autonomy – where art is produced for its own sake for a limited and highly specialised audience (high art) – and heteronomy – where art is highly commercial and favoured by those who dominate the field politically and economically (popular culture) (Bourdieu 1984). The value of the artistic objects or events and the status of those who produce and consume them varies as a result. In his detailed analysis of particular art forms, Bourdieu thereby linked artistic objects and activity to class, power, politics and taste.

Bourdieu's concept of cultural capital has allowed some in cultural studies and cultural economics to quantify and qualify the cultural industries and artistic products. John Frow draws on the notions of cultural field and regimes of value (Frow 1995, 1998) while Anne De Bruin uses Bourdieu's distinction between embodied, objectified and institutionalised cultural capital to assess the cultural production of a particular social group in Auckland New Zealand (de Bruin 1996, 1998a, 1998b). Both are useful to someone aiming for a workable concept of cultural capital by which the value and sustainability of the arts can be researched in place.

In trying to unpack the subjective dimension of artistic activity, John Frow has examined the way cultural objects are created through "regimes of value" – sets of social relations where desire and demand, reciprocal sacrifice and power interact to create value in specific social situations. He concludes, following Bourdieu, that every act of ascribing value to a commodity is specific to the regime which organises it; such that value formation is always the result of particular social relations and mechanisms of signification (Frow 1995, 1998; see also Baudrillard 1981). What such an analysis offers is a sensitivity to the ways in which social relations and social values impinge on the creation, ascription of meaning and consumption of a cultural object or activity. Beyond simple quantification, this view admits localised complexity, contestation and subjectivity in the process of value creation and reception. However, what would be helpful is a more nuanced and structured approach to the various elements which make up cultural capital and the field in which it is produced, circulated and consumed. This is provided by Anne De Bruin's use of Bourdieu to understand the cultural capital of Pacific Islanders in South Auckland, New Zealand.

De Bruin uses Bourdieu's disaggregated notion of cultural capital to analyse and facilitate community employment initiatives. She firstly considers embodied, objectified and institutionalised forms of cultural capital:

1. **Embodied cultural capitals** are the abilities, talents, styles, language, values, creative labour or images of people in a group – such as writers, painters, film makers or a particular ethnic group organising a self-referential festival. To mesh her analysis with that of Richard Florida, this embodied cultural capital ensures someone may be a member of the core creative class.

2. **Objectified cultural capital** comprises the cultural goods such as paintings, books, food, performances, films, heritage buildings and so on that are the result of conscious creative activity. They are the objects which are produced by individuals or groups, they express cultural identity and can be commodified (or not), circulated and consumed by others if they regard them as valuable. Adding here the insights of cultural geographers and tourist studies, their value as meaning statements is subject to the

field in which they are produced – by the embodied cultural capital that is within them, the social context in which they are presented to others and the political and institutionalised context in which they are circulated and either viewed or purchased. They in turn can be read as texts to derive their various meanings.

3. **Institutionalised cultural capital**, is where embodied and objectified cultural capital is directed into structures that can enhance an individual or group's social or economic position. This can involve a public showing of a film, video or paintings; the sale of a book manuscript, writing for a newspaper, patent and use of a computer game, a commissioned and built urban design (De Bruin 1998a). Following the analyses of the cultural economists and sociologists, such institutional interventions need to be analysed in terms of their costs and benefits as well as their role in supporting particular groups over others.

De Bruin took this framework and worked with Pacific Islanders in Auckland to identify particular aspects of their culture – organisational networks, music and artistic motifs – which were valuable to them and legible to others, to create new urban designs, a music recording company and an arts festival. As an economist, her interest was in the ways in which this cultural capital was converted into economic capital through concerted and innovative community action (1996, also 1998b). While de Bruin frames her analysis primarily in terms of embodied cultural capital, her analysis of the work undertaken by the Samoans in South Auckland is readily recast into Bourdieu's three categories of cultural capital and linked to the insights of David Throsby (Cultural Economics), Greg Richards (cultural tourism), Richard Florida (and the creative class) and cultural geographers (especially Kay Anderson and Jane Jacobs) to guide further analysis.

De Bruin's work indicates that utilising the three elements of cultural capital can offer a viable framework for unpacking the relational ways in which cultural activity is produced, circulated and apprehended by others. She shows how cultural capital is not only "valuable" when translated into economic capital, but has value through its links with social capital – networks, relations of reciprocity and trust. Here then is a mechanism by which to connect the material concerns of the political and cultural economist to the social, textual and spatial concerns of the social scientist. In her work there is also a notion of value in cultural activity and objects which is related to community pride, confidence, creativity and sense of place as well as in their aesthetic and critical roles. These forms of cultural capital can also be projected to and observed by others, as travellers and tourists. Contained within a power relationship of othering, such a dynamic is also contingent, in that a colonial relationship may exist or be transcended in the constitution of the event or cultural object. Such a framework can be utilised in the systematic study of particular cultural artefacts – the Guggenheim in Bilbao, heritage precincts and theatre in Singapore, design and city images of Glasgow, and waterfront redevelopment in Geelong. Such an analysis in subsequent chapters involves the following interconnected dimensions, across a range of scales:

Table 2.1   A framework for analysing c/Cultural Capitals

Embodied	Objectified	Institutional	Analytical techniques
Individual artist/ performer/art maker Motley crew of assistants	Individual art works	Policy framework Education/training Funding support Art market Audience – present and virtual Galleries and other spaces	Economic costs and impact Discourse analysis of texts and art works as produced and viewed Political citizenship
Groups of artists/ perfomers/art makers	Collective art works – theatre, film, gallery. Museum, park	Policy framework Education/training Funding support Art market Audience – present and virtual	Economic costs and impact Textual analysis of buildings, parks, performances Social impacts Citizenship
Designers, planners, heritage experts	Heritage buildings or precincts Galleries and theatres	As above + Arts precinct Cultural Industries	Economic costs and impacts Discourse analysis of texts Textual analysis of buildings, objects Social Impacts
Organisers and festival participants	Festival or event	As above + Space in which event occurs	Economic costs and impacts Social and political inclusion Cultural sustainability

Chapter 3
The Emergence of Cultural Capitals

A number of Geelong residents might scoff at the idea of a Guggenheim art museum coming to Geelong…The fact is Geelong does need to re-invent itself for the future. It cannot expect investors and new employers to come to Geelong rather than elsewhere without good reason. And so it must make itself an alluring destination to all manner of interests; industry, commerce, tourists, transport, education, researchers … experience overseas has shown significant boosts to regional economies where Guggenheim museums have been established. Geelong's economy, given the region's chronic and grossly under-stated unemployment problems, is in serious need of a major boost. (GA Editorial February 12, 2000).

This editorial in the *Geelong Advertiser*, endorsing the expenditure of significant funds for the pursuit of a Guggenheim Museum signals the continued potency and widespread endorsement of the Cultural Capital redevelopment strategy across the world. Geelong had long been a major manufacturing centre (see Chapter 7) but suffered a number of economic shocks over the 1970s and 80s so that efforts to restructure the economy and re-imagine the city were intensified, focusing firstly on the search for a new image, then on waterfront redevelopment and more recently on efforts to secure a Guggenheim museum and build a cultural precinct (Johnson 1990, 2002, 2006). In such moves, Geelong was echoing the experience and strategy of many cities around the world. This Chapter will examine the common pre-conditions for these strategies adopted by Geelong, but also Bilbao, Singapore, Glasgow, and many other cities as they searched for ways to move from industrial wastelands to re-inventing their urban image and economic foundation around waterfront redevelopment and the creative arts.

If the previous chapters looked at defining, conceptualising and mapping Cultural Capitals across the world, it is now appropriate to focus on their emergence at particular locations and times. Why was there a delineation of the Cultural Industries and moves to foster their development and that of Cultural Capitals from the 1980s? And what was the trajectory of these moves, both spatially and temporally? If Glasgow was one of the first cities to adopt this strategy (in the 1980s), Bilbao one of the most dramatic (in the 1990s) and Singapore and Geelong two of the most unlikely (from 2000), why did such an agenda emerge and why was it still considered a viable path to pursue by many cities across the world in the new century?

There are a range of academic scripts which describe and explain the last thirty years of urban change and socio-economic development. Such accounts by implication, if not explicitly, deal with the emergence of Cultural Capitals. These include narratives of globalisation – an acceleration in the movement as well as the heightened integration of capital, goods, people and cultures across the world. Globalisation builds on older discussions of imperialism and of a New International Division of Labour (NIDL), which charts the mobility of capital and jobs from industrial cities in the west to a number of "Third World" locations during the 1960s and 1970s. Such a re-sorting of investment created new centres of command and control in the global capitalist system and it is these World Cities and their regional counterparts, which both compete vigorously for their place in a global urban hierarchy and seemingly benefit most from it. Associated with such boom cities are others which bear the brunt of the other side of these developments – deindustrialisation. The abandonment of manufacturing, the demise of waterfronts and resulting social dislocation in cities, precincts and whole regions, present real challenges for governments in these localities, providing spaces as well as political imperatives to find alternatives. These alternatives include a post-Fordist transformation of work-places, support for the growth of services – including finance, retail and banking – but also the Cultural Industries and tourism which are based on a new cultural logic of late capitalism: post-modernity. The post-modern involves an architectural style, a critique of western knowledges, deconstructive analytical techniques as well as a view of goods and services as textual, symbolic and integral to identity construction. This post-modern aesthetic and economy becomes a fundamental foundation on which the Cultural Industries and Cultural Capitals were to be erected.

Associated with these developments in economic, social and cultural life go particular spatial effects; as from globalisation, post-Fordism and post-modernity emerges World Cities, cultural tourism, intense inter city competition, new internal geographies of industrial and port abandonment, and imperatives for urban renewal. In this context, the creative arts assume a status not just as an economic driver (see Chapter 1) but also a key way in which urban areas can be redecorated, redesigned, and redeveloped. Localised initiatives to boost the arts thereby become part of a larger agenda to deliberately create Cultural Capitals, spurred by sales pitches from academics and consultants such as Charles Landry and Richard Florida. It was Landry and others in Comedia who championed the creative city and Cultural Capital strategy over the 1980s and 90s, a strategy which received a new direction through the work of Florida as it was transformed into the Creative Class agenda for urban renewal from the late 1990s. Such recipes for renewal are received in very different ways by cities attempting to deal with economic change. For some, there is also a fraught colonial history which refracts the messages and shapes the ways in which the new global era is negotiated. In meeting the challenges of deindustrialisation, globalisation, and heightened inter-urban competition, there are a number of governance models, dominated by those around urban entrepreneurialism and neo-liberalism, but also involving socialist quests for social and spatial justice. These dimensions – of economic restructuring, new international divisions of labour, symbolic economies and the role of global consultants – are necessary for any understanding of Cultural Capitals, though each alone does not adequately explain the timing and location of each.

Unable to fully explain the emergence and precise locations of Cultural Capitals, but presented as powerful conceptual overviews of the recent past, frameworks such as post-modernity and the new international division of labour reveal a discursive confidence that, some argue, is poorly founded. For writers such as Katherine Gibson-Graham, this *will to know* ignores the groundedness of theorisation and the impossibility of constructing such overarching grand narratives. Post-modernity itself, along with feminism and post-colonialism, renders the quest for overweening social theory and its various abstract artefacts not only politically suspect but necessarily partial and incomplete. Further, any overall interpretation will tend to obliterate the difference, diversity, contestation, divergences, ruptures and fluidity that characterises the contemporary world. The quest for explanation and pattern is therefore doomed to fail; misguided, conservative and insensitive to the power dynamics involved in creating knowledge (Deutsche 1996; Gibson-Graham 1996).

One response to such a critique is to view the quest to explain the emergence of Cultural Capitals as a lost cause, to be replaced by localised narratives highlighting the particular, contested and diverse stories involved at each site. However, as the case studies will illustrate, while such local stories are vital to understanding the specific conditions which produce a cultural artefact, event or claim in any one location, they also have parallels and connections to international agencies, ideas and developments. Such patterns invite more general explanation. The designation of a Cultural Capital at any one place at a particular point in time occurs within a wider web of national and often international trends, discourses, flows and networks. Space, as Doreen Massey argues, is relational, with the local and the global mutually constituted in an ongoing, open-ended and empirical way which can be described and understood (Massey 2005). Sketching commonalities and international connections does not deny difference or contestation but rather establishes patterns and the basis for interpretation. For me, an attempt to forge an explanation for the emergence of not one but a large number of Cultural Capitals from the 1980s, in particular localities, is part of a will to know which guides feminist and post-colonial scholars as much as it does political economists. But it is also a political quest – part of a will to positively influence – which arises from the ethics informing this study. Thus as Chapter 1 outlined, if in the process of making a Cultural Capital, creativity is mobilised to effect political, social, cultural as well as economically sustainable outcomes, then the city and world become better places for it. Mapping and explaining this process as part of understanding it, can be a prelude to its replicability, while tabling unsuccessful or limited attempts offers cautions as well as insights to others. What follows therefore is an engagement with some of those who have described and attempted to explain the social, cultural and economic trends over the last thirty years which in turn have impacted on cities and generated Cultural Capitals.

Cultural Capitals have therefore been variously positioned within discourses around globalisation and World City formation, which heighten the competition between cities for investment; post-Fordism and post-modernity boosting the Cultural Industries, tourism and spectacles in cities; and new international divisions of labour and economic restructuring, creating crises for industrial centres, generating new imperatives for governments and new nodes of service sector activity. Such cities also need to be located within the ever-present dynamics of colonialism and post-colonialism. I will argue here that there are a number of preconditions for the emergence of Cultural Capitals operating at a global scale:

- Economic restructuring, the NIDL and the IT revolution
- Post-modernity, the symbolic economy and the emergence of the Cultural Industries
- Globalisation and inter-urban competition
- Urban entrepreneurialism, and
- Post-colonialism

It is necessary to acknowledge that such developments occurred across a number of countries from at least the mid-20th century so that such trends cannot fully explain the emergence of Cultural Capitals at particular localities. For as Chapter 1 indicated, Cultural Capitals are located in some places but not others and, as Chapter 2 detailed, the embodied class fractions that pursue and form the social foundation for them – as workers, artists and tourists – are also geographically localised as are particular enabling government policies and practices. It is therefore also necessary to focus on those particular times and places where Cultural Capitals emerged to develop localised explanations. What is needed then are an array of local biographies – on Glasgow, Bilbao, Singapore and Geelong – which can detail why Cultural Capitals emerged at particular times and places. Such is the purpose of later chapters.

Economic Restructuring, the NIDL and IT Revolution

The shift in western economies from manufacturing to services is a fundamental restructuring which has been occurring over the last thirty years with a range of profound social and spatial effects. For the advanced capitalist economies of Europe, North America and Australasia, the period from the 1950s to the 1970s was one of steady economic growth, rising standards of living, and a relatively stable system of democratic government with related interventions to ensure a welfare state and some support of the arts. But from the 1970s to the 1990s profits fell significantly across all sectors, but especially in manufacturing. While debate rages as to what impelled such a fall – with over production competition between capitalist countries (Harvey 1989a and b), new technologies (Castells 1989, 2000) and effective labour claims (Lash and Urry 1987; Hebdidge 1989) being the most common – the net effect was four fold (see Table 3.1):

1. the mass closure of industry across the western world
2. movement of much labour intensive production to parts of the "Third World" by multi-national corporations, encouraged by development policies and agencies in what became a few Newly Industrialising Countries
3. the extensive use of labour-displacing information technology and new ways of organising production to boost productivity in first world countries, and
4. the shift of investment and employment into the service sector in the west.

The demise of manufacturing and the rise of services involved capital investment in some localities and dis-investment in others (see Cooke 1989; Hudson 1989; Massey 1984). Thus, between 1977 and 1993, the USA lost roughly 2 million – about a tenth – of its manufacturing jobs. Britain was even more severely affected, losing 3.6 million – 45% – between 1974 and 1994 as did Australia and Spain (see Table 3.1). The brunt of this decline fell on the older industrial cities. In the USA these were concentrated in the north-eastern states. In the UK, by contrast, nowhere was immune, though northern and middle England, Scotland and Wales generally suffered more (Ward 1998 in Hall and Hubbard: 46). In Australia the major metropolitan centres but also a few key industrial provincial hubs felt the impact. The resulting de-industrialisation of cities and neighbourhoods marked such restructuring indelibly on the urban landscapes as did the inflow of investment and employment into services.

Sometimes services were concentrated along major roads in suburban office precincts, in what became labelled in the US as Edge Cities (Garreau 1991) but also into retail, recreational and tourist developments, within city centres and elsewhere. Associated with service sector growth and industrial dis-investment, went the technical revitalisation of some industry in developed countries but also the movement of much manufacturing production to lower cost regions (see Massey 1984) and to some low wage countries.

When explaining the parallel rise of the Cultural Industries in the 1980s, David Hesmondhalgh (2002) isolated three key developments:

1. A shift in political ideology and action towards neo-liberalism
2. The spatial fix of internationalisation or globalisation, and
3. New organisational forms, what is elsewhere was described as post-Fordism.

The notion of a spatial fix to the problems bedevilling developed countries in the 1970s was given theoretical weight by the notion of a New International Division of Labour (NIDL). The NIDL was seen as critical to the growth of manufacturing capacity in a few developing countries, which in turn generated import competition within western countries and led to the technological re-organisation, down sizing and abandonment of industrial plants and areas in those countries. In a trail-blazing text dealing with the West German textile industry, Frobel, Heinrichs and Kreye (1980) charted the moves offshore of German textile corporations in the 1960s and 70s. They related such patterns to the development of a world wide reservoir of labour power which was abundant, amenable and low cost – ultimately female, located in some third world cities and further concentrated in Export Processing Zones – the development and refinement of new technologies which allowed complex production processes to be broken down into elementary units, such that unskilled labour could be extensively used; and transport and communication technologies which rendered industrial location and the management of production largely independent of geographical distance (Frobel, Heinrichs and Kreye 1980: 13, 34–6; Johnson 1991; see also Cohen 1981; Higgott 1984; Jenkins 1984). The experience of the textile industry during the 1970s and 1980s was replicated by electronics, which moved away from the centres of their creation – the United States and Japan – into nearby underdeveloped regions (such as Singapore, Ireland, Mexico) for manufacture and assembly. Such moves were associated with the active creation of low cost and docile workforces – which were often female and racialised – by governments, foreign investors and intermediaries (see Elson and Pearson 1981; Fernandez-Kelly 1983; Mies 1986; Mitter 1986).

The idea of increasingly mobile capital moving out of developed countries across the globe in search of profitable investment opportunities was taken up by David Harvey in his seminal study of *The Condition of Postmodernity* (1989a). Connecting economic internationalisation to cultural and technical developments, Harvey's argument, like that of Frobel, Heinrichs and Kreye (1980), was infused with a Marxist political economy which prioritised economic over other imperatives. Thus for Harvey, US and European capitalists attempted to restore profits by investing abroad, to spread fixed costs and to make the most of cheap labour as wages rose at home. While off shore investment and internationalisation had a much longer history, with for example the United Kingdom investing heavily abroad from 1870–1914, this activity was highly concentrated in British colonies and based on extractive industries. In contrast, the waves of international investment of the 1970s and 80s were spearheaded by trans-national corporations, with the globalisation of production and distribution assisted by neo-liberal trade policies as well as the new communications technologies. It was for Harvey a different era of 'time-space compression' (Harvey 1989a) which ensured that cities in developed countries had to become more attractive to hypermobile capital; through government policies, urban spectacles and a de-regulated workforce.

The main effect in many cities was the closure of manufacturing plants, the dereliction of large tracts of industrial land and high levels of unemployment. This was very much the case for the steel and ship building industries of Glasgow and Bilbao, for textiles, clothing and footwear in Singapore and cars in Geelong and general manufacturing in the north eastern cities of the United States over the 1970s and 1980s. Creating massive unemployment and huge derelict areas, it was to be many of these industrial cities which adopted the Cultural Capital idea as one way to revitalise both their economies and de-industrialised urban precincts.

Table 3.1   Economic Structures of Australia, Canada, Singapore, Spain, UK and US 1970–2000 (Gross Domestic Product Composition by Sector)

Country	1970	1970	1970	2000	2000	2000
	Agriculture	Industry	Services	Agriculture	Industry	Services
Australia	(1974) 4.4	32.3	63.4	3.0	26.0	71.0
Singapore	3.5	30.1	66.3	0.0	30.0	70.0
Spain	(1981) 14.4	35.3	40.4	4.0	31.0	65.0
United Kingdom	(1980) 2	28	70	1.7	24.9	73.4
USA	4	29	62.7	2.0	18.0	80.0

Source: 2000 www.geohive.com.global/geo.php?xml=ec_sect (Accessed 8.12.05)

The growth in the service sector workforce – comprising workers in business, recreational, social and personal services – involves managers, professionals and technicians as well as many lower level workers in restaurants, shops, gyms, salons, offices, schools and so on. The service sector is therefore associated with a bifurcated workforce structure, with often very well paid if time poor senior members and a mass of usually low-paid, often migrant workers who provide lower level services (see Zukin 1995; Sassen 1998). Both groups have come to be associated with particular life styles, oriented to consumption, entertainment and the arts. Service workers both comprise and consume recreational, tourist, retail and personal services; which in turn boosts the size of this employment group (see Richards 1996a). It would be expected, then, that any Cultural Capital would have or aspire to have a high level of service sector workers and a full range of activities in which such service workers find employment as well as consumption outlets.

Beyond the major shift in the case study and other westernised countries away from agriculture and industry towards Services – with Australia, Spain, Singapore, the US and UK all having more than 65% of their Gross National Product coming from the service sector (Table 3.1) – there is a crucial question of what sort of services these economies were subsequently based on. Such a question is relevant to establishing what role Florida's "Creative Class" (especially the core group of those in high end computing, engineering, life sciences and education jobs as

well as in the creative arts) and those in tourism and recreation have within this
category. Finding comparable data for the service sector for all of the countries
involved in this study has proven impossible, as organisations such as the European
Union (which includes Spain and the UK) have different ways of delimiting the
service sector compared to the OECD (which includes these countries but also
the US, Singapore and Australia). Analysis across these two groupings reveals
the complexity of the service sector, especially its differentiated components,
productivity and growth rates. Such organisations also do not necessarily
distinguish the Cultural and Creative Industries from IT and Communication or
Recreation and Tourism Services. It is therefore necessary to rely on discussion of
these industries and on work more generally on the service sector for the following
observations.

Drawing on limited comparable data, then, and depending on just where
the line is drawn on who constitutes workers in the Cultural Industries, they
either constitute a major and growing sub-sector or are a relatively small and
insignificant part of the services sector – with workers in banking, insurance, real
estate, engineering, accounting and legal services (Producer Services), in Social
Services (medical, health, education, welfare, government) and Personal Services
(domestic, hotel, eating and drinking, and entertainment) being far more numerous
and structurally significant than those working in design, the creative arts (visual,
performing and media), and in related fields. Claims for the growth of the Cultural
Industries and the Creative Class therefore have to be approached cautiously and
may not necessarily underpin the designation of a Cultural Capital.

Associated with the decline of manufacturing and rise of services is the
emergence of what has variously been described as the information or knowledge
economy. Referring to somewhat different developments, they are united by the
importance of computer-mediated communications technology to transform and
speed up social and economic exchange. The information economy is tied to the
role of computers in accelerating the speed and extending the volume of information
which can safely be despatched around the globe. Such communications technology
allows the physical breakdown of any production system, the separation – across
cities, nations or the globe – of design from production, distribution from creation,
and control, from all other sites involved in the making or delivery of a good. As
well as facilitating a communications revolution, such technologies are permeating
more and more social and productive processes, transforming the way work is
performed as well as supervised. These technologies themselves have also become
consumer items – with the radio and television now supplemented by home
computers, mobile phones and personal digital music, information and image
carriers. Such developments bring the IT revolution home, creating a huge demand
not only for hardware components but also software content, all of which has to be
created within the Cultural Industries as part of the knowledge economy.

The knowledge economy refers to those who invented and now oversee the
information economy but who also developed entirely new industries out of its
technologies, convergences and applications – such as multi-media games, bio-

technology and nano-technology – which in turn generate further products and industries. Harnessing computer technologies to develop new industries is at the core of what many governments aspire to as they move beyond a dependence on older style manufacturing but also the first generation of service industries (Business, Social and Personal Services) into the newer Cultural but also Knowledge Industries. The quest to become a centre of a knowledge driven economy is common to a number of Cultural Capitals – especially Singapore, Glasgow, Boston, Brisbane, Geelong and Bilbao – which look to the creative arts as both a core and necessary support to such a development.

Depending on which authority one accepts, the information economy either creates a whole new world and changes everything into something very different or is being used to modify existing products, services and operations. Thus for Daniel Bell, when the computer converged with telecommunications, a new post-industrial service society emerged, dominated by professional and technical workers in the IT industries (Bell 1973). Alternatively, for Piore and Sabel (1984) information technologies constituted a "second industrial divide" which could have developed in at least two directions – towards revitalised mass production or towards "flexible specialisation". In reality, both directions have been realised. Either way, for Piore and Sabel (1984), the new technologies suffused all industries as well as created new ones. Whichever interpretation is adopted, it is clear that information and communications technologies have permeated the globe since the 1960s, altering the way work is done and how companies are organised and operated, creating new industries and fundamentally altering the nature of goods and services. The Cultural Industries have grown out of this economic restructuring, globalisation and the IT revolution but are also dependent upon a very different, symbolic economy for their value.

Post-modernity and the Symbolic Economy

If demand for labour saving domestic consumer goods had helped fuel the 'golden age' of the 1950s and 60s, western markets by the 1970s had become saturated. In the United States, companies benefited from the vast amount of high-tech research generated by the government in space and defence as a result of the Cold War. By the early 1980s, as Europe and North America faced economic recessions, and as Newly Industrialising Countries in Asia – such as Singapore – continued to achieve high levels of economic growth, the perceived advantages for Euro-American corporations of moving into new high-technology but also into the new Cultural Industries – such as computer software, film, design and advertising – were overwhelming. Such shifts were paralleled by the ongoing growth in advertising expenditure and a related growth in media outlets. The Cultural Industries were therefore a vital investment opportunity for a range of corporations. They were also prestigious, as the leisure and entertainment industries came to be seen as a key economic sector, at least in the UK and USA. Companies in other sectors – such as General Electric and Sony in electronics – also made significant investments in the Cultural Industries in the 1980s as this sector assumed an identity and record of profitability (Hesmondhalgh 2002: 89–92). The Cultural Industries therefore emerged as part of the new economy, merging the service sector with new forms of manufacturing as well as comprising an integral part of the post-modern city.

Frederic Jameson in a highly influential essay in the 1984 *New Left Review* suggested that late capitalism was not only typified by multinational corporations operating a decentred, global communications network, but that this in turn provided the material basis for a post-modern society based on the media, an architecture of pastiche and cities focused on spectacle (Jameson 1984). For him, Post-modernity thus became the logical outcome of post-Fordism. Joining Jameson, Mike Davis (1990) and Edward Soja (1986, 1989, 1996) portrayed Los Angeles in the early 1990s as the archetypical post-modern city. They argued that the city's high tech, defence, business services and IT industries with their well educated and well paid professional workforces, sat alongside migrant workers in garment sweatshops and an army of disenfranchised and impoverished service workers to provide the polarised economic base on which gated suburbs and fortified buildings, films, theme parks and shopping centres offered safety, entertainment, spectacle and escape. Here then was the post-Fordist economic base for the post-modern city *par excellence*.

Downtown, the Bonaventure Hotel became something of an iconic building to these three exponents of the post-modern condition (Johnson 1994a). Reading it as an archetypical text with its obscure entranceways, tiered interior, exterior lifts and towering glassed façade Jameson described the hotel as a "total space, a complete world, a kind of miniature city (constituting a new and historically original hyper-crowd" (Jameson 1984: 81). For Davis the hotel represented the darker side of the post-modern city where social polarisation led to the fortification of the building, a mirrored façade, elaborate security and a self-contained opulent world within for the jet-setting members of the business elite. In such a way, he maintained, the design of the building asserted its physical and social distance from the mass of child, racialised and immigrant labour on which the Los Angeles economy rested (Davis 1992, 1990). Surveying the same hotel, Soja confirms its social and symbolic value:

> … the Bonaventure has become a concentrated representation of the restructured spatiality of the late capitalist city: fragmented and fragmenting, homogeneous and homogenizing, divertingly packaged yet curiously incomprehensible, seemingly open in presenting itself to view but constantly pressing to enclose, to compartmentalize, to circumscribe, to incarcerate…The Bonaventure both simulates the restructured landscape of Los Angeles and is simultaneously simulated by it (Soja 1989: 243–4).

A building whose placement, use and design can be read in terms of the post-Fordist as well as the post-modern city, the Bonaventure also served as a film set – for example "In the Nick of Time" – where the spaces themselves became integral to the action as well as a statement on political life in the United States. Iconic buildings such as this join others – including the Guggenheim in Bilbao (see Chapter 5) – to become part of multi lingual narratives about themselves, as the symbolic economy both creates such spaces but also re-uses and re-interprets them through their circulation as texts and consumption as cultural artefacts.

As well as a site of social polarisation, celebrity buildings, blighted manufacturing as well as glittering service and tourist industries, the post-modern city is often associated with the creation of "spectacles" – be they associated with public performances in open spaces, those occurring within shopping centres or sporting arenas or within structures dedicated to them – such as theme parks, historical reconstructions, waterfronts, parks or squares. Some argue that previous sites of contemplation and education – such as parks, galleries and museums – are also part of these new "Fantasy Cities"; post-modern spaces of simulation, virtual reality and spectacle (Hannigan 1998: 4). For David Harvey, all have in common the creation of safe and enclosed spaces in which there can be ephemeral and participatory pleasures, where crowds gather to gaze at the spectacle and each other, and the commodity is king (Harvey 1994: 376). He connects the creation of such spaces to the stifling logic of post-Fordist accumulation strategies and growing class inequality, with waterfront redevelopment in Baltimore an exercise in defusing but not addressing class conflict and racial tension (Harvey 1994: 277). For Guy Debord, such spaces are also ones where unity is demanded, conflict and difference occluded and pleasure reigns over reflection and citizenship (Debord 1983).

The society and spaces of spectacle then are integral to the Post-modern city and, for Harvey, Hannigan and Debord as well as Michael Sorkin (1992/5) associated with growing inequality, the privatisation of public space and crass aesthetics. John Hannigan is one of the few commentators on such environments to admit the possibility of agency; of local authorities and community members asserting some control and gaining real benefits from this tendency to create urban spectacles. As Hannigan argues, signalling the importance of social, cultural and political sustainability to this process:

> Much depends … on cities themselves. Urban policy-makers need to be proactive rather than reactive, they need to become full collaborative partners with the private sector rather than supplicants who enter into flawed and costly development deals. And of equal importance, they must not fail to recognize and accommodate the cultural diversity in the community in favour of a generic model of …development which is only destined to succeed in a handful of tourist-rich cities (Hannigan 1998: 11).

The post-modern city is therefore typified by de-industrialisation and an expanding service sector, location within a globalised network of command and control systems, a boom in renovation and spectacle and social polarisation between the upper and lower level workers (often racialised, immigrant and female) in the newly expanded service sector as well as in the new knowledge and symbolic economy (Johnson 1994a: 54). In addition, structures such as the Bonaventure as well as the Guggenheim in Bilbao and the Esplanade – Theatres by the Bay in Singapore are built in a post-modern style.

Just what this means is subject to vigorous debate amongst architectural historians, but most agree that it is defined against its predecessor – the International Style of Modernism. This style saw the proliferation around the world of remarkably similar steel and glass office towers: airports, high rise housing blocks and hotels (Frampton 1980). Such structures defied local conditions, ignored heritage and the particularities of the local populace, elevated the architect to the status of hero and celebrated the machine age. In contrast, for Charles Jencks at least, post-modern architecture involves a double coding of the modern with other styles drawn from the past, the local environment or vernacular traditions (Jencks 1981). Post-modern buildings are populist, respecting and incorporating popular culture and traditions and often involve the community in some way in their creation. They can also be playful, eclectic and alive with metaphor, ambiguity, pastiche and humour with often a cacophony of styles (Jencks 1981; Rose 1991; Ley 1983; Johnson 1994, Ellin 1999).

Reading a building as a text in this way is consistent with techniques developed by cultural geographers (see Chapter 2) while seeing particular structures as archetypical of a range of processes – in the case of the Bonaventure Hotel as a statement in space of post-Fordist social relations and post-modern style – is an approach to be emulated here. Thus in Chapter 5 discussion will be of one of the more celebrated and recent manifestations of post-modern architecture – Frank Gehry's Guggenheim Museum in Bilbao – as a centre piece of this Cultural Capital.

If the post-modern city is epitomised by Los Angeles, it is also one whose many characteristics are present in Cultural Capitals – especially their placement in global networks of investment, migration and travel, economic foundation on services, social polarisation, post modern style and presence of the Cultural Industries. Such dimensions are related to each city's engagement with the symbolic economy.

The rise of the symbolic economy is related to a value shift in what is important to people – consumption rather than work – and how particular, "designer", commodities are related to new consumption priorities: for personal gratification, adornment and entertainment. Related to such social changes are structural shifts in the time available for recreation rather than work as well as higher income levels which allow greater expenditures on leisure, recreation, tourism, culture and personal services rather than necessities. Thus across the Western world over the last twenty years, expenditure on recreation has increased disproportionately to the increase in non-working time available (e.g. USA $93.8 per person pa in 1970 compared to $395.5pa expressed in 1992 dollar terms). In a much shorter period, there has been a doubling of personal consumption spending on recreation from 4.3 to 8.6% in the United States (from 1996 to 1998). There has also been the emergence and rapid proliferation of electronic and computer-based communication and entertainment devices which have become the must have consumer items across the world driving and symptomatic of the new media economy. Thus in 1975 sales of personal computers were negligible, but by 1983 they stood at 7 million around the globe and by 1987 were 50 million. Today they are ubiquitous. Other electronic devices such as CDs, DVDs, personal stereos, ipods and MP3 players have proliferated rapidly over the 1990s and into the new century.

Consumer electronics transnationals were a significant part of manufacturing internationalisation from the 1950s and have been critical in the creation and rapid dissemination of these products – along with shaping a desire for them (Hesmondhlagh 2003: 100-101). In addition to the production side of the Cultural Industries, it is also necessary to document the consumption of its goods – what these goods are, who might purchase, admire and give meaning to them – and the importance of place in their production as well as consumption.

The aestheticisation of life, cities, activities and of commodities is associated with the emergence of the symbolic economy. In a world where symbols and style matter in ways like never before – as a means of delimiting identities, declaring social status, defining a place and asserting a political position – culture has displaced politics and economics as a dominant discourse (Zukin 1995; Wark 1999). "Culture", while always ever present, has been commodified and personalised. The conscious definition and marketing of culture has been explicitly extended into all realms of life and is deemed by many to be central to an emergent economy, while also forming a crucial battle ground on which political allegiances are negotiated. For some cities, faced with a declining industrial base, localised but also globalised culture can be *the* source of economic and social salvation. Why this occurs in some places rather than others is related to the ways in which the above trends are negotiated and altered at each locale, the specifics of the local state and the ways in which local cultures are formed, mobilised, re-valued and commodified.

Living in the post-modern city – be it Los Angeles or London – has generated reflections on this experience which in turn gives insights into post-modernity. Thus Elizabeth Wilson writes of urban Britain as well as on contemporary film and literature (the two significantly merge):

> In postmodernism the city becomes a labyrinth or a dream. Its chaos and senselessness mirror a loss of meaning in the world. At the same time, there may be an excess of meaning: the city becomes a split screen flickering with competing beliefs, cultures and 'stories'. This play of unnerving contrasts is the essence of the 'postmodern' experience....Everything is the same and nothing is quite real (Wilson 1991: 136).

For Wilson the post-modern city is a place of contradiction – between sameness and difference, excitement and fear, pleasure and danger – mediated by media representations. Such openness to experiences is paralleled for Wilson by the possibility of creating new identities within the city. This possibility is especially exciting for women, long the subject of constraining and limited identity options. For Wilson then, the post-modern city is potentially a site of liberation for women but also for others who can seize the opportunities offered by new technologies as well as by a new view of individual identities to create themselves and new urban spaces. The symbolic post modern economy of the Cultural Capital is therefore not only for the consumption by tourists, but is actively engaged in by those who live in and move through the city.

If Wilson was refecting on living in the city, Michel Foucault scoured the minutiae of the French historical record to conclude that historical subjects, like their contemporary urban counterparts, were created by the discourses and power relations in which they were engaged. Thus his studies of institutional practices, spaces and regulatory regimes in mental hospitals and prisons lead to a view of people not as heroically individualised but as historically and discursively constructed subjects (Foucault 1973, 1977, 1979). Extended into feminism by Elizabeth Butler amongst others (including, for example, Nicholson, 1990) this view of identity insists that gender, along with class, race or youth, is a construct which not only has many different dimensions but these can be actively selected and performed (Butler 1990; Sedgewick 1993). While not outside of structured power relations – indeed options have to be created and presented by those with the power to do so – in cities saturated with styles, celebrities, fashion, and symbolic consumer goods, identities too become changeable and performative cultural artefacts.

In the post-modern city, it is the Cultural Industries that delimit the range of possible identities; with those working in film, the mass media, music, advertising, architecture, design and the creative arts, shaping the spaces as well as many of the identity options available to locals and tourists alike. The Cultural Industries are therefore vital to the post-modern city while the post-modern city is styled and represented by the Cultural Industries.

Engaging with the technology which has produced the flattened everywhere but nowhere imminence of the post modern city has been critical to two influential philosophers of post-modernity: Jean Baudrillard and Francois Lyotard. Thus Baudrillard has focused on the ways in which new media technologies, their saturation coverage and ubiquity have effected the ways in which people experience the world – as the image becomes real and the real increasingly known only through its representation (Baudrillard 1989). As reality is overtaken by its image and society ruled by the language of systems technology and advertising, the simulacrum emerges as dominant. Thus the image or the representation need not have a referent or original but becomes the currency by which people come to know the world. Restoring a Chinese shop house or a Charles Rennie Mackintosh building involves both a painstaking historical renovation but also a repackaging of the spaces for contemporary use and consumption. It is by definition new, but also old, a replica or simulation of the past in the present. How anyone learns about a culture, artistic artefact, building or a Cultural Capital is very much related to its representation and projection beyond the confines of its location. Creating historical precincts, mobilising heritage, formulating images – devising simulacra – and offering these to locals and international tourists is critical to the urban strategies of Singapore, Bilbao, Geelong and Glasgow (see Chapters 4–7). Chapter 8 revisits this idea of becoming a Cultural Capital as something that has been emulated and replicated already across the world, as successful examples are projected onto other places.

Considering the impact of computer technology not on the media but on the sciences, universities and research practice, Jean Francois Lyotard observed that knowledge, increasingly contained in data banks, is *the* commodity of our times and the main means by which power is attained and wielded (Lyotard 1984, 1986). Further, such knowledge no longer comprises a series of universal certainties endorsed by the state, but in the face of challenges to truths offered by feminists, Third World and black critics as well as chaos theory and relativity, is now producing not the known but the unknown. As a consequence "the grand narrative has lost its credibility" (Lyotard 1984: 37) so that science, like other bodies of knowledge, no longer has a claim to authority or certainty. Such a conclusion sends deep reverberations throughout the Western intellectual tradition which, since the Enlightenment, has built philosophical, scientific and moral certainties on the ability of reason to triumph in the creation of overarching theories of the human condition (Johnson 1994: 56). Such a view meshes easily with that of Wilson, Butler and Foucault as they speculate on the contemporary city, such that post-modernity itself becomes something of a new meta-narrative, but one which defies ready definition. However, as this account has indicated, the post-modern city (or at least some buildings within it) is distinguished architecturally, while the economy and experience of this city owes much to the Cultural Industries as well as to theorists of the post modern condition.

Building on the information technology revolution but also drawing on the insights of post-modern philosophy is the script which argues that the material or economic is increasingly fusing with the cultural or symbolic to create a new economic sector – a symbolic economy. For Allan Scott, just as culture is increasingly subject to commodification, so does contemporary capitalism infuse an ever-widening range of outputs with aesthetics and semiotic content. As noted in Chapter 2, his work documents the way the economic is embedded in the cultural but also how the cultural is increasingly tied to the economic (Scott 2000). Unlike the knowledge economy, the symbolic economy involves goods and services that are infused with broadly aesthetic or semiotic attributes whose function is primarily psychic gratification rather than utilitarian (Scott 1997). As such, the symbolic economy cuts across traditional economic sectors; forming part of the service sector – especially activities concerned with personal service (fashion, entertainment, hotels, restaurants); business services such as design, architecture, marketing and real estate – but also some manufacturing (high end textiles, gourmet food and designer furniture) and retailing. Thus Scott sees fashionable clothing, designer furniture, tourist services, jewellery, live theatre, advertising, interior design, recorded music, books and films as all comprising parts of the symbolic or, in his terms, the cultural economy (Scott 1997). As such they also involve the convergence of the creative arts with popular culture, design and consumer goods.

These are part of what have earlier been described (Chapter 1) as the Cultural or Creative Industries. As such, many have been around for a long time, but as Scott argues and earlier chapters have demonstrated, these activities and goods are now of greater economic as well as social importance. They function at least in part as personal ornaments, modes of social display, aestheticised objects, forms of entertainment and distraction, as well as sources of information and self-awareness (Scott 1997: 323–4, 2000: 3). Significantly for any discussion of Cultural Capitals, parts of the symbolic economy have become associated with particular places, such as the film industry with Los Angeles, Danish furniture, Florentine leather goods and London theatre (Scott 1997: 325). Such activities, along with a significant service sector fuelled by ICTs, would be expected to be at the core of any Cultural Capital and in turn associated with particular social groups and outlooks.

In describing what computer mediated technologies might mean for the organisation of production in offices and factories, Piore and Sabel (1984) coined the term "flexible specialisation", a strategy of permanent innovation based on flexible, multi-use equipment and skilled workers; in a community that limits competition, favours innovation and co-operation in regional conglomerations of workshop factories (Piore and Sabel 1984: 17, 265–7). Other theorists have labelled such a re-organisation of production "disorganised capitalism" (Lash and Urry 1987), New Times (Hebdidge 1989; Hall and Jacques 1989) and "flexible accumulation" (Harvey 1989a and b, 1994; Storper and Walker 1989). In this script, an allegedly dominant Fordist mode of mass production – with associated strong trade unions, a welfare state and mass market – was replaced by this new form of organising production – along with a non-unionised workforce, a neo-liberal state and highly differentiated market in the 1980s. Thus in the post-Fordist era, the assembly line is replaced by customised batch production worked by multi-skilled operatives, creating goods for niche markets (Johnson 1994: 53). While a general trend, model companies and industries have specific relations to places: including the Benetton fashion empire's connection to the Third Italy (Piore and Sabel 1984) and the Hollywood film industry (Christopherson and Storper 1989).

Considered two of the quintessential post-Fordist industries, film and fashion also have all the hall marks of the classic artistic product (see Chapter 2) – being high risk, often involving large investments of time and resources in their initial production but then highly economical reproduction, with a common dilemma of controlling copyright (from piracy and cheap reproductions) and generating a star system (of designers, labels, actors, directors) to differentiate one product from another in the market place. Also, as many studies have shown, these industries are the models for a post-Fordist future based on creativity, craft-like production relations in networked industrial districts while also having a global reach for their well differentiated products (see Caves 2000, Hesmondhalgh 2002). Significantly what also typifies these industries is their conjoining of the symbolic with the material, of styles from the past with new combinations for the present (double coding in a thoroughly post-modern way) and their dependence on both the engines of corporate capitalism (for production, distribution and sale) but also on the individual creative talents of designers, directors, editors and actors (Christopherson and Storper 1989; Crewe and Forster 1993; Crewe 1996). Such industries not only exist in particular localities but also emerge at particular times as part of the new post-modern and post-Fordist base of Cultural Capitals.Such cities also compete vigorously with each other.

Globalisation and Inter-urban Competition

Greater capital mobility has been accompanied by both urban decay and vitality – as always the patterns are uneven. The need to attract and retain such apparently mobile investment and the increasingly mobile tourist assumed a new urgency after the mid-1970s collapse of manufacturing to exacerbate competition between cities (Harvey 1989b; Hall and Hubbard 1998). As David Harvey wrote:

> Managerialism, so characteristic of urban governance in the 1960s, was replaced by entrepreneurialism as the main motif of urban action ... The rise of the 'entrepreneurial city' meant increased inter-urban competition across a number of dimensions ... (a) competition for position in the international division of labour; (b) competition for position as centres of consumption; (c) competition for control and command functions ... and (d) competition for government redistributions (Harvey 1994: 365).

Such a development became a key trigger in the formulation of strategies to differentiate and market cities beyond their borders to potential investors, but also to efforts to maintain populations and capital within any one city. For all cities became subject to such seemingly fickle investment and population movements. As well as seeking to court mobile investment, the quest also became to capture mobile populations, especially those with the skills and capital appropriate for the new information or knowledge economy, the economic foundation of the post-modern city. Particularly important to this city and one indicator of its success in the competitive stakes, was tourism.

As noted in Chapter 2 tourism as an activity has a very long history. Mass tourism, however as an industry emerged as a result of structural changes in the working week and year which gave paid free time to workers across a number of nations. Supported by an array of related service providers – places were increasingly packaged and marketed as tourist destinations. Staffed by new fractions of the service class tourist destinations over the later part of the 20th century have become increasingly differentiated but also have catered more and more to those seeking a cultural experience – be it of an anthropological or more formal type.

Alongside this differentiation of the tourist experience has gone a rise in the importance of the indirect, mediated and representational experience of places, which colours and at times replaces actual encounters. Some commentators thereby describe the post-tourist, someone who experiences other places and cultures vicariously – via the media and other forms of representation – but who also ranges widely across various activities, genres and cultures (Smith 2003). For Rojek (1993) the post-tourist has three main characteristics:

1. An awareness and playful engagement with the commodified tourist experience
2. Experience as an end in itself rather than the pursuit of self-improvement through travel, and
3. The acceptance and use of the representation of a site, event or culture as important as the experience itself.

The post-tourist is part of the contemporary post-modern world of representations, imageability and consumption, seeking out images as well as a range of "authentic" experiences across the globe. Such tourists are vital to the creation and sustaining of Cultural Capitals, as it is they who will visit and perhaps re-visit them, generating demand but also symbolic cultural capital for themselves and their class fractions in the process (see Chapter 2). Mass tourism, the rise of the cultural tourist and development of the post-tourist form therefore helps underpin Cultural Capitals.

If one aspect of globalisation is the greater mobility of people as tourists, so too is the heightened mobility of capital. Between the two, movement of people and capital, there is a third element – the city which aims to attract and keep both. Competition for urban investment, tourists and the command and control functions of the new capitalist order, has driven a new era of what Saskia Sassen labels, world city formation.

For Saskia Sassen (1991) and John Friedmann (1982) where hyper-mobile capital settled ensured concentrations of productive activity which in turn had to be regulated from somewhere. Such centres of command and control for international corporate networks became what they described as world or global cities. As Michael Smith also argued, capital flight, foreign investment, multinational corporate competition and the global interdependence of productive activities were all dimensions of the New International Division of Labour. This globalisation of economic relations impacted on migration flows – from third to first world countries and within developed countries – and produced an international network of World Cities (Smith 2003).

Such cities are primarily centres of corporate finance and control. Some, especially the World Cities delimited by Peter Hall in the 1960s, are also capitals of global culture. Thus in 1966 Hall published *World Cites,* defining them in terms of multiple roles: they were centres of political power, both national and international; centres of national and international trade, acting as entrepots as well as centres of banking, insurance and related financial services; centres of learning and the application of scientific knowledge to technology; centres of information gathering and diffusion through publishing and the mass media; and centres of conspicuous consumption, both of luxury goods for the minority and mass-produced for the majority. Such world cities for Hall, were centres of government, capital and culture. He argued that over the 20th century, these cities would grow in importance and as John Friedmann and Saskia Sassen have documented, this prediction has proven correct.

Friedmann and Wolf (1982) were the first to suggest a global hierarchy of such cities in which London, New York and Tokyo were "global financial articulations"; Miami, Los Angeles, Frankfurt, Amsterdam and Singapore were "multinational articulations" and Paris, Zurich, Madrid, Mexico City, Sao Paulo, Seoul and Sydney were "important national articulations". Such cities were not only vital in themselves but assumed their status as World Cities through their place within global networks of financial transaction and business services. In a similar vein Saskia Sassen argued that globalisation and informationalisation dissociated advanced business or producer services from actual production (Sassen 1991). She argued that as a result of a new global economy of production and exchange, there is a world wide market that needs specialised managerial work. In addition, privatisation and deregulation focuses a range of activities into corporations, while digitalisation means that leading sectors need state of the art infrastructure in major international business centres. Thus, she suggests, as production disperses worldwide, services are increasingly concentrated into a relatively few trading cities – global cities (initially three and now the big five of London, New York, Tokyo, Frankfurt and Paris) – and a second rung of about 20 cities, all of which are centres of financial services and headquarters of major production companies. Such cities may also be seats of major world-power governments (Sassen 1991, 2005. See also King 1990).

For Sassen, over the 1990s there arose a network of 30–40 "global cities" that concentrate command and control functions of international capital, including New York, London, Tokyo, Paris, Frankfurt, Zurich, Amsterdam. Los Angeles, Sydney, Hong Kong, Sao Paulo, Buenos Aires, Bangkok, Taipei, Mexico City, Seoul, Singapore and Shanghai. They also serve as production sites for finance and other leading industries of our post-industrial world and provide marketplaces where firms and governments can buy financial instruments and services (Sassen 2005). In the 1980s the upper stratum of this system – New York, London and Tokyo – accounted for 60–70% of world financial markets. In the 1990s, they were joined by Frankfurt and Paris. They were also joined by a second tier of cities to create an organisational architecture for global transnational corporate business. The intensity of transactions among these cities, particularly through the financial markets, trade in services and investment, has increased sharply in the new century as have the orders of magnitude involved (Sassen 2005).

There is intense competition between cities both at a given level in the hierarchy as well as between levels; such that Sassen had to add Frankfurt and Paris in the 1990s to her list of three dominant Global Cities (Sassen 2005: 2). Such a development illustrates the dynamism of the system but also confirms that the various capabilities for providing such high level services have to be produced and can be changed. Such capabilities may well be produced in cities other than those currently or deteriorate in the major centres. The contested and dynamic nature of the Global City hierarchy – despite a large amount of historic inertia (Hall 1997) – therefore invites the possibility of other cities replicating the higher level characteristics and entering the select list (Sassen 2005: 1). It also suggests that any world city, has to actively maintain that status in the face of ongoing competition as well as ongoing capital and labour mobility.

For Hall (1997: 7), the economic structures of these Global/World cities is also changing:

- They are divesting very large areas of economic activity – manufacturing, goods-handling, routine services – to other cities, regions and countries, and
- They are showing rapid growth in a relatively few related sectors – financial and business services (including architecture, engineering and fashion); command and control functions such as company headquarters, national and international government agencies; cultural and creative industries including the live arts and the electronic print media; and tourism, both leisure and business

He argues that these activities are highly synergistic. Such cities attract specialist business services – commercial law, accounting, advertising, public relations – and these in turn attract business tourism and related real estate functions. Business and real estate ally with leisure tourism, and " both are drawn to these cities because of their cultural reputations, with effects on the transportation, communication, personal services and entertainment-cultural sectors" (Hall 1997: 4). Hall thereby draws a direct link between a global centre for high order business services and a booming entertainment-cultural sector. So too does T.C. Chang who, writing from Singapore, notes how global cities not only help organise the world economy by directing capital flows, but they also shape cultural meaning and social norms in fields such as fashion, media and information, with such cities as much centres of dynamic social ferment and intercultural mixing as centres of capital transaction (Chang 2000a: 819). Hall, Chang and others, therefore, suggests a connection between a Cultural Capital and a global economic centre, one supporting the other. They also note the contested, dynamic as well as spatial and temporal specificity of this status.

Along with John Friedmann, David Harvey and Saskia Sassen, Hall offers a convincing description and explanation for the global city phenomenon. While the top cites have been explicitly excluded from this study because of their unassailable status, their position still needs to be acknowledged and explained. By their very existence and structure, global cities offer a model to others; while the active creation of capability and the contestation which produces the world city hierarchy, offers hope to other places aspiring to a place within it. It is of relevance to this study that Singapore, Boston, Sydney and Vancouver all make an appearance as regional centres of business service networks (Sassen 2000). Such cities have all courted the Cultural Capital title; seeking to secure or pursuing a higher place in the global hierarchy through the synergistic connections that Hall and Sassen described between international business service networks, the Cultural Industries and creative art resources. Such a possibility will be explored in later chapters, though it should also be noted that many of the cities claiming the Cultural Capital mantle are far too small and economically insignificant to enter the ranks of the global or regional city hierarchy. There is therefore no necessary connection between the two, though the synergy that Hall describes is certainly present in the policy frameworks that often guide those creating Cultural Capitals.

Entrepreneurial Governance

With the fall in manufacturing employment and recessions in the developed world over the 1970s, one widely experienced reaction was scrutiny of the role of government in economic regulation and social support as a prelude to the withdrawal of state support for these activities. What has since been labelled a neo-liberal, revanchist or economic rationalist agenda came to dominate Australia, Britain, Canada and the United States over the 1980s (see Bianchini 1993; Hall and Hubbard 1998). Such a political agenda has been associated with the creation of Cultural Capitals in these countries as cities become more entrepreneurial and compete more vigorously with each other for newly mobile capital investment, cultural tourists and mobile creatives. However, while widespread and connected by a number of commentators to the rise of Cultural Capitals (such as Hall and Hubbard 1998; Gibson 2003), this political agenda is not universal. Rather, when countries such as Spain and Singapore are considered both of which pursued a Cultural Capital agenda over the 1990s, very different political environments – socialist and state capitalist – are seen to prevail. There is therefore a need to look closely and without preconceived models, at the governance structures in each city and country that has engendered Cultural Capitals.

What *is* common amongst the case study countries is not their formal ideological orientation or governance structures but their view of the creative arts as part of or necessary to an emergent cultural or knowledge economy and a consideration of the arts as an economic sector which provides a vital creative milieu for other service and manufacturing activities and workers. For as Chapter 1 noted, the political context which created and supported Cultural Capitals was associated with a move to quantify the value of the arts in economic terms and to extend the definition of the creative arts to the media, entertainment, advertising, architecture and design; into a range of activities designated as a cultural or creative economy. Such a connection was often part of broader moves to engender service sector growth and to boost the overall profile of a city, region or nation in a more globalised world of hyper-mobile capital and professionals. In spite of rhetorical commitments to small non-interventionist governments in a number of countries, official support of Cultural Capitals often became part of a wider differentiating and developmentalist agenda pursued by socialist as well as liberal and authoritarian states.

The political connection of the arts to the economy parallels the academic linking of the two and their promotion to governments and communities through international consultancies and key thinkers. It was people such as Charles Landry, Federico Bianchini and Richard Florida who travelled the world offering an analysis and prescription for cities and regions to move from being moribund to vital through the mobilisation of the creative arts. Governments beset by the social, political and economic costs of industrial decline and with limited resources, saw such an agenda as a relatively low cost and safe way to progress alternative images and economic realities. It was these governments, especially city and regional ones, who often employed Landry's Comedia Group to conduct surveys and offer planning prescriptions to their councils and ratepayers. This certainly occurred across Australia – most notably in Adelaide, Melbourne and Brisbane – but also across Europe and North America (see Peck 2005). Thus, along with surveys on what the mobile middle class found attractive in a place and the need to differentiate and boost cities, these local governments moved to develop policies and provide resources to support their designation as Cultural Capitals.

The role of central, but especially local governments in designating and supporting such agendas in particular locations at specific points of time, is vital and is a key to explaining why, when and where Cultural Capitals emerged. Such actions were facilitated by the rise in importance of more localised rather than national competition and political actions. For alongside a move towards a less regulated but more entrepreneurial national political environment in some of the case study countries, went a decentralisation of power, decision-making and initiatives away from state and national capitals towards regional, local and city authorities (Bianchini 1993). It was often at this level that cities and regions entered a national and internationally competitive arena for recognition and investment. The political contexts in which Cultural Capitals emerged are diverse and certainly not confined to a de-regulationist policy frame – necessitating a detailed consideration of particular political environments – nationally but also locally – for each case study. What becomes obvious from each case study is their different location within a past colonial era but also their current negotiation in different ways with post-colonial challenges, It is both of these elements which are critical to explaining the particular form adopted by each Cultural Capital.

Post-colonial Cities

Post-colonialism is a political and cultural movement associated with struggles for political independence. While military invasion and colonisation have been part and parcel of all world history, it was not until the 16th century that European expansion reached the southern hemisphere – as Spain entered the Americas – and not until the 19th century that England, Portugal, Spain, France, Germany and the Netherlands expanded into Africa, Asia, the Americas and Australasia. European colonisation initially concentrated on the tropics – Spain in Central America, England in India and Malaysia, the Dutch in Indonesia – where native economies were re-oriented to trade and plantation agriculture. As a product of the "age of discovery" Australia was initially invaded to guard these trade and plantation interests. Thus the fortunes of England (and with it the ports of Scotland and Ireland), Spain, Australia, the Americas and Singapore became inexorably connected through the processes of imperial expansion; becoming either centres of imperial desire or subjected to it (Johnson 2000: 152).

These countries were also impacted by the imperatives that drove such an expansion – a set of Eurocentric, Christian and racialised views around whiteness, industrial development and Godliness which drove the quest for adventure, wealth, conquest and religious conversion. Such views were both vital to those countries subjected to colonisation but also shaped the construction of "Europe" as a unified and dominant society, as each looked upon and constructed the other (Said 1979; Chow 1996)

Since the mid-19th century and the growth of internationalism and nationalism, the dominant process has been one of decolonisation; European powers have either withdrawn or been forced to retreat from rebellious and autonomous states – England forcibly expelled from the United States of America in 1776 and Singapore in 1942; and negotiating a peaceful separation from Australia in 1901. Post-colonial thought recognises that these dual processes of colonisation and de-colonisation are central to all of the countries, populations and cultural formations involved; creating particular sets of economic, military and subject relations, displacing huge populations and producing global diasporas and fractured identities (Johnson 2000: 154). The dual processes are fundamental to all of the cities in this study. Thus Glasgow boomed as a consequence of its location within the British colonial system; utilising local iron, coal and a skilled workforce to build the ships which powered trade and naval prowess, and becoming a booming city as a result of the tobacco trade with the Americas. Singapore was the jewel in the South East Asian crown – a vital port and military bastion for the defence of trade routes which also absorbed three main ethnic groups from other parts of the British Empire – Malays, Indians and Chinese. Australian cities such as Sydney,

Melbourne, Geelong and Adelaide were also integral, not only as transhipment points for agricultural raw materials (wool, wheat) but also as affluent markets for the manufactured goods of Britain's industrial cities. Bilbao fulfilled a role similar to that of Glasgow – as an industrial and ship building city – but it was also a major source of iron ore and a port, funnelling trade from the Spanish colonies in South America into Spain and Europe. Bilbao thereby became a centre of the finance and companies which oversaw this trade. All of these cities have this colonial history imprinted on their urban fabric and within their social and political relations. Such histories are integral to understanding their contemporary problems and strategies taken to address them.

For Catherine Nash, "Post-colonialism interrupts the smooth historiography of modern European capitalism developing in the 'centre' and spreading to its 'peripheries' by making global colonial interconnection central rather than subordinate to a story of European development" (2002: 221). The story of Cultural Capitals, like all others, therefore also partakes of this colonial legacy.

The recent trends towards economic restructuring, an IT driven-knowledge but also symbolic economy, mass but also a highly differentiated tourism and entrepreneurial competitive urban governments, have shaped the emergence and widespread adoption of the Cultural Capital agenda. However, what also needs to be explained is the timing of its adoption at particular localities. For the initial idea of the creative arts driving rather than being a supplicant on the social economy emerged in the early 1980s, while its adoption by a few key thinkers and cities, had occurred by the mid-1980s. But how such an agenda then moved across the globe to be adopted by some places and not others, requires explanation.

Common Shape – Local Stories. Case Study Cities

Since the 1970s proliferation of information technologies, rise of mass tourism, economic restructuring and a shift from manufacturing to services, greater capital mobility and inter-urban competition, the scene had been set for alternative ways of seeing economic growth, governance and the role of the creative arts. However, the move to reconsidering the arts not as an economic mendicant but a driver of social-economic development and urban regeneration had to await the emergence of a post-modern symbolic cultural economy, the idea of a dynamic, contestable hierarchy of world cities and an articulated set of policies and practices for developing Cultural Capitals by an interventionist local state. The scene was set for a revaluing of the creative arts at a number of places from the mid-1980s, and from that time they were also linked to plans for urban and social regeneration. Why this occurred in places like Glasgow, Bilbao, Singapore and Geelong is detailed in subsequent chapters. The general and comparative context of each city is given below.

While the four chosen cities span the globe, have very different cultures and divergent histories, there are some remarkable parallels between them. All have at various points in the recent past deliberately marketed themselves to the world as Cultural Capitals – centres of the arts and cultural industries. For each city, such an orientation emerged during the 1980s as local and regional governments grappled with declining manufacturing industries – ship building, iron and steel in Bilbao and Glasgow, textiles and car making in Geelong, petrochemicals and electronics in Singapore. The New International Division of Labour – which took manufacturing from the First World and placed it in parts of the Third – and new technologies, decimated these industries. All four cities had landscapes on which de-industrialisation had been imprinted: Singapore with its ageing petro-chemical complexes; Glasgow its derelict steel and ship building plants and poor quality housing; Bilbao with industrial ruins along the south bank of the Nervion River and Geelong with its abandoned waterfront wool stores. All four also registered complex colonial histories: Singapore with its British buildings and older Malay, Chinese and Indian precincts; Glasgow with monuments to the US tobacco trade and later to building the pride of Britain's imperial fleet; Geelong with its long involvement with agricultural exports to Britain and then as a centre of a protected industrial economy; and Bilbao with its fraught political relations with a centralised Spanish state. All four centres subsequently have complicated post-colonial relationships, redundant landscapes and socio-political imperatives to move away from an industrial to a post-industrial economy.

If the four cities have comparable backgrounds, they also share remarkably similar strategies for renewal. The role of the local state (co-terminus with the national State in the case of Singapore), is critical. While viewed by many a critic as problematical (Smith 1996; MacLeod 2002), state intervention via explicit envisioning, deliberate policy, massive investment and public-private partnerships, has meant that leadership in the creation of these Cultural Capitals has come from government. Capital for the various initiatives has been mobilised locally but also, for Glasgow, Geelong and Bilbao, from the regional and national governments as well as the European Union and, for Singapore, from the State and multi-national companies. Fundamental to each vision and development plan, has been the active engagement of the city with globalisation – as each has utilised global advisers and chased international capital, tourists and recognition. Each city has also actively sought high profile international artists, performers, companies and designers for the creation and ongoing vitality of their Cultural Capitals. The role of famous architects is particularly apparent in Bilbao – whose regeneration projects read like a Who's Who of the international architectural scene – while Singapore has focused on attracting international performers to fill the vast Esplanade – Theatres by the Bay complex and Glasgow has sought out the international tourist via its Miles Better campaign and becoming an EU sponsored "City of Culture". Geelong as a much smaller provincial centre has tried and failed to engage at such level with the Guggenheim Foundation.

Table 3.2   Embodied, Objectified and Institutional Cultural Capitals in Bilbao, Glasgow, Singapore and Geelong 1980–2008 (Selected/ Published Examples)

Type of Capital	Bilbao	Glasgow	Singapore	Geelong
Embodied	Jorge Oteiza – socialist radical who did not exhibit after 1980. Local artists and performers	Worker's Action Garnethill Park Local artists and performers C.R. Mackintosh and McDonald sisters	Substation Theatre – Kuo Pao Kun 1985 Theatreworks creates "Singaporean Theatre" Alvin Tan "Necessary Stage" Books calling for artistic freedom State boost for arts/CI education	Jan Mitchell Pako Festa performers
Objectified	Gugenheim Museum (Frank Gehry) Museo de Bellas Artes Euskalduna Congress and Music Centre Abandoibarra Riverfront development (Cesar Pelli), Zubi Zuri bridge (Santiago Calatrava)	Merchant City – heritage, tourism 1983 Burrell Collection 1990 Royal Concert Hall, Scottish Exhibition Hall Kelvingrove Gallery McLellan Collection 1996 . Gallery of Modern Art Glasgow School of Design	Public art – TNC forecourts (international/ cosmopolitans) and river walk (local/realist) Urban regeneration/ heritage precincts – Little India, Chinatown and Kampong Glam English language theatre	Bollards around the Bay City Walk Plans for the Geelong Guggenheim GPAC Geelong Art Gallery Courthouse Youth Theatre Steampacket Place Pakington Street
Institutional	1989 Metropolis 30 Strategic Plan for the Revitalisation of Metropolitan Bilbao 2002 Bilbao 2010 Global City Plan - Knowledge industries, Universal Exhibition and Zorrozaurre Zone	Glasgow Action Group – 1986– 1990. Miles Better campaign. 1982 Mayfest – Annual Arts Festival 1983 Greater Glasgow Tourist Board 1989 + New inner city shopping plazas 1990 European City of Culture Lighthouse, Citizens Theatre	1989 Singapore to become a "Global City for the Arts" 1999/2000 Renaissance City 2002 The Esplanade – Theatres on the Bay Singapore Art Gallery National Association of the Arts (NAS) Heritage Council Educational programs, relaxation of restrictions on free expression, sexuality Fusionopolis within One-North	City by the Bay (1984) Steampacket Place Development Co Guggenheim Bid Co (1999) Cultural Precinct Plan (2007)

The various initiatives taken by each city can be categorised in terms of their embodied, objectified or institutionalised form of cultural capital with each empirically inter-connected in precise ways. To be detailed in subsequent chapters, a summary of key initiatives in developing these various Cultural Capitals is given in Table 3.1.

What is clear from a summary of various forms of cultural capital for the four cities is the dominance of large-scale objectified and institutional forms – spectacular infrastructure projects, government-derived policy frameworks and outside designations. In the case of embodied cultural capital, there appears to be a bifurcation between international iconic professionals and local (often resistant) groups. There is also a remarkable lack of interconnection between the different forms of cultural capital – indeed it is as though local embodied work occurs in spite of rather than because of the institutional frameworks that have been established. This raises vital questions abut how value is thereby generated and the sustainability of the various Cultural Capital projects as well as their interconnection with other economic sectors and development agendas.

It needs to be acknowledged that this summary has been derived from published and internationally accessible sources – which will by their very nature be over-represented by official statements. But academic assessment of these, while interested, is relatively free of pushing "official" lines. Therefore, within the limitations of available information, some further analysis can be undertaken of the *process* of creating and sustaining value for each locality. In relation to the creation and sustaining of economic value, the shift from manufacturing to services in all four cities has accelerated over the 1980s and this has been accompanied by larger numbers employed in the arts, creative industries and tourism sectors. Such growth has been associated with massive investment – with significant amounts of capital from outside the cities – in related infrastructure (theatres, galleries, hotels, shopping centres, airports, public transport and urban renewal projects). Also vital has been massive growth in international and national tourism numbers into the four cities, Whether such a visitation and employment growth will continue is an open question, but there is little doubt that economic value and some economic sustainability was achieved from 1980 to 2000 as a result of mobilising different forms of cultural capital. It now comes to look more closely at the process by which these general trends have impacted and been negotiated locally and how cultural capital has been defined, mobilised and valued within these cities to facilitate urban renewal.

Glasgow: Scotland with style

Chapter 4
Glasgow:
Cultural Tourism and Design

In its quest to become a designated Cultural Capital, Glasgow has the distinction of being one of the earliest cities to court the label and to engage in an ongoing effort to realise its agenda. When Merlina Mercouri, then Greek Minister for Culture, convinced the European Union (EU) to adopt a European City of Culture Program in 1983, it marked a shift from the EU's preoccupation with trade and regional development to more locally-based cultural concerns (Garcia 2005). While the first cities chosen in the program were major centres with undisputed reputations as Cultural Capitals – Athens (1983), Florence (1986), Amsterdam (1987), West Berlin (1988), Paris (1989) – the choice of Glasgow in 1990 marked the first time that such a small, second order city without an obvious claim to this status was selected. Indeed at the time, the image and reality of the city was as a blighted, abandoned industrial landscape riddled with mean streets and social disadvantage. It therefore signaled a significant move, with the Cultural Capital designation and related activities being more a means of generating positive change than a recognition of existing cultural capital. At the level of the European Union, across Britain and within Glasgow itself, the City of Culture designation was to be associated not only with a series of events, but a major shift in the image and nature of this city. Becoming a Cultural Capital was integral to remaking the economic as well as the urban and social structure of the city.

Why Glasgow chose this strategy and the sustainability of what has occurred subsequent to 1990 is the subject of this Chapter. It will begin by sketching Glasgow's historical background as the second city of the British Empire, before tracing its long term industrial decline and limited service sector expansion, as the city struggled to be positioned within a regional system of cities competing for capital investment and cultural tourists. What such a story highlights is the importance of history itself in shaping the city and in laying down a physical and cultural environment on which to build a Cultural Capital. In addition, such a narrative highlights the specific forms the general trends noted in Chapter 3 took in this locality: as placement in the British Imperial system generated great wealth, well endowed cultural institutions, magnificent buildings and particular industries with a radical working class politics, but then precipitated a catastrophic decline. As the global centre of ship building and steel making moved first to Europe and thence to Asian countries, Glasgow's economic and spatial restructuring exacerbated already intense socio-spatial polarisation and created huge challenges around its physical and social decay. It is from this history and from those who sought to address its negative consequences in the 1980s, that the quest to become a Cultural Capital emerged. It was a conscious response and alternative to the perils of socio-spatial economic restructuring and de-industrialisation. However, contrary to many of the critics of the 1990 program (such as Laurier 1993; Boyle 1997; Boyle and Hughes 1991, 1994; Maver 2000a and b; MacLeod 2002; Evans 2003), being a European City of Culture was not a one off, but became part of an ongoing quest to re-invent the image and reality of the city around consumer services, international and regional cultural tourism and a sustainable Creative Industry sector. From the historical overview, the Chapter will then examine the bid for and the experience of being the sixth EU City of Culture. From the perspective of 2007, the chapter will consider two particular sites of cultural capital formation: cultural tourism around Charles Rennie Mackintosh; and the contemporary expression of this tradition in one part of the Creative Industries – design – locating them historically and considering their embodied, objective as well as institutional forms across a range of scales, before assessing their economic, social and cultural sustainability.

Historical Context – Economic and Urban Restructurings

The site of what is now Glasgow began as a trade and ecclesiastical centre from around 600AD (McGrath 2006a). As a provincial market town on the west coast, it did not engage in the same level of export trade with Europe as settlements on the east coast. Despite being small – 1,500 in the 12th century – it was from these early times a city of learning, such that in 1451 the University of Glasgow was funded by Pope Nicholas V. The 17th century union of Scottish and English crowns facilitated an increase in trade, but river traffic was limited by the shallowness of the Clyde. In 1668 the town council developed Port Glasgow on the south bank and this allowed an opening of sea trade with the Americas, boosting wealth, building activity and the city's population to 14,000 (McGrath 2006b: 3).

The Imperial context for this phase of the city's history was critical. Over the 17th and 18th centuries, trade expanded to Europe and to the tropical English colonies in the West Indies – for sugar – and to North America – for tobacco. Merchant capital was invested in new factories which produced woollens, linen, soap, refined sugar and earthenware. Glasgow became a major *entrepot* of over 30,000 people by 1750, with a complex web of trade which focused on importing raw tobacco and re-exporting it to Europe for manufactured goods. In 1735, for example, 67 ships were Clyde-registered. Of these:

- 18 sailed to mainland America bringing tobacco and taking back manufactureds
- 9 went to the Caribbean taking manufactured goods in exchange for sugar, rum and cotton

- 14 went to Europe taking tobacco and returning with flax, hemp, iron, food and wood
- 20 sailed to Ireland taking linen, flax, skins and food and returning with textiles, glass, coal, tobacco and rum (Gibbs 1983: 58–61).

From an era dominated by tobacco, the independence of the United States saw the collapse of this trade and led to a broadening of markets – to South America, Asia and Australasia – and a shift to another staple, that of cotton and the textile industry.

In 1750 textile production was entirely domestic, with skilled self-employed men and women producing linen and woollen cloth in weaving villages on the periphery of the city and in riverside clusters. By 1830 it was based in factories located within the city and worked by Irish Protestants and Catholics as well as immigrants from lowland Scotland. A deepening of the Clyde and canal building along with innovations in steam engines, spurred the formation of an engineering and shipbuilding industry and with this the development of local iron works and coal mines. By the early 19th century, with an ongoing influx of migrants, the population passed 150,000 and that of Edinburgh, such that Glasgow became the second city of the British Empire (Fraser 2006).

From the 1820s steam power was applied to ships while wooden boats gave way to iron-hulled ones. What began as a relatively insignificant shipbuilding industry started to expand. By 1864 there were more than twenty shipyards in Glasgow and from 1851 to 1870, 70% of England's ships were produced on the Clyde with more than half of the British shipbuilding workforce based there (Gibbs 1983). Engineering skills were also applied to railways and from the 1840s, Glasgow firms were building customised locomotives for export around the world, but especially to countries in the British empire – including Australia and Malaya (Fraser 2006). In 1903 there were 39 shipyards with a workforce of 100,000, launching a ship a day. This comprised 1/3 of British and 1/5 of world ship production (Williams 1997:148). By 1913, Clydeside yards launched 757,000 tons of shipping, more than the entire production of Germany and the United States (Pacione 1995: 130).

At the height of its wealth, city merchants, local politicians and industrialists celebrated their achievements by hosting international exhibitions and supported the fine but also decorative arts; through direct patronage, by building up collections, constructing and furnishing lavish dwellings and by attending theatre, opera, philosophical discussions and musical recitals. Thus, for example, the McLellan Galleries opened in 1854 to house the personal collection of local industrialist and coachbuilder Archibald McLellan, while local shipowner and trader William Burrell amassed a massive collection of art works from across the globe. Glasgow became a centre of culture, as the creative arts became a well endowed by-product of industrial wealth.19th century Glasgow had numerous art patrons and dealers – who were some of the first to purchase the French Impressionists – a radical challenging group of "Glasgow Boys" in painting, and numerous theatres, music halls, orchestras and choirs. Its many theatres were boldly presenting the innovative works of Ibsen and Chekov, its orchestras and choirs gained international reputations and voluntary associations abounded. Gilbert Scott's towering Gothic spire rising on Gilmorehill in the 1880s distinguished a University which had become a centre of innovative thought and a place of international distinction. To acknowledge and celebrate the industrial and cultural prowess of the city, Glasgow hosted a series of international exhibitions of industry, science and art: in 1888, 1901, 1911 and 1938 (Kinchin 1988). The first attracted 6 million visitors and raised £257,000 for a new art gallery and museum. This was opened in 1901 at Kelvingrove Park as the centerpiece of another international exhibition. This gallery held one of the country's great art collections while the Mitchell Library built up one of the largest public book collections in Europe (Fraser 2006). As well as the wealthy building and displaying their cultural capital, The People's Palace and Winter Gardens were constructed in 1898 on Glasgow Green for the benefit of the industrial working people of the East End. The construction and furnishing of fine houses, expenditure on leisure and culture as well as a spirit of energetic industrial innovation, proved a fertile ground on which to build a local style of interior design and decoration. This emanated from the Glasgow School of Art and a circle around Charles Rennie Mackintosh and the McDonald sisters who both courted the local middle class as patrons but also actively engaged with European art movements. From such wealth, confidence and institutional supports, therefore, there emerged a quest to create, display and consume cultural as well as industrial capital.

While generating and indicative of great wealth, the city's rapid growth over the 18th and 19th centuries was also associated with poor housing and bad health. Massive immigration and ongoing housing subdivision saw the deterioration of living conditions in the inner urban areas, exacerbated by regular outbreaks of typhus, cholera and small pox, such that the city was described by Edwin Chadwick in 1842: "on the whole … both the structural arrangements and the condition of the population … was the worst … in any part of Britain" (Merchant City 2005a: 5). One popular response to such conditions was political agitation for franchise reform and repeal of the Corn Laws. At the political level, another response was to utilise the resources of the local state to improve the urban fabric. In a first for industrial Europe, from the 1840s Police Acts allowed municipal authorities to intervene to improve sanitation, control overcrowding and demolish decayed buildings. In 1866 the City Improvement Act made Glasgow the first British local authority to plan slum clearance on a major scale over an area twice as big as that attempted in Birmingham ten years later (Merchant City 2005a: 6). Between 1875 and 1888 such schemes displaced close to 35,000 people into significantly better homes (Gibbs 1983: 143). But problems continued to worsen along with higher levels of state intervention to alleviate them. Thus by the early 20th century gas, electricity, tramways and phones were all in municipal hands as the local state strove to improve the city and there was much talk of municipal socialism as a model for the future (Fraser 2006). Economic restructuring – from a mercantile to an industrial economy – had therefore been accompanied by an urban transformation as well as socio-spatial polarisation.

Despite the city's expansion over the 19th century, by the early 20th century the British empire was under challenge and with it the pre-eminence of Glasgow's industrial output. Shipbuilding had always been susceptible to fluctuations and by the early 1900s, there was increased competition from Europe, new off shore technologies – such as the oil driven diesel engine – and an increase in dependence on government orders. The economic base of the city rested narrowly on ship building, marine engine production, textiles and heavy engineering. The industrial base of the city was echoed in its workforce which gained great power but also vulnerability as a consequence. As World War I boosted military output and created a skilled labour shortage, pressures to increase wages and admit unskilled workers led to strikes in 1915 and 1916. Such militancy was even more evident in the general strike of 1919 when Glasgow workers repudiated the nationally negotiated 47 hour week agreed between the Confederated Unions and the shipbuilding and engineering employers. With huge pickets and rallies, up to 70,000 workers on strike and major factories idle, the employers called for military action. Five thousand troops and a tank regiment were dispatched to the city and on Bloody Friday – January 31, 1919 –the red flag was raised and the riot act was read in George Square. With the leaders arrested, the strike collapsed and the 47-hour week was accepted (Pacione 1995: 243–4). To Glasgow's image of a squalid urban-industrial landscape was added that of "Red Clydeside", to remain attached to the trade union movement and the entire city for the next half century. The socialist ideology which had inspired the actions was shifted into what became a tradition of local government urban intervention, as the Labour group assumed power and moved to ease the ongoing problems of unemployment and poor housing.

While World War I had led to an increase in demand for Glasgow's industries, the challenges to the British Empire remained and by the time of the 1930s Depression, coal and shipbuilding operated at half the pre-war level, pig iron production was down by two thirds and steel output was stagnant (Pacione 1995: 130). Interwar competition came from countries supporting their own industries – such as Germany, Holland, Sweden, Denmark and Japan – which in turn exposed the relatively high costs and low technology levels of Glasgow's ship yards and engineering factories. Measures taken in the plants to facilitate rationalisation meant both a loss of capacity and an even greater loss of jobs. As competition grew and government orders dropped off further, a shipyard workforce of 43,000 in 1919 fell to 29,000 in 1930, and thence to 24,000 by 1939 (Gibbs 1983: 147). As a consequence, Glasgow was one of the first large cities of the world to cease growing! A brief expansion during the second world war and immediately after could not stop the economic slide, to a point where in 1960 the region produced only 4% of world shipping tonnage compared to 20% in 1913 (Pacione 1995). Despite a Conservative British government giving a further £101 million of public monies to the industry over the 1970s, the decline of shipbuilding continued, taking with it the steel and engineering industries. Thus on top of the major interwar losses, Glasgow lost a further 40,000 jobs from 1978 to 1981 (Gibbs 1983: 148). Here then was a city deeply traumatised by economic restructuring and de-industrialisation as new global alignments of industrial production and military power impacted upon it.

Not only was the city reeling from industrial collapse, but the problem of social polarisation evident from the early 19th century continued to grow as the economy contracted. As with the economic malaise, the social problems were not alleviated by well meaning government action. The 1860s had seen the first concerted effort to improve the quality of working class housing. But ongoing in-migration and industrial decline meant that even new inner city housing was poor in quality and scarce. The census of 1911 revealed that 2/3 of the city's population lived in houses of only one or two rooms, a standard far lower than in comparable English cities. During the war, landlords increased rents in areas close to the shipyards, only to be met – in the context of "Red Clydeside" industrial radicalism – by a popular revolt. Led by the women's labour and housing groups, the mobilisation of whole localities and their alliance with the trade unions ultimately forced the British government to freeze rents at pre-war levels. The Glasgow rent strike forged a unique link between working and living conditions and confirmed the wider need for municipal housing (Pacione 1995). Despite such a commitment however, by 1914 16,000 houses had been demolished but only 2,200 had been built! (Middleton 1991). An estimated housing need of 5,000 after World War I had grown to 90,000 by 1939 exacerbating the socio-spatial polarisation of the city.

As in other parts of the world, the end of the second world war ushered in a period of social and political optimism and a commitment to improve pre-war conditions. In Glasgow such problems were defined primarily in terms of poor housing and health, most of which were concentrated in the inner city. In an era of grand planning, the ambitious 1946 Clyde Valley Plan aimed to reduce the city's population by 25%, largely by its relocation outside the city's boundaries. The need for such action was reinforced by the 1951 Census which revealed that while the city's living standards had improved, 44% of dwellings were still classed as overcrowded and 37% of city families shared a toilet with their neighbours. The Housing (Repairs and Rents) (Scotland) Act of 1954 forced local authorities to draw up plans for slum clearance and over the 1950s 29 districts were targeted for demolition and renewal. In Glasgow, The Hutchesontown-Gorbals Comprehensive Development Area was the first to be formally approved in 1957. The aim was to clear almost 100,000 dwellings and relocate 60% of the effected population from this near city industrial area, elsewhere. Some were moved to new communities within the city boundaries but others were shifted beyond the city limits. The result was that these two wards declined in population from 45,000 to around 19,000, destroying long established communities as well as major areas of 18th and 19th century housing (Maver 2006a).

With a history of municipal socialism, the responsibility to create better quality housing was readily assumed by the local state. In the context of a dominant Le Corbusier-inspired modern International Style of building, high rise public housing was seen as the solution. Beyond the inner areas and at a time when suburbanisation was associated with modernisation, great tracts of land on the periphery of the city were cleared to make way for four new high rise townships – Castlemilk, Easterhouse, Drumchapel and Pollock – into which were decanted between 30% and 50% of the city's entire population. As well there were moves to clear and rebuild the inner areas. In1958 Sir Basil Spence's scheme for 19-storey high blocks of flats was approved for the new Gorbals. By 1964 32,000 homes in Glasgow were closed or demolished and their populations moved to the peripheral estates. At their peak in the late 1960s and early 1970s the four large estates on the edge of the city accommodated around 200,000, almost exclusively in social housing. After an initial period of euphoria – stimulated by being in brand new dwellings with decent bathrooms and kitchens – these peripheral housing estates rapidly fell into disrepair while their populations continued to record high levels of poverty, ill health, unemployment and welfare dependency (Middleton 1991: 106). Most commentators agree that they created a new layer of spatial segregation superimposed on existing patterns of residential division (Mooney and Dansen 1997; Pacione 1990, 1995). If this was the fate of the new areas, in the inner city precincts, comprehensive planning, forced acquisitions, slum clearance and rebuilding schemes meant that there was now better quality housing but for fewer people. Such schemes also meant that the City Council came to own 170,000 houses or more that 56% of Glasgow's entire housing stock, thereby becoming Europe's biggest municipal landlord (Middleton 1991: 106).

By the 1970s then, the time most often associated with the beginning of western economic restructuring (see Chapter 3), Glasgow had already experienced long term decline in its core industrial activities – ship building, iron and steel production and heavy engineering. In 1955 such industries still employed close to 50% of the male workforce and, combined with textiles, employed 40% of women in the city. As they continued to contract, efforts were made to attract other manufacturing activity to the city. Special and Development Area policies over the 1950s and 60s – which included grants, taxation rebates and construction of buildings – encouraged companies to occupy newly created industrial estates as well as tap into the peripheral labour markets created by slum clearance. As a result by 1960, the Glasgow region contained 18 new industrial sites employing 65,000 people in the engineering, car and electrical industries (Pacione 1995: 142). Action by the local state to boost employment and support new industries therefore has a long history – the entrepreneurial local authority is definitely not a new development in Glasgow (Maver 2006b).

In addition to this growth in new manufacturing, there was also an expansion in the service sector. However, as with the new manufacturing, it was anything but an automatic process, but one facilitated by the local state. As Michael Pacione details, from 1961 to 1981, the proportion of the city's workforce employed in services rose from 48% to 68% and thence to 77% in 1991. By 1985 Glasgow had become the principal business centre in Scotland and the seventh largest commercial office centre in the UK. Within this sector health, education and public administration ("Non-marketed services") formed the biggest employer, ironically perhaps as the social problems of industrial decline spurred the growth in those services charged with easing the related problems. The social services were followed by transport, communications, wholesale and retailing (what Pacione calls "Distributive Services") and then Producer services (banking, insurance, property, business services and advertising) and Personal services (leisure and recreation, hotels and restaurants, pubs and clubs) (Pacione 1995: 147–8). Those sub-sectors that expanded the most from 1981 to 1991 were business services along with advertising, financial services and public administration, with very little growth in what would later be defined as the Cultural Industries – which were buried within Communications and Personal Services, in hospitality and tourism related activities, or not identified at all.

The growth in light manufacturing and services was nowhere near enough to absorb those workers displaced from heavy industry. From 1971 to 1983 the city endured a loss of 78,000 manufacturing jobs while service sector employment actually *declined* by 18,000 (Boyle and Hughes 1991). Over the next decade – 1981 to 1991 – losses from manufacturing totaled 39,000 while the growth in services added only 2,800 extra employees (Paccione 1995: 146). The city may well have been viewed as moving from manufacturing to services, but the percentage change was related far more to the collapse of industry than the buoyant growth of producer and consumer services. As a result, by 1982 unemployment reached a post-war high of 76,400 or 20% of the city's economically active population (Boyle 1995: 455). By 1987 54% of unemployed males and 39% of unemployed females had been out of work for more than a year while 16% of unemployed men and 6% of unemployed women had not worked for over five years. There were even higher levels of unemployment for the young (50% for women under 25, 33% of boys) while the peripheral estates of Drumchapel, Easterhouse, Castlemilk and Pollock all had levels at or above 20% and Glasgow city had 27% of its population unemployed in 1993 (Pacione 1995: 150–152), indicating patterns of ongoing deprivation that became infamous across England. So too on the housing and health fronts; social deprivation was registered across space. Despite huge investments and actions to clear and rebuild areas, by the mid-1980s 45,000 houses were still below "tolerable standard", the city had a mortality rate 12% above the Scottish average and deaths from lung cancer ran at 40% above the Scottish average (Middleton 1991: 106). Glasgow was, in economic and social terms, unsustainable.

Glasgow then, has a long history of economic adversity and social polarisation but also of enrichment and cultural fluorescence. Such a pattern is strongly connected to the city's shifting place in the British empire: processing sugar, cotton and tobacco from the 17th and 18th century trans-Atlantic trade and then in the 19th century supplying the heavy engineering and shipping needed for further imperial trade and military expansion. As a city of wealth and taste in the 19th century, the creative arts as well as more popular sites of cultural expression all flourished, while the exuberance of the city late in the 19th century was evident in a series of radical art movements, including the Glasgow Style of design. Civic confidence and innovation in industry, the arts and sciences was registered in the international exhibitions that were held in the city from 1888 until 1938, in the public and private buildings that were erected, as well as in major cultural institutions, including the university, libraries, private collections and galleries. A range of institutional and objective forms of cultural capital were therefore created out of the industrial wealth of the 19th and early 20th centuries, a legacy that was to prove invaluable in the latter part of the 20th century.

But if the history of Glasgow is one of economic expansion in parallel with that of the British empire, the wealth generated was never spread equitably, with the city associated with sectarianism, poor quality housing, widespread poverty and brutal working conditions. It was such conditions that spurred the "Red Clydeside" reputation while also stimulating concerted local and national government intervention to boost the economy and to improve urban conditions. Such interventions led to some successes – as new manufacturing plants were established along with some call centres and business services while some of the worst inner city tenements were demolished – but in general, state interventions were associated with poor judgement and failure. Best illustrated by the destruction of inner city areas such as the Gorbels and the decanting of their population to poorly serviced, low quality, high rise housing estates, a Labour controlled local state oversaw ongoing economic decline and social polarisation. This then was the city that was chosen – somewhat incongruously – as an international beacon of culture in 1990. Why, how and with what consequences is the subject of the next section.

Glasgow: The 1990 European City of Culture

The quest to become a European City of Culture emerged from a city undergoing a painful process of economic restructuring away from manufacturing but not very successfully towards consumer and producer services. From the dizzy heights of the late 19th and early 20th centuries – which had engendered a rich array of cultural assets – subsequent years had witnessed industrial decline and increasingly acute social problems. Most planning energy and resources had gone into addressing the housing problem via inner city clearance and peripheral estate construction. By the 1970s, however, this solution to the city's woes was not only looking ineffectual – as the many social indicators of deprivation remained stubbornly dire – but aesthetically repugnant and naively deterministic. As modernist high rise was rejected, the alternative of renovation and restoration emerged amid a new aesthetic of valuing "heritage" buildings. Having mobilised heritage, the idea of re-building the city from its core – rather than by emptying the centre to a modern edge of housing estates, industrial parks, ring roads and new towns – was embraced, along with different strategies to grow new industries and the consumer service sector. Key to this strategy was both a re-imagining of the urban image and the mobilisation of both popular and high culture. Such moves built upon the existing but undervalued cultural capital of the city, but also added considerably to it, especially through objective and institutional forms – by the construction of galleries, theatres and exhibition spaces as well as a series of major events and targeted investments to attract cultural tourists. Culminating in the 1990 designation as the European City of Culture, the immediate and longer term impact of such a shift in strategy in creating an economically, socially and culturally sustainable city is still being debated. But I would argue that, because of its historical underpinnings and ongoing trajectory in relation to cultural heritage, image-(re)making, cultural tourism and the design industries – in shifting the city's physical form, economy and social structure towards these parts of the service sector – this Cultural Capital strategy is proving successful and sustainable.

If the 1950s and 60s had been the apotheosis of high rise housing and inner city "slum clearance", by the mid-1970s there was not only popular resistance to demolitions but a more general loss of faith in wholesale modernist planning. In 1964 the New Glasgow Society was formed along with the Scottish Civic Trust (in 1967) and both lobbied successfully for laws to give local authorities powers to designate conservation areas. Instead of being identified with an ugly past, Victorian, Edwardian and Neo-Classical buildings acquired a new value as "heritage", to be celebrated, conserved and re-used rather than destroyed (Frey 1999). A 1971 report concluded that Glasgow was "the finest surviving example of a great Victorian city" (quoted in Pacione 1995: 215). Such a change in perspective led to a number of heritage surveys – in 1972, 1974 and 1987 – and the designation of conservation areas, primarily around the cathedral-Glasgow Cross axis of the old city as well as the Georgian, Edwardian and Victorian precincts nearby. The Merchant City precinct was added to the Central Conservation Area in 1976, to become vital to the re-imagining of the city and its creative arts strategy. In parallel with these council actions, Assist Architects – emanating from Strathclyde University – started a program in Glasgow to demonstrate the possibilities of rehabilitating rather than demolishing Victorian tenements. This re-valuing of older dwellings, civic buildings, warehouses and industrial architecture by members of the creative class was accompanied by more widespread recognition of the critical legacy of the 19th century "Glasgow Style". Thus the inner ring road was re-routed to avoid Mackintosh's Martyrs School (1895), while the more general shift towards renovation rather than demolition led to the dropping of plans for the Stonehouse New Town and redirection of funds into the Glasgow East Area Renewal Program (GEAR) (Rodger 2006).

Thus between 1976 and 1987 GEAR renewed all tenement houses in an area covering 1,600 hectares or 8% of the city. The site included a disused steel works, 20% vacant land and 12% abandoned housing, from which 85,000 people had fled – through choice or slum clearance – leaving a population of 55,000, mainly elderly, unskilled and unemployed people living in single or two roomed dwellings (Middleton 1991; Pacione 1995). The integrated project involved the public (local and regional, health and housing departments), community (via housing associations) and private sectors, with the overall aim to halt population outflow, re-establish industry and improve the quality of the area's environment. With an investment of nearly £200 million of state and £20 million of private capital, 4,000 tenements were rehabilitated by local housing associations, 8,000 interwar houses were modernised by the City and Scottish Special Housing and 4,000 new houses were built, half each by the council and private sector. In addition, new parks and sports facilities, shopping centres, retraining schemes and industrial estates were created, including the Templeton Business Centre for electronics and telecommunications (Middleton 1991). Despite such actions, critics point to the ongoing high levels of out-migration, unemployment, single parents and pensioners in the area, a set of problems that were to re-occur across the city (Pacione 1995; Middleton 1991). For the purposes of this discussion, the significance of this development was the widespread revaluing and refurbishment of inner city housing, the effective partnering of government with the community and private sectors, the continued association of poor economic and physical conditions but also investments into new, non-industrial, high technology knowledge – if not cultural – industries.

With GEAR all but complete, a history of municipal intervention to improve housing, and with a reputation as "Red Clydeside", it was something of a shock that in the 1977 local elections, the Labour Party lost power to the Conservatives in Glasgow. For Mark Boyle, the resulting reflections on policy meant a shift away from the pre-occupation with housing towards dealing more directly with the problem of job creation. With this went a new development strategy based on improving the image and transforming the economic base of the city towards sunrise industries and services. Thus in 1981 the re-installed Labour Council established an Economic Development and Employment Committee with the sole purpose of generating employment (Boyle and Hughes 1994: 456–7). Initially, its main tools were retraining schemes, upgrading local office and industrial land and providing financial help to local businesses. Efforts along these lines to attract light industry had been tried in the past and had not delivered the necessary scale of activity to boost employment or overall economic activity in the troubled city. Clearly a different strategy was required to stimulate economic development, physical regeneration and employment growth.

Past failures to attract new investment had become linked to the negative image of the city. In a survey of civil servants in the south east of England by Michael Pacione in 1982, London was viewed as bustling and cosmopolitan while Edinburgh also assumed a positive image around its castle, festival and military tattoo. In contrast, the overwhelming impression of Glasgow was negative, with a clustering of images centred on violence, depression and slums and the Gorbels appearing as the archetypical site of environmental and social decay (Pacione 1995: 237–8). Reinforced by novels such as *No Mean City* (1935), regular newspaper articles and the highly popular *Rab C. Nesbitt* and *Taggart* television series, "Glasgow was seen as the City of mean streets and mean people, razor gangs, the Gorbals slums, of smoke, grime, of drunks, impenetrable accents and communists" (Taylor quoted in Williams 1997: 152). The failure to attract new business was thereby linked to the negative image of the city.

A new image, it was hoped, would both boost local pride but also attract tourists and investors to the city. Thus from 1980 to 1984 Lord Provost Michael Kelly took on the role of roving ambassador with the "Glasgow's Miles Better" slogan. Modeled on an earlier (1977) "I ♥ New York" promotion, the jocular double meaning of the phrase – miles better/smiles better – and the smiling Mr Happy cartoon became potent symbols. The message was disseminated locally, nationally and internationally via colour newspaper supplements, international business magazines, posters on the London underground and on buses, multilingual bumper stickers, millions of tee-shirts and the travels of HMS Glasgow. Videos documenting how the city was really miles better won prizes at the New York International Film and Television Festival for three successive years and celebrities lined up to be part of Scotland's biggest ever marketing campaign (Ward 1998: 31). For Fisher and Owen, such actions signalled "a city that badly wanted to reinvent itself; here was a town its residents were desperate to love" (Fisher and Owen 1991: 44). Most analysts of urban marketing agree that the campaign was highly successful in altering the local and outsider's perception of the city. While not translating directly into business investment, it was held responsible for boosting the rate of tourist visits to the city from 700,000 in 1982 to 2.2 million in 1988 and thence to between 3 and 4 million in 1990 (Fisher and Owen 1991: 43–4; Middleton 1991: 117). While opinions differ on the numbers, the dramatic upward trajectory of this tourist inflow is not disputed. But there was more to such increases than a re-invented image, for these people were coming to see things that the city now offered to them – and critical to the growth of tourism in Glasgow was that cultural capital assets were assembled from the past and re-presented to the cultural tourists of the 1980s.

Accompanying the re-imaging of the city, went a deliberate effort to boost its cultural infrastructure. The 19th century ship owner and trader Sir William Burrell had amassed a collection of 8,000 art objects, ranging from Ancient Greek amphora and Chinese vases, to French impressionist paintings and Medieval tapestries and armour, over his long life. Donating them all to the city of Glasgow in 1944, he then gave the Glasgow Corporation £450,000 for the construction of a building to house the collection, insisting that it be at least five miles from the city centre and in a rural setting. It took until 1967 and the bequest of Pollock House for a suitable site to be found and in 1971 an international architecture competition selected the design by Barry Gasson to house the collection. Somewhat fortuitously, it was during the Miles Better campaign that the massive Burrell Collection was opened in 1983, at a final costs of £23 million. But in one stroke, the city gained a major public art collection and mecca for cultural tourists, 1.2 million of whom visited the gallery in its first year, propelling it to the number one tourist attraction in Scotland (Friel 2004; Middleton 1991: 117; Williams 1997: 153).

However, with only one major attraction, it seemed that the city offered little else to the burgeoning cultural tourism market (see Chapter 3). The newly created

Regional Tourism Board noted that the city basically shut down from June to August, the biggest tourist months for overseas visitors. The Board therefore set about creating a number of events and festivals to attract people to Glasgow. Building on the success of the Burrell Collection, the strategy was to continue to grow the link between the creative arts and tourism. Thus the Director of the Tourist Board Eddie Friel (British American Arts Association 1989), instituted an annual arts festival – Mayfest – as part of an event and cultural approach to Glasgow's urban redevelopment and economic revival. Significant in the elaboration of such a strategy were three reports completed in the mid-1980s by John Myerscough (economic adviser to the British government on the economic value of the arts), Gordon Cullen (internationally renown architect) and multi-national consultancy McKinsey and Co. Comfortably located with a neo-liberal Conservative national government led by Margaret Thatcher, here then were national and international "experts", brought in to advise on how to create the post-industrial city: around a new image and major events but also, through the renovation of the inner city, a re-valuing of cultural heritage and the promotion of the creative arts through a partnership between the private and public sectors.

Thus in 1985 the international management consultancy firm McKinsey and Co-commissioned by the Scottish Development Agency – suggested the city embrace a post-industrial future and use place marketing projects as a tool by which such investment could be lured (Boyle and Hughes 1994: 457). They also recommended that the city centre should be rejuvenated using the cultural industries in particular and the consumer services sector more generally (Williams 1997: 152). Their report on *The Potential of Glasgow City Centre* concluded that: "if Glasgow is to reach its full potential as an international business and service industry centre, it must have a vibrant and cosmopolitan city centre" (quoted in Reed 1999: 189). Following a visit to Minneapolis in the US, McKinsey and the Scottish Development Agency proposed that private sector involvement in the plan would be vital. A new group – Glasgow Action – was created as a result in 1985 (and lasted until 1991 when it was replaced by the Glasgow Development Agency). Comprised of three full time employees and led by Lord Norman McFarlane, Chairman of United Distilleries, all members of Glasgow Action were drawn from national and international companies and formed an informal business club to lobby local and national government as well as other business leaders. While seen as relatively ineffectual by Boyle and Hughes (1994), Glasgow Action was actively involved in a number of city projects, beginning with their commissioning of internationally renown architect Gordon Cullen to re-imagine and re-design the centre of the city. Cullen had spent time over the 1960s and 70s developing an empirical townscape alternative to what Peter Reed calls the "austere axioms of modernist town planning" (Reed 1999: 190). His plan for Glasgow comprised three main elements:

1. Buchanan Street was to become the major artery of the city, with key cultural institutions and shopping malls at either end and the "sturdy precincts" of Blythswood New Town and Merchant City on either side,

2. Consistent with existing planning priorities within the city, the waterfront around the River Clyde was to be redeveloped into a Riverside Chain – or string of pearls – comprising rehabilitated housing, multi-use facilities, hotels and office blocks, and

3. The M8 motorway running around the city centre was to be developed as a visual metaphor of the medieval walled city (Boyle and Hughes 1994: 460).

Boyle and Hughes conclude that this idyllic and clearly top-down plan aimed to re-aestheticise the city centre as a means to enhance property values, boost the city's image and extend (or perhaps make!) Glasgow's reputation as a centre of stylish consumption. Visiting the city in 2005, it was obvious to me that Buchanan Street was indeed the retail axis of the city and that it had been successfully anchored by cultural institutions – including the Royal Scottish Concert Hall – and major undercover shopping centres, the Buchanan Galleria at one end and the new St Enoch Centre at the other. To the east was Merchant City with its mix of warehouse residences but also galleries, boutiques, restaurants and bars. Here then was a plan and ultimately a reality to connect old with new cultural institutions – as Cullen's plan of 1984 shows – with the Glasgow School of Art, joining the Royal School of Music, Strathclyde University and Glasgow Film Theatre at the apex of the design, restored heritage precincts bisecting it and other renovated buildings and new developments along the riverside (see Figure 4.1). While now somewhat more spread out and more reliant on retailing than the original plan, the 1988 Annual Report of Glasgow Action could observe that "activity in Glasgow city centre has related closely to the vision developed by Dr Cullen. Not only were the polar buildings of the Buchanan Street axis under construction, but proposals were also in hand for the materialisation of his 'riverside chain'" (quoted in Reed 1999: 191). A contemporary tourist map of the city shows just how much of the original plan was realised, suggesting that such visions and those who promoted them, did indeed shape the city (MacLeod 2002; Author's field notes 2005).

Building onto and complementing such work, in 1988 the key advisor to the British government on the economic value of the creative arts (see Chapter 1) was commissioned by the Glasgow District Council to assess the importance of the arts in Glasgow. John Myerscough affirmed the wisdom of the city seeking regeneration through tourism, arts and service sector development while also concluding that tourist expenditure *alone* would not be sufficient to generate a substantial number of service jobs (Boyle and Hughes 1994). In his report Myerscough noted: "There was good evidence that Glasgow had tapped new markets through the influence of the arts. In Glasgow 71% of cultural tourists were first-time visitors (and) the response of visitors to Glasgow's cultural facilities was especially strong" (quoted by Wishart 1991: 46). He goes on to argue that the arts are a major source of economic activity, with each job in the arts giving rise to another 2.7 in the region (Wishart 1991: 46).

The report by Mysercough joined those by Cullen and McKinsey and Co. in offering a consistent argument about building a new image for the city and

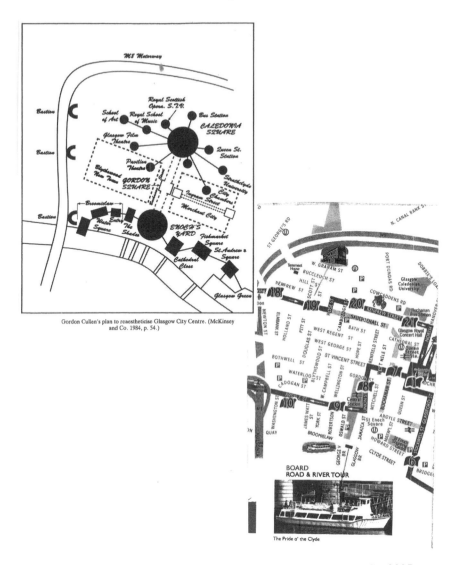

Gordon Cullen's plan to reaestheticise Glasgow City Centre. (McKinsey and Co. 1984, p. 54.)

Figure 4.1   Gordon Cullen's plan for Glasgow City Centre and a 2005 Tourist Map

Source: Boyle and Hughes 1994: 461; Scottish Tourist Board 2005.

in taking real steps towards mobilising cultural capital as *the* way to further grow tourist numbers, activate the city centre and to stimulate the shift towards the consumer service sector. Such reports meshed with existing local planning policies, the interests of those already working in the creative arts in the city – as practitioners and administrators – but also with elements of business, especially those in retailing and hospitality.

While the city had already begun investing significantly in its cultural resources with the Burrell Collection, the combined weight of arguments rendered by Myerscough, Cullen and McKinsey and Company meant that the local state sought to inject internationally renown cultural capital into the city – by way of eminent architects – and to boost the institutional infrastructure on which the creative economy would be developed. From the late 1980s then major investments were made in a new Royal Concert Hall (1990) by Sir Leslie Martin and RMJM, the £36 million Scottish Exhibition Centre (1990), a new home for the Royal Scottish Academy of Music (1996), the £7 million Gallery of Modern Art in the restored neo-classical Royal Exchange building (1996), the Tron Theatre – redeveloped by RMJM in 1998 – and the renovation of Mackintosh's Scottish Herald Building as the new site for the National Centre of Design – the Lighthouse (by local firm Page and Park in 1999). In addition to these public investments and in the context of Margaret Thatcher's drive to reclaim the inner cities, efforts to re-animate the city were undertaken by private capital through the building of a series of major shopping centres, including the Forge (1988), St Enoch Centre (1989), the Italian Centre (1990) and the Buchanan Galleries (1995). Along with a string of international hotels along the riverfront, Williams estimates that between 1985 and 1991, 150 cultural, retail and other developments with an overall value of £1.8 billion were completed in the city centre of Glasgow (Williams 1997: 153).

As well as these public and private investments – all of which reversed a long term trend of capital flight from the city and contributed to the massive upsurge of tourism and retailing in the city – there was also the embrace (or perhaps the rediscovery) of the major event as a trigger for further physical restoration and economic transformation. With the opening in 1985 of an exhibition and conference centre, festivals of choral, folk and jazz music as well as dance were created to enliven the summer months (Law 1993: 105). In 1987 a festival unit was established in the city council and it moved more decisively to build on the long tradition of hosting major events in the city. In 1888 Glasgow had been the venue for the first in a series of international exhibitions. The last, in 1938 had attracted 13.5 million visitors. It was to be in 1983, as the quest to reinvent the urban image of the city and to re-orient its economy gained support and direction, that this strategy was rediscovered and the city bid to host the third National Garden Festival – after Liverpool (1984) and Stoke-on-Trent (1986). German in origin, the idea of such a festival was to reclaim derelict land through landscaping and generate short term benefits in the form of tourists. In Glasgow the abandoned Princes Dock on the south bank of the Clyde was renovated and the event staged at a cost of £41 million. The 4 million visitors, however, only generated £23 million in revenue and left a net cost to the public purse of £19 million along with a renovated site that, ten years on, was still unused (Williams 1997: 154). In 2006, however, such a site was earmarked for a new digital city, and will, the planners clearly hope, be the place for a major Creative Industry cluster. While some in Glasgow regarded the Garden Festival as a poor investment, for others it was a model to be further developed into systematic claims for international recognition and cultural capital. This was to occur via the bid to become the European City of Culture.

Throughout the 1980s, then, guided by a series of external consultants, international models – especially the examples of Boston, Baltimore and Minneapolis – reflection on past policy failures and before intractable levels of unemployment, industrial decline, poverty and physical abandonment; image, the creative arts, retailing and major events were mobilised to refashion the city. Consistent with David Harvey's observations on the quest by industrial cities in the United States to reinvent themselves through waterfront renovation, urban spectacles and retailing from the 1970s (1989a, see Chapter 2), what was somewhat different in the case of Glasgow was the centrality of cultural capital in the strategy. The symbolic economy was clearly being elevated above the industrial one in the quest to be the European Union (EU) City of Culture. Over the 1980s in Glasgow then, along with the mass steam cleaning of buildings went the opening of a host of cultural institutions, new shopping centres, warehouse housing and riverside hotels (Mooney 2004: 329). It was on this foundation that the city bid to become the sixth EU City of Culture. Chosen by the British Government over Bath, Bristol, Cambridge, Cardiff, Edinburgh, Leeds, Liverpool and Swansea, the Glasgow District Council successfully argued for the importance to the city of developing its cultural tourism sector as a tool for economic regeneration (Williams 1997: 155). Those members of the Office of Arts and Libraries who made the initial evaluation of Glasgow were not immediately convinced that this gritty city was the best candidate. However, on their return, a paper by the local well-established network of arts workers and administrators pointed to the annual arts budget of £24 million, the list of national arts companies resident in the city – Scottish Opera, Scottish Ballet, the Royal Scottish National Orchestra – and the annual Mayfest international arts festival, along with seventeen major museums, twenty five galleries and nine major theatres (Wishart 1991: 44). The city therefore had a lively contemporary arts scene as well as major cultural institutions and a drive to mobilise the arts further to change the image and socio-economic as well as physical reality of the city. The historical legacy as well as recent revaluations of cultural icons and investments in institutional and objective forms of cultural capital, conveyed by those who both embodied and administered much of it, was critical to Glasgow becoming formally designated a Cultural Capital.

The 1990 City of Culture was but another step in the process of re-imagining and consciously directing the economic restructuring of the city. Being a high profile exercise, it attracted a host of praise and academic attention but also some spirited criticism, especially from those who spoke on behalf of the "Workers City". With a total budget of £54 million – £35 million from the local council, £12 million from the regional council, and half a million pounds from the European Union – over 3,800 events were held. The Festival Office had three main objectives:

1. Cultural objectives: to co-ordinate the development of existing facilities and cultural organisations in the city; to provide incentives and encouragement for artists; and to extend cultural objectives (internationally).
2. Economic objectives: to improve the regional economy by creating employment opportunities; to increase visitor numbers and expand the number of participants and spectators in cultural events.
3. Social Objectives: to provide increased opportunities for participation in cultural activities with the emphasis on groups often ignored by mainstream cultural institutions; and to provide fun and entertainment for the citizens of, and visitors to Glasgow (Sayer 1992: 69–70).

Significant amounts of funding was directed to securing and presenting high profile international acts – such as Frank Sinatra, Luciano Pavarotti, Peter Brook's epic Mahabharta and the Bolshoi Ballet – but also in assembling the "Glasgow's Glasgow" exhibition, tracing the city's 800-year history in the newly refurbished central railway station (a major loss maker), while one million pounds was spent on the Big Day rock and pop festival. As the program was about image as well as the arts, £4 million was spent commissioning Saatchi and Saatchi to market the year, primarily to south east England and Europe (Williams 1997: 155). Sayer maintains that only 1% of the 15 million pound City Council's contribution was spent on funding local events (Sayer 1992: 72). But if one of the major objectives was to use culture as a marketing tool and for boosting tourism, the year also included promotion of community arts, ethnic minority arts and art in socially and culturally deprived neighbourhoods. Theatre groups and arts centres from peripheral housing estates organised plays and photographic competitions, artists in residence were located in the Gorbals, while the Jewish and Irish communities organised extended arts programs and commissioned public sculptures. The scale of the community arts program suggests that resources were indeed spread across the city as local artists and groups were supported along with marketing into Europe (Williams 1997: 156–7). While not big ticket items, such localised arts activity was significantly boosted by the funding and promotion offered by 1990.

From the beginning though, there were pockets of stident opposition to the Cultural Capital idea. Emanating from self-appointed spokespersons of working class culture – "Workers City" – this group of forty was a loose collection of Left-orientated local artists and celebrities. As Boyle and Hughes (1991, 1994) detail, its members included Booker Prize winning writer James Kelman, author Alisdair Gray, local museum curator Michael Donnelly, academic Sean Damer and investigative journalist David Kemp – a host of notables with considerable amounts of embodied cultural capital. While not representative of the wider Glasgow population but clearly an important sample of the local arts community, they successfully organised opposition meetings and marches, accessed the local press for ongoing coverage and compiled a collection of essays critical of the 1990 events – *Workers City: the real Glasgow stands up* (1988) and *Workers City: the reckoning* (1990). Boyle and Hughes summarise the groups arguments: that the year had more to do with capital than culture, that in a bid to re-present Glasgow in a positive light, the reality of working class life and cultural heritage was ignored and trashed, the events brought no economic benefit to the average citizen and the whole package confirmed the willingness of the Labour council to partner with and even more systematically advantage capital over labour (Boyle and Hughes 1991: 214). Central to the Worker's City case was that the year did not capture and celebrate the essential nature of the city's history and culture, which was of a tough, radical working class community that had endured and struggled for survival. For example, Damer noted:

> Glasgow is of all British cities, the industrial city *par excellence*. It is one whose identity – not image – is secure because it is cemented by its history of tough living and working conditions ... This bonding was ensured by common poverty, which in turn resulted in a common culture of survival. Glaswegians define this identity as socialist. Nobody denies that Glasgow is a tough city. This toughness is the unwanted outcome of the people's history of having to survive harsh working and even tougher living circumstances (quoted in Boyle and Hughes 1994: 465).

In contrast, the group argued that the City of Culture assumed "the character of hype and spectacle geared towards the tastes of middle class and tourist consumers" which, Damer argued, reflected nothing of the traditional radical and socialist working class culture and politics of the city. Such sentiments were echoed by some of those working within key cultural institutions in the city. Thus another critic was Assistant Curator of the People's Palace. Faced with having what some argued was a pro-industrialist, celebratory and sanitised version of the city's history reproduced as the "Glasgow's Glasgow" exhibition (Sayer 1992: 71), Michael Donnelly wrote to the *Glasgow Herald*:

> If Glasgow is to avoid some of the worst aspects of urban decline ... it must base its future on a sound and critical analysis of its cultural and political past and present. To face up to that task ... was a unique challenge implicit in the award of the City of Culture title. But that opportunity was rejected and instead the District Council allows itself to be highjacked by the concept cowboys and mythologists of the public relations industry. Their object was not to hold up to inspection and critical analysis the radical past of this city and its unique contribution to socialism. On the contrary, they considered this past to be inglorious and anaethemistic to those who take pride in its achievements (quoted in Boyle and Hughes 1994: 466).

In addition to querying its symbolic meaning and value, Workers City also questioned the economic value of the City of Culture, arguing that it would only profit mobile capital and benefit the affluent (Williams 1997: 157). Here then were members of the Cultural Industries and the creative class, offering a stinging critique of the effort to make Glasgow a Cultural Capital. The irony is all too apparent. What they were pointing out, in part, was the tension between those who have high levels of embodied cultural capital – the middle classes who would attend many of the new cultural institutions and events – and those that, in Bourdieu's terms, had little, the working class of Glasgow whose rich industrial history they argued was marginal to the year and whose taste and resources meant their exclusion from most of the year's activities. Anxiety then focused on whose culture was being represented and celebrated as well as who was going to benefit economically as well as discursively from it. While there was a broader concern with the apparent complicity of the Labour Council with the market-led, revanchist agenda of Margaret Thatcher, it is useful to test the various claims made by the group – on the exclusive nature of the events, their orientation primarily to those who already had recognised cultural capital and their limited and exclusive economic impact.

For Williams, it is telling that Workers City disbanded soon after 1990, while many of its protagonists now praise the developments that have taken place (Williams 1997: 157). Ruth Wishart points to the essential arrogance of the Worker's City group who assumed, from their somewhat privileged class positions, that they were "qualified to be keepers of the city's socialist conscience and working- class traditions" (Wishart 1991: 46). So too Gerry Mooney notes how the Worker's City group neglected to recognise the extent to which Glasgow, like any other place, is always being imagined and re-imagined and has diverse and often conflicting histories. There is also an assumption in the critique that the often low paid service sector jobs which emerged from the Cultural Capital agenda were inferior to those that had been lost in ship building. The Workers City argument, ignored if not romanticised, the dreadful conditions and low wages associated with Glasgow's heavy industry (Mooney 2004).

Booth and Boyle also note:

> The criticism of Worker's City needs to be seen in the context of an extensive community events programme that attracted widespread support during 1990 ... more than five hundred exhibitions, local gala days and theatrical events brought the year of Culture closer to the public, especially into the peripheral public housing sector housing schemes (1993: 39).

Indeed as the Myerscough report on the year noted, there was a 40% jump in attendance at theatres, halls, museums and galleries over the year while another 1.7 million took part in outdoor events. The program touched the lives of four out of five adult residents in the region. 54% went to the theatre or to a concert hall while 61% visited a museum or gallery. The programmed events spanned over 700 Glasgow organisations and up to 22,000 people had some sort of involvement in their organisation (Centre for Cultural Policy Research 2004). Over the year, attendances at events and attractions reached 6.6 million, 74% attending museums and galleries and 26% theatres and concerts (Law 1993: 105). Here then are figures which suggest a huge expansion in popular engagement with institutional and objective cultural capital by those deemed to have a serious deficit in it – in Bourdieu's terms at least. Clearly, much of the program, engaged locals and worked to enhance their embodied cultural capital, not necessarily by denying it. For as Mark Boyle (1997) details, following a key objective of the Festival Office, there were many *local* projects that received support through 1990 – including the Glasgow Sculpture Studio's efforts to connect local communities (including Drumchapel and Govan) and artists together in creating a series of representative Milestones; a play on housing dampness developed by the Eastall Theatre Group (an offshoot of the Easthall Residents Association) and the Drum Kitchen developed by the Gorbals Unemployed Worker's Centre artist in residence, and a series of banners by another artist in residence, this time in the predominantly Asian community of Woodlands. Wishart points to the 100,000 teenagers in George Square and Glasgow Green who attended The Big Day series of concerts and the 10,000 children marching with their home made lanterns through a sodden and cold October day as part of the year's events (Wishart 1991: 50).

Sayer (1992) also notes how the cultural focus on 1990 spurred Glaswegians to think about their own cultural heritage and facilitated a revival of local traditions and cultural practices. She gives the example of the Easterhouse Feis in 1991 which included lectures, art shows and murals, Gaelic football, traditional dance and music, Ceilidhs in local halls, music in local bars and a broad ranging engagement by those on a much demonised peripheral estate with their own cultural capital.

As well as the artistic and community effervescence that accompanied the year, there have been ongoing artistic outcomes. Most obviously this includes the major cultural institutions which were constructed for the year. Permanent legacies include the new McLellan Galleries, the Tramway Theatre, a new front for the Citizen's Theatre and the great concert hall sitting atop Buchanan Street (Middleton 1991: 118). Atttributed to the sheer energy and determination – some also said the ballooning ego and Stalinist authoritarian rule of the Lord Provost for the year Pat Lally – this structure signified to Workers City members the abrogation of democratic rights that the year brought. But for others it was a triumph, anchoring the inner city revival while also giving something to Glasgow that Edinburgh – that rival for the title of Cultural Capital in the inter-city competition stakes – did not have! Cultural institutions as well as what they housed became symbols of both civic pride and arrogance and signaled a new level of international and national orientation towards the creative arts by the people of Glasgow.

Festival director Bob Palmer did indeed bring in major international artists, but strove to keep ticket prices relatively modest – a maximum of £75 for Pavarotti and Sinatra – and put these alongside the thousand of community-based events as evidence of significant local ownership of the year. Palmer saw 1990 as a way to kick start cultural activities that would continue well beyond this magical year, arguing in 1989:

> My view if that the people of Glasgow must feel that the cultural year is theirs and that it is not imposed upon them. They must contribute to the planning of it … Fundamentally, our work involves the coordination and assisting of many hundreds of local groups, to celebrate Glasgow's culture in their own terms rather than in our terms (Quoted in Boyle and Hughes 1994: 462).

Neil Wallace, his deputy in the 1990 Festival Office and working in 1992 to develop the Tramway theatre, pointed to the touring "Call that Singing" choir and the ongoing "Street Biz" festival of street theatre and buskers as evidence of the ongoing nature of such local artistic developments, dating from 1990 (Wishart 1991: 49–50). In addition, three million pounds was invested on behalf of the city's art galleries, with the interest still available for new and ongoing purchases (Middleton 1991: 118).

As well as the ongoing artistic outcomes of 1990, it is notable that Glasgow people did not back the opposition groups en masse. Despite the vehemence and visibility of the Worker's City's objections, as the year went on, to suggest that being European City of Culture was a mistake was to criticise Glasgow itself. Glasgow had won the title with a socially inclusive agenda. For all the column inches generated by the protests, there was a constant unreported level of activity at a community level, most of it generated by people who simply wanted to be part of it. 1990 redrew the boundaries of the word 'culture' for many. Cultural capital was spread far wider than before and indeed underwent a definitional expansion in this city, to include much of its industrial and design history as well as engaging much of the population. The year ensured an accelerated investment in major cultural institutions but also gave recognition to the broad cultural heritage of the city – the magnificent civic art collections, the architecture of Makintosh, the Citizens Theatre – putting them on an international platform while also supporting the growth and expression of a range of local artistic activities.

If the artistic and cultural outcomes from the 1990 City of Culture are significant, what of its economic contribution – both short and long term? Having been important in setting the agenda, John Myerscough was brought in again to assess its success – or otherwise. In a study conducted for the City of Glasgow in 1991 he noted:

- £54 million of investment had brought a net return of £10–14 million
- The year had created over 5,300 'person years' worth of jobs

Other studies documented how hotel and guest house occupancy rates had risen significantly as did the sheer numbers and levels of expenditure by tourists. Thus Williams notes how between 1983 and 1989, the average number of overseas tourists to the city was 264,000 spending around £71 million per annum. From 1991 to 1994, 455,000 on average visited – a rise of 42% from pre-1990 – spending on average £112 million per annum – an increase of 37% (Williams 1997: 159). Between 1991 and 1998 visitors increased further by 88% and in

2002 tourism sustained 21,000 jobs (OECD 2002: 96). Tourism was one of the longer term growth sectors which benefited from 1990. But if tourism has grown substantially on the back of the re-imagined city and its cultural resources, what of the city's overall economic structure?

In 1985 Williams estimated that the arts in Glasgow were a £204 million industry, employing 14,700 people (2.25% of the working population), more people than built ships on the Clyde (Williams 1997: 158–9). The Centre for Cultural Policy Research at Glasgow University observed in 2002 that the cultural industries – which they define as "the art trade, music industry, designer trades, film and television etc." – were estimated to have grown between 1986 and 1990 by 3.9% (Centre for Cultural Policy 2002: 4). However, in a survey completed by the OECD in 2002, the Cultural Industries did not rank a mention, except in terms of future growth and as a site for EU investment (OECD 2002). Other economic audits of the city in 2003 and 2004 for Scottish Enterprise and the Glasgow City Council tend to focus on the fate of manufacturing and the broader service sector, rightly emphasising the importance of employment growth in business services as critical to the ongoing restructuring of the city (OECD 2002; EKOS 2003a and 2003b; Experian 2003). Indeed that ever visible if not overly reliable recorder of public information – Wikipedia – reports that since 2000 more than 150,000 jobs have been created in Glasgow and that it sill accounts for more than 60% of Scotland's manufacturing exports, especially in ship building, engineering, food and drink, chemicals and textiles. It also notes significant growth in opto-electronics, software and bio-technology, knowledge industry sectors of the new economy. Such data puts the hype associated with the Cultural Industries in this city into perspective.

Dedicated assessments of the Creative Industries do offer some insight into the longer term legacy of the Cultural Capital strategy and indicate a modest if not overly strong contribution to the urban economy. In any such assessment, problems of definition inevitably arise. In two major surveys, both consultants – EKOS and Experian – use the 2001 British Department of Culture Media and Sports Creative Industries Mapping Document (2000) definition of the Creative Industries, being: "those industries which have their origin in creativity, skill and talent, which have a potential for wealth and job creation through the generation and exploitation of intellectual property". Moving from this broad definition the focus of discussion by both EKOS and Experian is on four main activities, with their 2001 employment levels (Experian 2003) shown:

Motion picture and video activities	-	540
Radio and television activities	-	1,540
News agency activities	-	110
Other service activities (including personal services such as hairdressing and recreational services)	-	4,680
Total	-	6,870 (for Metro Glasgow)

Notable institutions which swell these numbers include BBC Scotland – both TV and radio production centres – and large newspaper offices in Glasgow. What is *not* included in such a listing is "Architecture and Engineering Services" [6,190] and "Advertising" (1,310) (both considered Knowledge Industries and members of the creative class along with new manufacturing, pharmaceuticals, telecommunications and business services) as well as those employed in "Library, archives, museums and other cultural activities" (830). In addition to those in what I would call the Cultural Industries (see Chapter 1), there are those employed in Retail (37,000) and Tourism (28,500), sectors which have grown significantly in the region and can be seen as relevant indicators of the long term success of the Cultural Capital agenda. So while direct employment in what can be delimited as the Cultural Industries – around 15,200 or 1.4% out of a workforce of 1,100,000 – is very modest, related industries are significant employers. It is also possible to argue that the growth in business services and new manufacturing can be related in small part, to the improved cultural assets and physical appearance of the city. Despite such modest levels, however, the place of the Creative Industries remains prominent in any assessment of the city's future economic growth and in its planning, with most references being incredibly upbeat (see for example Experian 2003; Kane nd; Glasgow City Council 2006). How sustainable such a strategy is will be considered in the final part of this chapter.

For those surveying the outcomes of 1990, in addition to the short and medium term economic impacts and the effects on the creative and Cultural Industries, are considerations relating to the socio-economic well being of the city as a whole. And here, the assessment is profoundly negative. For while the inner areas of the city have continued their physical and cultural regeneration, this has been accompanied by gentrification: as an inflow of relatively young, single or childless couples who are also well off, displace those who are poor from these refurbished and now revalued sites (Seo 2002). Indeed the investment in institutional and objective cultural capital in the inner city can be seen as matched by an inflow of those with far higher levels of embodied cultural capital than those who once lived there. And on the other side of the social-spatial ledger, the statistics of social disadvantage continue for Glasgow as a whole and for the peripheral estates in particular. In spite of employment growth and the continued shift to a service economy – which provided 82.5% of employment in 2003 (Mooney 2004: 334) – there are other figures that point to ongoing high levels of unemployment – 25% in 2002 – well above the level for Edinburgh (10.6%) and the UK (9.5%). Across Glasgow there remain high rates of people on sickness and disability benefits – 72,000 in 2003 – with 34% of the metropolitan population claiming some sort of social benefit in 2001–2 (Mooney 2004: 335). Research for the Scottish Executive showed that 55% of the entire population continues to live in areas classified as deprived, with Glasgow accounting for 16 of the 20 most deprived areas in Scotland in 2003. 41% of households live in poverty with most of these households located outside the inner city (Mooney 2004: 336). The social and spatial polarisation of Glasgow then, has not been appreciably eased by the Cultural Capital agenda. Indeed it could be seen as exacerbating it, undermining the social sustainability of the strategy.

Short term, with the adoption of a Cultural Capital agenda, Glasgow saw new cultural infrastructure and a city centre renaissance, along with a boost to the arts, retail and cultural sectors, a broad ranging engagement with and growth in local cultural capital, widened and strengthened international cultural contacts and an improvement in Glasgow's image in England and Europe which stimulated a growth in tourism. Longer term, there has been a positive change in the inner city's physical fabric, a change in the scale and nature of the cultural institutions and the image of the city, registered in London as well as in Europe and expressed most strongly in ongoing tourism expansion. But there are serious questions as to whether the Cultural Capital agenda has had a major positive impact on the continuing high levels of unemployment as well as the social and spatial deprivation of the city. While the platform may well have been provided for the development of the Cultural Industries, this sector, even if linked to tourism and hospitality, is unlikely to generate the number of well paying jobs or scale of economic activity and physical regeneration in the right places to address the ongoing problems faced by so many of Glasgow's population. Whether the agenda has actually worsened these problems, however, is debatable. There has indeed been an increase in the levels of cultural capital within the inner city but it has not been without its broadening and there has also been an increase in valued cultural activity in the peripheral regions. The discussion of 1990 has not only highlighted the broad scale and scope of the many events of that year, but has noted the transformation of the inner city as a site for leisure, recreation and shopping for those who live in greater Glasgow. Such developments have also fed into the more positive image of the city and undeniably made it more attractive to those inside the city as well as from outside – travelers, students, investors and potential residents. There has been major shifts in the valuing of the cultural resources of this city – especially its heritage buildings and established cultural institutions – as well as the promotion and creation of other cultural activities – including major galleries, concert halls but also performance spaces and companies which have broader appeal. There has therefore been an appreciable growth in the cultural capital of Glasgow, especially since 1990, but there remain real questions about the longer term economic, social and cultural sustainability of the Cultural Capital agenda. This will be furhter explored by looking at more recent strategies to re-imagine the city and the current state of the cultural and design industries.

Re-designing Mackintosh

Travelling to Glasgow in 2005 as a cultural tourist and student of Cultural Capitals
and staying in the refurbished Central Quality (Railway) Hotel (1879) adjacent to
Merchant City, a number of things were obvious about this city (Author's field
notes 2005):

- A great deal of effort had gone into valuing and restoring the Victorian
  heritage buildings, which were clean and fully utilised;
- Shopping was a mass activity and involved flows of people across traffic
  free precincts that went from the Merchant City up Buchanan Street to each
  of the major undercover malls and the retro "Glasgow Style" complexes
  such as the Italian Centre and Princes Square Shopping Centre;
- With some effort, you could *do* a Mackintosh tour, having sourced maps
  with the appropriate information and traversed the city to see the many
  buildings, galleries and tea rooms that not only displayed his work but that
  of other members of the "Glasgow School";
- Clearly there remained an edginess in this city, most obviously registered
  in the number of young people, inevitably dressed in black and heavily
  adorned with silver jewellery who hung around two main precincts – the
  steps of the Gallery of Modern Art and adjacent streets, bars and coffee
  shops – and around the Glasgow School of Art just to the west of the city.
  Close to and part of these precincts, there were indeed galleries and small
  design businesses as well as more up-market retail and social spaces;
- Such edginess for a woman traveling alone was even more evident and
  palpably threatening when a weekend soccer match saw Scotland pitted
  against a European team. As the game was played the streets emptied, only
  to be filled anew at game's end by groups of drunken and kilted young men
  shouting, singing and claiming the inner city as their own. Spirited and
  patriotic yes but also aggressive and not the style of cultural capital that I
  could relate to;
- But on other days, the banners fluttering in the main squares and along the
  major boulevards pronounced a new slogan for the city – "Scotland with
  Style" – that invited further exploration

From 1990, those who planned and attempted to bring economic development to the
city of Glasgow – the city and regional councils, the European Union but also after
devolution in 1999, the Scottish development authorities – remained engaged with
the Cultural Capital agenda. As Glasgow became a model of arts-led re-imaging
and urban regeneration and as other cities emulated its strategies and the mantle
of City of Culture moved to other places, it was apparent that competition for
cultural tourists and the cultural industries would only intensify. Having initiated
such an agenda, it had to be regularly reviewed and, if assessed as successful,
renewed and refreshed. The necessity for such actions not only came from the loss

of momentum after 1990, but also by events such as a 1992 gangland murder trial and a 1995 series of violent attacks in the city which reminded those within and beyond Glasgow of the fragility of the new image as well as its perilous social sustainability (Mooney and Dansen 1997). This return to a gritty negative image was reinforced by movies set in Glasgow and by ongoing official assessments and actions on social deprivation. While there had been a large expansion of new services over the 1980s and 90s – banking, insurance and finance, public and private administration and personal services – all promoted as key elements of the post-industrial economy, such growth had overwhelmingly benefited commuters from outside the city and still remained insufficient to absorb all unemployed workers or to boost the overall economy of the city. By the mid-1990s, then, older images and ongoing negative realities of Glasgow had been re-asserted.

The response was to re-imagine the city anew and, significantly for this discussion, the basis of such re-imaging was the cultural resources of the city, both historically and as they were developing from the 1990s. While in 1992 the idea of "Glasgow's Alive" was touted, along with its viability as a conference venue (Law 1993), in 1994 it was the visual arts that received prominence while in the same year Glasgow was nominated as the UK City of Art and Design for 1999. This formed part of the decade of annual celebrations that were promoted by the Arts Council of Great Britain. Competition for this title was fierce, with the 17 cities that originally competed for the designation finally being reduced to a choice between Glasgow and its east-coast neighbour and capital of Scotland, Edinburgh. At stake was £400,000 from the Arts Council, plus the opportunity to generate much more income through future funding bids, sponsorship, grants, tourism, exhibitions, and sales.

Two years after the election of Tony Blair and the creation of the "Cool Britannia" image, the 1999 Festival of Art and Design in Glasgow was to celebrate excellence in architecture and design from around the world, to promote awareness in the people of Glasgow, its communities, organisations and business of the cultural and economic importance of the design process, and to highlight new thinking to help position Glasgow as a major European city of ideas. It was, as Bell and Jayne later theorised, a co-ordinated effort to put design at the centre of the local economy across a number of fronts (Bell and Jayne 2003). In order to do this, the Glasgow 1999 Festival Co. Ltd created a programme of individual projects and events which showcased what design could mean and promoted the economic significance of design and architecture for Glasgow's businesses and institutions. Further to this, the Festival was to leave a legacy to the city in the National Centre for Design in the form of the Lighthouse Centre for Architecture and Design which was located down an alley in a newly refurbished C.R. Mackintosh building (see Figure 4.2) originally constructed for the Glasgow Herald.

Events and projects over 1999 included exhibitions, conferences and displays; the development of the Lighthouse centre; the Glasgow Collection project that helped to fund new product ideas to prototype stage; education and community programmes; *Homes for the Future*, a project to build a new low income residential area incorporating innovative design principles near Glasgow Green; *Millennium Spaces* to develop high quality public spaces designed by artists in consultation with local communities; and the Partnership Fund to support various small scale projects with goals compatible with the aims of the Glasgow 1999 Festival. This time, instead of looking to the United States for inspiration, the model was Barcelona. Here a major event – in this case the 1982 Olympic Games – had been connected to internationally renown architects designing flagship buildings, a celebration of the architectural heritage of the city's most famous sons – including Gaudi, Domenech and Cadafalch- and a more positive image as well as other policies aimed at stimulating economic and social regeneration (Bell and Jayne 2003). The parallels with Glasgow were clear and emphasis fell upon the heritage of Charles Rennie Mackintosh and the Glasgow School of Design.

One of the more enduring outcomes of the 1999 event was the Homes for the Future competition. Here on a site adjacent to The Merchant City and Glasgow Green and masterplanned by local architects Page and Park, a range of innovative social housing units were designed and erected. It was to be a model of new brownfield housing and when the first units went on sale for £55,000 to £135,000 people spent the night queuing for them. The brief for Stage 2 of the project demands high density and mixed uses integrating public landscaping with hundreds of dwellings offered as a mix of social, rental and private housing. Here then was a practical application of international design expertise with the social and physical needs of the city.

The Lighthouse was the largest and most high profile Glasgow 1999 project. Its refurbishment cost nearly £13 million – funded by the Heritage Lottery Fund, European Structural Funds, the Scottish Arts Council, Arts Council of England, Glasgow Development Agency, Glasgow City Council, Historic Scotland and private sponsors. The conversion of the original Mackintosh building was by local architects – Page and Park – who had also designed the Centre for Contemporary Arts, the Italian Centre in the Merchant City and cutting-edge housing in the Gorbals and Glasgow Green. With interiors by renowned designers Sam Booth, Gareth Hoskins and Graven Images, its very form was trumpeted as a veritable mecca of design. In operation, its aim is to "combine excellence with accessibility", introducing architecture and design to a mass audience, alongside specific programmes tailored to appeal to children, schools and colleges, architecture and design professionals and the business community. Within it there is a gallery space, rooftop café and education facilities and the centre serves as a focal point for international design exhibitions, conferences as well as network and funding opportunities for local and national designers. The Lighthouse is meant to give leadership for design not only in Glasgow but across Scotland, campaigning for it and the Creative Industries to be given a far higher priority politically and economically. To provide support for this disparate sector, the Lighthouse established a Creative Entrepreneur's Club which in 2006 had 850 members Scotland-wide. This provides an organised network, talks and workshops offering advice on finance, intellectual property and business planning. The Centre also has Creative Collaborations and a student version – Platform – both aiming to match practitioners from different parts of the creative industries to produce new business ideas.

The Lighthouse operates as a business and in this it has moved away from the traditional model for cultural centres with government subsidy representing only 10% of its £2 million turnover. It aims to bring together commerce, culture, education and social activities. It also invests £1 million each year in the Creative Industries by commissioning exhibitions and posters, accommodating and seeding design companies – with the Glasgow and Digital Animation Group based there – along with educational tools websites, conferences and other events to aggregate

Figure 4.2   Mackintosh re-discovered – The Lighthouse and Mackintosh Festival

value (MacDonald 2004: 29). The Centre also ensures that Scotland is represented at international design fairs.

In its operation, the Lighthouse is about boosting the role of design in the Creative Industries but also across the board of the Glasgow economy. In 2006 for example, the Lighthouse organised the Six Cities Design Festival which connected Aberdeen, Dundee, Edinburgh, Glasgow, Inverness and Stirling in an international design festival promoting and celebrating Scottish design. In launching the £3 million initiative, Scotland's First Minister Jack McConnell noted that Scotland had the largest creative industry sector outside of London and the South East (www.thelighthouse.co.uk 2008). In their evaluation of design and urban regeneration more generally, Bell and Jayne conclude of the initiatives emanating from the Lighthouse:

> While Glasgow has clearly sought to foster links between creative design practitioners and the city's remaining manufacturing and industrial businesses in order to bring about new product development, diversification and post-Fordist small batch production, it is not as yet clear how such design activities are successfully contributing to the profile of all economic sectors in the city. Furthermore, there seems to be little proliferation of design-led projects beyond the city centre – in terms of either improving the city's housing stock, transport, streets or parks, or new business start-up, economic diversification or job creation (Bell and Jayne 2003: 272).

Despite such cautionary evaluations, Scottish Enterprise extols and promotes the value of the design industries as part of the broader cluster of Creative Industries. Thus in a number of presentations (Tibbetts n.d.: Kane n.d.), Glasgow is located into a network of "digital cities" which are variously developing the Creative Industries – design, publishing, music, film, TV, radio, advertising, architecture, the cultural industries, digital media and games (Tibbetts n.d.). Each has its own spatial niche – Edinburgh [administration, finance, EdVEC), Dundee [interactive entertainment], Ayrshire [music], Livingston [Silicon Glen] and Glasgow – BBC Channel 4, Pacific Quay, Glasgow Science Centre and Digital Design Studio. . Scottish Enterprise estimates that the Creative Industries support between 70 and 100,000 Scottish jobs or 4% of GDP with growth at an annual rate of between 5% and 20% (Tibbetts n.d.).

Despite the divergence of assessments of such activity, there are considerable government resources – by Scottish Enterprise and the EU – being channeled into the Creative Industries, via the Lighthouse, various celebratory events but also through the building of Creative Business Parks in Glasgow and Dundee, the Screen Industries Strategy Group and into the Creative Entrepreneurs Club. Thus from 2006 £25 million is to be invested over 3–5 years to grow these various clusters by 10-20%pa to thereby create 2000 new jobs and increase exports. To encourage the realisation of such targets, Scottish Enterprise has set up a number of "Business Gateways" one stop places for all business development services and a "Cultural Enterprise Office", a Business Gateway for artists and pre-start cultural practitioners, staffed by artists and cultural practitioners trained in the facilitation of business development and located in areas frequented by artists. These are seen as good for practitioners, as they involve less dependence on public subsidy and good for other industries such as tourism, for the Scottish economy and for the overall quality of life via a vigorous cultural scene (Tebbitt 2004).

The Creative Industry sector then, with design as a vital part of it, is therefore seen as a major growth driver in its own right as well as a stimulant to other sectors. With eerie parallels to the early years of the 20th century, design is seen as both an expression of and a driver of industrial innovation – as the arts assume new value as an economic stimulant. The creative arts recede in such discussions, as the digital and commercial side assume economic and political priority. It is from this direction that planners clearly see positive economic transformation coming. No longer tied directly to cultural institutions, the Creative Industries are about business and economic development, not through the enhancement of the physical and cultural environment, but by providing commercial tools, services and ultimately jobs. It is therefore by engaging directly with the symbolic economy that design assumes new value and becomes more sustainable in Glasgow.

But if this is one direction the Cultural Capital agenda has gone in Glasgow, there are at least two others, one which builds on the foundations laid in 1990 – around images and cultural tourism – and another which relates to a different valuing of the arts, this time as the means to not only generate economic salvation but also social inclusion. Thus in its ongoing quest to have a positive but also fresh image and in the face of falling tourism numbers – which have gone from a high of 4.3 million in 1990 to 3.2 million in 2006, in 2004 Glasgow declared itself the new black as it launched a £1.5 million campaign to give itself a more cosmopolitan image – "Scotland with Style". The objective is to create 1,000 new jobs and attract £42 million of investment from 2004 to 2006 through a celebration of the legacy of C. R. Mackintosh. In the way that Barcelona celebrates Gaudi and Chicago Frank Lloyd Wright, the project is to feature on line advertising and a year long promotional campaign across the United Kingdom, Europe and the US. The logo is a "modern homage to Mackintosh" and the aim is to project a new and confident image of the city on the world stage. Eddie Friel, still Chief Executive of Greater Glasgow and Clyde Valley Tourist Board said in 2006, that having rebuilt its reputation the city now needed to project a unique image – not simply a slogan – and capitalise on a point of differentiation that no other city can claim – Mackintosh. The new brand will do what no other campaign has done – it will speak to Glaswegians, to what is constructed as the city's key external audiences and clearly identify Glasgow with Scotland. He notes how the city has a history of reinventing itself according to the needs of its customers. One of the adverts promotes the city's shopping and fashion credentials under the slogan – "Glasgow: the new black", another highlights the city's arts and architecture with the slogan: "Discover Mackintosh's Art Nouveau masterpiece. It's called Glasgow'. (Glasgow unveils £1.5 million rebranding'.) Time will tell just how effective such a campaign will be, though it is clear that once again the city's historic cultural capital – in the form of the reputation and work of

Charles Rennie Mackintosh – is central to it, as his embodied capital is linked to its various objective manifestations and retro copies to become fully institutionalised though this campaign. In all of this, there is a disturbing lack of reference to other members of the Glasgow School, especially the many women who comprised it, as well as a detachment of the image of the city from other creative and cultural activities. Nevertheless, in linking the new image of the city to its design history, cultural sustainability on this front at least, is ensured.

In contrast, the final other use of the creative arts within the city echoes a wider shift towards seeing them as a vehicle for healing social boundaries. While present to some extent in the 1990 celebrations, the 2006 *Cultural Strategy* is located within a view of the city competing successfully in the global economy but it also aims to encourage participation, to enhance infrastructure and events, and develop a vibrant and distinctive city which is attractive to citizens and visitors alike (2006:1). While recognising the Creative Industries as a key growth sector, the expanded Cultural Strategy notes how: "Competing in a global economy, where cultural tourism is estimated to account for 37% of all tourism, our commitment to enhancing the city's cultural infrastructure and events program will help Glasgow achieve a strong and unique position in the global market". Significantly, though it notes that the City: "also aims to have a broad and inclusive view of culture combining equality and access with excellence and quality" (Glasgow Cultural Strategy 2006: 2).

The strategy covers dance, music, visual art, theatre, community recreation, museums, heritage, libraries and information, sport, parks and open spaces, events and festivals, along with activities such as architecture, design, film and video (all termed in the *Cultural Strategy* part of the Creative Industries). In developing the strategy, the City Council acknowledges the link between cultural involvement, economic redevelopment and providing better opportunities for the people who live in Glasgow. "We want Glasgow to be economically competitive, a vibrant and creative city that is successful, but we also want to make sure that everyone who lives in the city shares in its success" (2006: 2). The economic and physical regeneration agenda is thereby linked to the social inclusion one. Therefore much of the Strategy and its specific actions are to facilitate the young, disabled, minority and the elderly being more involved in sport, leisure and arts activities. In these ways, the creative arts become part of a social sustainability agenda and assume new value in these terms.

From such a plan and with a faith borne from experience in the major event to boost reputation and the economy, considerable energy was subsequently devoted to successfully winning the 2014 Commonwealth Games for Glasgow, but also to ensure that Kelvin Grove was re-opened and efforts were put into improving the city's status as a world class cultural tourism destination (Cultural Strategy 2006: 6). Further extending the connection between physical and artistic regeneration, there are detailed plans for 2008 through to 2010 (2006: 8) for King Street and the Briggait in Merchant City to be redevelolped as a visual arts centre and a Film City Project to open in Govan Town Hall. In 2009 the Riverside Transport Museum – designed by the internationally acclaimed Zaha Hadid – will open, along with an Indoor Sports arena (in 2010). In addition to the grand edifice and gestures, however, there are also annual festivals to promote mutual understanding and respect amongst the different communities, including Black History Month (Cultural Strategy 2006: 8). Over the next five years, the River Clyde will also be developed as a 'vibrant, cultural and recreational resource', the Merchant City will become a focus for the visual arts and the creative and cultural industries, while a city-wide lighting and public art strategy as well as a local history strategy will also be developed. The most recent cultural strategy for Glasgow therefore connects image to the creative arts but also to major events and social inclusion. It is a huge agenda and one that extends the ameliorative role of the creative arts from the cultural to the economic and social. Such an extension bodes well for its sustainability.

From the mid-90s, then the various forms of cultural capital have been split apart in Glasgow to perform different functions within this post-industrial city. The more traditional creative arts have been redesignated vehicles for social inclusion as well as forming the foundation for urban and economic regeneration. In addition the Creative Industries – meaning here design, film, and digital media – have been hived off and consciously grown as a new and vital business sector increasingly unrelated to the creative arts, while the foundation of the city's image from the 1990s on a broad notion of being a City of Culture has been narrowed to focus on Charles Rennie Mackintosh and a vague notion of edgy cool. Whether these definitions and forms of cultural capital are sustainable is the subject of the final part of this chapter.

Glasgow – Sustaining Scotland with Style?

The cultural re-development of Glasgow has involved official planning, public-private partnerships, the construction of a number of flagship cultural institutions and the revitalisation of the inner city. The restoration of the Merchant City has involved the renovation of abandoned warehouses and their conversion to up-market housing, boutiques, wine bars and restaurants, the classic experience of inner city precincts subjected to officially sanctioned investment, gentrification and in-migration (Sayer 1992; MacLeod 2002). However, along with the conscious push to make Glasgow "Scottish for Style", this precinct has also become the centre of an edgy fashion and graphic design industry that has put Glasgow on the Cultural Industries map and, according to some authorities at least, generated thousands of jobs. Some of the buildings in the Merchant City area are now galleries but also art spaces where new work and networks are emerging. Companies such as Timorous Beasties – founded by two graduates of the Glasgow Art School and specialising in designer fabrics and wall papers – are located in this area. As well as these new spaces, the re-invention of the city has been accompanied by a concerted effort to connect with its middle class as well as working class past. Attention and investment has been directed into the regeneration of working-class housing estates and historical traditions

– best represented by the People's Palace museum, The Worker's Theatre and recognition of the early 20th century design work of Charles Rennie Mackintosh and Margaret Macdonald (Laurier 1993; Garcia 2003, 2005). Connecting these strategies has been a series of major events and re-imaginings of the city. Building on the tradition of hosting international arts, science and industry exhibitions, Glasgow held the national Garden Festival (1988), and has been the European City of Culture (1990) and the national City for Architecture and Design (1996). All of these events have been associated with bidding against other English or European cities, the reclaiming of blighted urban sites, significant public and private sector investment, new images and the accretion of cultural capital – in the from of objective buildings, art objects, performances and events, institutional arrangements and skilled individuals, thereby ensuring the transformation of money capital into cultural capital and thence back to higher and broader amounts of cultural capital.

How sustainable such strategies have been and will be into the future is difficult to assess. Beatrice Garcia's work has confirmed that there has been a long-term positive boosting of the image of Glasgow as well as a sense of the city being a far better place to live in, work, create and invest in since 1990. Efforts to broaden the foundation of cultural capital, its use in new designs for low income housing and ongoing cultural activities in peripheral not just inner areas, suggest that the social sustainability of the city has been enhanced by the Cultural Capital agenda. So too does the more recent shift to seeing the creative arts as the basis for social inclusion and with it active policy interventions to involve the aged, the young, minorities and the poor in the creative arts. The ongoing success of places like the Citizen's Theatre also attests to the broadening – in both class and geographical terms – of cultural capital in Glasgow. Thus the theatre has reduced ticket prices for residents of the Gorbals as well as actively reaches out to its community through workshops and community projects (www.gorbalslive.org.uk 2006). In addition, the London based *Observer* newspaper could note in 2003 that "Around the world, the city's stock has rocketed, not necessarily as a destination for the visual arts, but as a cradle of talent producing it (Khan 2003). Such a recognition of the growth and extension of cultural capital in Glasgow does not ignore the challenges posed by ongoing social and physical deprivation which has been exacerbated – or perhaps just relocated – by the gentrification, population displacement and scale of cultural investment into the inner parts of the city. Clearly such developments continue to raise serious questions as to the social sustainability of Glasgow as a Cultural Capital.

Undeniably, though, the huge investments in cultural infrastructure has boosted the institutional and objective cultural capital of the city and made it both a richer place to live, a dynamic creative art and design centre and a vital cultural tourist destination. Inner city renewal and renovation has not only meant a revaluing of magnificent architecture but its re-use and rejuvenation as places of consumption, leisure, business and housing. On the basis of the new image of the city but also these investments there has been a boost in city confidence for residents and businesses which, for those in Scottish Enterprise at least, offers a platform for future growth (Kane n.d.). There has been a growth in those economic sectors connected to the Cultural and Creative Industries as well as others related to cultural tourism. In particular there has been a growth in tourism and hospitality – in terms of numbers employed, turnover and visitation rates and therefore multipliers – and the design industries in the city, facilitated by The Lighthouse but also built upon the embedded cultural capital in the Glasgow School of Art and the traditions surrounding the Glasgow Style.

The foundation for the Cultural Capital label is therefore a rich and historically deep one which has therefore enhanced the economic sustainability of the city. Such a claim, however, needs to be tempered by the limited scale of such Creative Industry development and put into the context of a much broader expansion of service sector employment. While trumpeted as an unbridled success story, a close examination of the evidence for a booming Creative Industry sector suggests that it remains relatively small and in the planning stages rather than fully realised, except around a few key institutions and sub-sectors – such as design. For despite the hype, huge and ongoing investments and concerted campaigns, when Richard Florida and the DEMOS group visited Glasgow, they ranked the city below Edinburgh and Leicester on the Bohemian Index of creative cities (MacDonald 2006: 29). So too the 2002 OECD report noted that there were still massive amounts of social deprivation and the city held 60% of Scotland's worst off communities, a figure which had actually increased since 1991 (OECD 2002: 39). Within the greater Glasgow area. there are still very high levels of poor quality housing, unemployment and abandoned sites as well as ongoing depopulation and socio-spatial polarisation. Some would argue that on this foundation, there is only limited scope for cultural sustainability. Indeed it could legitimately be suggested that the government funds that were directed to the 1990 City of Culture and into subsequent cultural institutions and their buildings, could have been better spent on clearing derelict industrial sites, attracting other forms of employment and dealing with the more important social problems that continue to bedevil the city. Would these have made the city more attractive to investors and therefore more economically and culturally sustainable? Or is the future with high level service industries which need vibrant Cultural Capitals to even begin to compete for their investment and as a site for their workers?

For at least some commentators – Macleod 2002; Evans 2003 – Cultural Capitals are part of a neo-liberal revanchist agenda which re-asserts the power of the state to stifle democratic processes while assisting capital investment and withdrawing support from social welfare activities. Such actions inevitably involve exacerbating social division and benefit only the few with a commitment to images rather than substance, the middle class rather than the workers and the cultural over other industries. The preceding analysis has shown the story to be more complex than this, with a relatively crude view of the state working only in the interests of a narrow middle class belied by ongoing efforts to ease housing problems, boost employment, value a broad range of cultural traditions and to involve many publics in the process and their use. The foundation of Glasgow's bid as a Cultural Capital in 1990 has been significantly boosted and broadened by the experience and by subsequent efforts to build on this agenda and on the city's cultural assets – not only Mackintosh and the Glasgow Style but also on the creative energies of visual artists and those in design. As a Cultural Capital then, various forms of cultural capital have been defined anew, mobilised, projected into and beyond the city in ways that are, in general, proving to be socially, politically, economically and culturally sustainable.

Guggenheim: Bilbao

Chapter 5
Bilbao:
The Guggenheim and Post-modern City of Spectacle

Previous chapters have established working definitions of cultural capital(s) (as value and as places), sketched their areal extent and considered various explanations and theorisations of their timing and form. Having examined the global and national dimensions of Cultural Capitals and considered the first second order European city to formally adopt this mantle – Glasgow – it now comes to look more closely at other case studies and to consider if and how they create sustainable value. This chapter will focus on what has become, along with Glasgow's marketing image – a successful archetype – another European industrial city that has this time used an art gallery as the cornerstone of its redevelopment strategy. Frank Gehry's Guggenheim Museum is an architectural masterpiece, located on the site of a former steel works on the Nervion River in Central Bilbao, north west Spain. A branch of the New York-based Solomon R. Guggenheim Foundation, it is both a franchised arm of a cultural multinational and a local monument to the arts, urban entrepreneurialism and post-modernity. A photogenic structure, the building along with its architect, has achieved celebrity status around the world. As such it has been the subject of adulation, critique as well as conscious emulation. In Bilbao, it forms the centrepiece of a co-ordinated strategy that has mobilised cultural as well as other forms of capital to fashion a new image for the city, reclaim a derelict industrial waterfront, restore the historic core of the city, improve urban infrastructure, shift the economy away from iron ore and metallurgy towards the service sector and help build a more peaceful community renown for its violent secessionist politics It produced what is known as "the Guggenheim effect" (Igelsias 1998).

The aim of those who commissioned the gallery – while not expressed in these terms – was for economic, cultural, political and social sustainability. Within the theoretical framework of this book, the main vehicle – in many ways like Glasgow – was the mobilisation of embodied, objectified as well as institutional cultural capital locally, nationally, from within Europe and internationally, to realise not only the Gehry gallery but a host of other initiatives. Taking inspiration from other re-developments in Europe and the United States, I will argue that the Guggenheim in Bilbao goes well beyond what critics have derided as a shallow spectacle. Rather, in being a sustainable moblilisation of cultural capital, my suggestion is that, along with Glasgow, Bilbao offers a model Cultural Capital. After first considering the timing, form and location of the Bilbao Guggenheim in terms of sustainable cultural capital, this chapter will directly address its status as a post-modern archetype.

The Guggenheim in Bilbao

Surveying the museum in 2004, Joan Ockman wrote:

> In 1997, virtually overnight, "Bilbao" appeared on the map. Frank Gehry's dazzling design for a far-flung branch of the Guggenheim Museum was not just an extraordinarily audacious architectural achievement, nor was it merely another new destination for the art-world jet set and a global ego trip on the part of its ambitious New York director. The museum immediately became synonymous with an entire city and a symbol of regeneration for a troubled region of Spain (2004: 227).

The context of such a development is related to the broader trends of globalisation, decolonisation, de-industrialisation, urban entrepreneurialism, mass cultural tourism and the fusion of high, popular and symbolic culture described in Chapters 2 and 3. However, this was also a very specific initiative, an architectural wonder and trigger for urban revitalisation yet to be replicated anywhere else in the world. To understand this particularity, it is necessary to connect localised developments (of de-industrialisation, unemployment, cultural autarchy, political separatism, tourist development and internationalism) with particular *embodied* personalities (architects, museum directors, outward looking local and national government officials, resident artists and critics) and to link these to various *objective* forms of cultural capital – galleries, but also well designed infrastructure and the work of indigenous artists – and to particular institutions (the European Union, the Guggenheim Foundation, Spanish as well as regional and local governments), their histories, priorities and trajectories. Such connections across various scales allow comprehension of the local, regional and international embodied, objectified and institutional elements which came together in this place from the mid-1980s. Whether this development has led to a sustainable Cultural Capital will be considered in the course of the chapter.

International dimensions

Imperialism and decolonisation   The village of Bilbao, situated in the valley of the Nevion, 20 kms from the Cantabrico Sea, was formally created in 1300 by Diego Lopez de Haro V, Lord of Biscay. At that time it was a seafaring village, acting as a port for foreign merchandise on its way to the fairs of Castile and a point of departure for wool exports to central and northern Europe. Adjacent to the Santiago Way, the coming and going of the pilgrims gave rise to intense commercial and cultural activity and connected the area to the artistic richness of Europe (Prieto 2003: 3).

As a port, trade between Seville, northern Europe and the Americas was important to its prosperity. The early history of the town was linked to Spanish imperialism in the Americas and was also shaped by the relation with central Spanish authority (Collins 1986: 235; King 1990). The Spanish regions had a contractural rather than a subordinate relationship with the Castilian centre. In the Basque country there were *fueros*, collections of local laws and customs and special economic and political dispensations recognised by the kings of Castile/Spain in return for political allegiance to the monarchy (Heiberg 1989: 20). What was critical to the fragile unity of the state known as Spain was military control over the seas and the colonies. Each region had different and specialised connections to the operation of the Spanish empire. The Basque country was oriented towards the Americas, Castile towards North Africa, America and Europe, Aragon and Catalonia to the Mediterranean (Collins 1986: 2). This historical connection to South and Latin America is consciously maintained in current Bilbao with, for example, the major visiting exhibition in August 2005 being on The Aztecs, a show accompanied by a trade fair for Mexico (Author's Field Notes 2005). One of the major directions in national cultural policy is to become a centre of Spanish-language publishing that can be sold into the Americas, including the United States (Real Instituto 2004). Imperial connections were therefore important in shaping the history of the Bilbao port and in establishing trading and cultural patterns which are maintained today.

The main problem for 18th and 19th century rulers was the loss of the Spanish empire along with independence movements in the United States, the disastrous war with England (1796–1802) and Napoleon's invasion (Heiberg 1989). Loss of empire undermined central Spanish authority, allowing an upsurge of movements for regional autonomy. It also curtailed economic development across the country. With the failure of the Spanish Empire, the fate of Bilbao became linked to that of Britain and her Empire, continuing a tradition of interconnection with colonisation and de-colonisation which has persisted over the history of this city.

Evident in the history of Glasgow (Chapter 4), the British Empire was built on the exchange of colonial raw materials for its manufactured goods and capital. Be it cotton from India and North America, wheat and wool from Australia or tropical goods from Asia and the Pacific, the relationship was similar. To fuel the manufacturing juggernaut that was England and its outlying regions such as Scotland, sources of basic inputs had to be found beyond its borders and, in the case of iron ore, beyond the empire. It was to northern Spain that the British came to both invest surplus capital and ensure ongoing supplies of iron ore. Basque industrial potential lay in the rich deposits of high quality iron ore located in the mines near Bilbao. Liberalised local laws led to British investment in these mines so that by the 1870s, 50% were owned by foreigners. Basque and other foreign capital combined to increase iron ore extraction, so that by the end of the 19th century, Spain was producing 21.5% of the world's output of iron ore, with most of it coming from around Bilbao. Because of the small domestic market, Bilbao's easy access to the sea and long established commercial links between Bilbao and England, 90% of all production was exported and of this 60–70% went to Britain

(Heiberg 1989: 39). In the early 20th century, Bilbao supplied 2/3 of Britain's iron ore creating a relationship of wealth but also dependency not unlike that created for Glasgow's ship building industry (Zulaika 2001:5).

The economic link to Britain was accompanied by cultural exchange. The expansion of Bilbao across the Nervion in the 19th century was funded by mining wealth. The Bilbanos also admired and emulated British men's clubs, dress and hotels. Thus the imposing Carlton Hotel was modelled on the Ritz in London. Built in 1926, it is centrally located on the rim of the Ensanche's garden-adorned traffic circus (Bartolucci 2000: 2). With British capital, the port of Bilbao was also modernised and became one of the largest and busiest in Europe. Aided by readily available supplies of Basque timber and iron, Bilbao became a major centre for ship building. Industrial development was supported by a high tariff wall and central state subsidies, while the capital generated through industry stimulated banking and what became the country's second stock exchange. By 1900 45% of Spain's merchant fleet, nearly all of her production of iron and steel and 30% of Spanish investment capital was in Basque hands. Within 20 years, Basque or rather Bilbao industrialists and bankers (a mere five families) had become the single most powerful interest group in Spain (Heiberg 1989: 40). The echoes with the history of Glasgow – with the dominance of its tobacco and trading barons and links to the fortunes of overseas interests – is remarkable. As Joseba Zulaika notes: Basques have a long and successful tradition of joint ventures with international capitalists, initially to exploit their mining and iron industries and more recently, of course, in the cultural industries (Zulaika 2005: 162).

Industrialisation of Bilbao attracted large numbers of unskilled rural and non-Basque immigrants and by 1900 the vast majority of the population were relatively un-educated. There was no Basque university or theatre and limited development in the arts. Although European influences were enthusiastically absorbed in Barcelona, Bilbao by contrast, remained proletarian in appearance and attitude. Urban conditions, especially around the inner city, were very poor with crowding, high mortality rates and poor water supplies. Such conditions stimulated unionism, ongoing industrial action (35% of all labour conflicts in Spain were in this region [Fraser 2005: 49]), the growth of socialism and Basque separatism or nationalism (Heiberg 1989: 43–4).

The dependence on Britain and its imperial system meant that when this exchange regime began to falter, so too did Bilbao's mines and ship building. Shielded from international competition and technological imperatives by the Spanish state through high tariffs, heavy industry endured but at the cost of relatively inefficieny. If Basque industry was forced to engage directly with a global market or higher technology producers, it could not compete. As with much of the industrial west – but not Glasgow! – the down turn began in the 1970s and accelerated thereafter. The trigger was the fall of the Franco Regime in 1975 and the ascension of Socialists to power in Madrid. In an effort to modernise the Spanish economy, tariffs and industry subsidies were lowered, exposing the country and its regions to the new international division of labour.

New International Division of Labour   Once the pinnacle of industrial power, the pride of an advanced region and magnet for Andalusian and Gilician migrants, by the late 1970s Bilbao and its outskirts constituted one of Europe's most depressed urban landscapes. Designated by many observers as a "tough city" owing to its history of labour unrest, violent political separatism and brutal industrial landscape (Zulaika 2001), the label attained even more resonance as economic restructuring began in earnest. Bilbao and its hinterland province of Bizkaia saw around 95,000 jobs lost in manufacturing between 1979 and 1985, especially in ship building, heavy engineering and iron and steel production (McNeil 2000). One of the demands by the European Union before allowing Spanish admission was the further withdrawal of government protection for industry. This immediately ensured the exposure of Spanish industry to the far more efficient European producers and the situation in Bilbao became even more acute. From the mid-1980s, unemployment rose further and the closure of industrial plants accelerated. Even the downtown Euskalduna dockland, until 1970 the site of the city's most powerful factory, lay in ruins by 1990 (Crumbaugh 2001: 41). By 1993 unemployment in the city had reached 25%, far worse than at any time during the 1980s, and rates were even higher in the working class riverside areas. With the collapse of mining, steel and shipbuilding from 1970 to 1990, the metropolitan area lost 20% of its population and 47% of its industrial jobs. The impact on the urban fabric was profound. The city contained 465 hectares of industrial ruins, up to 50% of the total industrial land in some municipalities. Entire valleys were devastated by pollution, with hills dotted by toxic ponds of flooded open-pit mines and a river reduced to a bubbling ribbon of orange sludge. (Fraser 2005: 47).

Clearly some sort of response was required and it came from the local state allied with right wing regional business interests accessing local, Spanish and European Union funds. In seeking solutions, the Basque government looked to models offshore, hosting conferences and symposia to canvass the experience of other industrial cities in Europe and America. This included Glasgow – with many parallels noted by the Spaniards in its history, image and economic structure which had, counter-intuitively, led to it being designated Europe's 1990 City of Culture (see Chapter 4) (Baniotopoulou 2001: 3) – but also Pittsburgh, Baltimore and Manchester (see Chapter 8) . From such comparative work, the government and its business elite identified a strategy to turn Bilbao into a post-industrial centre for services, finance and tourism. Using various planning groups and agencies, such as Bilbao Metropoli – 30 a public-private partnership with many of the key businesses in the city – a metropolitan plan was devised and implemented. This was augmented by Bilbao Ria-2000, an urban development corporation dedicated to clearing old industrial land for new investment. (McNeill 2000: 486).

The new international division of industrial labour had taken its toll on this city, but it also offered models for shifting the economic structure from manufacturing towards services as well as a transformation of the industry that remained. Within such a transformation and with a relatively autonomous local government, direct engagement with the international arena was the strategy adopted.

Guggenheim Foundation: globalising a museum   Established with a bequest
and initial collection from Solomon R. Guggenheim in 1923, the Guggenheim
Foundation was in deep financial trouble in the early 1990s. With its leading
museum in New York closed for renovation and its failure to find financing for
a project to open a new museum in Salzburg Austria, it had sunk into a profound
operating deficit (Azua 2005: 77). Extensions to the Frank Lloyd Wright building
in New York eventually cost US$18 million more than projected, while the
Guggenheim in SoHo had a cost over-run of US$4.6 million By 1993 the US
$10.5 million operating budget of 1988 had risen to US$23 million (Haacke
2005: 115–6) exacerbated by interest payments of over US$6.5 million on a US$5
million bond issue meant to finance the expansion plans. Bad debts were made
worse by poor business decisions designed to ease them.

In 1990 the Guggenheim director Thomas Krens had acquired Count Guiseppe
Panza di Biumos collection of 300 minimalist and conceptual works for a reported
gift price of US$30 million. He raised funds for this by selling a Chagall, a
Modigliani and a Kandinsky at Sotherby's for US$47.3 million. Again in 1999 and
2000 a further US$15 million worth of art was de-accessioned and US$10 million
was deposited in a restricted fund. This fund was investigated by the Association
of Museum Directors for a possible breach of its code – which prohibits the use of
art work sales for anything other than the purchase of new works (Haacke 2005:
116). Not only was the Guggenheim in financial meltdown in the 1990s, but the
tactics used by its director to generate income were increasingly seen as highly
questionable and ineffective.

Overseen by the German art historian Thomas Messer from 1961 to 1988, the
Guggenheim had always actively pursued corporate sponsorship. But by the 1990s
it was clear there needed to be a further injection of funds and a new strategy to ease
the ballooning levels of debt and encumbrances. His successor, Thomas Krens,
was a graduate in studio art and management. Previously he had worked with the
architect Frank Gehry to transform the sprawling and somewhat remote Sprague
Technologies in North Adams into the Massachusetts Museum of Contemporary
Art (MassMoMA). In a manifesto published in 1997, Krens describes the changing
nature of the contemporary museum and his own institution:

> The new Guggenheim must ... be at the forefront of an evolving cultural project
> in its widest sense: it must construct great buildings; it must organize great
> exhibitions; it must collect and administer great works of art; and it must invent
> new administrative methods to foment and aid these creative activities (Quoted
> by Guasch 2005: 192).

In the Strategic Long Term Plan for the Guggenheim Foundation (2004–2014),
the policy of the Museum is spelled out:

> To collect, conserve and exhibit modern and contemporary art, within the setting
> of a flagship architectural work...striving to reach the highest standards of

artistic excellence and the widest audience in order to educate society about art as a foundation for the values of tolerance and freedom, and serving as a symbol of the economic and cultural vitality of the Cities, Regions and Countries in which our facilities are based (Quoted in Azua 2005: 83).

In 1989 the primary assets of the Foundation were its collection and image. The tactic of de-accessioning some works to raise funds had created controversy and was indeed being investigated by the authority overseeing museums in the United States. So instead of selling more, Krens moved to *rent* the works of the Guggenheim collection – much of it unseen in warehouses – to itself, developing in the process a new business model for the operation of his museum. In a way similar to a multi national corporation, branch museums would be built and financed by foreign governments and companies. Their collections and shows would be directed entirely from New York and the remote museums would pay the Guggenheim Foundation for loaning parts of its collection and for curating travelling exhibitions. The museum could capitalise on its collection and the brand power of its global image. Like many corporations in the 1990s, its expansion allowed it to draw new investment that could cover debt from existing operations (Fraser 2005).

Plans to expand the Guggenheim brand offshore were therefore pursued from 1988, first with Berlin's Martin-Gropius-Bau for a joint venture and then a branch in Salzburg to be built inside a mountain by Hans Hollein – which did not come off – and a later arrangement with the Deutsche Bank which did eventuate. As well as going off shore, two branches of the Guggenheim were to be opened in the United States, one in a Las Vegas Casino and another in Lower Manhattan, New York. Other possible locations were pursued, including in Spain.

The Guggenheim's Curator of 20th century art in New York was Carmen Gimenez. Formerly the Director of National Exhibitions for the Spanish government, she provided a direct link from the Guggenheim to Spain and it was she who took the idea of the branch museum to cities in her country (Baniotopoulou 2000: 5). Several cities in Spain were approached, including Seville, but none took up the offer. But then Bilbao came along offering (Haacke 2005: 117–8):

- US$100 million for the construction of a major gallery
- US$50 for new acquisitions
- US$20 cash "licence" fee up front, and a
- US $12 million subsidy for the museum budget

Krens had first journeyed to Bilbao in 1991 with a colleague who had worked with him in North Adams, Massachusetts – Frank O. Gehry – and also with Carmen Gimenez. Inspecting what the city had long planned as a site for the new museum – an abandoned wine warehouse located in the centre of the city – the Alhondiga – Gehry and Krens both agreed that it was far too congested a site and inappropriate as an exhibition space (Baniotopoulou 2001: 6).

All subsequent negotiations between the Guggenheim Foundation and the city of Bilbao were conducted in secret and surrounded by the style, urgency and intrigue which came to be associated with Krens. At one point, local politicians and artists requested a copy of the agreement but were denied; raising profound questions as to the political sustainability and local accountability of the entire process and the final decision. For Zulaika at least, this was one of many signs of the contempt with which the city was held by Krens and the supplicant status that the region assumed (Zulaika 2005). As Zulaika recalls: Kren's first reaction was: "Bilbao? Are you crazy?" (Zulaika 2005: 149). Describing himself as a change agent, (Fraser 2005: 55), Krens likened his style to that of a seductress; offering to others what they wanted – for a fee. As Zulaika quotes Kren's: "Seduction: that's my business … I don't earn money, but I raise it, and I do it by seduction. I make people give me gifts of \$20 million. Seduction consists (of people wanting) what you want without asking for it. It is a transference of desire. I am the greatest prostitute in the world" (Quoted by Zulaika 2005: 152). In the light of the huge amounts offered by the city, Krens is reported to have said to his staff: "The Basques are coming to eat from my hand. I can't believe it!" (Zulaika 2005: 151). For the Guggenheim Director, the city may well have been "tough" to look at, but it was certainly easy to deal with, a place easily seduced.

The cash-strapped New York based museum was therefore coming to Spain. As part of its global expansion strategy, the museum was to be transformed along with the city in which it was to be located. For the Guggenheim Foundation, Basque money was the only fresh infusion of cash that allowed it to survive while carrying out its expansion and renovation (Zulaika 2005: 165). Driven by its Director, the initiative suited a desperate museum but also a desperate city. It mobilised significant amounts of accumulated production and finance capital from within Bilbao and in return, infused the city with a vast amount of cultural capital – internationally renown architects, borrowed items from the Guggenheim's collection of European but especially North American modern art, sole connection to the Guggenheim brand and its associated merchandise, links to the New York art, business, fashion and financial scene, curatorial expertise and blockbuster exhibitions. The coming of the Guggenheim to Bilbao was the transformation of productive and finance capital into cultural capital in the hope that this strategy would lead to a healthy return – in the form of further cultural capital but also to other forms of capital growth. If such investment was ongoing, the circuit would be economically sustainable.

Table 5.1   Guggenheim Bilbao, Impacts (2003)

Guggenheim Global Attendances	New York	893,532
	Bilbao	874,807
	Berlin	143,628
	Las Vegas	205,957
	Venice	250,000
	TOTAL	2,367,964
Direct expenditure generated by the museum	154 million Euros	
Income for the Basque treasury	27.7 million Euros	
Employment (direct and indirect)	4,547 jobs	
Visitors	1997 1,400,000	
	1998 1,360,000	
	1999 1,265,000	
	2000 1,000,000	
	2002 857,500	
	2003 834,000	
Friends (Members)	14,800	
Corporate members	160	
Students	28,124	
Library users	2,130	
Acquisition budgets	1997–2000 US $40 million	
	2000–2004 US $33 million	
	2004–2007 US $30 million	

(Adapted from Baniotopoulou 2001: 7; Azua 2005: 87–88)

The Bilbao project was but one part of a larger globalisation strategy for the Guggenheim Foundation. Other Guggenheim branches subsequently opened or were linked to the New York operation in St Petersburg, Venice and Berlin as well as in the Venetian Hotel-Resort-Casino in Las Vegas. Many others were bid for, the most advanced being one proposed for Rio de Janeiro, Brazil. There was also a serious bid mounted by an Australian provincial city – Geelong in Victoria – that sorely tested both the globalisation model and the Cultural Capital agenda. It is explored in detail in Chapter 7. Completed in 1997, though, the Guggenheim in Bilbao has been the most successful of the branch museums; in terms of visitor numbers, membership, employment and its educational program as Table 5.1 summarises.

However, such success did not solve the ongoing problems besetting the Guggenheim Foundation, which still had expenditures well above its income. Thus in 2002, staff had to be cut – from 391 to 181 – major exhibitions were postponed, hours of opening reduced while the lower Manhattan gallery was abandoned, SoHo was closed and one of the Las Vegas spaces was also closed

(Haacke 2005: 122).The global museum, basically invented by Thomas Krens, has not proven profitable for the Foundation which backed it. The strategy, though, has transformed the nature of contemporary museums and galleries. As Haacke concludes: "Less flamboyantly than Krens, but just as determinedly, many of his peers are expected to pursue similar strategies to turn cultural capital into monetary capital" (Haacke 2005: 123).

Frank O. Gehry and the Guggenheim Museo Bilbao – International superstars

A key element in Kren's proposed Museum for Bilbao was the utilisation of internationally renown architects. Thus in announcing how its designer would be chosen, the Guggenheim indicated that there would be a closed three week architectural competition between three specified offshore firms: Arata Isozaki (designer of the SoHo branch), the Austrian collective Coop Himmelblay, and Frank O. Gehry, each of which would be given $10,000 and one visit (Baniotopoulou 2001: 6). Consistent with the Strategic Plan of the Guggenheim Foundation, this strategy of importing "major" architects was also shared by the city of Bilbao. Thus for those moving to re-imagine and rebuild the economy and urban fabric of the city as part of its strategy of becoming an international Cultural Capital, only the best international architects were to be used. Such a strategy connects key individuals to "signature" buildings and reinforces an international star system for architects which in turn allows the city to claim global cultural status.

As a Canadian Frank O. Gehry moved at 16 from Toronto with his family to Los Angeles. There he completed planning and architectural studies at the University of Southern California. Exposed there to "great southern Californian modernists" in the 1960s he also came into contact with a group of innovative artists and made his mark by using an array of local materials and a bold design to remodel his own home. By the 1980s he was collaborating with New York artists Richard Serra, Claus Oldenberg and Coosje van Bruggen on interior designs and furniture. In 1988 he designed the Guggenheim's "Art and the Motorcycle" show, before that working with Thomas Krens on plans for the Massachusetts Museum of Contemporary Art. As an innovative architect, well connected into the US *avant garde* art worlds and friend of Krens, it was therefore not surprising that he accompanied Krens to Bilbao in 1991 and was the winner of the commission to design the Guggenheim there. While well known in the United States, this commission and the building that resulted is deemed by most critics to be the turning point in Gehry's career, propelling him to international stardom and celebrity status. As Friedman (1999a) notes: With the opening of the Guggenheim in Bilbao Gehry seems to have crossed an invisible line. International awareness and admiration of his work has subsequently taken on proportions known to very few architects – in LA he is a reluctant celebrity and now he spends half his time travelling around the world visiting his various commissions.

While a relatively simple brief – for 100,000 square metres, of which half would be exhibition space – Krens also wanted a central atrium – inspiring like a

Gothic cathedral, with metaphorical echoes of Fritz Lang's movie "Metropolis" and the sculptor Constantine Brancusi's Paris studio. What was also required was one very large gallery space (150 metres long) for the work of a Guggenheim favourite – Richard Serra – and a host of smaller gallery spaces. What Gehry designed has become the stuff of architectural legend. Echoing his work for the Walt Disney Music Hall in Los Angeles and drawing on previous explorations with sculptured metal, the articulated bodies of fish and the possibilities offered by computer aided design, Gehry's design resembled nothing that had gone before. It is truly magnificent; positioned on the river, surrounded by water on one side and an intense urban landscape on the other. It either gently rises around a bend of the Nervion or surprises as a vista at the end of a street in the old city. With its mix of golden blocks of stone, soaring glass panels and twisting, luminescent titanium, the building itself is clearly an attraction in its own right, readily overshadowing the art within. Visiting in August 2005, it was clearly a special place; somewhere that people sat around, gazed upon and were photographed in front of; an iconic and symbolic construction that was a must for any tourist gaze. As Michael Sorkin notes, he who famously learnt about contemporary design and architecture from theme parks (Sorkin 1992/5): The evanescence of the reflective façade achieves the feeling of motion via literal animation... It is a masterpiece (Sorkin 1999).

Located in the centre of a cultural district formed by the Museo de Belles Artes, the University de Duest and the Old Town Hall, the museum functions as a local centre for cultural activity. In addition to the exhibition galleries, the Museum has a 350-seat auditorium, restaurant, café, museum store and offices. The latter are accessible from within the museum but also from the main plaza, enabling them to operate independently of the museum's hours and to function as an integral part of the urban life of Bilbao. As a structure, then, it is connected and integrated into the city.

It is most famous though as a masterpiece in international architectural circles, one designed not be a local or Spanish architect, but by a resident of Los Angeles commissioned and stocked by a gallery based in New York. It is very much a product of international sensibilities and imperatives. However, this is but one side of the story, for the Bilbao Guggenheim also emerges very much from local imperatives.

Local context

Political separatism   Why a relatively small industrial city in northern Spain would approach the New York Guggenheim Foundation with a very large amount of cash and persuade it to create a signature building there, is an international story but also a very local one. To explain why Bilbao made such a move – in the same way as it was not expected that Glasgow could become the sixth European City of Culture – it is necessary to examine Spanish history as well as local economic conditions, visions and personalities.

Spanish unification (Reconquista 718–1611) arose from an unstable alliance of independent Christian kingdoms pushing southward against Islamic invaders. Neither the Catholic kings (1469–1516), the Hapsburgs (1516–1700) nor the Bourbons (1700-1800) tried to force a unified royal administration on the Iberian peninsula. As a result, the Basque provinces maintained distinct legal codes and autonomous political institutions – the *fueros* (Heiberg 1989:1).

Scholars and polemicists remain divided on just how unique the Basques are, with some asserting a racial distinctiveness registered in blood types, others claiming an archaeological ancestry that makes the region's populace the oldest and purest of the European tribes, and still others emphasising the distinctive and wide use of the Basque language – Euskera – as an indicator of cultural and ethnic uniqueness (Collins 1986; Heiberg 1989). The fact that such debates continue and emerge with varying degrees of intensity over the history of northern Spain and southern France is testimony to the vital role played by various incarnations of local identity and autonomy in the region. The chequered if violent history confirms the contested nature of the Basque nation as it is enacted around various assertions of language, culture, race, religion and history over the years.

The clearest statement of a separatist ideology dates from the late 19th century and the writings of Salano de Arana-Goiri, founder of Basque nationalism as a discrete political doctrine and its most revered ideologue. Born in Bilbao, Arana disliked late 19th century capitalist industrialisation, seeing Bizkaia in an advanced state of moral, political and ethnic decay as a result of the untrammelled growth of a Basque industrial oligarchy, massive in-migration of non-Basques and the growth of non-Catholic socialist ideology. Arana in contrast mobilised and celebrated Basque Catholicism, customs, *fueros*, the Euskera language, rural life and character, and demonised the rule from Madrid (Heiberg 1989: 49–51). From the 1960s, such views and feelings coalesced around the violent political tactics of ETA (Euzkadi Ta Askatasuna [Basque Nation and Liberty]) as it struggled to gain political separatism from Madrid, adopting the tactics of Third World countries dealing with what it regarded as comparable colonisation (Salvado 1999). While never representing the majority of the Basque population, the violence of ETA claimed many lives and negatively coloured the image of the region to the world.

For Marianne Heiberg tracking *The making of the Basque nation* (1989), the dynamics behind Basque history involve the drive to maintain autonomy and an egalitarian mode of life. For her, the region's history also reflects the tension between two co-existing social orders: urban, Hispanicised, complex, prosperous, multi cultural and powerful; and the other, the majority of the population, being rural, Euskaldun (Basque speaking), relatively impoverished and largely unable to effect events in the wider world (Heiberg 1989: x-xi). Any idea that the Basque region is unified over time and space is therefore misplaced, though the sense of struggling for autonomy is very real and remains a vital force in the region's history and contemporary policy towards the outside world. Such a struggle reached a critical point with the end of the Franco dictatorship in 1975. After hundreds of years of sporadic fighting and fifty years of Franco's centralisation, recognition was achieved – formally at least – with the negotiation in 1979 of a regional autonomy agreement. This created a Basque government and parliament and one of the highest levels of self-government in Spain and Europe (Fraser 2005). Violence by ETA subsequently receded in the face of this greater level of regional autonomy.

It was therefore a semi-autonomous state, confronted with mounting economic and social problems as a result of de-industrialisation, that had the power as well as the sense of regional identity, autonomy and pride, to devise its own regeneration strategy and approach the European Union and the Guggenheim Foundation for assistance in the 1980s. Like many regions of Europe – including that around Glasgow – the Basques moved to engage globalisation directly, but unlike most of these regions, this one had a separatist (if also dependent) history and identity to draw on (McNeil 2000).

De-industrialisation and local politics

Earlier discussion has noted how Bilbao's 19th century industrialisation was strongly related to developments in Britain; which provided the finance and major markets for the city's iron ore, ships and steel. With new international divisions of labour in the 1970s, such markets evaporated, while the entry of Spain into the EU in 1986 boosted competition and thereby hastened the collapse of local industry. In the face of soaring unemployment and industrial abandonment, the right wing government of Partido Nacional Vasco, the Basque Nationalist Party or PNV developed a vision for the future of the city and mobilised local and international capital to realise it. In that this vision included a focus on cultural tourism as well as on industry – both metal-based and the Cultural Industries – relates to the economic as well as social history of the region.

The PNV is a party of conservative business interests which is also strongly nationalistic, concerned with the preservation of the Basque language and protection of regional heritage. Co-governing with the Socialists from 1986 to 1990, the PNV had control of the Department of Culture and initiated a series of conferences and symposia to explore what could be done to revitalise the city, with an emphasis on culture. Already a centre for trade fairs and exhibitions, Glasgow's experience as the European City of Culture in 1990 as well as that of Manchester in its inner city revitalisation, provided models against which to envisage an alternative economy and image for the city (McNeil 2000: 486; Baniotopoulou 2001: 3). A 1990-91 strategic analysis – commissioned by the Department of Economic Development and Planning and the provincial government – highlighted the importance of cultural centrality and tourism for the city's future.

According to MacCannell, a core grievance in the Basque struggle was resentment at being exploited as a rustic and backward tourist attraction by the Spanish government, France and the rest of Europe. Even as they grew more economically dependent on tourism, the Basques resented being portrayed as descendents of the Cro-Magnons, as the "Indians of Europe". The secessionists argued that the Basque Country should not just be the playground of the rich from distant cities, coming to gaze at them as a historical aberration. They affirmed this view by blowing up travel agencies, real estate offices that sold vacation chalets and the non native palms planted around resorts (MacCannell 2005: 23). With the creation of Eusko Juarlaritza, or the Basque Autonomous Government in 1979, tourism development was transferred from Madrid to Euskadi. The new tourism planners dropped references to the Basques as rustic primitives and shifted their emphasis to what they saw as the desirable cultural resources of the region: natural beauty, food, culture and music. The previous tourist image remained, however, and overall the economy continued its decline. "The only economic hope, tourism, remained a contested domain both culturally and politically (MacCannell 2005: 23).

Such a contest was usurped by the PNV in the late 1980s. Exploring ways of moving from the double bind of deindustrialisation and crippling terrorism (McNeil 2000: 481), the approach involved a fierce defence of cultural particularism and political and economic autonomy. It was a Bilbao representative of the PNV who raised the city as a possible location for a major international museum, one that would act as a very different magnet for tourists and support local economic as well as cultural development.

Local agendas and strategies   In the face of collapsing employment and closing industries, threats of violence from political separatists and a decaying urban fabric, what Arana-Goiri once labelled the liberal industrial oligarchy of the city of Bilbao, formulated a strategy. Called the Revitalisation Plan (1989) it was developed at the request of the Basque (regional) government and the Bizkaia County Council. The vision was for the city to be open, plural, integrated, modern, creative and cultural. It was a plan to move the urban economy from an industrial to a post-industrial base and from a local and national focus to an international one.

The Plan identified eight critical agendas to revitalise the decaying industrial city:

1. Investment in human resources via education (including a University closely bound to the economic and industrial structure of the region)
2. Creating a service metropolis in a modern industrial region via up to date infrastructure but also "an agreeable environment" which included culture and leisure facilities as well as industrial diversification
3. Mobility and accessibility for the population via public transport, rail and road connections to Europe so the city would be central to the Atlantic Arc, a relocated port from the city centre to the river mouth and upgraded airport
4. Environmental regeneration through improvements in air and water quality, waste management and the regeneration of degraded areas

5. Urban restoration via available housing, infrastructure that will provide "an excellent urban habitat and high quality of life"; "various emblematic buildings which would contribute to social and cultural centrality of the metropolis and to improving its external image and appeal", good urban management, "recovery of the damaged urban infrastructure through the exploitation of obsolete or abandoned spaces and the rehabilitation of the old town" and "an estuary that constitutes the vertebral axis and integrated element of the metropolis"

6. Cultural creativity; mechanisms of cultural and recreational information – to inform and "as a channel for a greater cultural formation". The city would offer financial incentives to become an obliged focal point of reference for international cultural circuits and industries; have an education system with a greater presence of culture; and be a centre of cultural creativity and infrastructure which allows all to access culture

7. Coordinated management by the public and private sectors

8. Social action for the common wealth of all citizens. Personal well-being will be the fundamental priority of urban development, involving the gradual removal of the structural causes of exclusion, pluralist management of Social Action under new relations between the State and Civil Society (Revitalisation Plan 1989).

In short the 1989 *Revitalisation Plan* for the City of Bilbao was a blueprint for the city's economic, political, ecological, social and cultural sustainability. Economic regeneration was to occur through education and training, new infrastructure (especially in road, rail and air facilities along with a relocated port), the modernisation and diversification of existing industry in the context of private-public partnerships and an attractive cultural and physical environment; political sustainability through being an elected government, prioritising personal well being and strategies for social inclusion; ecological sustainability by cleaning up the Nervion and abandoned industrial sites; social sustainability through political inclusion, improved employment prospects, better infrastructure and a pluralist outlook; and cultural sustainability through education, inner city renovation, social inclusion, cultural accessibility and by becoming an international Cultural Capital and centre for the Cultural Industries.

The aim was to grasp the challenge offered by globalisation and membership of the EU to "attain a position of centrality in the European system of cities" as an international cultural centre. City planners envisaged a high quality Centre of Art and Congresses based on good services, a prestigious university and key organisations in a metropolis where important international contests, fairs and festivals would occur. All of this was to happen in a city supported by "a long cinematographic and lyrical tradition… a powerful cultural industry, a high level of cultural assets and an external image associated with art and culture" (Revitalization Plan 1989). The sites for many of these new constructions were the abandoned industrial plants on which the early wealth of the city had been built. Thus Bilbao Ria 2000 – the agency charged with planning particular sites in the city – envisaged a riverfront area at the heart of the central city – formerly the El Campo de los Ingleses steel works – as the site for the Guggenheim – with the Euskalduna Concert and Conference Hall on the old Euskaldune ship building works (McNeill 2000: 486; Banitopoulou 2001: 4).

In 2000 Deputy Mayor Areso stressed that there was more to turning around the rustbelt city than a new museum, "We were forced to face a change from an industrial city to a post-industrial one. That doesn't mean that we want to renounce industry, that's where our know-how is. But we had to see that this industry, now high tech, wasn't going to generate lots of jobs. Wealth yes. So we had to find areas – banking, communications, tourism – to distribute this wealth in the form of jobs. To attract people you have to have the right surroundings and facilities". Hence there was a need not just for a major museum but a new metro, port, airport, roads and rail connections etc. all of which would cost a very great deal; funds which necessarily had to be drawn from the city, from the private sector, the national government and the EU. Thus the metro (cost US$800 million), cleaning up the river (US$500 million) and the new airport were all funded locally and by Madrid, the re-development of the port is being paid for by its users, while other monies were derived from local taxes and Brussels (EU) regional redevelopment funds (Usher 2000/01).

The Regeneration Plan, borne out of dire economic and social circumstances, predates by one year Glasgow's City of Culture (1990) and by two years the beginning of negotiations for the Bilbao Guggenheim. It was therefore a local vision informed by engagement with other European industrial cities – including Glasgow and Manchester – and one which connected cultural regeneration to overall economic and urban renewal. In its realisation, the Plan involved an injection of over $US1.5 billion, including funds from the EU, the Spanish government as well as from the Bizkaia and Bilbao governments into a broad array of projects, only one of which involved a major art gallery, but many of which were related to the notion of creating a Cultural Capital.

By 2002, this Plan had mainly been realised. The city is therefore in a second phase of planning for further regeneration. Thus Bilbao in *Global City 2010*, "seeks to be one of those local areas in the globalised world where value is created. Innovation, culture, quality of life and globality are the distinguishing features" (Global City 2002: 2). In this new plan, the city is considered as a sustainable system centred on three main pillars: people, economic activity and its attractiveness. The aim is to build on the knowledge industries via people (their education, research, leadership, life long learning, new social capital), strong economic activity (especially in engineering, biomedical studies, IT, communications and business management), and the attractiveness of the city (via physical regeneration of inner and outlying districts) to foster the integration of people into the community (2002 Plan: 26–7).

The 2002 plan notes how the renewal of the city's human capital undertaken in the 1990s, is changing the city's "economic base…away from heavy industry (towards an) advanced services industry and a network of technological and innovation centres" (Global City 2002: 9). Internationalisation is to be boosted by communications technology, research, quality universities, the International Exhibition Centre and Euskalduna Convention Centre. The Plan also envisages Line 2 of the Bilbao Metro, new facilities at the port, a tramline from San Mames and Atxuri, further urban renewal via the Guggenheim, energy diversification and zoned enclaves for hi-tech business including the Zamudio Technology Park and the Abandoibarra, support for major fairs and events but also for local festivals, pedestrianisation, traffic control, better public transport at night, better street lighting and improvement in community policies. The aim, then, is to move the economic base of the city towards greater internationalisation, new industry, including the knowledge – but not necessarily the Cultural – industries but also towards quality local services and environments which are sustainable.

Cultural capital – international and local   Central to the vision of Bilbao being a centre for international culture is the use of world renown architects for all major projects. Thus, the new Metro system was designed by Norman Foster, a foot bridge over the Nervion and the new airport terminal by Santiago Calatrava, a transport interchange by James Stirling and Michael Wilford, the Euskalduna Congress and Music Centre was designed by Santi-Soriano and Dolores Palacios and the Abandoibarra Riverfront development – including "advanced services, high income housing, shopping, leisure and culture" and one million square metres of office space and a shopping mall was designed by Cesar Pelli, (Fraser 2005: 48; Zulaika 2002: 5). This was all additional to but clearly complemented Frank O.Gehry's design for the Guggenheim. All of these functional but also iconic structures are presented as stylish attractions to international cultural tourists, business visitors and investors through promotional booklets and expositions (see Bilbao Exposition 2002).

But to become a sustainable Cultural Capital, not only is it appropriate to engage with international trends and iconic figures, but regional and local creativity also has to be supported. While there was local disquiet from artists about the terms and resources devoted to the Guggenheim, its development has been accompanied by vigorous artistic activity, burgeoning visitor numbers to all galleries and museums and a sense of urban pride that is palpable. After the signing of the agreement with the Guggenheim Foundation, more than 400 Basque artists and intellectuals presented a letter protesting the deal and requesting a copy for public scrutiny. Along with the request from the Basque Parliament it was refused, on the grounds that it would violate the secrecy clause in the agreement! (Zulaika 2005: 151). A picket of unemployed locals shouting "thieves", "scoundrels" and "fewer museums and more jobs" attended Gehry's public showing of his design to the city (Zulaika 2001: 12) and local artists remained deeply and rightly distressed by the diversion of 80% of the city's cultural funding into the Guggenheim's coffers to pay for the museum.

One of the most vocal critics of the Guggenheim proposal was Jorge Oteiza. A Basque nationalist and socialist, Oteiza was also an abstract sculptor of international renown who rejected the Guggenheim and attempts to buy and exhibit his work there unless it was accompanied by other Basque artists (Zulaika 2001, 3–4). Oteiza protested vigorously against what he called the new American Disneyfication of art. He pointed to the cruel paradox by which New York's artists consider him as their equal – with Richard Serra and Frank Gehry calling him the greatest living sculptor – but the terms of the Guggenheim franchise reduces him to a local artist whose value is negligible against American modernists. So too with another Basque artist – Eduardo Chillida – whose work Krens refused to buy, though the New York Guggenheim exhibited his work in 1981 and bought it then. Under protest, Krens later relented on Chillida and the Guggenheim Bilbao is now committed to purchasing some local works (Zulaika 2005: 161). This too has generated some concern, with the Director of the Belles Artes Gallery citing the need to broaden and diversify the art offerings of the city rather than tie them to Basque work (Viar 2005). Oteiza was also an interested player in the design of a new gallery for Bilbao, having been approached by the city's administrators but later rejecting the city's efforts to house a modern art collection in the Alhondiga. From this rebuff the city rulers then turned to an international architecture competition, the Guggenheim and another riverside site.

Thus, well before the commissioning of the Guggenheim, the Center of Contemporary Art was proposed in an abandoned wine warehouse. Invited by Bilbao's mayor to design it, Oteiza made a bare, minimalist design, comprising a glass cube grafted onto the old building with another on top of it linked by an elevated footbridge. Rather than a museum, it was to be a multidisciplinary centre of culture, contemporary art and aesthetic investigation. It was to be, in the words of Anna Guasch, an "art factory whose aim was to stimulate cultural creation" (Guasch 2005: 200–201). After two years, the project failed – mainly due to political infighting between the Autonomous Basque Government and the mayor, concerns over the damage that the design would do to the original building, its cramped location and Oteiza's clashes with local officials (Viar 2005: 102; Zulaika 2005: 161). The site was also rejected as an option by Thomas Krens and Frank Gehry in 1991. In a 2002 exposition on the city shown in the Australian city of Geelong – then seeking its own Guggenheim (see Chapter 7) – it was proposed that the Alhondiga become a sports centre – with swimming pools on the roof – and a great library. Combining recreation with culture, the aim is that: "The whole complex will be a meeting place for the city's inhabitants, a place to socialise and seek information for the whole metropolitan area" (Bilbao Exposition 2002).

In addition to plans for the Alhondiga, Bilbao also has a long established Fine Arts Museum and active arts scene which has been variously supported as part of the regeneration strategy for the city. Thus despite 80% of the budget for cultural development in the city being diverted to the Guggenheim (Zulaika 2005), other funds, policy frameworks and institutions have encouraged the development of local artistic production. Thus just before the opening of the Guggenheim the

ARSenal gallery had a show by123 artists with 155 works in different media, distinguished by its festive, incisive and ironic tone. (Guasch 2005: 191). The Euskal Museoa is a specialist museum on Basque history and culture, whose visitation rates and public profile has grown significantly since the late 1980s (Bartolucci 2000: 3). The Belles Artes has also received strong support and is proudly differentiating itself from the Guggenheim.

As with Glasgow, when Bilbao was at its industrial zenith in the early 20th century, a group of prominent businessmen had endowed the city with two museums, one for traditional and one for modern art. These later merged into the Museo de Belles Artes. It has a mix of European masters, Spanish and Basque master pieces, including Goya, Zurbaran and Velazquez along with Jorge Oteiza sculptures (Bartolucci 2000). Its collection is therefore primarily historical and regional rather than modern. Javier Viar, Director of the Fine Arts Museum described the Guggenheim as a neat complement to his gallery (Viar 2005). He further notes how the Guggenheim adds to the city, through its expertise, collections and profile. Having a New York-based institution in the city means that it can bring in masters that the local gallery cannot afford. The Belles Artes has 1,600 friends compared to the Guggenheim's 14,000, indicating a high level of local support if not a status factor in being associated with the imported institution. Viar also notes how the number of friends for the Belles Artes has grown significantly since the Guggenheim has been present in the city (Viar 2005: 105). Over this time, the gallery has also increased its workforce – from 41 to 53 permanents and subcontracted staff from 17 to 33 and its annual budget has grown from US$2.7 to US$7.1 million along with increases in attendance of 20% in 1998. He further reports that such visitors come primarily (80%) from the region; in contrast to the Guggenheim which draws only 10% of its visitors from the city (Viar 2005 106). Weighing up the value of the two institutions, Viar concludes: "People of Bilbao have never had such an abundance of the highest-quality contemporary art so close at hand" (Viar 2005: 107).

From the perspective of local artists and galleries, then, the overall effect of the Guggenheim in Bilbao has been paradoxical – draining off funds and attracting the lions share of international attention, but also boosting the overall level of interest in the creative arts within the city, along with the quality and quantity of what is shown. Within the context of a Cultural Capital, the combination of ambitious international works and local artistic production ensures at least one aspect of cultural sustainability in the city. This burgeoning of creative works has to be seen within the institutional framework created by the city of Bilbao itself with its various revitalisation plans and funding from the city, the region, Madrid, the European Union and, of course, the Guggenheim Foundation. A somewhat unique confluence of imperatives – for the city of Bilbao to address its collapsing industrial base and for the Guggenheim to reverse its financial fortunes via a strategy of globalisation – meant that the many objective cultural capital elements in the city, including the Museo Bilbao but also the Belles Artes, the concert hall and other well designed urban infrastructure, was built. Rather than being solely

Table 5.2   Embodied, Objective and Institutional Cultural Capital in Bilbao, Spain

Form of Cultural Capital	Local/City	Regional	National	International
Embodied	Iron ore miners Factory workers Local gov't officials Bilbao Metropoli-30 Janner Viar Local artists Jorge Oteiza Eduardo Chillida Gehry in Bilbao	Basque separatists	Carmen Gimenez	Thomas Krens Frank Gehry
Objective	Riverside factories Nervion River Allondhiga Old city Belles Artes ARSenal Gallery Guggenheim Museum	Nervion River		
Institutional	Bilbao Ria-2000 Bilbao Council 1989 Revitalisation Plan	ETA Euskadia Council Basque Parliament	Spanish Government – autonomy agreement (1979) – cultural policy	Spanish Empire British Empire European Union Guggenheim Foundation

the outcome of a globalising metropolitan museum, the quest by Bilbao to become an international centre of culture around signature buildings and institutions, was part of a well researched local plan for social, urban and economic revitalisation, one which mobilised and accelerated the further creation of cultural capital. Table 5.2 summarises the key actors across the various scales and dimensions of cultural capital involved. The next part will consider directly, just how sustainable and post-modern the Guggenheim and the city of Bilbao have become as a result.

The Guggenheim and post-modern style

For many commentators, Bilbao has become the quintessential city of spectacle, the Guggenheim a signature post-modern building and Frank Gehry the post-modern celebrity architect *par excellence*. Such designations are usually more than innocent descriptors but are loaded with negative connotations. However, I will argue that such evaluations miss much of the point of the Guggenheim in Bilbao, for being a post-modern city of spectacle is integral to an overall, locally devised redevelopment strategy which has been vital to creating a sustainable Cultural Capital. In short, celebrity status is grounded on a far deeper history as well as a political, economic and social agenda particular to this Cultural Capital.

Chapter 3 gave an overview of the multi-faceted development known as post-modernity. In summary, it can be seen as comprising:

- A critique of Western knowledges and deconstructive textual practices;
- A post-industrial, service, information and symbolic economy, dominated by business services, but also personal, social and welfare services; all of which are mediated by information technology. Alongside – and for some cities a dominant growth sector – goes tourism, recreation and the Cultural Industries;
- A post-Fordist form of production built on niche markets, batch production, non-unionised labour, computer mediated technology with decentralised often globalised production systems co-ordinated by a few centres of control;
- Cities differentiated across the globe into a few command and control centres (Global Cities) and a mass of other cities competing for mobile capital investment and visibility;
- Urban forms characterised by de-industrialised port and core areas (at least in the 1970s and 80s), various forms of regeneration – gentrification, port reclamation, waterfront revitalisation – and urban spectacles as a means to capture hyper-mobile capital and the Creative Class;
- An architecture characterised in opposition to the Modern – international, formal, white/steel/glass/tall, designed by heroic architects, where form follows function – with double coding occurring on facades, and buildings more whimsical, playful and organic while being connected to their locality and populace.

The identification and rise of the symbolic economy fuses post-Fordist forms of production with the post-modern city of spectacle and the Creative City of cultural capital. In approaching the Guggenheim in Bilbao, it is appropriate to look more closely at this structure as a post-modern building but also to locate it within the broader notion of post-modernity described above, in particular, considering it as part of a city of spectacle and part of a new post-Fordist economy as a means of evaluating its economic, social and cultural sustainability.

Gehry's architecture attracts tourists but also accolades from the global architectural press. For many it is a quintessential post-modern structure, in its embrace of deconstruction, engagement with but also transcendence of local history and flight into the extraordinary. For MacCannell, it is not founded on a fantasy of controlling history, culture or nature but rather opens dialogue with these realms (MacCannell 2005: 36). As such the building conforms with Charles Jenck's definitive view of post-modern architectural style (Jencks 1984/1991). For Jencks, the double coding of past and present does not imply a lazy eclecticism but an original engagement with it. So a building can have historical referents but also engage with the present, fast-changing society with its new materials, technologies and ideas. Such originality means that the post-modern building may well be a beautiful thing in itself rather than a structure subservient to practical ends (Klotz 1988). It is, in the words of Paolo Portoghesi, the architecture of communication, an architecture of the image for a civilisation of the image (Portoghesi 1983: 8).

If the Gehry Guggenheim appears to satisfy many of the criteria of post-modern style, it also fails on numerous fronts. For the Bilbao structure is not a historical quotation, is far more than a decorated façade, is autocratic rather than democratic in its origins, is not strongly connected to a traditional, vernacular tradition or to local populism, nor is it legible and human in scale (Ellin 1999: 111–12). Such divergences perhaps confirm the contradictory and divergent nature of those writing on post-modern style and suggests a caution in using this term as a talisman for any sort of evaluation.

But the Gehry Guggenheim does join a number of signature structures by international architects in Bilbao. The creation of such a stylised urban environment, for Kroker and Cook at least (1986), is consistent with the trend for "the spreading outwards of aestheticised production in the form of designed environments" (Kroker and Cook 1986: 18) such that in the words of Nan Ellin (1999), post-modern urbanism may well be triumphing in this city of spectacle.

The Guggenheim and the city of spectacle

For David Harvey writing on the United States, urban spectacles of the 1960s occurred in relation to oppositional political movements – for black civil rights, against urban renewal and the Vietnam War. However, from the 1970s Harvey notes how urban spectacles were captured and used by the powerful in cities to stifle dissent, create diversions, activate capital and differentiate one place against another in an increasingly fierce battle for mobile investment. He gives the example of Baltimore – one of many models for Bilbao – wracked by race riots in the 1960s which threatened the viability of investments made there. He continues:

> The leaders sought a symbol around which to build the idea of the city as a community, a city which could believe in itself sufficiently to over-come the divisions and siege mentality with which the common citizenry approached downtown and its public spaces (Harvey 1989a: 89).

The solution was to create the Baltimore City Fair and then Harbor Place, a science centre, an aquarium, a convention centre, a marina, innumerable hotels, "pleasure citadels of all kinds" which required a different architecture. Harvey continues:

> An architecture of spectacle, with its sense of surface glitter and transitory participatory pleasure, of display and ephemerality…became essential to a project of this sort (Harvey 1989a: 91).

Faced with hyper-mobile capital as well as civic unrest Harvey describes a city of spectacle in a way that could be readily applied to post-1997 Bilbao. While asserting the need to unpack and to understand the process by which cities are impelled towards such a strategy, Harvey also clearly disapproves of it, suggesting that such developments are but one more way capitalism destroys social equity, good design and the urban fabric. However, my research and experience in the city of Bilbao in August 2005, suggests a different reading.

In Bilbao to see the Guggenheim during a week in August, my visit to this iconic museum lasted only one day. I also spent considerable time in the old city, in the Belles Artes, along the waterfront, in the new Euskaldua shopping centre and in other galleries – being a concerted cultural tourist. In the evenings the city along the river lit up with spectacular fireworks, while during the days, there were parades, street performers and a great deal of music and dancing. One stage was set up adjacent to the Guggenheim and here the young of the region dressed, sang and danced their dialect – a display and celebration of deep, highly localised cultural capital (Figure 5.1). What I encountered was indeed a city full of spectacle, but not one solely or even primarily geared to the new international artistic icon, but one focused on an ancient religious event – the Semana Grande or Aste Nagusia – a week-long festival in honour of the Virgin, one of three held in the major Basque cities (Prieto 2003: 79). The vital question, then, is whose spectacle – in this case a very local one, widely appreciated and lavishly funded – and to what ends – for in August 2005 the main objective seemed to be the realisation and celebration of Basque tradition.

This sort of celebration is not what Harvey was referring to in his evaluation of Baltimore. His comments resonate with the observations of Bilbao by Joseba Zulaika. Zulaika noted how in 2000, the Bilbao planners were not averse to a Disneyfied spectacle. He continues:

> The economic logic of postmodern cities is perhaps best described as one in which "the urban wasteland has been positioned within the circuits of international finance capital and recoded as a site of consumption and the pursuit of leisure … The process requires an ideology of urban regeneration and gentrification of neighborhoods in decline. The planners find it essential to create the myth of a brand new waterfront reality …The spectre of industrial decline and the threat of historical abandonment are mobilized to drive the belief in the new utopian vision of "Bilbao 2000"…Transport policies, architectural decisions,

Figure 5.1   August Festival in the City of Spectacle 2005

Photograph by the author.

urban design, emblematic buildings – in the end they all hinge essentially on the politics of sight and spectacle (Zulaika 2002: 9).

In evaluating such an assessment of Bilbao as a city of spectacle, it is appropriate to consider what appear to be the two main critical elements of both Harvey and Zulaika – that spectacle implies escapism and superficiality and a loss of economic control. I will consider each in turn.

The Guggenheim as a celebrity Meaghan Morris suggested that in the 1960s, everything seemed "arrestingly political", but then in the 1980s, "everything turned obscurely cultural"; with culture the site where competing views of the world battled it out whereas before it had been religion, the family, community or politics (Quoted in Wark 1999: 20). With the elevation of culture in/as popular discourse, people and, I would suggest, buildings became popular preoccupations as the celebrity architect was invented. For Mackenzie Wark, celebrity involves the celebration of someone, via the wide circulation of their image. They become a celebrity partly because of their extraordinary appearances or statements, but also because no matter how otherworldly they may appear, they are also ordinary as well. As Wark observes: "Celebrity is not just a trace of the extraordinary in the ordinary. What makes it tangible is that it is also a trace of the ordinary in the extraordinary" (Wark 1999: 49). Celebrities affirm individual ambition and a break with their community, but also collective belonging (Wark 1999: 48). As such, they have power, which for David Marshall "structures meaning, crystallises ideological positions, and works to provide a sense and coherence to a culture" (Marshall 1997: x). Celebrities involve "a system for valorizing meaning and communication" (Marshall 1997: x). This includes a larger than life person (or structure), an audience and intermediate means – increasingly the electronic media – of connecting the two. The pleasure for the viewer involves a reciprocal link between the everyday and the fantastic, the banal and the magical, which gives the celebrity their "temporary immortality and ubiquity" (Wark 1999: 53).

For Marshall and Wark, the celebrity is a focal point of flakiness, of false value; as success is dissociated from achievement and feeds off itself. In Baudrillard's terms, the image becomes the total reality and the reality the image; the ultimate post-modern creation (see Chapter 3). Marshall connects the contemporary celebrity with efforts to contain the power of the democratic mass in a way that also involves the consumption of commodities and therefore the expansion of capitalism (Marshall 1997). As with Harvey, he sees celebrity as inevitably linked to the negative social relations of capitalism. Sustaining celebrity status is an ongoing and fraught task; one that needs constant renewal and re-circulation to maintain currency and vitality.

The Guggenheim in Bilbao and its architect – Frank Gehry – fulfil many of the characteristics of the celebrity. In the case of the structure, it has elements of uniqueness and magic that elevate it to the status of architectural icon. It is written about and reproduced endlessly in the professional architectural press

– journals, magazines, books – with its construction techniques, enigmatic look and originality the main focus (see for example Cuito 2001; Bardham-Quallen 2004). Gehry too assumes the status of elusive genius who has a history – as a Jewish Canadian moving to California to train, live, work and ultimately triumph. Marginal to the American architectural mainstream, Gehry makes his reputation through the design of his own home, by working in the office of internationally renown architects (such as Victor Gruen) and by working for high profile clients (such as the Walt Disney Corporation). His working class background and status as a self made practitioner allows Joan Ockman to ascribe to him an affinity with Bilbao's tough urban landscape (Ockman 2004: 230). So too the fact of living and working in Los Angeles – that city of quintessential post-modernity – means that for many commentators, Gehry has absorbed some of its essence – be it an openness to dazzling light and benign climate but also respect for practical spaces (Forster 1999) or imperatives to build inward looking fortresses for the elite (Davis 1995: 167–69). The ordinary life thus becomes enmeshed with the extraordinary city, to produce leading edge buildings which are prophetic in both positive and negative ways; but always larger than the present and everyday life.

The celebrity status of the building is also related to its mass circulation as an image and setting for things other than art works. Thus the Bilbao Guggenheim joins other iconic/celebrity buildings – such as the Eiffel Tower, New York's Chrysler building, Pei's Louvre extension – to be included in movies, music videos and fashion shows. As Georgeni Poulakidas notes:

> The Guggenheim Museum Bilbao quickly became as popular as some celebrities. Film makers, musicians and even fashion designers wanted their works associated with the museum. It was used as a backdrop during the opening sequence for the James Bond action film The World is Not Enough. The music group Simple Minds used one of the museum's galleries as a setting for their music video "Glitter Ball", designers Carolina Herrera and Paco Rabanne used the central atrium as a fashion show catwalk to introduce their new clothing collections (2004: 37).

Celebrity also encapsulates collective wills in individual personas, and perhaps also, into buildings constructed in a place. The Bilbao Guggenheim is at once strongly connected to the city but clearly also apart from it. Architectural critics cite the use of metal and local stone, the addition of Basque blue to the administrative wing, engagement with the river, the city and bridge and a design resonant of a ship's prow, as evidence of a strong connection to the locality and its industrial history. A sure sign also of its post-modern credentials. Others emphasise the use of military technology, titanium, glass, stainless steel – all imports to the area – as indicative of Gehry's wish to engage with international rather than local agendas (Ibelings 2003). In addition, the similarity of the Bilbao Guggenheim to other Gehry structures – such as the Experience Music Project Seattle (1995–2000) and the Walt Disney Concert Hall in Los Angeles (final design model 1987–2003) and the now-abandoned Lower Manhattan Guggenheim – for me at least, belie his oft repeated commitment to express the locality and its striking originality.

But perhaps the search for "evidence" to confirm celebrity status or local resonance is unnecessary. For what matters is the way in which the building is represented; conveyed by word and image as integral to this city and its history of cultural autonomy and industrial development; but also apart from it, as a far greater structure, part of the canon of remarkable international architecture. And in this, the words of Jeremy Gilbert-Rolfe are typical:

> One would be truly indifferent to the visual as a source of pleasure…not to see that the Guggenheim Museum in Bilbao is a great event – of structure and lightness, mass and movement…It fits into the city perfectly while being quite unlike it…Others have also immediately identified it as a definitive work of contemporary architecture (2001: 101).

Here then is one source of its post-modernity and also its cultural sustainability. For this building, emerging from fractious local and international politics and meshed in an ambitious urban and social renewal program, is clearly in and of this place but also a transcendent international icon. It is a place to visit, to gaze at, to marvel; for locals and international cultural tourists alike. It may well contain few local art works – though a whole gallery is devoted to them – but as a stimulant for expenditure and visitors, as an art space and magical object, this is a building which reflects the local as well as the global. As a result this building is indeed a post-modern structure and celebrity, but as such it has collected together a huge amount of cultural capital in a way that appears sustainable. It is also part of a fundamental economic transformation of this city which, from the outside in 2007 at least, appears to be sustainable.

Bilbao's post-Fordist economy?

A 1996 study by Arantxa Rodriguez, Galder Guenaga and Elena Martinez documented how service employment had grown in Bilbao, to replace those jobs lost in industry from 1975 to1996. Combined with other data, the trend from 1975 is clear (see Table 5.3).

Within such a structural change, there is also the issue of Business Services, those parts of the Service sector that are most strongly identified with the Creative Class and World City status (see Chapter 3). On this front, there has also been a marked expansion – from 2% in 1985 to 7.2% in 1996 – with this old industrial city equalling the Spanish average by 1994 (Progress Report 1998). This change has also been accompanied by a fall in unemployment – from 25% in 1993 to 18.7% in 1998. Accompanied by the re-use of many older industrial sites and spectacular case studies of local entrepreneurs made good – such as Mikel Urizabarrena and his Panda software empire (Usher 2000/2001) – the city of Bilbao joins a region undergoing a broad renewal, but one not disconnected from its industrial past.

Table 5.3   Bilbao – A Post-Fordist Economy? 1975–1996

	1975	1990	1996
Manufacturing	45.5	32	26.9
Services	41.7	52	65.2

(Adapted from Fraser 2005: 48 and McNeill 2000)

Thus, in the context of their industrial history, EU membership, free trade, plans for industrial revitalisation, higher education, skill development and venture capital, the three Basque regions (Bizkaia, Gupuzozkoa and Alava) with their two million people continue to house 50% of Spain's capital machinery sector, 90% of the nation's special steel production, 80% of its machine tools and 25% of the aeronautical sector. The region also has a high proportion of university students, with 25% enrolled in tertiary education (Euskadi Essential 2005: 3). The city of Bilbao, then, as part of the Basque region, remains a major centre for manufacturing, while also shifting decisively towards services, including Business Services. Such a broad economic structure with a new emphasis on Services provides a solid foundation for economic sustainability.

Critical to this economic sustainability is the Cultural Industries, especially the connection of the fine arts to tourism. Thus, tourism has become a major industry for the city of Bilbao, especially in the aftermath of publicity surrounding the Guggenheim. Visitors to the gallery have been as high as 1.4 million (in 1998) and in 2003 stood at over 850,000 (see Table 5.1). The tourist board registered a 28% rise in tourists in the first quarter of 1997. 85% of visitors to the city to visit the museum extended their stay, all of which contributed 0.47% of annual GNP to the region in 1998. (NcNeill 2000: 486). Over three years, the museum lured 3.5 million visitors to the city, 85–90% from outside the region and most from France and England. A KPMG study indicated that in these years, its economic impact – $500 million – was five times its cost and partly as a consequence, the vast majority of the city supported it. Ten years before 99% of the population were against it as crazy profligacy in desperate economic times (Usher 2000/1). The Guggenheim museum therefore generated economic activity that added 47% to the gross regional product in its first year of operation, contributing to the maintenance of between 3,800 and 8,900 jobs, mostly through tourism (Banitotoulou 2001; Fraser 2005). While tourist numbers have been falling from such dizzy heights- from 1.4 million in 1988 to 850,000 in 2003 – the place of tourism in the local economy has grown significantly. While questions are legitimately raised as to the sort of jobs these are, with the sector associated with many part time and contractual employees, there is no doubt that the Guggenheim and the related tourist influx, has directly contributed to employment, tax revenues and improvement in the image of the city, to the point where 85% of the population are proud to live there and Bilbao is very much on the international cultural tourist map.

In addition to being a highly profitable spectacle, the Guggenheim is only a part of the tourist experience with other elements of this city, including different spectacles, cultural heritage, food, coastal beaches and landscape also vital. Further, in contrast to Harvey's argument, the evidence suggests that in having urban spectacles, the city has generated significant inflows of people and capital that would not have come otherwise. With a number of spectacles and with its move from an industrial to a broadly based service economy, Bilbao like Glasgow, is mobilising and valorising its own as well as imported cultural capital for its economic and cultural betterment.

A Sustainable Cultural Capital?

This discussion has isolated a number of different forms of cultural capital which are, in different ways, continuing to various forms of sustainable development. Embodied cultural capital in the form of the expertise and international connections of Thomas Krens and Frank O. Gehry were imported into the region by an elite group of Basque business and political figures. Whilst they enraged many local artists and intellectuals, these individuals and groups mobilised cultural, productive and finance capital to firstly create a magnificent museum but also to support a broad based urban and economic regeneration agenda. While initially contrary to the principle of political sustainability, subsequent elections and relative quietude from separatists, have confirmed the political acceptance and hence sustainability of this strategy.

The resulting objectified cultural capital – in the form of the Guggenheim Museo Bilbao and Guggenheim collection, but also in commissions for local art works, support for other galleries and international as well as local interest in the arts – has meant that cultural capital has taken a material form which is also enduring. This is most evident and arose from an array of institutional supports for this process – the Revitalisation Plans, various public-private partnerships to realised their objectives, the role of different levels of government (city, regional, national, the EU) and, of course the role of the New York-based Guggenheim Foundation.

The issue of whether the resulting transformation is culturally and socially sustainable is the most contested. For many critics – such as Joseba Zulaika, Evdoxia Baniotopoulou and Andrea Fraser – the Guggenheim Bilbao is the result of a "franchised asymmetry" whereby a powerful, American institution basically ripped off a relatively naïve and desperate city, to render its citizens impotent in the process and its artists bereft of support and status. The resulting Cultural Capital is, for these critics and within the frameworks offered by David Harvey, Frederic Jameson, Michael Sorkin and Mike Davis, of necessity tainted with the post-modern brush – a shallow spectacle, dependent, crass and exploitative. My argument, however, is that contrary to such views, the Guggenheim Bilbao is but a small part of a localised agenda of urban renewal and economic transformation;

Esplanade Theatres by the Bay, Singapore

Chapter 6
Singapore: Post-colonial City of Cultural Heritage and Performance

Cultural Capitals, even more than other contemporary cities, are situated within a globalising economy and infused with the many dimensions of post-modernity. As the examples of Glasgow and Bilbao have demonstrated, both globalisation and the symbolic economy shape the value which accrues to the creative arts in each place. Many Cultural Capitals are also enmeshed in a maze of colonial and post-colonial relationships which infuse the creation and reception of art works. Thus as Chapter 4 illustrated, the history of Glasgow was intricately linked to the rise and fall of the British empire, while Chapter 5 detailed how the city of Bilbao too was integrated into the British Empire in the 19th century through its provision of iron ore, shipping and investment sites. These relationships were etched onto each city's urban fabric through factories, mines and housing. In Bilbao, the British imprint as well as the Latin American one continued in the 20th century through civic architecture, urban design, trade and cultural orientation. The terms of EU membership and connection to the Guggenheim Foundation continued this unequal but mutually beneficial metropolitan- peripheral relationship. So too with Glasgow as it moved from being captive to the fate of the British Empire to being part of an assertive and autonomous region of the United Kingdom, negotiating directly with Europe and securing much sought after national and international designations. The relations between states within and beyond their empires during and after colonisation is therefore a part of understanding the city of Bilbao as well as Glasgow, including how they secured some of their most valuable cultural assets – the Guggenheim Museum and the various cultural capital labels lavished on Glasgow.

If the history of Bilbao and Glasgow can be read through the lens of colonialism, so too can that of Singapore and Geelong. For the colonial and post-colonial experience is one that variously permeates most cities of the world – either as a centre of imperial expansion or as places created or modified by colonial activity. The port city in particular is a key staging post and element of empire and, in the case of Singapore, remains vital to its post-independence reality. In the post-colonial era, representing and expressing the city through cultural artefacts – be it public art, performances or heritage precincts – will inevitably engage with this colonial past. How this past is constructed and how it relates to the artistic values created, is heavily inflected by the views of the Singaporean state. What sort of Cultural Capital thereby emerges in this authoritarian democracy relates primarily to the political conditions which structure its creation and visibility. In Singapore, the question of how sustainable the arts can be is limited by issues of cultural, social and political representation; for the economic and political agendas drive all others in this city state. In the context of its developmentalist agenda (see Chapter 3), this chapter will consider Singapore as a colonial and then post-colonial city and chart how its theatre and heritage buildings have become valued in this context. The focus will be on the relationship between The Esplanade – Theatres by the Bay and other performance spaces; and the re-construction of Chinatown, Little India and Kampong Glam as ethnic heritage enclaves as Singapore strives to become a Global City of the Arts.

Singapore as a Post-colonial City

Chapter 3 introduced the post-colonial perspective as one that can usefully inform the examination of the creative arts in at least some – if not all – Cultural Capitals. While a debated notion derived from both Marxist-inspired world-systems frameworks and post-structural literary theory (Jacobs 1996; Gandhi 1998; Hall and Tucker 2004), post-colonialism is a powerful and relevant lens through which to view contemporary Singapore. The colonial experience as well as how independence was attained shapes the current definitions of Singapore; with its British and multi-ethnic origins the foundation for its triumphal march towards economic and political autonomy. Subsequently the main drivers of this city state have been economic development, ongoing rule by the People's Action Party (PAP) and forestalling social fracturing along ethnic and class lines. This history is registered in public narratives – in the "Singapore Story" told to those who visit the Asian Museum (in 2000 at least, Author's field notes 2000), in local theatre and in sculptures along the Singapore River. How Singapore's post-colonial status is defined and realised is also evident in current economic as well as arts policy and in the treatment of heritage precincts within the city. This chapter will argue that the post-colonial nation/economy/community building agenda prescribes the creation, value and sustainability of the art that is produced in this city. It also profoundly limits the relationship between the creative arts and the Cultural Industries as the former are limited by moral prescriptions, political censorship and orientation to a superficial tourist gaze. However, the chapter will also show how, once permitted to flourish, even on relatively narrow economistic terms, the creative arts are difficult to contain. In the case of Singaporean English-language theatre, that produced by The Necessary Stage evinces a radical autonomy that bodes well for the creativity of the nation as well as the cultural sustainability of its artistic communities.

For Jacobs, "colonialism ... entails the establishment and maintenance of domination over a separate group of people, who are viewed as subordinate, and their territories, which are presumed to be available for exploitation" (Jacobs 1996: 16). In addition to involving the exercise of political and military power, 19th century colonialism involved a cultural incorporation into a web of Eurocentric, racial and religious stereotypes. In a critical contribution to conceptualising this process, Edward Said documented the many ways in which European scientists, anthropologists, geographers, explorers, traders, novelists, journalists and politicians constructed a world of exotic "Others" in Asia; in a process that he describes as Orientalism (Said 1978). He distinguished between Imperialism – as the theory, attitudes and practice of a dominating metropolitan centre ruling a distant territory – and Colonialism – a specific articulation of imperialism associated with territorial invasion and settlement (cited by Jacobs 1996: 16). For Said both imperialism and colonialism are uneven, contested and messy processes which create particular European societies as well as colonised ones. While thereby rendering a complex military, political as well as cultural process a site of conflicting ideas, Said writes:

> Neither imperialism nor colonialism is a simple act of accumulation and acquisition. Both are supported and perhaps even impelled by impressive ideological formations which include notions that certain territories and people *require* and beseech domination, as well as forms of knowledge affiliated with that domination (Said 1993: 8).

Said goes on to describe the generative but also negative power of the nationalism that often arose to eject colonial powers. Thus in the words of Leila Gandhi: "Said's *Culture and Imperialism* stands out for its relentless disavowal of the "third worlds' post-imperial regression into combative and dissonant voices of nativism" (Gandhi 1998: 108). Such nativism is often a key part of defining the nation; a critical post-colonial project, one in which the creative arts and definitions of heritage can assume a central role.

The creation of Singapore is the result of imperial rivalries and economic agendas while its post-colonial history is very much concerned with an aggressive nationalistic developmentalism. This colonial and post-colonial context is vital to understanding the role creative arts have assumed in this city state and provides an important means to ascertain its value.

Colonial Singapore

The island now called Singapore has a history linked to the fortunes of Asian empires as they variously expanded, fought and contracted across the Malay and Indonesian archipelago. In this sense, colonialism is not an invention of 17th century Europe, but part of long term Asian empires emanating from Srivajaya in Central Sumatra as well as from China and the Majapahit of Java. From the 19th century these empires were joined by European ones in determining the island's fate.

Singapore's history was and remains linked to its strategic location, on the main trading route between India and China. In 1330 a visitor from China reported that an island named Long Yamen or Dragon's Tooth had Chinese living there.

Locals tell stories of Malay pirates lying in wait for wayward junks to pass the Dragon-Teeth Gate before they struck (McKie 1942:78). By the end of the 14th century the Sanskrit name – Singapura or Lion City – became commonly used. At this time, Singapura was caught in the struggles between Sumatra's Srivijayan Empire and the Java-based Majapahit Empire for control over the Malay Peninsula. By the 18th century, Iskandar Shar, a prince of Palembang, founded the Malacca Sultanate from which he ruled Singapura. At this time, the island was a small port oriented to India and China with around 100 Malays and Chinese earning a living through piracy, trade and fishing (Economist.com 2006).

Into this multicultural mix came trading and colonising European powers – the Dutch, English, Portuguese and French. Already present in India and Indonesia through its East India Company, the British were extending their dominion in India and expanding their trade to China. The company saw a need for ports in the region to refit and protect their merchant fleet. They also had a need in the era of intense imperial rivalry to forestall any advance of the Dutch in the East Indies. As a result, they established trading posts in Penang (1786) and captured Malacca from the Dutch (1795). The end of the Napoleonic Wars in Europe – in 1815 – changed the environment in which the British were operating. From then on, the aim of the British government was to forestall any repeat of French expansionism. To achieve this, they moved to strengthen the Dutch economy and empire, a policy that both secured British interests but also threatened those of the East India Company (Webster 1998). The government and its commercial agents also needed to boost industrial exports. In this context, the then governor of Belconnen, Stamford Raffles, saw the need to expand British influence in east Asia and to secure access for Indian commodities at a time when they were losing ground in Europe (Webster 1998: 70). He wrote:

> To ensure a market for the manufactures of India, and thus promote its industry and prosperity, and give an advantage beneficial to the energy of its people becomes an object of great and increasing importance. The extraordinary advance of British manufactures having in a great measure excluded those of India from the European market, it is to the populous and less civilised countries of the further east that we can alone look to for a permanent demand (Quoted by Webster 1998: 71).

Summoned by Lord Hastings, Governor General of India, to discuss how to deal with a Dutch resurgence in the region, Raffles was given approval to establish a trading station on the tip of the Malay Peninsula. This port was to control the new opium trade between India and China as well as ensure an outlet for Indian manufactured goods and secure the interests of the East India Company against the Dutch. Raffles landed at Singapore on January 29, 1819. This island had the advantage of fresh water, timber for refitting ships, a location on the main trading route from India to China, was unoccupied by the Dutch and had only a small, mainly Malay settlement. At the time, the Dutch had secured the island through a treaty with the Sultan of Jahore. Raffles concluded treaties with the local Malay ruler and then with the Sultan's brother and contender to the throne – Tunku Hussein of Jahor – in return for formal recognition and money. While contrary to official British foreign policy, in the light of the success of Singapore as a trading station, Raffles' negotiation was later legalised by the British government in two treaties. Thus in 1823 Raffles signed a treaty with Sultan Hussein and the Temenggong which extended British possession to the whole island – except for the residence of Sultan Hussein Shah, at the istana (palace) in the heart of what was later to become the Malay enclave of Kampong Glam – in return for modest ongoing payments. The island would henceforth come under British law, with the proviso that Malay customs and religions would be respected. The 1824 Anglo-Dutch treaty divided the Indonesian and Malay archipelagos into Imperial spheres of influence. The cession of Singapore to Britain thereby emerged from both great power and local rivalries. Significantly, it was established as a free port and therefore was attractive to those attempting to by-pass Dutch trading duties. As news spread across the archipelago Bugis, Peranakan Chinese and Arab traders flocked to the new settlement (Webster 1998).

Singapore speedily began earning revenue and by 1823 its trade surpassed that of Penang. By 1827 the Chinese supplanted the Malays as the largest ethnic group. Especially prominent were the Peranakans; well to do merchants and descendents of those Chinese who had long settled in the archipelago. They were joined by Chinese coolies – male, poor and uneducated – from southern China. The Chinese were actively encouraged by Raffles who noted that "my city of Singapore is already attracting the peaceable, industrious and thrifty Chinese". At this time Malays remained concentrated in agriculture and fishing, the Chinese dominated commerce while Britain imported labourers and soldiers from India. Some of the Chinese and Indians were educated in English to become civil servants or business people (Tamney 1996:3); moves which accelerated the emerging racial and class-based structuring of the city. The boom economy and its masculine bias led to a relatively lawless society; rife with prostitution, gambling and drug abuse, all of which was overseen by powerful Chinese secret societies. In a deliberate effort to forestall any united opposition to British rule, Raffles organised the city into functional and ethnic subdivisions. Under the *Raffles Plan* of 1822 ethnic groups were corralled into different urban quarters, such that race, space and economic role came together. Urban geography was therefore a tool of imperial social and political control from the earliest days of colonisation.

Singapore joined Malacca and Penang in becoming the Straits Settlements in 1826 under the control of British India. By 1832 Singapore was the centre of government and in 1867 became a Crown Colony under the London Colonial Office. Trade was boosted by the opening of the Suez Canal in 1869, by steam transport and the development of Malaya's rubber plantations. Singapore became the main port and sorting centre in the world for rubber. British rule was military and bureaucratic, cemented by the co-option of local leaders and by keeping the different racial groups apart – economically and spatially. The colonial

office ensured that economic development served British interests; such that
no manufacturing industries could be opened that would compete with British
industry (Tamney 1996: 3). The nation's economic structure assumed that of a
trading city, primarily a service economy with a small manufacturing component.
The population grew rapidly – from 5,000 in 1820 to 60,000 in 1850 up to 81,000
in 1860 and thence to 223,000 by 1901 – and was heavily differentiated by race,
dominated first by Malays but then increasingly by the Chinese, with Indians and
to a lesser extent European minorities (see Table 6.1).

In many ways, Singapore was the primate city of Malaya (Buchanan 1972:
34); dependent upon the primary producing Malayan hinterland – especially its tin
mines and rubber plantations – and heavily reliant on European investment. It was
also the shipping, financial and commercial centre of the region (Buchanan 1972:
34). The city's economic structure changed little over the first half of the 20th
century, with a dominant trade-related tertiary sector generating around 70% to
75% of Gross National Product and 80-85% of its employment. There was a much
smaller manufacturing sector, commanding around 10 to15% of employment and
generating 5–7% of domestic income (Buchanan 1972: 35). Well before the advent
of the Western service economy in the 1980s then, Singapore was dependent on
the tertiary sector for its very existence. Such a foundation allowed population
growth to continue – from 220,000 in 1901 to double by 1920 and double again by
1947 leading to over 2 million people in 1969.

Like the 19th century, the 20th century history of Singapore up until 1965, was
primarily shaped by British foreign and trade policy as well as its relationship with
Malaysia – with which it was formally integrated in the 1940s and again in the
1960s. From these colonial positions had come not only economic dependency but
significant wealth and a social-spatial structure that reflected a political strategy of
multi-ethnic rule which connected ethnicity to class and economic development.
Social services and infrastructure were, however, limited as the colonial
government valued economic over other concerns. Progress was measured in trade
volumes and roads built, so that schools, hospitals and housing were left to either
philanthropists, local religious organisation or the private sector (Ho 1997: 214).

Table 6.1   Ethnic composition of Singapore 1850–2000 (%)

	1850	1860	1972	1988	2000
Chinese	53	61.9	75	76	77
Malays	27	13.5	14	15	14
Indians	12	16.1	8	7	7.6
Europeans (Others)	2	8.5	3	2	1.4

(Buchanan 1972: 165; Milne and Mauzey 1990: 12; Tamney 1996: 2; Marshall 2003: 153)

Independence and development

For Singapore the movement towards decolonisation was a protracted and, for some commentators, a reluctant one. It was a process linked to the weakening of the British empire worldwide before the challenges to its economic and political power offered by Europe and Japan from 1900 to 1945. Withdrawal of Britain from Asia was accompanied by the growth of leftist movements within the region. Thus after the inglorious "Fall of Singapore" before the Japanese advance in 1942 and the island's occupation, Singapore was returned to the British and became part of the Malayan Union from 1946 to 1948. From this time, the level of local representation in the ruling parliament gradually increased – a consequence of British withdrawal and local demands for greater autonomy. The newly formed leftist and nationalist People's Action Party (PAP) – an alliance of English-educated professionals and left wing Chinese school teachers and unionists – promised to end colonialism, establish democracy and abolish inequalities in wealth and opportunity (Tamney 1996: 4). Its main political competitor was a union and working class based socialist party – the Labor Front – which grew in strength in parallel with communist parties in China, Indonesia and Malaysia. The first free elections in 1955 saw the leftist Labor Front win ten seats, the People's Action Party three along with smaller numbers for the Malay's National Organisation and the Malayan Chinese Association.

Conservative Singaporeans joined with the British government in reacting anxiously to this growth of worker organisations and leftist politics. As Tamney observes: "(b)ecause the British would not allow communist-influenced groups to gain political power in the region, the left in Singapore needed the nationalists, who were allowed to control the PAPs executive committee" (Tamney 1996: 4). It was the British Secret Service who subsequently orchestrated the arrest of leftists within the PAP and who then supported the party's leader – Lee Kuan Yew – in his moves to isolate leftists within the party and beyond. Granted home rule by Britain in 1959, the PAP won a majority of seats with 53.5% of the vote in the 1960 election. The PAP proceeded to dominate the political life of Singapore – winning all seats in 1972, 1976, 1980, losing one in 1982, two in 1984 and four in 1991 – developing what has been variously labelled "authoritarian capitalism" (Lingle 1996) and "democratic socialism", a unique blend of one-party authoritarianism, bourgeois liberalism, devout anti-communism, state welfarism, unbridled free enterprise, and Chinese chauvinism (Buchanan 1972: 19) within a "corporatist socialist economy" (Langenbach 2003: 8).

When Britain conceded self-rule in 1959, Singapore's location and its trading history ensured that it was the pre-eminent economic centre of the region. Despite its ethnic mix, its colonial heritage guaranteed English as the principal trading language. This colonial history also ensured privileged access to trading with the West and the British Commonwealth and the establishment of a highly regarded legal and commercial code. In the mid-1960s, Britain transferred its substantial housing stock previously provided for military personnel to the Singaporean state. This in turn lowered development costs for the new republic and allowed taxes to stay low. The British also left behind the Central Provident Fund (CPF) which provided the regime with access to low interest funds (Lingle 1996: 64). Colonisation and the process of de-colonisation was therefore relatively beneficent to those who had built their wealth, class and political position on links to the British. Singapore was very much a product of the imperial relationship and retained many links and ongoing benefits of the British connection with decolonisation.

Despite ongoing ties with Britain, economic interdependence led to regular discussions with Malaysia on political integration. The last of these occurred in 1961 when Malaya proposed closer political and economic ties via a Federation of Malaya, Singapore, Sarawak, North Borneo and Brunei. Supported by the PAP, this integration was approved by referendum in September 1962. The hope was that such a union would boost economic activity and security while also easing unemployment. Opposed by left-leaning Chinese within the PAP – fearful of being overwhelmed by Malays – the federation was also actively opposed by Indonesia. Interpretations vary as to how the situation was resolved, with some suggesting that Singapore opted out of the Federation while others point to its forced removal. Thus for Yeoh and Kong: (I)n the early 1960s Singapore wrested independence from the British colonial power and became a sovereign State (Yeoh and Kong 1994: 19). Others point to a one-sided process of expulsion whereby the Malay parliament voted against the wishes of Singapore and its Prime Minister 126–0 for separation. The online encyclopaedia Wikipedia concludes its discussion of the process: "Singapore became the only country in the history of the modern world to gain independence against its own will" (Wikipedia 2006: 15). The securing of political independence by Singapore – from Britain and from Malaysia – is therefore variously constructed as a triumph of local nationalism and a messy process of staged decolonisation, regional engagement and reluctant autonomy, leaving a small and economically fragile state.

The priority of the newly independent nation was economic development and political stability. Within this agenda, the arts were insignificant. In pursuing investment and employment, Singapore followed a policy leading to its successful integration into the New International Division of Labour (see Chapter 3); courting the movement of capital and jobs from Western to "underdeveloped" countries that was to devastate Glasgow, Bilbao and Geelong. Thus in 1961 an ambitious industrialisation plan was announced; with the creation of the Economic Development Board and an expansion of port and other infrastructure. From 1965 a program was developed to attract export-oriented industries; with Singapore offering its strategic location, political and economic stability, efficient infrastructure and low-cost, highly productive and disciplined workforce to multi-national corporations from the West (Singapore '73). The first Prime Minister – Lee Kuan Yew – toured the world offering Western and foreign investors tax holidays of 5 to 10 years, low tax rates and full profit repatriation. A restive labour force was tamed by the consolidation of trade unions into a government affiliated National Trade Union Congress and new industrial relations laws. The government created industrial estates, complete with state of the art infrastructure, compliant workforces and tax incentives. The education system was also revamped and oriented to the needs of employers with a focus on technical and vocational schools. In an effort to transcend ethnic divisions and following on from colonial tradition, English was promoted over Chinese as the language of instruction, politics and commerce.

It took until the late 1960s for such a strategy to be realised. For Buchanan, industrial estates were incidental to the main attractions of Singapore: its location, cheap and regimented labour force and its generous fiscal incentives to foreign enterprise (Buchanan 1972: 69). The indigenous manufacturing sector had a large number of very small and marginal backyard industries. With the inflow of foreign capital – especially from Japan and the US but also from England – these indigenous operations were joined by large, labour intensive plants, especially in electronics assembly, plastic products, textiles and wig making. Electronics alone accounted for 4,000 new jobs in 1969. This workforce was comprised almost entirely of "unskilled" female labour, many of whom had come from domestic service, confirming the New International Division of Labour as both a racialised and gender divided one (Buchanan 1972: 83; Mies 1986). By 1969 manufacturing comprised 15–17% of GNP and 20% of the labour force (compared to 10–15% in 1960). It was characterised by a few large foreign controlled export-oriented concerns and many small locally owned enterprises (Buchanan 1972: 61–2).

Despite such developments, the manufacturing economy remained weak and the nation continued to be dependent on overseas investors, trade and tourism. Even with formal decolonisation, Britain was by far the largest foreign investor – in 1967 British investors and the British government owned two oil refineries, a motor assembly plant, a print and publishing house, ran 500 buses, metalwork and chemical factories and a large number of food and beverage plants. British firms controlled mosts of the international trade going to and from the Malaysia-Singapore region, though this proportion declined over the 60s – from 80% in 1965 to less than 60% in 1969 – as the US and Japan moved into the region (Buchanan 1972: 93).

Over the 1960s and 70s then, Singapore's government moved to stimulate industrialisation, foreign investment and export-oriented development, especially of oil-related products, electronics, machinery, textiles and transport equipment. There was little emphasis on the arts or on conserving older parts of the urban fabric. What cultural policy there was, focused on art for nation-building with its primary role being to negate the damaging effects of a decadent West. To broaden the economic base of the country, tourism was also encouraged, to the point where in 1966 it was the 4th largest foreign exchange earner and by 1969 the 3rd (Buchanan 1972: 137–9)· Despite frantic hotel building over these years though, the industry was limited. There were relatively few hotel beds compared to Hong Kong and Bangkok, and as a destination Singapore had limited tourist-oriented activities. There was local resentment towards foreign tourists, high priced shopping and what Buchanan described as a "rampant Puritanism" which limited the growth of bars, resorts, and entertainment venues (Buchanan 1972: 137–9). This led to official moves aimed at recasting the image of the place – as "Instant Asia" – but also as stable, attractive, exotic and clean, with new tropical vegetation planted along the main roads, hawkers cleared out, night clubs encouraged and locals urged to welcome outsiders (Buchanan 1972; Phillips 2000). In addition there were plans to build tourist resorts, one on a separate island with a casino, greyhound racing stadium, massage parlours, Turkish baths, cabarets and a 100-room hotel. Such developments were exclusively for foreigners, especially Malays and Americans, with Singaporeans present only as workers, because of the alleged moral risks involved (Buchanan 1972: 140). The role of the state as moral guardian of the nation is evident in these early moves to promote tourism and it continues to impact on policies towards tourists and the creative arts. The state also focused on facilitating social harmony through its management of poverty, the labour unions and ethnic difference. Often these elements merged, as they did with actions of the Housing Development Board (HDB) and latterly with actions towards the ethnic enclaves of Chinatown, Little India and Kampong Glam.

Socio-spatial segregation   The early segregation of settlement along ethnic lines persisted after independence, with Chinese, Indian, Malay and European communities localised along the lines of Raffles's original zoning. Thus South Indian chettiars clustered around the city centre, Telego and Malayan groups concentrated near the docks and railroad station and a main centre for Tamils was in the Senangoon Road area, while the Chinese were close to the river in Chinatown (Milne and Mauzy 1990). Along with this ethnic localisation went a concentration of workers in a few central areas close to the port and a peripheral sprawl of elite residential districts and administrative quarters (Buchanan 1972: 166; Ho 1997). The quality of worker housing, especially along the river, rapidly deteriorated as in-migration accelerated. Thus, writing in 1937 R.C.H. McKie observed of Chinatown:

> Festering under grey slate roofs, houses half a million people, a vast sink of hunger, disease, laughter and murder side by side. Streets and lanes tangle like snakes and ladders on a game board; red and black and orange characters hang on scarlet and white banners, climb up walls, splash windows...radios blare into streets thick with refuse, torn paper scraps, slither of fruit skins, lanes are jammed with a hundred races breathing a thousand stinks into smoke and dust-laden air (McKie 1942:43).

To ease such conditions and as part of the nation and economy building task, the PAP charged the Housing Development Board (HDB) with re-housing the slum population. In a way echoing the policies and practices of Glasgow's modernist planners, from 1955 to 1965 housing absorbed 22% of the country's capital formation as the Singaporean government embarked on a massive rebuilding program. In 1960 the HDB began its first five-year building program, the first phase of the most ambitious housing scheme in the world (Buchanan 1972: 68). The appalling physical state of Singaporean housing was documented in a 1966 Sample Survey of Housing conditions. This showed that in less than ten years, 29% of the population lived in Housing Board flats, but that 33% lived in "temporary" *attap* or zinc roof houses. Over half of the population lived in "deteriorated or dilapidated" structures of which 46% were overcrowded (Buchanan 1972: 191). Many of the housing units in tenements, *attaps* and shop houses had no kitchens and inadequate bathing facilities. In contrast, the population of public housing estates were materially well endowed compared to residents of shop house slums or squatter colonies, though 27% lived in one roomed flats (Buchanan 1972: 190–196).

Facilitated by the 1966 Land Acquisition Act, areas such as Chinatown were excised to "prepare for growth and ultimate progress" of the newly formed State. In the process, shop-houses were declared unsightly, uneconomic and redundant, while the whole area was proclaimed a slum. Again echoing the assessments made of areas like the Gorbels and Govan in Glasgow, all of the inner riverside areas were to be replaced by below-cost public housing and medium-cost private housing with a mix of ethnicities (Yeoh and Kong 1993: 20). Within 10 years the majority of the population were housed in high rise HDB blocks. Contrary to the colonial policy of separating out ethnic groups by geography, each HDB block deliberately had a mix of ethnic groups comparable to the overall population. Thus the housing and urban redevelopment program of the 1960s and 70s aimed to foster racial harmony by grouping the different races together in the same estate while also destroying ethnic concentrations and poor quality housing across the city. By 2000 80–90% of the population lived in HDB apartments, a triumph of modern high rise housing design, urban renewal, housing poverty alleviation and social integration. The costs of such efforts was high, as communities were torn apart, vast areas of the city razed and a historically unique urban fabric all but destroyed. Such environments were deemed physically but also morally degenerate. In being declared slums, the urban landscapes of Chinatown and Little India in particular, were demonised and devalued with no conception of their possible restoration or preservation.

Such views were similar to those which impelled the public housing advocates of Geelong in the 1950s (see Chapter 7), Glasgow in the 1960s (Chapter 4) and Bilbao in the 1970s (Chapter 5). Indeed, the building of high rise housing estates to erase social and urban problems was a common strategy adopted across the world from the 1960s until the 1980s. While now abandoned in many countries, in land poor and populous Singapore, this housing strategy continues; with emphasis now on improving the quality of the housing stock and providing more community and cultural facilities. The Singaporean housing program was part of an overall developmentalist strategy which did indeed improve the physical quality of life for the majority of the population.

From this post-independence agenda of demolish and rebuild in pursuit of a modern economy as well as urban form, a new middle class also emerged which, paradoxically perhaps, came to engage with preservationist discourses. Thus it was from within the architecture and planning professions that concerns were first voiced about the destruction of the old city. For Kong Chong Ho a sense of a city and society lost was a class-based anxiety which ultimately emerged as a concern for cultural heritage. Thirty years of unbridled urban development but also mass education had created a class of well-educated and vocal Singaporeans. It was they who joined a group of architects in the 1980s to mobilise sustained support for urban conservation. In this they built on the creation in 1966 of an Urban Renewal Department within the all-powerful Housing and Development Board to create the Preservation of Monuments Board (1971) which, by the early 1980s, moved beyond their limited work on individual sites to study areas such as Chinatown, oversee the pedestrianisation of the Emerald Hill area and intervened to preserve a heritage precinct at the Peranakan Corner (Kong and Yeoh 1994; Yeoh and Huang 1996). Subsequent conservation plans were done for more than 100 hectares of old Singapore – including the central civic precinct, Chinatown, Little India, Kampong Glam and the Singapore River. Such a change was stimulated by professionals and a middle class who, in the words of one of the proponents: '... already have their homes. The next best thing to fight for is their roots, some place in time and space that they can identify with' (Wei, quoted by Ho 1997: 218). But it also came at a time of growing general concern that massive demolition had destroyed a city that no longer reflected an "Asian identity". Further, a downturn in tourist numbers was attributed to the fact that Singapore had "removed aspects of (its) Oriental mystique and charm" in its efforts to become a modern metropolis and that to win back international tourists, Chinatown and other historic sites would have to be restored (Kong and Yeoh 1996).

Thus in the 1980s there began a re-valuing of urban heritage, all but destroyed through urban renewal and the drive for modernisation. This was accompanied by a rediscovery of ethnic "difference" which celebrated hyphenated identities – such as Singaporean-Indians, Singaporean-Chinese – over ethnically specific groupings. In a belated post-colonial turn, Singapore moved to create cultural heritage enclaves within the city. Such a move involved revaluing the urban landscape; a shift in values that can only be understood in the context of a mobile nation-building developmentalist agenda and a move to engage with international (cultural) tourism and the politics of difference. It was also the outcome of members of the creative class defining landscapes in heritage terms and using their class power to see their visions realised (see Chapter 3).

Re-presenting the (Post)colonial City – New Asian Landscapes

One of the major promoters of Cultural Capitals around the world, Charles Landry (see Chapters 3 and 8), noted in 2000 that the possibility of Singapore becoming a city of the arts by mobilising cultural heritage had been squandered by insensitive urban redevelopment. Landry lamented the virtual destruction of the old city, especially of shop houses in Chinatown. Indeed for many, the idea of approaching

Singapore as a centre for cultural tourism and the creative arts, including as a place where cultural heritage was valued, was something of an oxymoron, impossible in a country pursuing modernisation, ethnic integration and the international style seemingly at all costs. When Ian Buchanan wrote of Chinatown and Serangoon Road in the early 1970s, he wrote of a world that was soon to pass. Thus he muses on two parts of what the tourist authority had then designated "Instant Asia":

> There is the cramped and clamorous shop-house district of Chinatown, where washing-poles hang like a million flags over narrow streets choked with taxis, trishaws, hawkers, shoppers and cluttered rows of market stalls; where the whole population seem to live in the streets, in escape from the tiny, twilight worlds of 6' by 10' cubicles which are the homes of thousands of households, large and small; where business is an obsession simply because most people are poor; where every shop has its jos-stained altar to bring good luck and every shop-keeper gambles; and where the secret society is inextricably woven into the fabric of social and economic life (Buchanan 1972: 188).

(Then ...)

> There is the more subdued and fragrant Indian world of Serangoon Road, where the curry-grinder clanks away next to the jeweller's shop with its glittering show-cases; where curry shops abound and every coffee shop has its thosai-seller frying rice pancakes over an open griddle; where the air is heavy with the mingled aroma of sweet incense, curry powder, and temple flowers sold in tiny doorway stalls along the five-foot way; and where – at any time of day – we will always see more men than women, for many wives remain at home, in India, while their husbands earn, in Singapore (Buchanan 1972: 188).

Having marked separate quarters for the different "native" communities, including a Chinese *kampong* on the south-west bank of the Singapore River, the *Raffles Plan* ensured that Chinese immigrants gravitated towards this area. It was in Chinatown that support services such as clan-based accommodation, welfare institutions and the control of particular occupations were established. By 1900 Chinatown's two square kilometres contained 33% of the city's population (i.e. 66,000) of which the overwhelming majority were Chinese (Yeoh and Kong 1994:18). In the 1970s this same small area accommodated 130,000 people in grossly overcrowded shop houses, many of which were over 100 years old. 96% of the population there were Chinese with small concentrations of Indian merchants and money lenders on the periphery. It was densely populated – up to 1,000 people per acre – crowded, with small scale commerce, and overwhelmingly poor. The buildings were typically southern Chinese in design, with narrow fronts, overhanging "five-foot ways" and an elongated structure extending back from the street (Buchanan 1972: 184–5).

While Chinatown had been designated part of "Instant Asia" for the benefit of international tourists in the 1970s, the role of tourism in the Singaporean

Figure 6.1   New Asian landscapes in Singapore

economy remained relatively peripheral until the 1980s. Indeed tourism was seen as a threat to cultural uniqueness and by the mid-1980s with numbers falling, this was recognised as a problem only in the aftermath of the island nation's first recession. Thus in 1985, the price of oil fell and Singapore's major ASEAN trading partners experienced an economic slowdown. The response was a Government-led restructuring of the city state to become "a total business hub". This involved a reduction in corporate tax rates (from 40% to 33%), decrease in employer's pension contributions and incentives to the electronics and service sectors, including tourism. The possibility of expanding tourism was related to the quality of life in the city and its overall attractiveness to foreigners; as workers, investors and managers of mobile multi-national corporations. Connected to this rethink was a consideration of the creative arts as part of what a sophisticated modern city needed to offer outsiders – as tourists and investors (Kong 2000a). Such a rethink included a more explicit valuing of cultural heritage as something of interest to foreigners and tourists. Fortuitously it occurred at the same time as the discourse of cultural heritage was being heard in the halls of the urban redevelopment authority. As a 1983 Tourism Taskforce noted: "in our effort to build up a modern metropolis, we have removed elements of our Oriental mystique and charm which are best symbolised in old buildings, traditional activities and bustling roadside "activities" (Quoted by Chang et al. 1996: 294). It was these which the authority suggested had to be restored, involving a new localised definition of "Orientalism" in the process.

Thus in 1986 a Tourism Product Plan was developed. Its main aim was heritage enhancement and conservation, coupled with a redefinition of Singapore as a modern Asian – not Western – state (Tamney 1996). With a slogan – "Surprising Singapore: A Magic Place of Many Worlds" – the image presented the island as a combination of modernity with Oriental mystique and cultural heritage. The Plan included development of the "Exotic East" in the form of designating and refurbishing Chinatown, Little India and the Raffles Hotel, developing Sentosa Island as a tourist destination and presenting the city as clean and green and centre of international sporting events (Chang 2000b: 39).

It is significant that alongside these changes in economic and cultural policy went moves to define and affirm national values. Such a correlation between economic and cultural policy can be read as one move offsetting the other, as the potentially unsettling effects of mobilising ethnic difference and history was countered by nationalist ideologies and a renewed drive for wealth creation. At the same time as Chinatown and Little India were (re)designated and their populations exhorted to rediscover their ethnicity, architects and planners moved to codify and restore the beauty and nobility of the shop house, and tourists were educated into the attractiveness of heritage and "the Orient"; a National Ideology Committee delimited Shared Values (Tamney 1996: 19). Thus as one part of the State highlighted "difference", another part drew on Confucianism to delimit five elements of unity:

- nation before community and society above self
- the family as the basic unit of society
- community support and respect for the individual
- consensus not conflict
- racial and religious harmony

What became known as the Singapore School places the interests of the majority ahead of the individual. The individual is seen as intrinsically bound up in family, kinship, neighbourhood, community, nation and state with the person ultimately subservient to communitarian interests. These values were presented as the basis of economic growth and social stability. Concern for individual human rights was connected to the liberal democratic system of government and associated with a decadent and decaying West. For Baden Offord, post-colonial Singapore is thereby pursuing a form of Occidentalism where the West is demonised and seen as the font of economic and moral decline, especially in relation to its views and actions on pornography and homosexuality (Offord 2003: 135–37).

In this post-colonial nation, then, the priority is economic development, one party rule and social harmony. The latter was achieved initially through the destruction of ethnic enclaves and the merging of ethnic groups into larger collectivities – as for example Hokkien, Cantonese, Teochow, Hakka and Hainanese speakers become "Chinese" in HBD blocks and Chinatown – which also acted as welfare agencies and the source of national values (Tamney 1996: 96–7). However, an economic slowdown and a need to boost the attractiveness of Singapore to foreign investors and tourists, along with a professional group engaging with an international heritage discourse, led to a re-valuing of heritage architecture and prescribed elements of ethnic culture – food, clothing, decorative and performing arts. Such elements were therefore rediscovered, connected to particular localities and projected into a commercial market in a deliberate effort to engage the symbolic economy and gaze of the foreign investor and cultural tourist. At the same time as "difference" was being rediscovered and valued, however, national values, the English language and strict censorship laws were affirmed. The apparent correlation between tourist, cultural and citizenship policy continues and is summarised in Table 6.2. Together such policies delimit the value of the cultural artefacts that emerge but also pull them in different directions; as areas of ethnic identity are reconstructed and celebrated at the same time as national unity is affirmed. So too creativity is extolled simultaneously with the enforcement of censorship laws.

Chinatown, Little India, Kampong Glam – New Asian Landscapes

Chinatown   Chinatown was the first area to be re-valued within the policy framework of creating New Asian Landscapes. The area was to be divided into three sub-areas, rendered highly legible by colour coding:

1. Greater Town was to be predominantly red and house a new theatre, museum and themed streets;
2. A Historic District was to have mainly gold motifs with its original temples and clan associations and
3. Hilltown with a proliferation of boutique hotels, pubs, cafes and gardens, will be green.

Streets were renamed to indicate their particular role within this new themed precinct. Thus the existing Pagoda Street was to become Bazaar Street, complete with a shopping strip of Chinese craft shops, the old Smith Street was to become

Food Street with an obvious bias towards dining, Temple Street with its craftspeople and merchants will be renamed Tradition St and Market Square will be a new fully enclosed space for fresh produce. In addition there was to be a Cultural Heritage Interpretative Centre to house indigenous artefacts, five gardens to represent elements of Chinese mythology and a Village Theatre for opera performances, poetry readings, calligraphy and traditional exercises. In launching the S$9 million plan, Richard Hu the Finance Minister suggested that is was not about "recreating" Chinatown but rather "recalling and revitalising the Chinatown spirit" (quoted in Chang 2000b: 40).

Chang notes how the popular reaction to these plans, registered in newspapers and public meetings, was one of outrage. The plans were criticised for being overly rigid, an imposition of order, which would fatally tame Chinatown's haphazard lifestyle and destroy much of its charm. In the words of the Singapore Heritage Society (established only in the 1980s), it will be a "new district that is distinct, not only for its sharp delineation of boundaries, but also in its uniformity and superficiality" (quoted by Chang 2000b: 40). The new Chinatown was also criticised for representing a sanitised view of history, with no mention of the back lanes, brothels and death houses which typified old Chinatown "an Orientalist caricature of itself". For those who lived there, the plans meant displacement and the destruction of a familiar social and physical environment. As one shopkeeper explained:

> We were born here and this is home for us...We don't want to do business in the basement of a market complex. It would be like going to hell. We like doing business on road level (quoted by Milne and Mauzey 1990: 38).

So too a writer to the *Straits Times* noted:

> In connection with the continuing discussion of what makes Singapore "home" and not just a hotel and the debate about turning Chinatown into a "theme park" (it is already one, doesn't anyone realise that?) surely one important criterion must be the presence of collective memory (as government plans for conservation) do not always reflect public feelings (quoted by Wee 2002: 226).

For T.C. Chang researching boutique hotels in the area, the policy of renovating and re-using old shop houses allowed an uneasy but productive accommodation to emerge between tourists and locals – providing a unique short stay experience, a local entrepreneurial opportunity and an upgrading of whole neighbourhoods (Chang 1997). Writing of the same area three years later Chang was more critical, noting how the new Chinatown "celebrates a reified image of Chinese culture, one which is distant and distinct from the lived culture of early immigrant life". (Chang 2000b: 40).

As such Chinatown has assumed a value akin to Chinatown's in Australia and Vancouver (see Anderson 1991), emerging through comparable if particular

Table 6.2   The Institutional Framework for the Arts, 1820–2006

Dates	Cultural Policy Creative Arts/Heritage Key Organisations	Tourist Policy	Other key policies/developments
1820-1960	Support for British culture. Physical separation of "Asian" groups. Chinese and Western art taught in a few academies	Trader and administrator as tourist. Adventurers as tourists No real tourist policy	British colonial rule Raffles Plan divides city into ethnic and class enclaves
1959/65	Culture for nation-building Anti-the decadent West	Tourism eschewed in the interests of protecting cultural autonomy	Self rule and Independence
1968– 1980	Western culture as dangerous. Some night spots closed, censorship introduced Core infrastructure established or boosted for the high arts – Art Galley, Symphony Orchestra, Central Library 1967–76 first flowering of (political/leftist) theatre eg 1967 *Hey, Wake Up* by Pao Kun	"Instant Asia" Hotel building, shopping, some nightclubs. Clean green Singapore	Economic Development Board established. Singapore in the NIDL – low wage, low taxing export-oriented manufacturing. Shift to oil refining, chemicals, electronics and finance HDB begins urban redevelopment/slum clearance. Ethnic groups together in blocks 1973–5 oil shocks Ministry of Trade and Industry established 1979 English the main language of instruction
1981–89	Arts as part of the Cultural and Entertainment Service Sector. Support for festivals, TV, film. Artists Housing Scheme Urban Redevelopment Authority creates a Conservation Master Plan Conservation Manuals for Little India, Chinatown, Kampong Glam The Necessary Stage 1988 Artists Village 1988 Ravindran Drama Group (Tamil Indians) 1989 Ong Teng Cheong Report recommends the National Arts Council (NAC), Esplanade Theatres, Heritage Board 1989 Teater Kami (English and Malay plays) 1989 Agni Koothu avante garde Tamil theatre	Tourism declines in 1983. Tourist Product Plan – To protect and enhance heritage Exotic East (Chinatown, Little India) Colonial heritage (Raffles Hotel) Sentosa Island, clean-green garden city, international sports	1983–89 first openly gay nightclub operates 1985 bulldozers in Bugis Street 1985 First recession Singapore redefined as as a Total Business Centre 1988 Shared Values announced 1989 lifting of rent control, ethnic quotas in HDB blocks

Table 6.2 Continued

Dates	Cultural Policy	Tourist Policy	Other key policies/developments
1990–95	NAC established Sub –Station rehoused Review of Censorship Creative Services Development Plan 5th Passage Artists Ltd Global City for the Arts 1993 Tresors art auctions 1995 Theatre Ox 1993 Sub Station annual arts conferences begun	Strategic Tourist Plan Nostalgic, rustic, colourful, stylish Singapore complete with nightlife, spices, family theme parks	Goh Chok Tong succeeds Lee Kuan Yew. Less authoritarian, more inclusive and consultative 1991 Living the Next Lap report with business, living, leisure, transport and nature highlighted
	Staging of gay plays Josef Ng Sing Chor Event Banning of Forum Theatre		1991 Review of Censorship Policy Relaxation/enforcement Singapore = "gracious society"
1995–99	Action Theatre New Asian Landscapes Chinatown themed 1994–6 Forum Theatre	Tourism 21 Singapore as a Tourism Capital – as a business centre with entertainment district, theatre walk, museum and heritage trail, malls. Ethnic Singapore	Creation of Ministry of Communication and IT
2000–03	Renaissance City for the Arts Public Sculpture Plan		Singapore 21. Future in Knowledge industries – Creative Industries Biotechnology
2003–06	CIs to be supported	Tourism 21 +	Hee Hsien Long PM One North and Fusionopolis created

Sources: Buchanan (1972); Chang et al. (1996); Krishnan (1997); Chang (2005); Nathan (2002); Kong (2000b)

processes of racial construction, heritage conservation and place theming. All such staged activities tend to obliterate complex and unseemly pasts while creating an environment detached from that past and oriented to a highly politicised and commodified present (Hauser 2001). Thus in the words of Lily Kong and Brenda Yeoh: conserving Chinatown as a repository of tradition, history and culture can be understood as a means of upgrading the built environment and rendering heritage in material form, but the conserved Chinatown landscape also serves the socio-political purpose of binding Singaporeans to place, to the city and ultimately to the nation (Kong and Yeoh 1994: 29). Place theming Chinatown has both upgraded and transformed its physical environment and disrupted its social order. In the process Chinatown has become something of an antique: distinctively charming but impractical and unaffordable. One result has been the obliteration of slum dwellings as well as the restoration of many parts of the area. In this exercise, spaces have been created for boutique hotels, gays and artists who have newly colonised the gentrified area. Thus as a consequence of cultural restoration, locals have been excluded and property values increased but also new groups have been admitted, some of them boosting the area as an alternative social and creative space. There has therefore been a mix of intended and unintended effects of the conservation move. This has also occurred in the process of (re)creating Little India.

Little India   Early Indian settlement had concentrated – like the Chinese – around or within the city centre. Thus South Indian Chettiars and Moslem Tamils established an enclave adjacent to the business centre of the city – a community of financiers, money-lenders and petty traders concentrated in the High St. area. Sindhi, Gujerati and Sikh textile traders also concentrated in the High St. area; South Indian dock workers and railwaymen around the docks and Tamil shopkeepers moved into the Serangoon Road area to establish a large Indian community there (Buchanan 1972: 185). For Milne and Mauzey, the survival of this latter area depended on low wages, long apprenticeships and controlled rents – all of which were systematically removed over the 1970s and 80s – along with the shop houses that combined living, working and selling spaces (Milne and Mauzey 1990: 37).

In July 1989 it was not the High Street areas that were declared ethnic enclaves, but 13 hectares around Serangoon Road encompassing 900 shop houses that were gazetted as the Little India Historic District. Once designated as a heritage site, any property owner required government approval for alterations. A conservation manual was published and shop owners were given incentives to enhance Little India as a "distinct historic district within which dwells the heart of the Singapore heritage" (Quoted by Chang 2000b: 41), especially through requirements to have shop houses undergo adaptive re-use, restoration and use by profitable businesses.

In 1997 under the aegis of the "Thematic Development Unit" within the Singapore Tourism Board, stakeholder meetings and a Little India Forum were held to elicit views on how best to "theme" the area. A geographer from the University of Singapore, T.C Chang attended this forum and also surveyed residents and shop-owners in the area. From these observations Chang described three ways in which the area was "tamed" – but also revalued within the Cultural Capital – converted from a dynamic and diverse environment to one limited by tourist needs:

1. There was a decline in traditional retailers and outlets as emphasis was shifted to new and economically viable merchants who often have tenuous links to the district. This occurred via adaptive reuse which ensured restoration of the building but also the payment of high rents, often beyond the reach of local, multi-use merchants;
2. By the alienation of parts of the community as their views were solicited but then ignored, and
3. Accentuation of an Indian-ness which is deemed inaccurate by many of the locals, as traditional shops are displaced, housing limited to high rise blocks and diversity curtailed through regulation.

When interviewed by Chang, most residents believed the government's efforts had yielded a pleasant mix of old and new activities, but that there was a predominance of the new. Most retailers were indeed new with only a minority having shops in the same location or nearby. They were chosen on the basis of a colour blind policy which meant that Chinese and Malay shops were entering a region previously the province of Tamils. Most shops were now selling goods to tourists – such as trinkets, souvenirs and food – rather than serving the diverse needs of the nearby – mixed race – HDB blocks. Retailers were less happy with, for example, the hawkers now corralled into being rentiers in the well regulated arcade selling tourist ware rather than the yoghurt of old. The consequence is that, for Chang at least, Indian culture has been reduced to a set of marketable images; something that sells, something that is seen rather than lived or felt (Chang 2000b: 43). By selectively choosing which area and history is included in the precinct and which remains either hidden or is transformed state conservation and redevelopment practices are involved in simultaneously erasing but also inventing heritage.

For Chang, because of the adaptive re-use requirements, the building stock is indeed being restored but in the process, rents have increased to the point where only non-Indian and non-local businesses, including multinationals such as the Body Shop, can afford them. Like so many gentrifications, the transformation has involved a displacement of low income, working class residents by higher income occupiers. In their activities, selling various incarnations of Indian-ness, the shops have also been changed in a process that involves post-modernisation rather than Indianisation. As Chang concludes: "The very essence of Little India – its old style shop houses and buildings – has been given a western touch in the name of conservation…Everything looks so new and westernised, the flavour of India seems to be missing" (Chang 2000c). While such a transformation raises larger questions as to the very purpose and nature of conservation – namely is it about preserving some past or imagined state or about overlaying the old with viable elements of the new (see Chang 1997) – the re-valuing and re-presentation of buildings and their cultural associations as cultural capital in particular ways, is of critical importance to the tourist and socio-political agenda in Singapore.

Accessing the area via the Little India Cultural Centre and touring the Little India Arcade, the tourist engages roadside story boards and tour it yourself brochures to create a "sanitised, safe and user-friendly landscape" (Chang 2000b: 45). With its array of designer shops, Little India is catering to a culture of conspicuous consumption rather than a culture of lived experiences. Chang's survey further indicated that even tourists see Little India as becoming irrelevant to local residents. As one is quoted as musing:

> I feel that the shops have been upgraded and have lost their historic mood, the feeling is not the same as it used to be.

Like Chinatown, Little India is becoming removed from the practicalities of people's daily lives (Chang 2000b: 45). Tourists come to see the architectural facades, visit temples, take photos and window shop. As one of those tourists in 2005, the story boards were actually hard to find, the precinct difficult to discern with its mix of shops and nationalities spilling across what on the maps looked like clearly demarcated boundaries. For me, despite an obvious ethnic diversity – present since the earliest days of this area – there was also the definite presence of shops oriented to an Indian clientele. Thus curry smells hung in the air, shops were crowded with gold jewellery and wedding saris as well as an Indian clientele. As Chang observed, local visitors still come for speciality items like saris, religious items, spices, Hindu videos and CDs, jewellery and they find such goods easily and the whole experience is very positive (Chang 2000b: 46). For Chang, it is local residents – now in the high rise Zhu Jiao Centre – who find it most problematic as their local shops supplying cheap food have now gone.

What has also appeared in this precinct is another ethnic concentration – of Koreans – who on weekends come together in the streets and squares to meet, talk, exchange food, dance and hear music. Present in Singapore as low paid construction workers, the Koreans have added to the ethnic complexity of this area, complicating its presentation as Little India. There is also an array of racial tensions – a strong anti-Chinese sentiment expressed by Indian merchants and an equally strong anti-Indian feeling harboured by Chinese residents towards South Asian labourers (Chang 1997, 1999). Into this mix has also come a new gay quarter, attracted by the area's cosmopolitan feel, ethnic diversity and relatively cheap rents and services (Author's field notes 2005). Such developments fall well outside the carefully stage managed and regulated efforts to present this area as ethnically homogenous and to theme this part of Singapore for the consumption of local and international tourists.

The experience of this place and in Chinatown raises the difficult question of what constitutes heritage and its "value". For the preservation of areas like

Chinatown and Little India as they were in 1970 involves maintaining oppressive activities (such as sweat shops, prostitution, secret societies), sub-standard buildings and a ways of life that in many ways are undesirable and subject to legitimate calls for change. As the Urban Renewal Authority's Chief Planner T.K. Lu observed:

> There is no earthly reason why you should freeze at the point of restoration because lifestyles have been changing ever since the building was built. Moreover, the lifestyle in these old areas is undesirable. The residents are old and poor, the trades are dying and many of the buildings are fire hazards. We have to bring in viable social and economic life so that not only is there money to pay for the restoration, but there is money to maintain the buildings. Our view is that we want to build for uniqueness, for history (quoted in Chang 2000b: 42).

As the Minister for National Development affirms: Our approach is simple: "restore the buildings and let a new tradition emerge" (Quoted in Chang 2000b: 42); a view which ensures that the material fabric of the city, its built cultural capital, is sustained but the intangible heritage of those who previously lived there is modified and may well disappear. However, Chang also documents how the formal processes of consultation led to the mobilisation of the local community and their engagement in re-defining both their streets and cultural identities. The designation and re-valuing of Little India within a post-colonial developmentalist and nationalistic context involved official re-valuation but also localised engagement and diversification. If the overall effect was the maintenance and enhancement of built heritage at the expense of local economic activities, intangible social values and relationships, the value of the site derives from its blend of maintained and recently appreciated building stock but also their diverse occupants and activities. For without the two the area has no utility to locals or tourists nor to the all-pervasive State.

Kampong Glam   In ways similar to the delimitation of Chinatown and Little India, the designation of the Kampong Glam Historical District stimulated controversial discussions on what constituted Malay heritage and culture. Kampong Glam was officially allocated to the Malays and other Muslim traders from the Malay Peninsula in Raffles' original 1822 plan. Centred around the Sultan's Palace and Mosque, the area boomed and grew in the latter part of the 19th century, with wealthy Arab traders creating schools and mosques across the various kampongs (Yeoh and Huang 1996: 417). Designated a conservation area as part of the 1980s planning process, the delimitation of the site involved both the inclusion and exclusion of vital parts. Brenda Yeoh and Shirlena Huang note how such a geographical delimitation may have been spatially tidy and socially homogeneous, but it also excluded major sites of Malay cultural and social significance, in particular the Muslim Cemetery, and the Madrasah Aljuniied Al-Islamiah (or Islamic school) with deep roots in the history of Kampong Glam. Built in 1927 on walaf land

– ceded in perpetuity by its legal owner to Allah – and by one of the earliest Arab traders, the school has played a sustained role in Islamic education in the area. Despite this deep and significant history and the professed commitment to heritage conservation by the authorities, the school was earmarked for demolition in 1996 to make way for an urban park (Yeoh and Huang 1996). Particularly problematic was also the eviction of the descendants of Sultan Hussein Shah, the 19th century pre-colonial ruler of Johor and Singapore, from their ancestral home at the istana (palace) in the heart of Kampong Glam. This was to make way for a S$16 million state-driven restoration project to convert the Istana Gampong Glam into a Malay Heritage Centre. In an effort to showcase "the history, traditions, culture and future challenges of the Malay community", one of its main politically, charged pre-colonial sites, was to be transformed and the original descendents evicted!.

Further contested decisions about what constituted legitimate heritage surrounded this area as its boundaries demarcate what is heritage and what is not. Yeoh and Huang note how such a geographical delimitation may have been spatially neat and relatively homogeneous, but it also excluded major sites of Malay cultural and social significance, raising questions of what is legitimate history and culture as well as who decides (Yeoh 2005: 953). The value of this heritage precinct thus lies not only in its recently appreciated shop houses and interpretation centre, but also in being rendered small and relatively insignificant in comparison to Chinatown and Little India. More so than the other sites, the politics of physical and cultural heritage at Kampong Glam are all too obvious and render it culturally unsustainable.

Thus in post-1980s recession Singapore, heritage conservation constituted one element of a multi-faceted redevelopment strategy designed to stimulate, direct and satiate tourist interest in Asian uniqueness, improve urban aesthetics and transform degraded environments while enlivening their local economies (Chang et al. 1996: 294). The moves to revalue Little India, Chinatown and Kampong Glam should be connected to the economic shift from manufacturing to higher end services, the need to attract and retain global talent and to deal with the downturn in tourist numbers (Yeoh 2005: 948). Such origins along with the limited consultations involved and the economic, social and cultural displacements that have resulted, raise profound questions as to the sustainability of these heritage precincts. For while the newly refurbished areas may be economically viable – as the market has decided which activities stay and which close – they are part of a policy framework which limits cultural definition and expression in place and, as a consequence, can be seen as both culturally unsustainable and politically unstable. In the context of political priorities for social cohesion and economic growth, urban spaces and those who live in them have been re-valued. Located within all embracing policy frameworks, each area also registers ruptures to the well laid plans – as artists and gays move into Chinatown, local traders resist the gentrification of Little India and Koreans complicate its homogeneous image and Malays join academics to dispute the social and physical delimitation of Kampong Glam. The "valuing" of ethnicity and heritage in these precincts has occurred in an aggressive developmentalist and socially unifying post-colonial environment which, while producing sites of rupture, also ultimately limits their value and sustainability.

Performing the Post-colonial: English-language Theatre

Until the 1980s the Government treated art as a reservoir of cultural markers to entertain tourists who wanted to experience "Instant Asia" or to publicly affirm the multicultural composition of Singapore. From the recession in 1985, however, the creative arts were explored for their possible role in a restructured economy, especially one more geared to tourism and the Cultural Industries. In 1988 an Advisory Council on Culture and the Arts was established and in its1989 report, it recommended the creation of a range of physical and organisational infrastructure to support the creative arts. In particular the Cheong Report recommended the establishment of a National Arts Council (NAC) to regulate funding to individuals and groups, a Heritage Development Board to oversee the five existing and any new museums and a massive theatre and performance centre – The Esplanade – Theatres by the Bay. In the light of experiences documented for England (with the Myerscough Report regularly cited), the United States, Hong Kong and Australia, Singapore was to pursue the new knowledge economy by becoming an international centre for the arts (Tamney 1996: 154).

The aim was to become a thriving arts, cultural and entertainment centre. As a Global City for the Arts (1992) and then as the Renaissance City (1999), policies and practices were to further a set of socio-cultural and economic objectives. First a cultured city was to forestall the out migration of talented locals and foster national pride. Secondly the policy shift was also part of a socio-economic strategy of attracting tourists and competing for corporate, high skilled "foreign talent". In the face of globalising and mobile corporate capital, the policy was a response to a sense that Singapore was sterile and dull, lacking in the cultural attractions necessary to attract but also retain high level professionals and corporate executives. Such a move was impelled by figures which revealed that in 1992 100,000 Singaporeans were living and working overseas and a 1997 Master Card International survey which reported that one in five Singaporeans wanted to emigrate.

But the policy also emerged from an internal assessment of the island's economy and society, which noted that once a high level of personal material well being had been attained, then it was possible to pursue and support the creative arts. It was Lee Kuan Yew who in the late 1980s observed, following the theories propounded by the psychologist Abraham Maslow, how a human being has first to satisfy their physical needs like food, water, clothing. Second they seek safety, to feel secure and protected. Third, a person needs to belong, to be accepted before seeking esteem and recognition. Fifth, they need and seek self-development, intrinsic fulfilment of their artistic, aesthetic, or creative nature. For Yew, following Maslow, the lower of these five needs must be satisfied before they and the nation pursue the higher needs (Quoted by Tamney 1996: 18). Having single-mindedly pursued economic development, physical renewal and social integration from 1965 to 1985, it was highly appropriate in this linear and developmentalist view and in the face of slowing growth, to now foster the arts. Later the new Prime Minister Goh Chok Tong in his 1999 National Day speech noted: "If Singapore is a dull, boring place, not only will talent not want to come here, but even Singaporeans will begin to feel restless" (Chang 2000a: 820). A new official emphasis on the creative arts was therefore part of a dual social and economic agenda; one primarily driven by the need to restructure the economy but also to enrich the society.

Subsequently the arts were expected to contribute to the symbolic economy via three nodes:

1. An art and antique trading and auction centre,
2. A theatre hub of South East Asia, and
3. An entertainment destination for tourists and leisure seekers (Yeoh 2005: 949).

The twin aim was to nurture local arts appreciation and aesthetics and to support local and overseas creative talents via "our Asian heritage …even as we evolve a Singapore identity" (Yeoh 2005: 949). As a Renaissance City and a Global City for the Arts, Singapore is to become a place where local, regional and international arts and culture can be displayed and consumed in a "cosmopolitan city plugged into the international network where the world's talents and ideas can converge and multiply" (STB 1996: 9 Quoted by Chang 2000a: 1). However, as Chang observes: to be a Global City of the Arts involves developing world-class venues for cultural events while also ensuring that local arts, needs and values are not compromised. He further argues that this global-local nexus may be achieved in three ways: by striking a balance between the economic and humanistic objectives of the arts; by encouraging the global export of local talents alongside the import of foreign artistic talent, without Singapore becoming the Borrowed Arts city; and by realigning local regulations and mindsets in line with international best practice, especially in relation to censorship laws (Chang 2000a). I would go further and suggest that such an ambitious set of objectives requires a new national character, one already recognised as needed by the Singaporean State – adventurous risk takers, independent, creative thinkers unfettered by physical and social restrictions. As Tamney observes, public discussion has moved from the need for discipline to the need for creativity (Tamney 1996: 70). But as he himself painfully found out, as an academic, if opinions and actions diverge from official lines, the personal consequences are high, in his case, the loss of employment, threat of imprisonment, involuntary exile and massive fines (Tamney 1996). There is therefore a fundamental contradiction at the heart of Singapore's ambitions to be a Cultural Capital – between State regulation of the arts and the stated need for the arts to be at the core of a new creative economy. Such a contradiction makes the agenda unsustainable despite the success of its realisation on a number of fronts – with the city now a regional centre for international performances and auctions

– but not yet a city where local theatre or visual art has the requisite freedom to flourish.

The global comes to Singapore

Having moved to actively support the creative arts, the short term aim is to become a regional arts centre – to match Melbourne and Hong Kong – as a step towards becoming a global Cultural Capital akin to London and New York (Chang and Lee 2003: 130). Building on its experience as a regional trading entrepot, Singapore is to become a regional centre at the intersection of Asian travel and tourist routes, by firstly courting major international – ie Western – acts. Thus, during the 1980s *Les Miserables, Miss Saigon, Phantom of the Opera, Aida, Saltimbanco, Chicago, Cats* and *Masterpieces from the Guggenheim Museum* were brought to the island. The success of such strategies were confirmed when Michael Jackson's two day concert in 1993 attracted many Indonesians and Malays, to earn the hotel industry $S1 million in a single weekend (Chang 2000a: 826). Popular and profitable musicals and blockbuster art shows from the centres of Western culture – London and New York – are therefore bought into the region by Singaporean entrepreneurialism. Housed in the new Esplanade – Theatres By the Bay or in the major art galleries, such shows reveal both an engagement with global culture and a neo-cultural colonialism, in many ways akin to that shown by the Guggenheim in Bilbao and by those organising the performing arts agenda of Glasgow 1990. Similarly Singapore has also encouraged the art auction houses Southerby's and Christies along with Tresors, an international art and antique fair, and the head office of Cirque du Soleil to locate and operate in the city, further engaging the city with major Western art and performance organisations.

The value of such events and activities to Singapore is primarily measured in terms of economic turnover and regional profile as a centre for entertainment tourism. However, as a post-colonial nation, such a strategy has strong neo-colonial resonances as the highest artistic values are ascribed to imported Western products. Singapore is to be a regional centre of the arts by being at the cross roads of Western cultural trade, not by initiating and supporting its own high quality work. It was this importing agenda which was to receive most official financial and other support. Engagement with the global Cultural Industries was to be made possible and boosted by the building of the gigantic *Esplanade – Theatres by the Bay*.

On six hectares of prime harbour-side land, the complex is an assemblage of several theatres and performance spaces in a spectacular building on the water, a building which visibly transforms the city's skyline, waterfront and aerial view (Yeoh 2005: 949). Costing over S$S400 million, it is a major investment, designed to put Singapore on the global map for arts and cultural tourism. Inspired by the local Darian fruit, it comprises five performance spaces: a 2,000-seat Lyric Theatre, a 1,800-seat Concert Hall, three smaller studios and a range of outdoor performance spaces. It was designed to "usher in a new Asian Renaissance" (quoted by Yeoh

2005: 949). At the time it was announced, arts practitioners expressed concern that with its high rentals and scale, the Esplanade would only be available to blockbuster events such as foreign pop concerts and Broadway shows and would be far less accommodating towards smaller, local, experimental and non-profit productions. In the words of one critic: "It will be a salubrious venue for top performing groups from the developed world as they cycle through Asia while having no benefit for Singapore experimental art" (Chang 2000a: 824).

When in Singapore in August 2005 the major show being promoted was *Stomp* "currently celebrating its 11th year on Broadway and its 3rd year on London's West End...Internationally famous on Broadway, this award-winning British-created production repeatedly induces thunderous applause from delighted audiences and sold-out houses world-wide" (Brochure 2005). While confirming the necessity to import high profile and obviously successful acts from the global centres of Western culture, such a show is also necessary to fill a 2,000-seat auditorium and fulfil Singapore's ambitions of being the regional centre for (Western) arts. With citations from Melbourne, Chicago, London and New York papers, the provincialism of such a performance is obvious. The prices for attendance – students at S$50 up to S$110 for premium or S$320 for a family package – also confirm the relative exclusivity and affluence required to engage with such an event and further suggests that an international not just a middle class and affluent domestic market is being targeted.

The Esplanade though, does have a number of smaller and outdoor theatre spaces and has become part of a broader policy of encouraging and educating Singaporeans into the creative arts. Thus at the same time as *Stomp* is being performed, a series of free lunch time concerts and weekend performances were being promoted. These included local bands, performance groups and musicians doing movie music, love songs and jazz. For as the 1989 Report noted and subsequent plans confirmed, there is a need to ensure audience education in Singapore and therefore an active outreach program. Thus as Chang and Lee note: To realise its social objectives the National Arts Council organises many accessible art activities, by organising regular arts festivals, establishing an arts radio station and taking art activities to parks, shopping malls, office buildings and HDB blocks. In 1998 a total of 143 outreach programs were organised attracting an audience of over 99,000 (Chang and Lee 2003: 135). They also note that despite such activities, the level of popular participation and awareness in the arts is low with a series of interviews and surveys indicating that only the Singapore Arts Festival, the two major art schools – the Nanyang Academy of Fine Arts and Las Salle – and the Singapore Museum were known by over 80% of respondents (Chang and Lee 2003: 136).

While the *Esplanade-Theatres by the Bay* was known by 62% of respondents in 2002, it was not attended by many. Thus only 25% of Singaporeans have ever attended an arts/cultural performance compared to more than 33% in Hong Kong and almost 100% in Melbourne (MITA 2000 quoted by Chang and Lee 2003: 136) with cost, aesthetic distance and sense of class exclusivity being the main deterrents. Indeed, when I visited the Esplanade on a weekday morning, most of those around me were foreign tourists photographing the space and the building itself. Entering the theatre complex during the day time via tunnels under the major roads, I encountered an array of homeless people sleeping along the walls. In this vast, pristine, white space; this walkway from the car park to the air conditioned theatre, which only the wealthy could afford, was some of the underbelly of this very modern city. Along the riverside walk which runs adjacent to the theatre complex, apart from the open spaces and restaurants, there was a demonstration by Falung Gong members against their treatment in China. Illegal under Singaporean law, such a show of political protest in this popular tourist haunt, confirmed its utility as offering a public space in which all types of performances could occur. As with Chinatown and Little India, what then occurs on these tamed and well regulated places, is often well outside what is intended (Author's field notes 2005).

As an aspiring global city and Cultural Capital, then, Singapore is adopting a systematic strategy of building major infrastructure and engaging with the metropolitan centres of performance art and cultural tourists in a way very similar to Bilbao. In this sense, as part of a tourist agenda, venues such as The Esplanade are sustainable economically if not culturally. However, in another component of the theatre world in Singapore, in the smaller scale performance sector, the local side of this globalised arts agenda is shown to be present but highly prescribed, to the point of being limited in its value and sustainability but also vital and questioning.

The oppressive locality – Forum Theatre, gay theatre and censorship

If Singapore is to become an international centre for the creative arts, it not only needs an official commitment to the task and high quality infrastructure, but also an open and tolerant society. One indicator of this is not the shows that appear in the Esplanade, but the ways in which social minorities and contentious social issues are performed – be these to do with the ethnic mix of the country, its politics or being gay. As part of the moves to become a Renaissance City for the arts, Singapore has become far more relaxed about such matters, but as a number of cases indicate, there remains a sense that artistic freedom has to occur within State sanctioned boundaries of moral rectitude and social acceptability, with the costs of crossing those boundaries being extraordinarily high. In such a context, I will argue that Singapore cannot become a sustainable Cultural Capital – as a place actively pushing artistic boundaries and connecting these to innovative Cultural Industries. As an arts capital, because of the ways in which the creative arts are over-regulated Singapore is unsustainable politically and culturally but not economically.

Such a judgement emerges primarily from a consideration of the political context in which the creative arts have to operate. So while there is an apparent wealth of funding and infrastructure, there is not a social and cultural milieu which fosters creative arts practice. Thus in the 1990s, censorship involved three organisations – the PELU (Public Entertainment Licensing Unit), the Censorship

Division of the Ministry of Industry, Technology and the Arts (MITA) and the National Arts Council (NAC). The PELU is part of the Criminal Investigation Department, staffed by police charged with overseeing public order issues. In their work with the arts and public performances they are guided by lists of Dos and Don'ts – mostly don'ts – such as: don't use the word "fuck", don't allow any language or gesture that appears to encourage gay behaviour, don't make fun of civil servants, don't simulate the sex act, don't criticise the government, don't encourage communists (Yeo 1994: 54). As part of the apparently more relaxed and consultative style of Prime Minister – Goh Chok Tong – and in the light of efforts to become a Global City of the Arts there was a review of such censorship policies and a relaxation of them in 1991 (Yeo 1994: 59). With the easing of censorship rules, greater freedoms were accorded, if the age limit of audiences was assured (ie over 18), nudity and ouvert provocation avoided. After the relaxation of rules there was a flood of soft porn movies from Hong Kong and a growth in movie attendances. Subsequently a new code eliminated these films under a policy of "prudent liberalization" (Tamney 1996: 155). Such policies also impacted upon gay and lesbian theatre – an off limits subject matter for public performance art and activity in Singapore, with very few exceptions, up until the mid-1980s (Heng 2005). I will consider the treatment of gay subjects in theatre as an indicator of social and political tolerance in the Global City of the Arts. For as Richard Florida has convincingly argued, if a society is tolerant of social difference, including around issues to do with sexuality, then it offers the milieu in which creativity may flourish. If it does not, it cannot expect to be a Creative City (Florida 2002).

Gay theatre   In 19th century Singapore, following on from its Victorian inheritance, homosexuality was deemed illegal via section 377 of the Indian Penal Code. In 1938, as war in Europe loomed, these laws were made more explicit with the enactment of Section 377a which criminalised male homosexuality. Despite such laws, there was a transgender scene around Bugis Street in the 1950s. Famous for its ouvert transvestites, many came to this part of the city in search of sexual freedom. Moved on by police in the early 1980s, the street remained a site for sexual transgression such that in 1985 it was bulldozed in the name of urban redevelopment. There were a few gay bars in the city centre around Orchard Road, but most had been closed or forced to move during their invariably short history over the 1960s and 70s (Heng 2005). As Singapore moved to be more open to international ideas and tourism, in 1983 the first full time gay disco was opened in the Far East Plaza on Orchard Road. Within a policy agenda that was actively encouraging the creative arts, the late 1980s saw gay plays being written and performed. Such activity was further encouraged by the 1991 relaxation of the rules to secure a permit for any public performance and licences for any bars. In 1992 there was at least five staged readings and eight fully realised productions of eleven plays with gay, lesbian or transvestite characters or themes (Peterson 1994: 65). Under the new rules all new plays did not have to send their scripts to the PELU but could 'self-censor'. From this time, one play was allowed to proceed provided it limited access to those over 18, another was banned and upon appeal allowed to proceed as was a further one.

Compared to the financial support provided to the Esplanade, that available to other, smaller theatre groups and artists is miniscule – around S$3 million compared to S$400 million in 2000. However, despite the limited financial backing, Singaporean theatre has been very active and innovative since its revival in the 1980s. Before then, there had been classical Chinese theatre and smaller groups associated with the Malay and Tamil populations as well as a long history of derivate English language theatre (Birch 1997). Once English was made the major language of education, it was in this arena that a number of key organisations emerged. Thus in 1985 the cross cultural *Theatreworks* was established, the bilingual Chinese-English *Theatre Practice* in 1986 and in 1987 *The Necessary Stage*. *Theatreworks* was the first English-language professional theatre company in Singapore. It explicitly aimed to decolonise local theatre by putting Singapore characters, situations and language on stage. It borrowed readily from Western and Eastern dramatic traditions and has exchange programs with Malaysia and the United States (Birch 2004).

Theatreworks was one of a number of independent theatres which consciously attempted to push the boundaries of what was acceptable performance art in Singapore. This included engagement with the always risqué subject of sexuality. Thus *Private Parts* by Michael Chang was a serious comedy about transsexuals. The play concerned the emotional – but tactfully the non-physical – relationship that develops between a man who undergoes a sex-change operation and a heterosexual male with whom the transsexual falls in love. The director Ong Keng Sen wrote:

> The gender tension and ambivalence in transsexuals allow us to explore social liberalization in the Singapore of today, societal acceptance, tolerance and ultimately society itself. But finally *Private Parts* moves beyond the peripheral world of this small minority and speaks of human frailty, our need to be accepted and our fear of rejection in social interaction.

For William Peterson, surveying the fraught portrayal of sexual minorities in Singaporean theatre: "Given the social and legal constraints which militate against the open expression of homosexuality in Singapore…Chang's play becomes a moving plea for greater tolerance by the general public for same-sex relationships" (1994: 67). Despite – or perhaps because of – its risqué subject matter, the play's two-week run sold out.

Despite the artistic and commercial success of plays such as *Private Parts*, efforts to push the boundaries of the new censorship regime quickly revealed its fragility. At the Artist's General Assembly, a week-long art festival that took place at the *Fifth Passage Galley* in the Parkway Parade Shopping Centre from December 26, 1993 to January 1, 1994, there was a mix of installations, live music, poetry, readings, videos, performance art and a forum on the state of alternative art. Organised by *The Artists Village* – founded in 1988 by Tang Da Wu – in two acts, Shannon Tham vomited on stage and in another Josef Ng Sing Chor turned his back to the audience and snipped his pubic hair. Both artists declared that their actions were in protest at the arrest of 12 men for allegedly committing homosexual solicitation and the unfair press reporting which accompanied the arrests. They defended their acts as performance art (Langenbach 2003). Press reports in Chinese and English papers and sensational photos led some members of the public to protest vehemently, calling on the NAC and the government to act against vulgar performances. Academics from the National University also condemned the performance, while admitting they had not seen it. The NAC wrote: "The NAC finds the acts vulgar and completely distasteful and deserve public condemnation. By no stretch of the imagination can such acts be construed and condoned as art. Such acts, in fact, debase art and lower the public's esteem for art and artists in general" (NAC quoted by Choy 1994: 4). They went on to note that the *Fifth Passage* and any other organisation that staged such performances could not expect to receive any kind of assistance in future from the NAC and pursued the artists with individual charges in court. Ng was fined $S1,000 for performing "an obscene act in public". Iris Tan was also fined while Joseph Ng and Shannon Tham were "banned" from performing or exhibiting art in public (Choy 1994).

While not diverging from surveyed popular views on sexuality, the role of censorship has had an overall dampening effect on the Singaporean art scene while also perpetuating a hostile climate towards sexual difference. Thus a national survey in the mid-1990s – the time when the city proclaimed itself a Global City of the Arts – indicated that 48% wanted a complete ban on the depiction of homosexuality, with 40% suggesting that a "Restricted" category be used for non-artistic films that had sexual or violent scenes (Tamney 1996: 156.) Other surveys indicate that sexual conservatism may be most strongly supported not by tradition-oriented Chinese but by Christian and Muslim Singaporeans. Such views may indicate that bans on homosexual activity and representations may indeed be culturally sustainable, in that they are well supported by the broader population. However, this is not to condone them as right or to admit that such views do not damage the creative arts and Creative City agenda. As Richard Florida argues, the Creative Class is attracted to and comfortable with technology, talent and tolerance. Without the latter, such people go elsewhere or are stifled. Such a prediction is confirmed by the experience of Madeleine Lim, a Singaporean film maker and lesbian who now lives in San Francisco (Lim 2005). In a 1997 interview she tells of her decision to leave:

> I wanted a lesbian community around me to organise within, to be an active part of. Since that was not possible in Singapore, I decided to explore other countries (quoted by Offord 2003: 153).

While openly gay bars and precincts were observed and noted by others in Singapore in 2005, the ongoing intolerance towards ouvert displays of political, ethnic and sexual difference is part of what I would argue is an unsustainable and non-creative culture. The actual stifling of individual self-expression – depicted as a Western vice – is integral to the nature of the Singaporean State and its engagement with the realities of artistic work. This is painfully obvious in policies and actions in relation to Forum Theatre.

Forum Theatre   Because of the nature of performance art – no script, little equipment, no stage and with few resource needs – it is hard to police. After the Ng-Shannon episode, the government stigmatised an entire art form as having the potential to "agitate" the public, "propagate" deviant messages and "subvert" the government (Langenbach 2003: 3). As a result organisers of script-less public performances are now required to provide a synopsis when applying for a licence; if approval is given the organiser will have to put down a security deposit (Tamney 1996: 155–6). Anxiety about performances that cannot be scrutinised in advance extended to another form of work conducted without scripts – Forum Theatre – which has been explicitly linked to political subversion. Thus two highly respected Singaporean artists – the Director of The Necessary Stage Alvin Tan and the resident playwright Haresh Sharma – were reported in the Straits Times as having attended the Marxist-inspired Brecht Forum in New York where they learnt about the change-oriented and political nature of Forum Theatre. Learning about theatre of the oppressed was, by definition, suspect, let alone putting the techniques into practice.

In a reflective essay on the two Forum Theatre events staged at *The Substation* in 1993, Sanjay Krishnan describes how the opportunity for the audience to participate and direct the course of action in the plays led to "an extraordinary transformation both of the theatrical space and of the audience" (Krishnan 1997: 201). Thus in the performance space, previously controlled and directed by actors and directors was a mix of "humour, emotion and reflection" as the audience became involved, accepted responsibility and were moved. "They freely spoke their minds and took the risk of acting before strangers. Art had opened a space for dialogue and self-expression…what I saw was the transformation of audiences from passive consumers to active producers of meaning" (Krishnan 1997: 203 and 206). With this sort of agenda unremarkable in the theatres of Scotland, Spain, North America and Australia, it is both extraordinary but perhaps also not surprising that Forum Theatre was banned in Singapore from 1994 until 1996.

In 1994 the Ministry of Home Affairs and the then Ministry of Information and the Arts issued a joint statement to ban script-less art forms such as Forum Theatre because the government was worried that such performances "may be exploited to agitate the audiences on volatile social issues, or to propagate the beliefs and messages of deviant social or religious groups, or as a means of subversion' (Quoted by Chow 2005). However, as Krishnan makes clear, the only serious threat was one of scrutiny and control when what is needed is "an atmosphere of trust and tolerance" as a foundation for addressing issues crucial to the growth of the nation (Krishnan 1997b: 211). As the eminent Singaporean director of Chinese and English theatre and founder of The Substation and The Practice Performing

Art School Kuo Pao Kun noted in an *Arts Magazine* article reprinted in *The Straits Times*: "State management has been greatly suffocating in spirit and political in orientation because their allegiance requires them to be subservient to government politics", such that strong government control over the arts undermined the objective of making Singapore an arts hub (Chow 1996). The value of such work is very low, ascribed to the few who produce it, critically engage with it and who attend performances – small in number and falling – in contrast to those who attend the Esplanade blockbusters (Tan 2004).

Sustaining the Creative Arts in Post-colonial Singapore

Post-colonialism is a dispersed set of discourses "which negotiate the ideological, social and material structures of power established under colonialism" (Jacobs 1996: 25). Post-colonialism acknowledges that places emerging from the colonial experience not only have imprinted on their landscapes and societies this legacy, but that they seek to interpret and remake those landscapes and social relations.

Anne McClintock (1992) and Gyatri Spivak (1993) both argue that the emphasis by writers such as Edward Said (1978) on the power and discursive project of Europe in creating something called a colonised Orient, once again places Europe and heroic masculinity at the centre of Asian history. So too Homi Bhabha's (1990) focus on the troubled meshing of imperial and colonial subjects to generate mimicry or create hybridity attests to a triumphalist view of the Imperial project and the inevitably lesser role that a colonial agent might play. But another reading is possible. For Leila Gandhi, "postcolonialism can be seen as a theoretical resistance to the mystifying amnesia of the colonial aftermath. It is a disciplinary project devoted to the academic task of revisiting, remembering and, crucially, interrogating the colonial past" (Gandhi 1998: 4). Such an interrogation needs to acknowledge the agency and power of those involved, including that of the colonising nation. So, as Gandhi continues: "the cosmetic veneer of national independence barely disguises the foundational economic, cultural and political damage inflicted by colonial occupation" (Gandhi 1998: 7). In the case of Singapore this "damage" was basically the creation of a particular economy and society which became politically independent in 1965. A post-colonial perspective involves recognising the importance of the colonial relationship to the history of this city as well as detailing the terms of its post-colonial present. With Singapore, the very creation of this place as a town and port was fundamentally connected to the trade, security and investment priorities of the British and its great power rivalries before the shifting dynamics of Asian empires. That the island was populated by Chinese, Malays and Indians was also related to the economic and social relations the British had established with these countries and the ideological baggage attached to each ethnic group, all of which facilitated migration, provided a source of employment and wealth for some and thereby largely shaped their place in the emergent social order.

The post-colonial agenda of social stability through wealth creation, the management of ethnic and class differences and assertion of national values and the political dominance of the PAP has all been variously imprinted on the urban landscape of Singapore. Most recently, the need to shift the economic structure away from manufacturing towards (or back to) high order services has involved the mobilisation of the creative arts and cultural heritage. With a new view of the arts has gone financial support of arts infrastructure and a globalised perspective as well as the re-valuing of heritage precincts and the construction of massive theatres, museums and galleries. A more recent emphasis on "soft infrastructure" has led to investments in smaller theatre companies, artists villages, out reach activities and arts festivals. However, mobilising the creative arts as a vehicle for economic development and social cohesion, also of necessity involves allowing individual creativity as well as international engagement. Pulling in one direction then is a regulatory State wishing to ensure social unity and political control but in the other direction is a Creative City and an arts sector that is both supported and systematically encouraged The tension is indicated in the following assessments of the arts in Singapore:

> The true (artistic) subject in Singapore is fear (of being thought different, of our true selves, of our neighbours, of those in power –many facets of the same fear) that has disabled so many of us from self-expression. This fear has found its natural ally in materialism. The accumulation of goods has been both a bribe for political conformity as well as the only approved outlet for expression (Quoted by Tamney 1996: 157).

> … the performance controversy in 1993–4 meant that there were still limits indicating that playwrights have been and will continue to test the censor's tolerance, given greater liberalisation…they should discover what the limits are. The government and the NAC though should strike a balance between its desire for greater political and artistic openness and the preservation of values that stress authority and consensus (Yeo 1994: 60).

My suggestion would be that despite being in a culture where artists are fearful and shape their work with an eye on the censor, funding bodies and authorities, quality work and ruptures will still emerge. Overall, though such a regime is doomed to be culturally and politically unsustainable. Such a view is supported by the ways in which the creative arts – especially performance art – is valued such that internationally validated work assumes high value and that produced locally is not unless tied to either an acceptable political agenda or to the Cultural Industries while ethnic cultural expression and heritage precincts also assume real value when proscribed and profitable. Such then are the limits on this particular ultimately unsustainable Cultural Capital.

Geelong bollards and waterfront

Chapter 7

Geelong as a Cultural Capital?
Down Under Echoes

The examples of Cultural Capitals discussed in the previous chapters involve cities well recognised for their self-proclaimed status as centres of international architecture (Bilbao), cultural promotion (Glasgow) and cultural tourism (Singapore). While not large World Cities, they nevertheless connect into regional networks of investment and ideas which have in turn been directed towards their transformation through the creative arts. In particular ways, their arts have been revalued and these processes along with their sustainability have been central to this discussion. Each city is located in webs of relations associated with imperialism, globalisation and symbolic economies. Despite these commonalities, each also has particular histories and geographies that make them unique while the ways in which their arts have been (re)valued has, in many instances, led to unpredictable outcomes. While there is still disagreement over the boundary between the creative arts and the creative economy, these examples show how the two intersect and in the process raise fundamental questions of citizenship and socio-cultural sustainability. Whether it be support for a major international gallery franchise like the Guggenheim, a range of decentralised activities of a European City of Culture or the promotion of cultural heritage and performance in Singapore, becoming a Cultural Capital primarily for economic reasons tends also to reaffirm the socio-cultural originality of the creative arts. Official instrumentalism thereby sits alongside local agency and artistic innovation in any analysis of Cultural Capitals, the two often contradict but also reinforce each other.

Despite the ambivalent links between creative activity and non-artistic objectives, the lure of being a Cultural Capital continues to exert its magic. While dating from the mid-1980s and attaining its European and North American zenith by the mid-1990s, the quest to become a Cultural Capital still resonates in the Asia-Pacific region as Singapore as well as Australia and New Zealand seek to mobilise the creative arts in the interest of urban, social and economic development. In what follows, the example of a small regional city in Victoria, Australia will be used to illustrate the ongoing pervasiveness of the Cultural Capital discourse. The case study will show how the various elements of the Cultural Capital idea has been manifested locally to direct official policy and investment towards waterfront revival, the design of a cultural precinct, heritage tourism, urban festivals and in the quest to secure a southern hemisphere Guggenheim museum. Here then are many of the elements associated internationally with being a Cultural Capital consciously drawn together in a regional Australian city to rebuild a local economy decimated by manufacturing decline. Even in 2008, the Cultural Capital agenda thereby retains much of its potency, spurred by successful international examples – like Bilbao and Glasgow – and by the promotional efforts of its key apologists – such as Charles Landry and Richard Florida. Embraced as a panacea by local government as well as a long-neglected arts community, Geelong has sought to become a Cultural Capital since the early 1990s. More recently, and in line with developments elsewhere, the newer discourse of innovation/IT/knowledge capital has modified and broadened the initial emphasis. Nevertheless, the agenda retains its hold over urban planning and regional promotion, a testimony to its resilience as well as the potency of emulation. To understand the ways in which the Cultural Capital idea has emerged in this one Australian centre, it is first necessary to locate Geelong within the political economy of Australian manufacturing and in cultural policy before focusing on the development of the local Cultural Capital agenda and how it revalued particular urban spaces and the arts in this region.

Down Under Context – From Colony to Post-colonialism

Settled in the 18th century as a British colony, the economic foundation of Australia was on land seized from the indigenous population and its development by free convict labour. Along with British capital, such foundations underpinned the export of raw agricultural products – especially fine wool and wheat – and the development of pastoralism, agriculture, towns and cities in the separate colonies of New South Wales (NSW), Victoria, Tasmania and South Australia. As the "workshop of the world" and Australia's coloniser, Britain's trade, expertise, immigrants and investment set the terms for Australia's development. It was predominantly as a supplier of woolen fleece that Australia assumed importance to the 19th century British economy (Johnson 1991). Whereas in 1800 90% of the wool used in the Yorkshire mills was home grown, by 1860 imports had overtaken home production and 40% of these came from Australia, rising to nearly 70% in 1886, making Australia by far the biggest supplier of this huge industry (Hyam 1976).

The role of artists in the new colonies of Australia was initially limited by the demands of colonisation itself. Thus most of the earliest activity was associated with the task of documenting and exploring the new continent as well as in building the dwellings and public buildings needed. As Serle writes: "An immense quantity of graphic records were produced – of flora, fauna, topography, Aborigines and the general progress of the colony" (Serle 1973: 9). Some artists could attain a living through such activity. So, for example Conrad Martens traveled as a scientific artist on the Beagle with Darwin. He later settled in Sydney where he was a fine topographical painter and managed to live by his art through sales and teaching (Serle 1973: 11). Others like Augustus Earle, world traveler and Royal Academy trainee, spent 1825–28 in NSW and opened an art school there, painting two governors, leading citizens and landscapes full of "noble savages" and heroic frontiersmen. He also held an exhibition which, according to the *Sydney Gazette*, was "much visited by the youth of the Colony, and must have had considerable influence in promoting good taste among the rising generation" (Serle 1973: 11). From about 1840 local painting and other arts had acquired a small audience; with a market for lithographic views and patrons happy to commission works. Amateur painting became a frequent past time, art exhibitions viable and colonial architects proficient (Serle 1973: 14).

As for the institutional foundation of such activity, the first Schools of Arts or Institutes were modeled on those established in Edinburgh and London in the 1820s. In Australia, Hobart Town led the way in 1827 followed by Sydney in 1833, Newcastle in 1835 and Melbourne in 1839. In the next fifty years, hundreds were formed in almost every township, aiming for the intellectual, social and moral improvement of the population. In Sydney the main functions were the library, instruction classes, debates (excluding politics and religion) and tuition in essay writing. Pitched too high for many artisans, the classes soon ended and the halls converted to meeting centres as well as dance and billiard rooms. These early Schools of Art or Mechanics Institutes were the first state sponsored artistic organisation – supported by the colonial governments through cash and land grants. They reflected an official view of intellectual activity as fully derivative – with all content British – as well as morally uplifting and necessary for the relatively uneducated populace. Here then the arts, sciences and education were merged and deemed of value by their association with British culture and through their contribution to social and moral order. Such organisations thereby confirmed what AA Phillips was later famously to label a national "cultural cringe" whereby local culture was always deemed lesser than the superior British (Phillips 1958).

If wool was the mainstay of the East Australian colonies up until the 1850s, for ten years, gold supplanted it in economic and ultimately social importance. Thus a mid-century gold rush saw a huge influx of people from many countries – most notably England, central and northern Europe, China and North America. For the southern colony of Victoria, this meant a massive six-fold increase in population: from 77,000 to 540,000 between 1851 and 1861 (Regionalism 1985). Many found their fortunes on the alluvial fields and down the deeper reef mines of central NSW and Victoria, while many others profited by supplying the enlarged population with necessary food stuffs, building supplies and tools. As the gold waned, there was widespread anxiety about future gainful employment as well as a necessity to invest the capital dug out of the ground. There was a concern among the old pastoral and new middles classes that large numbers of unemployed would not only succeed in their clamor to "unlock (their!) land" but they could pose a threat more generally to social order. In the face of such a threat – made real by the miner's revolt at the Eureka Stockade – many more Mechanics Institutes and Schools of Arts were established in major towns and cities and, along with the "free public libraries" had their role to civilise and educate through British values and cultural capital, affirmed (Gibson 2001; Rowse 2005). Landholders also joined ex-miners and local workers in demanding protectionism for infant industries so that it could absorb the looming unemployed. Through the imposition of import duties, manufacturing expanded, becoming one of the most rapidly growing sectors in the east Australian colonies from the 1860s to 1880s, though it still only accounted for 15% of the total workforce and 11% of GDP in 1881 and remained relatively small until the 1920s (Jackson 1977).

The gold rush not only increased the population but changed its class composition, bringing in a far more educated and skilled people, who subsequently supported a wealth of quality newspapers and journals as well as a lively music and performance scene. Even in the 1840s in Sydney and Melbourne there were musical recitals, dramatic performances and choral societies. Sydney held its first major music festival in 1859 while opera was well established. Until the Depression of the 1890s, Melbourne had at least one opera season per year – which was not to happen again for most of the 20th century. From the 1870s Australian theatre was lively, dominated by a small group of actor-entrepreneurs exploiting a large market for imported melodrama.

The wealth that the gold rush generated allowed the further emulation of English institutions, including universities and major museums and galleries. Thus the Melbourne National Gallery was opened under Redmond Barry's tutelage in 1864, the New South Wales galley in 1876, South Australia in 1881 and Queensland in 1895 (Serle 1973: 28–9). The wealth was also invested in cultural institutions in regional areas, and so the Geelong art gallery was established in 1896 along with others in Ballarat and Bendigo with fine collections of British work but later Australian. Associated with these galleries were well supported art schools, again modeled on the British academies. Despite such activity in creating institutions there was little original writing or painting; with artistic activity circumscribed by a lack of patronage, the ongoing quest for material wealth, limited education, provincial deference to British culture and a small colonial market (Serle 1973: 56).

Nineteenth-century "policy" towards the arts by government was therefore limited, confined initially to supporting the artist as a scientific calligrapher involved in recording the landscape and "native populations" as well as building the public and private buildings needed for the imperial project. While Arts and Mechanics Institutes proliferated, and in the latter half of the 19th century, individual art schools, artists and patrons all emerged, official support only occurred through major institutions – such as the colonial galleries, libraries and universities – which were primarily involved in transferring British culture to the Antipodes through their staffing, canon, collections and curriculum. Along with the Mechanic's Institutes, their role was as civilizing and uplifting agents of a colony bereft of any but imported culture. It was only late in the century that more original output emerged – in the form of the Heidelberg school of painters, bush balladists, novelists and a vibrant popular press – but it tended to be based on the work of isolated individuals rather than deliberately supported by government finances or policy.

Federation and national arts

Governed as separate and competing colonies, Victoria and New South Wales had witnessed a massive inflow of capital and people into towns and cities after the gold rush and it was these colonies which drove the agenda for a national market, united defense and exclusionary immigration policies – for the Chinese and Pacific Islanders – in the form of Federation and the Immigration Restriction Act of 1901 (Hall 1998). Such a wave of investment and population also provided the critical mass for an outpouring of original cultural activity in the two largest cities of Sydney and Melbourne. Thus, in the 1880s Sydney's widely circulating *Bulletin* newspaper supported a range of original writing on the nature of bush and urban life, while Melbourne's Heidelberg School of visual artists questioned British academic dominance of the art scene with its *plein air*, European inspired impressionist work.

Under the influence of the dominant colonies of NSW and Victoria, the newly federated nation embraced trade protectionism. Initially seen as a vehicle to raise revenue and guarantee "fair and reasonable wages", the 1908 Lyne tariff on woolen goods, iron, steel and agricultural implements, set a framework and rationale that was to persist well into the century. In the aftermath of World War I, further initiatives were taken by the federal government to boost manufacturing (Connell and Irving 1980). The Tariff Board was created in 1921 and a range of tariffs were imposed on imported industrial goods. The local industrial base expanded to include agricultural machinery, iron and steel making, processed agricultural goods – such as textiles, clothing and footwear – and tariffs encouraged overseas investment into the mainstays of a modern manufacturing economy – especially car and truck making and later into electrical goods and other consumer durables (Linge 1975; Rich 1987). Such investment went primarily to the major capital cities, but also to a few regional centres, including the Ford Motor Company which in 1925 established a plant in Geelong, Victoria. This early 20th century foundation of the Australian economy and society became known as "the Australian Settlement" and comprised political and later military and economic location within the British Empire, a White Australia immigration policy, a generous welfare state, high wage levels and a raft of trade barriers to ensure the development of a protected industrial sector and full employment.

The active role of the newly formed Commonwealth government in protecting local industry was not extended to the creative arts, with only the new technology activities of film and radio considered in any way as industries. While in 1908 Alfred Deakin established the Commonwealth Literary Fund to provide pensions for impoverished writers, such support was but a token effort compared to the policy energy directed toward film and radio. Film had arrived in Australia in 1896 and had been supported mainly by theatrical entrepreneurs out to diversify their offerings, and by the public who flocked to the new picture palaces (Collins 1982). However, by the 1920s, United States interests had captured distribution outlets and through them their superior product began to swamp local production. A Royal

Commission was established in 1927 and charged with examining the fate of the Australian industry. Focused primarily on the place of Australia within the British Empire – but at least now seeing this as a cultural challenge rather than only an asset – it recommended a quota on Empire films. In doing so the Commission effectively ensured the ongoing flood of higher quality American films into Australian cinemas and had the effect of crippling local feature production (Serle 1973; Dermody 1982).

Radio had begun in Australia in the 1920s. Theatrical entrepreneurs – such as the Taits and JC Williamson Ltd – owned many of the first stations and through them made frequent direct broadcasts of their own concerts, opera and vaudeville. In 1928 the Commonwealth announced its intention of taking over the "A" class stations and then in 1929 formed the Australian Broadcasting Company with exclusive rights to them. In 1932 this was replaced by the Australian Broadcasting Commission (ABC) which set about not only expanding its broadcasts but supporting music and musicians to provide their content (Serle 1973: 156). By 1946, with subsidies from State governments and city councils, permanent full sized orchestras were established in Sydney and Brisbane followed soon after by the other major cities. In 1942 the Broadcasting Act was amended to require that at least 2.5% of musical content be Australian – moving to protect the local industry through trade restrictions. The ABC became the main agency commissioning and broadcasting musical productions as well as radio plays and organising tours by overseas artists, becoming in the process a massive concert promoting agency. In contrast to film and radio – and through them music and performance – other creative arts were not given official protection or direct subsidy. As Serle lamented in 1973: "Every Australian industry, except the arts of course, was protected or subsidised; in the great age of protection, governments did not for a moment consider literature for possible assistance. Painters were protected by the difficulty of importing pictures for sale" (Serle 1973: 134).

In addition to actively supporting radio, music and performance and regulating Australian content, the other major role assumed by the new Federal government was over the moral and political standards of artistic expression, though its constitutional powers over communication and international trade. Before the 1930s there were few efforts to ban books, but from 1929 the government tried to protect Australians from anything that attacked the values of the patriotic family man or woman. James Joyce's *Ulysses* was the turning point as the three grounds for censorship – obscenity, sedition and blasphemy – were mobilised. By 1936 5,000 books had been prohibited, including communist texts as well as ones banned on the grounds of public decency and morality. Protests by civil libertarians and the rebellious youth generation of the 1960s led to a relaxation of political censorship, so that by 1970 most restrictions had been eliminated (Serle 1973). But the role of the State in regulating the moral order through culture had been asserted and would re-appear in less obvious guises in the 1970s, through funding organisations, in the ongoing office of the censor and through broadcasting standards authorities.

Stalled briefly by the 1930s Depression, economic growth began anew after World War II and manufacturing continued to expand on its 1920s foundations into the 1950s and 60s. Most industrial activity was centred on the metropolitan capitals but there were also notable concentrations of manufacturing in regional centres – with Geelong in Victoria becoming a centre for textile, clothing and footwear as well as car and truck manufacturing, Newcastle and Wollongong in New South Wales were coal and steel making towns and Whyalla in South Australia a steel and ship building centre (Linge 1975).

As the Australian economy geared for peace in 1945 and the beginning of an unprecedented long boom in consumer capitalism (Groenewegan 1972; Rowley 1972), industry as well as construction encountered a severe labour shortage. Coupled with anxieties about the low birth rate, the spectre of Asian invasion and the need to grow the post war economy, post-War Federal governments embarked on a massive program of population growth – with the aim to boost Australia's population of seven million by 2% per annum – 70,000 from natural increase and 70,000 by overseas immigration (Borrie 1994; Collins 1991; Jupp 2001). Preferring at least 80% to come from the United Kingdom, policy makers reluctantly had to draw from a broader range of nations as the available numbers nowhere met the target. Accessing the Displaced Persons Camps in Europe, immigration officials later joined with manufacturing employers in directly approaching the governments of Greece, Italy and Yugoslavia for potential migrants. While initially explained in terms of the humanitarian acceptance of war refugees, the systematic encouragement of European immigration was carefully linked to the expansion of Australia's industrial base (Collins 1984). Forming 14% of the Australian population in 1954, the overseas born climbed to 20.2% in 1971 and thence to over 24% in 2001. Significantly, many migrants from non-Anglo-Celtic countries tended to work in manufacturing, generally as unskilled or semi-skilled labourers. Thus in 1971 nearly 40% of the overseas born workforce were in manufacturing compared with just over 20% of the Australian-born workforce (CURA 1976: 2). Such a diversification of the Australian population not only impacted on the economic structure but it changed the cultural and creative foundations of the nation in both urban and regional areas.

Such a change was also prefigured in policy circles by post-war reconstructionists who envisaged a new cultural order which had to meet the challenges presented both by the rise of US cultural output as well as by communism. The solution they saw in active support for Australian creative arts and they proposed a cultural council to oversee a touring performing arts company, traveling exhibitions, community art centres, and a national theatre and film board (Johansen 2008). With a move from progressive to conservative post-war governments, such plans were not immediately enacted, but they did provide a model for later actions to support the arts as a bulwark against foreign competition.

Cultural policy emerges – 1950–1970

As affluence grew and the population diversified in the 1950s, knowledge of art and possession of paintings became an adjunct to gracious living, a status symbol. Gallery societies, formed first in Melbourne, attracted many thousands of members. Establishment approval helped educate taste and widen public support. Within the Federated nation, the Commonwealth government had constitutional power over inter-state communication as well as external relations – and therefore regulated immigration, trade and defence – but also gained widespread taxing powers which it could and did use to great effect in relation to supporting organisations such as the ABC. The States had responsibility for service provision within their borders – especially health, education and police – but also assumed responsibility for those cultural institutions that had been created in the colonial period. Local government existed only at the behest of the states, to deliver local services within their limited financial resources. But local government did have a close political connection to their communities, oversaw critical cultural institutions such as libraries and, once they became larger entities in the 1990s, could and did actively intervene in cultural policy.

From the early 1960s a new wave of scholarly art publications emerged and a new class of art dealers joined them, so that individual artists could make livings through their craft. Theatre continued to thrive via private companies but in the 1950s there was a movement to sustain the theatrical arts and secure public funds via a "national theatre". In collaboration with the British Council, Tyrone Guthrie was brought from England to advise on how best to develop local theatre, but he argued against a national theatre. Rage from locals did not stop Anglophile Prime Minister Menzies agreeing, but in 1954 H.C. Coombs of the Commonwealth Bank, J.D. Pringle of the *Sydney Morning Herald* and Charles Moses of the ABC launched the Elizabethan Theatre Trust; to commemorate the Queen's visit, support indigenous drama, opera and ballet, and to realise the ideal of a national theatre. Securing small amounts of Federal and State funds the Trust created a Sydney-based theatre along with a national opera and ballet company. The Elizabethan Theatre Trust epitomises the first phase of what most commentators identify as cultural policy in Australia. Tim Rowse (1985, see also Radbourne 1993) calls this phase "voluntary entrepreneurship" – the efforts of a diverse group of self appointed altruistic cultural leaders lobbying for a range of cultural activities, including the Elizabethan Theatre Trust and the Australian Film Institute, with some Commonwealth support. Proving that government support for the arts was not akin to socialism, spurred by the success of the Elizabethan Trust, and lobbied by those involved in it, the Commonwealth government moved to support other creative arts by establishing the Australian Opera (1956), the Australian Ballet (1962) and the National Institute of Dramatic Arts (1958), therefore ushering in the second phase of cultural policy development – that of official statutory patronage. The Elizabethan Trust further argued for an Australian Council for the Arts as an additional step towards increasing official as well as popular support for the arts

(Johansen 2008). Despite these developments, the level of public interest in the arts remained low and confined to a cultural elite, though it did involve an official valuing of some creative arts and their subsidisation as public goods (Craik 1996: 188).

The limited popular engagement in the arts was to be addressed through the creation by the Liberal Federal government of John Gorton of the Australia Council for the Arts (ACFTA, later the Australia Council) in 1968 with funding of A$1.66 million. Based on an English model, the Council was to ensure arms length funding and peer review. Its initial focus was on those creative arts already well supported – drama, opera and ballet – but also film, which received additional support through the Creative Development Fund, the Film Investment Fund and the Australian Film and Television School. Here then was the active engagement by the Federal government in the higher arts as well as film – all arenas that had long been the subject of state regulation and support from the 1920s. But now the scale was far larger, the amounts more significant and the objectives broader – to involve not only the survival and expansion of a select array of high art forms but support for an Australia film and television industry as vehicles of cultural nationalism.

From the late 1950s there had been an expansion of higher education – with university enrolments rising from 30,000 to 120,000 from 1955 to 1970 (Serle 1973: 211) – as well as mass European migration, so that a market for a broad range of artistic activity as well as a quest to create new material had emerged, especially in independent theatre and modernist painting. Interest in the creative arts and in the newer forms of communication led to greater official attention. Arguments centred on the need for employment and professional careers for artists, for Australia to have its own production capabilities, on the need for a national culture and for broadening the offering to and education levels of audiences. The coming of television in 1956 gave these arguments a new urgency as the dominance of offshore programming raised the need for Australian input and highlighted the vulnerability of audiences to being swamped by outside material. The Vincent Report (1962), confirmed the dominance of imported programming and the need for regulation to support a local production industry to meet local content quotas (Bennett and Carter 2001: 12; Johanson 2009).

The 1960s and 70s thereby became a turning point in cultural policy, with the intervention of the Federal government to create a range of funding and regulatory organisations. These were models of arms length intervention which ensured that support from government was mediated by peer review but also linked to a range of national policy objectives (Radbourne 1993). Flagship institutions were thereby associated with public subsidy rather than regulation alone as well as with a range of civic aims. Along with artistic excellence went a concern for the promotion of a national culture (Bennett and Carter 2001: 12). Creation of the ACFTA and the Australian Film Development Corporation occurred at a time when new technologies, audiences – constitute by technology rather than through actual attendance – and economics, meant the emergence of new cultural forms. For Gaye

Hawkins, it is significant that at this time, "Art" was taken under the caring arm of the state. Not only were there now official organisations for the Arts but, there was a separation between art and mass culture which, for Hawkins at least, "became the cornerstone of this new public cultural field" (Hawkins 1993: 7). Such a simple depiction is complicated by the massive increase in financial support for a broad range of arts, its deliberate diffusion across new sectors in the 1970s – including community arts, indigenous arts and multicultural arts – dedicated support for film and a conscious effort to boost access and community cultural development.

The 1980s have been characterised as a time when this relatively new regime of regulation and public subsidy settled. Utilising institutions created in the 1970s, the regime involved a mixed system based around local content requirements for TV and radio, finance support for film, strong support for national broadcasters, "protection" for the performing arts, visual arts and literature, and expanding programs to support popular music and emerging new media (Bennett and Carter 2001: 13). At a time of trade liberalisation and a "guided market" approach to industries, the main Hawke government agenda to open the Australian economy to more foreign competition was tempered by measures to stimulate research and development and to encourage "sunrise industries". It was in this context that arts advocates began to use terms such as the "arts industries" and the "cultural industries" (Johanson 2009: 145).

For Stuart Cunningham – charged with the creation of a Creative Industries precinct in Brisbane – the main criticism of this era was a lack of *integration* between arts and communications policy (Cunningham 1992). Significantly this was reversed in 1992 with a report on *The role of the Commonwealth in Australia's cultural development* and the creation of the Federal Department of Communications and the Arts with its minister holding a Cabinet place and the 1994 *Creative Nation* statement. These developments mark the arrival of the cultural industries model in Australia where the definition of culture was broadened, the economic value of the cultural industries was explicitly recognised and the "content" dimension of media technologies was emphasised, with their "value" assessed in terms of access and participation, creativity and excellence, cultural diversity, economic viability and export performance (Flew 1997: 173). The arts thereby moved over the 1980s from being about broad ranging creative expression and high brow consumption supported by a benevolent state to an industry that would ultimately drive a different economic future.

From Creative Arts to Creative Nation – 1970–2008

Australia entered the 1970s as a post-colonial country. Developed on land stolen from the indigenous population and with a long history of racialised immigration policies, these foundations supported a vital 19th century pastoral and agricultural economy but also fuelled the expansion of manufacturing over the 20th century. In a post second world war climate of fear about invasion and the need to "populate or perish", racialist anxieties gave way to stronger drives to expand the population, grow the suburbs and staff the burgeoning factories of the long boom. As a consequence significant numbers of non-Anglo Celtic migrants – firstly from northern and southern Europe in the 1950s and 1960s and then, more reluctantly – from Asia and the Middle East from the 1970s and 1980s entered the country. Along with these changes in immigration policy went shifts in settlement policies: from an insistence on their assimilation as "New Australians" in the 1950s and 60s to a multicultural agenda recognizing and celebrating difference from the 1970s. By the 1960s there was also a renewed commitment to addressing past injustices to indigenous peoples – with their admission to citizenship rights, and by the early 1990s the securing of land rights and, for a time, a self governing administrative Body; ATSIC or the Aboriginal and Toorres Strait Islander Commission. Australia, then, can be seen quite formally but also informally as becoming a post-colonial nation, though with ongoing questions about the inequitable social position of indigenous peoples and the place of non-English-speaking migrants. These issues register in cultural policy – primarily through the creation of separate Boards within the Australia Council and the multi-lingual Special Broadcasting Service (SBS) – and in later approaches to and within Cultural Capitals.

Articulation of a broad-ranging cultural agenda had to await a crisis in the manufacturing economy. As in Western Europe and North America (see Chapter 3), the long boom did not falter until the early 1970s. Along with other developed economies, Australia was hard hit by the rise in crude oil prices in the early 1970s, by successful union demands for higher wages, world wide recession and by what David Harvey (1989a) called a "crisis of accumulation" amongst domestic producers. The Whitlam Labor government met such challenges by beginning the process of opening Australia to the global economy; by cutting domestic tariffs by 25%, devaluing the Australian dollar and relaxing the restrictions on the entry and operation of foreign banks. These and subsequent decisions to remove trade barriers meant that Australian industry began a massive decline. Thus whereas in 1960–61 29% of Australia's GDP was derived from manufacturing, by 1988–89 it was 18% (Juddery 1990: 56) with an estimated job loss of well over 100,000 (BIE 1985). At the same time, the economic and political importance of mining and finance grew. A series of government reports offered comparable diagnoses and recommended more of the same as economic rationalism and neo-liberalism took hold (BIE 1985; Bernasek 1986). An Industries Assistance Commission (IAC) Report (1976) approached the performing arts in a similar way, arguing that the arts were like any other industry whose contribution to the economy was measurable and whose subsidisation had to be fully accountable in economic terms. It argued that government support for the arts was inefficient and undemocratic and should therefore be withdrawn. Echoed in other reports on music (1978) and publishing (1978) the IAC argued that government funds would be better spent on strengthening distribution and growing demand (Johansen 2008). The arts therefore had to justify their existence as a public good. Seeing not just film and television but also the arts more generally as an industry had begun. This was affirmed when, from 1995 the Australian Bureau of Statistics (ABS) began to calculate the economic value of the arts.

Moves to further integrate Australia into the global financial system continued to be made over the 1980s and 90s by both the progressive Labor and conservative Liberal-National coalition parties. Based on the formal endorsement of "competition", neo-liberalism and free trade, measures included the floating of the Australian dollar, abolition of exchange rate controls, further trade deregulation (with quotas phased out by 1993 and tariffs lowered to 20% by 1996 and thence to 10% by 2006), bilateral free trade agreements, privatisation of state assets, labour market deregulation, local government amalgamation and public sector employment cuts (Wiseman 1998). Over the 1980s and 90s, the decline of protected manufacturing employment proceeded apace – though with some counterveiling investments to internationalise and technologise what remained of the car, whitegoods and textile industries – along with a concomitant expansion in the service sector, including tourism and what became labelled the *cultural industries*. Such declines were to impact particularly hard on those regional centres that had been built on industry, such as Geelong in Victoria.

The new ideological and economic agenda was also associated with a new approach to cultural policy. From the 1950s, there had been two distinct forms of government assistance to the arts – one involved direct subsidy via the Australia Council or via state and local government support for arts groups, spaces and activities; and the second was the quota system, whereby a certain proportion of radio or television broadcasting had to be of Australian-made material – applied to radio since the 1940s and TV since the early 1960s. Accompanying such quotas has been direct government funding of the ABC and, since 1980, of the multicultural Special Broadcasting Service (SBS) in radio and television – all of which consumes 60% of federal funding. There has also been ongoing support for the Australian film industry, since the 1970s taking the form of government finance corporations and subsidized studios – at Federal and State levels – and occasional tax subsidies. But, from the mid-1980s as the neo-liberal agenda broadened and deepened, the arts in Australia were re-defined as an industry to be assessed as such and held accountable; by government agencies such as the IAC but also by artists besieged by funding cuts and demands to justify their utility and subsidisation. But the arts also maintained their distinctiveness as a social good which had broader cultural roles to play – in relation to national identity – and remained supported through massive government subsidies and tax concessions. As Stevenson argues "As an industry sector, the arts are required to generate economic and symbolic wealth and contribute to national prosperity" (Quoted by Bennett and Carter 2001:2).

As a result policy makers, producers, practitioners and analysts started to use the notion of the *cultural industries*. Once used to indicate the mass-produced and therefore inferior nature of mass culture such a term was now used positively as a way of seeing culture as not only a matter of individual creation and private consumption but the product of complex institutions, sophisticated technologies and specific economic relations leading to public goods (Bennett and Carter

2001:2). The key document and policy setting framework was provided by Labor Prime Minister Paul Keating's *Creative Nation* (1994). This marked the full arrival of the cultural industries model in Australia, where the definition of art was broadened, the economic value of the cultural industries was explicitly recognised and the "content" dimension of media technologies was emphasised, with their "value" assessed in terms of access and participation, creativity and excellence, cultural diversity, economic viability and export performance (Flew 1997: 173).

Creative Nation was the first Commonwealth cultural policy document in Australia's history. Aiming to protect the distinctiveness of Australian culture from global influences, the economic potential of culture was an ever present theme as the document noted how "culture creates wealth" and was essential to "economic success" (1994: 7). One of its objectives was to create the conditions which would integrate "cultural and economic life" allowing art and cultural industries "to achieve sustainability" (1994: 19). This was to be achieved by training indigenous artists to recognise the importance of international visitors (1994: 21), to increase copyright protection for the contemporary music industry (1994: 28) and coordinate international cultural activity with Australian trade and investment (1994: 93; McCleay 1997). Allocating A$250 million in additional funding, the Australia Council was boosted and its entrepreneurial role extended – as its funding was made triennial, it was directed to engage in more international marketing, develop a sponsorship program and create a Major Organisations Board to ensure support for flagship arts institutions. The policy also argued for the creation of a Foundation for Australian Cultural Development (Craik 1996: 189–190).

Creative Nation represented for many the high point in the Federal government's recognition of the value of the creative arts: a sense of culture as more than the arts alone; as it recognised the arts as an industry and constructed an economic argument for culture's significance to the nation. This was an argument based on national identity defined in terms of creativity and national independence. It also included a cultural export/diplomacy argument and a vision that linked culture and national identity to the new electronic multimedia technologies (Bennett and Carter 2001: 5). *Creative Nation* (1994) therefore also allocated $60 million to the Commercial Television Production Fund, $13 million to SBS for local programs and $84 million for emergent multimedia.

Here then was a policy document backed by institutional arrangements and funding that connected the creative arts to the creative industries, seeing them as interconnected and vital for both national identity and economic growth. The policy was questioned by artists anxious lest they be complicit with the official agenda or face a withdrawal of funding. There was also a concern that their work would have to bear the load of national expectations which could never fully be realised while most additional funding went into the large professional companies and institutions. In addition, many were concerned that the policy moved the Australia Council too far towards a market model rather than supporting its role in fostering creative activity (Flew 1997: 175). In rolling culture and tourism together for the first time *Creative Nation* also defined the value of the arts not only as an industry and creative activity but as a set of activities which directly related to and boosted other economic sectors.

The 1990s saw tourism on the national political agenda – having been present but relatively unimportant since the 1970s. As its economic and national image grew – especially in relation to major events like the 1987 defense of the Americas Cup in Fremantle, the 1988 World Expo in Brisbane and the 2000 Olympics – tourism was also embraced as an economic driver. In 1998, the Bureau of Tourism Research reported on the characteristics and value of *cultural tourism* to the Australian economy, and noted that around 60% of all tourists to Australia visit cultural attractions, spending more than the average visitor (Craik 2001: 95). But while tourism was now seen as an industry, cultural tourism continued to fall into cultural and arts policy, meaning a diffusion of effort, budgets and policy as well as a divergence of interests. As Craik observed:

> The tourism lobby essentially is interested in 'bums on seats', bodies in beds and dollars at cash registers, while the cultural lobby is interested in cultural employment, elite cultural improvement and cultural development…In light of the cowboy mentality of the tourism industry and the elitism of the cultural industries, the degree to which genuine partnerships and sustainable programs between these two sectors can be reached is minimal or cosmetic (Craik 2001: 96).

While early studies exhorted the value and potential of indigenous tourism, attention was minimal until the 1990s when the federal department and ATSIC developed an indigenous tourism strategy. Its recognition as something unique in terms of culture, customs, art and habitus was acknowledged overseas long before it was at home but once recognised, its growth has been rapid (Craik 2001: 107).

In contrast to the approach taken by Paul Keating through *Creative Nation*, John Howard's more conservative Liberal-National party government (1996–2007) was opposed to cultural policy being linked to national identity with rhetoric and some actions fueled by an ideological commitment to small government as well as a hostility to the arts community. Despite such a stance, however, and a series of investigations into major organisations with the intention of withdrawing support for them, the outcomes of the reviews were usually to tighten accountability but also to increase finding. Thus under Howard there were reviews of the ABC and Commonwealth assistance to the film industry, but both recommended ongoing – if less – support, noting in relation to film that: "to achieve cultural objectives within a commercially driven Australian film and television industry, there will be a continuing need for government assistance and non-commercial rates of return on its investment (Gonski 1997: 6, quoted by Flew 1997: 177). Australia Council funding was reduced by 12% and support lessened for what was labeled "minority arts" but after further reviews more funds were directed towards major "flagship" theatre, dance, multi media and musical organisations. The Howard government also funded a national museum and portrait gallery in Canberra and overall provided 66% more to the cultural sector that its predecessor under a policy best described as elite nurturing. Despite their apparent political divergences then, the coalition of John Howard placed culture within a comparable economic framework to that of Paul Keating (McCleay 1997).

There are also continuities between Keating and Howard in relation to valuing the arts as an industry. Thus the 1990s saw the emergence of cultural policy as a means of integrating different areas of arts and media policy and linking these to other policy objectives, such as social and economic policy. There was also a change in emphasis to support audience and enterprise development along with a move from a subsidy based (supply) model to an industry development (demand) model (Katsonis 2001). Under Keating this was accompanied by a more interventionist and directive view of culture compared to the Howard coalition which rhetorically signaled a lighter hand while also maintaining much of the institutional and financial supports. The focus then was on audiences rather than practitioners and on the peripheral benefits of the arts – employment creation, cultural tourism, cultural exports and the multiplier effect of cultural activity. These were the (economic) benefits of the arts which made them worthy of support. Both parties therefore saw cultural policy as an element of industry policy and therefore subjected to cost-benefit analysis. But as many cultural enterprises would fail such a test, then other justifications needed to be found for the huge transfers of public monies to the arts. Under Keating these justifications – or frameworks for establishing value – included expressing national identity and forming the foundation of the new economy. For Howard they were more conventionally associated with the value of the elite arts to a more amorphous idea of the nation, but also value as an earner of export income on the "level playing field" of a newly globalised world (Norton 1996: 109–110; Craik, et al. 2003: 22; Caust 2003; Craik 2008).

Relating the creative arts to emergent economic sectors was not the centerpiece of the Howard years, however, nor is it central to the "Federal Labor Arts Policy Discussion Paper" of 2007 (ALP 2007). For here while there is recognition of the importance of "creativity" to "new knowledge-based, information-rich industries and that new media forms …will play a crucial role in this growth" with artists "well placed to be new cultural entrepreneurs" creating content of economic value in cinema, television, popular music and online, there is also a recognition that this is well developed in Britain and Japan but Australia "needs to move towards self-sufficiency in cultural capital and become an exporter rather than just an importer of niche and popular arts" (ALP 2007: 3). In other words, there is a hard headed recognition of the potential for, rather than a booming creative industry sector in Australia, and an affirmation of the creative arts as valuable "in their own right" with access, equity, education, excellence and innovation the foundation principles for both an arts policy and a healthy democracy (ALP 2007: 2). The Federal government has therefore prefigured an arts policy once again concerned with access and equity as well as excellence evaluated without political interference. While Creative Australia (2008) became one of the subjects for the exploratory *2020 Summit of Ideas* – with discussion on the growth of the creative industries, arts education, the film industry (and its failings), digital technology and "democratizing content creation", the popular embrace of but also barriers to cultural engagement, the role of the ABC and SBS as well as the fragmentation of government action – to date there has not been a strong statement of commitment to supporting their development from the new Federal government. Rather, most action on this front has occurred at the lower levels of State and local – especially metropolitan – governance.

Creative Industries and Cultural Capitals in Australia

A 1996 assessment of government funding for cultural facilities and services in Australia revealed that, State governments contributed half, local government a third and the Federal 20%; with libraries receiving most support, followed by museums, galleries, heritage facilities and performing arts spaces (Craik 1996: 193–4). In 2005–6 the A\$5 billion of government funding for the arts and culture was divided pretty equally between Federal (38%) and State (43%) governments (with around \$2 billion each) with local government providing close to \$1 billion (19%). Dating form their colonial era support for major cultural institutions, the level of involvement by the States changed markedly from the 1960s as they became more engaged in boosting their regional economies and state capitals in the face of greater globalisation. Beginning with the first Adelaide Festival of the Arts (1960), the South Australian government later supported this festival through new venues and generous subsidies. Aiming to bring the best of Australian and international creative arts to Adelaide every two years, the festival is one which effectively permeates the city and has become the foundation on which major urban developments around North Terrace and a more general campaign to make South Australia "The Festival State" has been built (Taylor 1994). Other major cities followed suit, sponsoring their own arts festivals as vehicles to enhance their images, cultural tourism and status within the increasingly competitive global urban system (Hawkins and Gibson 1994).

From the late 1970s as manufacturing decline accelerated and the central city office boom faltered, State governments began investing more in inner city cultural projects in a quest for tourists and to deal with the impacts of economic restructuring. Inspired by overseas examples of waterfront and inner city renewal, State governments therefore joined some of the more progressive local governments in seeing the arts as a vehicle to boost not only community development and international profile but also to stimulate social and economic development. Here then was newly heightened capital city competition being realised in Australia as cultural policy was seized upon as a means to address "problems as diverse as the effects of industrial restructuring on inner city areas, the consequences of increased global migration for local and national communities, and ... the negative effects of unemployment" (Gibson 2001: 122). Often located close to or in the Premier's office, state arts ministries not only offered advice but were responsible for flagship institutions, venues and organisations, policy development, administration of funding and liaison with communities and other levels of government. Their core activity was to support and therefore privilege the high arts – visual and performing arts, music, film, dance and literature – in all states. While there was some regional emphases – on nature and the arts in Tasmania, art and higher education in South Australia – by the 1980s, all of the states were using art and arts policy to differentiate their state from others in terms of quality of life and cultural supremacy (Stevenson 1999: 76).

Well before the Federal government embraced the creative arts as an economic driver, the states and their capital cities had noted offshore models – especially around waterfront and festival place developments – and proceeded to remodel their cities accordingly. This competition and emulation extended well beyond the creative arts to include mega precincts and major events which in turn were linked to larger development agendas, which included tourism, industry development, touring programs, indigenous arts, multimedia and multicultural arts (Stevenson 1999: 77). Over the 1980s and 90s, then, State governments worked to attract hall mark cultural and sporting events to their respective cities – including the Formula One Grand Prix first to Adelaide and then to Melbourne, the Commonwealth Games (to Melbourne in 2002) and the Olympics (to Sydney in 2000) and in underwriting cultural precincts, events and festival marketplace development such as Melbourne's Southbank, Crown Casino and Docklands, Sydney's Darling Harbour and Brisbane's Expo (1988) and Southbank arts precinct.

As with a number of the other cities considered here – especially Singapore – the role of Cultural Capital proselytisers was critical in crystallizing this agenda, as both Charles Landry and Richard Florida were invited to visit, speak, advise and generally enthuse metropolitan and provincial authorities with their visions. Thus Landry advised Brisbane on its "Creative City Strategy" in 2002 and had earlier been a key note speaker to the national "Portraits of Planning Conference" (in 1996), was a guest of the city of Adelaide as its "Thinker in residence" in 2003 and highly visible at Canberra's "Ideas and Innovation Festival" in 2004. Richard Florida has also spoken in Melbourne (2002 and 2004) and in Sydney (2004). His ideas had impacted even earlier as his "Creativity Index" was used in the national local government association's 2002 "State of the Regions Report" (Atkinson and Easthope 2007). The Creative Industry agenda was formally incorporated into state planning documents from the beginning of the 21st century as Queensland declared itself the "Smart State" and Victoria's capital Melbourne announced itself a Cultural Capital.

The shift in this direction in the manufacturing centre of Australia – Victoria – had begun ten years earlier. Thus in the face of a moribund and near bankrupt Labor State government, the conservative Jeff Kennett assumed the premiership of Victoria in 1993 promising to revive the state economy and boost the status and reputation of Melbourne through the imposition of an ambitious neo-liberal agenda. As well as cutting the public sector and privatizing state assets, Kennett personally supported the arts through encouraging private enterprise sponsorship, "easing restrictions", better marketing, challenging the Sydney-centric bias of the Federal government, recognizing indigenous arts and acknowledging the relation between cultural activity and other activities – such as tourism, sport, recreation and leisure. His *Arts 21* agenda did not talk about the Creative Industries but rather about an Information Age to which the arts could contribute by being "a creative force in the media and communication sector of the future"; by stimulating content production, developing new titles, utilizing broadband and by adding value to the education, entertainment and tourism sectors (*Arts 21*, 1994). For Kennett, all of this was to occur primarily through investment in the city of Melbourne. As *Arts 21* notes:

> The Capital City vision – Melbourne with a revitalized riverside, major new civic works, and providing world class commercial, social and recreational infrastructure – will create a dynamic picture of a growing, energetic city positioned to expand its role in the Asia-Pacific region (1994 *Arts 21*: 5).

To realise this vision, Kennett embarked on an ambitious building program – commissioning two new museums (the Immigration Museum and new Museum of Victoria in Carlton Gardens), supported a massive casino and leisure development along the south bank of the Yarra River and the redevelopments of the Docklands precinct, complete with a state subsidised film studio and centre for the moving image. There was also support for festivals and ambitious plans to boost attendances at, for example, the Melbourne International Comedy Festival and Melbourne Writers' Festival.

With a change of government in 2001, new policies built on these and emphasised making Victoria the cultural centre of Australia. The aim was to ensure Victoria's reputation as a vibrant and dynamic arts centre and to establish the state as the nation's cultural capital (Katsonis 2001). In the aftermath of the politically repressive Kennett years, this was to be achieved by fostering artistic innovation and creative freedom, ensuring that Victoria was a centre of excellence for film and television and encouraging access and equity as well as regional inclusion (Katsonis 2001). A few years later *Creative Capacity+* became the policy framework in which this was to be realised, arguing:

> Developing creative abilities is of fundamental importance in meeting the challenges of economic development…the arts can play a key role in the transition to a knowledge-based economy and a culture of innovation (Arts Victoria 2003).

Victoria has therefore moved from being a State which somewhat benignly supported those major cultural institutions inherited from colonial times – especially its public galleries, libraries and museums – to a far more entrepreneurial actor, actively using the creative arts to firstly revive the faltering image of the metropolitan capital (in the early 1990s), to then form the core of a waterfront renewal strategy along with a broader economic revival package (in the mid-1990s) and thence to become both a sector in its own right and the centre of a cultural industry agenda based around film and the knowledge industries as well as leisure tourism in the new century. If this then is the state level policy framework, located in turn within a changing Federal landscape, how then does the idea of being a Cultural Capital get embraced by a declining industrial centre in regional Victoria and with what consequences for valuing the arts and sustaining a social as well as economic and physical transformation of the city?

Geelong, Victoria as a Cultural Capital?

Located 70 kilometres south west of the Victorian capital city of Melbourne, Geelong began as a wool port and agricultural processing centre before becoming a major car and truck manufacturing city in the mid-20th century. With an array of related industrial operations – oil refining, aluminium smelting, car components and glass making – as well as significant textile, clothing and footwear production, the city was hard hit by the decline of Australian manufacturing from the 1970s. Partly offset by the growth in service sector activities in health, education, research, finance and community welfare, the city is also looking to the arts, culture, tourism and recreational industries, for its future (Johnson, 1991; 2003; 2006).

While industrial decline began in the 1970s and accelerated in the 1980s, local policy responses initially focused on halting and dealing with the decline – exacerbated by the failure of a major local financial institution – by boosting the central business district and its related retail and business operations. In the 1980s it was accepted that the city was over-reliant on old and declining manufacturing industries, and local planners realised that the city had to become more attractive to emergent industries associated with education, tourism and new technology, though no one initiative – such as the construction of the Geelong Performing Arts Centre (GPAC) in 1981 – had been sufficient to trigger any thoroughgoing transformation. In 1981 the *City by the Bay* plan was developed to revitalise the sagging economy by boosting central Geelong's retail role. This was to occur via a re-orientation towards Corio Bay and through this, the city would capture the tourist traffic which journeyed from the State capital – Melbourne – over summer towards the coastal resorts west of the city. The plan was to extend the Central Activities Area (CAA) – which was placed well away from what was once a bustling and working port – past the empty woolstores down to the foreshore using pedestrian promenades and a recreational and retail complex, along with a range of tourist attractions that could act as a "catalyst for new investment and development" (City by the Bay 1987). With ongoing manufacturing closures and the financial crisis engendered by the collapse of the local Pyramid Building Society in 1986, however, little came of such plans until the 1990s.

From the early 1990s, Geelong more actively engaged international revitalisation agendas. In this, Geelong drew consciously and sequentially on what Stevenson describes as the two main models of inner city/waterfront redevelopment developed in the 1970s and 80s (Stevenson 1999: 89):

1. America's festival marketplace model with its emphasis on theme parks, retailing, street theatre, exhibition spaces and "life style" experiences for locals and tourists. The achteypical examples of this strategy were Baltimore and Boston in the US but also Darling Harbour in Sydney, Docklands and Southbank in Melbourne and Newcastle's Honeysuckle redevelopment, and

2. The cultural precinct or European model based on local culture and difference. The best example of this strategy was Glasgow but Manchester, Dublin and Dundee were also cited as exemplars.

In pursuing these agendas, Geelong was up to two decades behind its North American and European counterparts, but nevertheless adapted these agendas to its particular circumstances while variously affirming the value of its cultural capital to urban revitalisation. In pursuing its new status as a Cultural Capital, this regional city went beyond a re-designed waterfront to pursue major events, a cultural precinct and, extraordinarily, a local branch of the Guggenheim Museum.

Geelong's festival waterfront

While primarily focused on making Melbourne an international Cultural Capital, the neo-liberal state government of Jeff Kennett not only forced local government amalgamation onto Geelong (as well as the rest of the state) to create the City of Greater Geelong (COGG), but also extended his urban revitalisation agenda to the regional city's waterfront. Building on the original City by the Bay idea, consultants were commissioned by the state and local governments to develop plans for Waterfront Geelong. The central feature was to be *Steampacket Place* – a multi purpose pedestrian space linking the foreshore to the Central Activities Area. Tourism once again was the great economic hope and attracting more visitors the main objective. Every effort was to be put into attracting *big* events and along the waterfront, pedestrian calming, public art and accommodating redesign was to be installed. Proposals to attract tourists and endear locals included a Fisherman's Wharf as a dockside restaurant precinct, making the old Customs House into a Maritime Museum, a calm water harbour and possible underwater aquarium. The model explicitly invoked was Boston and its waterfront redevelopment, though ten years on. Cunningham Pier Plaza was to be developed and linked to open space and the new Deakin University's Waterfront campus in a restored woolstores building. This plan and its orientation stimulated the redevelopment of two city blocks in the late 1980s – Market Square in 1985 and Bay City Plaza in 1988 – which had the effect of moving the retail core of the city towards the bay while also destroying part of the heritage urban fabric in the process. The ideal was to be spectacle, cultural edifices and urban design, if necessary at the expense of heritage, all of which was expected to generate investment, retail activity, tourist stops and prosperity.

Concern over "delays" and the "complexity of existing planning schemes", led to COGG placing the area into the hands of the Steampacket Place Development Board in 1995. Such a move was consistent with other such developments in Australia – such as Darling Harbour in Sydney (Berry and Huxley 1992) and Docklands in Melbourne (Dovey 2004) – as well as in Europe and North America (see Hall and Hubbard 1998) where local representative bodies were replaced by overarching and unaccountable statutory planning agencies. Here, as with other examples of such governance structures, there was strong central or state government representation and restricted local input. Limited public comment was possible on the concept plan as it was displayed for six weeks and the 59 objections, while dealt with by an independent panel hearing, were not registered in the final draft. The community was more actively engaged via market research and an aggressive and ongoing marketing campaign to promote the idea of the festival place (COGG 1994).

The resulting *Waterfront Geelong Concept Plan* (1994) included detailed traffic analyses and a design and development code. Subsequently implemented in a scaled-down form, the Marketing Manager of the city could enthuse in 1997:

> The Waterfront Precinct has breathed new life into this once run-down section of city wharves and is in fact leading a revitalization of the whole city. This new focus has led Geelong to cast off its tired rust-belt image and embrace education, tourism and technology (Geelong Business News 1997).

When launched in 2001 *Waterfront Geelong: The Future is Here* (COGG 2000), had altered significantly from the original plan – with the aquarium gone along with the seafood precinct and extensive boardwalks, while a waterfront pavilion had become a plaza in which there was an old carousel. Much of the open space and urban design elements had been included, along with themed public art – including Mark Stoner's "North" and Jan Mitchell's bollards (see Johnson 2006). Public art was integral to the new waterfront, as a way to beautify the space but also to add a critical element of local distinctiveness. In this the work of Jan Mitchell was vital.

A member of the Art House Collective (created in 2003), Jan Mitchell was something of a visible but lone voice in the Geelong art scene. She was distinguished within that collective by the extent of her formal training, her interest in the legal side of intellectual property rights and by the nature of her work (Mitchell 5.5.06). Mitchell's most public work in Geelong comprises 106 bollards located at historically appropriate sites around the Waterfront Walking Trail. Using wooden pillars from the demolished Yarra Street wharf and drawing assistance from a regional builder and fellow artist, the Melbourne trained graphic designer, illustrator, painter and print maker turned her hand to three dimensional sculptures in the early 1990s. Trialed at a local primary school as an Arts Victoria Artist in Residency in 1990, the images which are variously inscribed on the bollards, are taken from detailed research into the history of Geelong – people, events, places, institutions and moments that have been important in making the place.

The bollards were produced on commission from the City of Greater Geelong as it moved decisively in the 1990s to rejuvenate the waterfront. Presented as a highly polished and professional submission from someone with an existing track record and image, they were to form a vital part of the pedestrian upgrade of the foreshore. Mitchell knows about and is excited about the history of Geelong and finds it personally rewarding to bring this to the public through appealing and accessible work (Mitchell 5.5.06). The bollards include images of a nurse from the earliest Geelong Hospital, Sisters of Mercy, sea bathers, mayors and surveyors, volunteer firemen, ship captains, life savers, members of the Volunteer Rifle Band, Peter Lalor (the leader of the Eureka Rebellion who came to Geelong to nurse his wounded body) and Nancy Nattyknuckers sitting astride her velocipede. While other bollards have been made for the nearby Avalon Airfield and for Melbourne's Tullamarine (international) Airport with a small number for an apartment building in Sydney, Mitchell is adamant that her work remains connected to the Geelong region – with bollards in other places signifying Geelong and her output consciously limited by this commitment (Mitchell 5.5.06). The web site for the city has the bollards prominent as a symbol of the city and they are massively reproduced on post cards and on city publications. The web site for the city enthuses "The Bay Walk Bollards have reached the significance of national and international identification for the City of Greater Geelong".

There is therefore a value to the City and region of such work – in the generation of a successful image, in the creation of a tourist attraction, but also in giving a sense of Geelong as a culturally sophisticated city with institutions, precincts and a culture which supports inventive, playful and real creative work. The bollards in particular have become a symbol of Geelong, marketed as an integral part of its revitalised waterfront and progressive image, especially to tourists but also to potential investors and residents. Here the creative arts have value primarily as a vehicle to represent, differentiate and add a symbolic quality to a regenerated part of this manufacturing city, struggling to change its image and economy.

Such public art along with urban design was critical to the redesign of the Geelong waterfront, though its main objective was to bring in visitors and sustain related commercial activity in hotels, restaurants and theme-park like activities. In 2001 COGG announced that Waterfront Geelong had attracted A$140 million in private sector investment (COGG 2000: 4), mostly in the form of upmarket residential developments – including a waterfront hotel and apartments, Here then was a redevelopment for the rich to occupy and others to visit, but in this the vision had been achieved and, as elsewhere – including Glasgow, Bilbao and Singapore – provided the spatial foundation for further revisioning the city. In a 2003 City Progress update insert into the local newspaper, the *Geelong Advertiser*, local boosters note how such development links the city, waterfront, gardens and arts precinct noting how the "vibrant waterfront" with more than $230 million invested, has involved new attractions, restaurants, promenades, walking/cycling paths, major artworks and landscaped gardens, antique carousel, bollards and Steampacket Gardens along with a refurbishment of the art deco ocean pool at Eastern Beach. While modeled on examples from elsewhere and spurred by retailing, the redevelopment of the Geelong waterfront has indeed been vital to the re-imagining of the city, if not its economic revival.

Festival city and cultural tourism

If the city had pursued tourism and re-imagining of its waterfront as a key strategy to meet the challenge of manufacturing decline, the association of these developments with art and cultural development was fundamental. The commissioning of the Bay Walk bollards by Jan Mitchell was a critical part of this development and this occurred during the 1990s when other discussions were occurring at federal as well as state level on the role of the arts in economic regeneration. Even more direct connections between art and urban revitalisation were to be made over this decade in Geelong. Thus in 1994 a community group prepared a report entitled: *Geelong 2010: A preferred Future* (CCC 1994) where they noted that the Council had moved to see Geelong as an *"Arts City"* focused on the bay and committed to working with regional arts groups, organisations and institutions to boost the Arts Precinct and support a Summer Theatre Music and Arts Festival. This report joined two others – *Cultural Vision and Strategy* (1995–6) *and a Cultural Tourism Development Strategy (Draft) by Geelong Otway* Tourism (GOT 1995) – in highlighting the value and opportunities in the region to develop cultural tourism. While accompanied by the development of some related brochures, however, this strategy never moved beyond the draft stage and today cultural tourism remains but a small part of an overall tourism strategy. The Waterfront remains at the centre of all major events and festivals as part of the revitalisation strategy. But this flies in the face of other elements of local cultural celebration, including one local festival held at a very different location, the Pako Festa.

In 1995 a Major Event group was created within the Cultural Development Unit in the City of Greater Geelong. Following the creation of Melbourne Major Events within the Kennett government, here was a local equivalent to bring tourists and capital to the city as well as to boost the image and confidence of the region through urban spectacles. Sponsored by local businesses, the radio station, the council and State government, festivals and events were seen as ways in which public confidence could be displayed and enhanced. Major events were also seen as a vehicle to get the locals spending and outsiders to notice an industrial provincial city desperately trying to shake off its "Sleepy Hollow" image. Thus in 1998 Geelong Major Events was formed as an advisory committee to council with a mandate to attract new events, grow a calendar of major events and maximise the impact of the major events program. It was also the body assigned the task of managing the Council's funding support program for the arts – thereby linking the creative arts clearly to events and tourism. That year I counted 24 festivals across the region. Of these seven were in the Steampacket Place precinct and the others were scattered across the city in older, more traditional venues, such as the showgrounds, major parks, indoor stadia and at the racecourse. Most of the outdoor and waterfront events were in the summer, three were explicitly to do with music – the Celtic Folk Festival, the Rock Eistedford and Schools of Music – and the same number were also identified with ethnicity – the Celtic Music Festival, the Scots Highland Gathering and the Pakington Multicultural Festival. In 1999 there were even more music festivals – the Murgie Music Festival, Jazz by the Bay and Offshore Music Festival, two new food based festivals – Seafood Feast and Barwon Winter Wine Festival – and one specifically focused on the creative arts – Momenta 99 – bringing the number of festivals to 30. In 2000 "Major events", which included sporting as well as cultural activities, numbered 50, with one occurring each week! One of the largest, most enduring and ultimately challenging, was the Pako Festa (Author's field notes 1998–2008).

Begun by a small Migrant Resources Centre in 1983 as a celebration of an ethnically diverse heritage suburb under siege from redevelopment, the Pako Festa is a combination of local communities, traders and schools, ethnic food and dance, all overseen by the Geelong Ethnic Communities Council in the main street of Geelong West – Pakington Street. The street is closed off for much of its length, with anchor parks and hotels at each end and along it, there are stages, stalls and a major parade on the first day of the festa. In 1999 50,000 people attended, in 2000 and 2001 even more came to what is usually a warm February long weekend. The Chairman of the Pako Festa Committee George Ballas in 1999 intoned:

> I invite everyone to join in the celebration of our diverse cultural heritage. Pako Festa is the best opportunity the people of Geelong have to experience the color and richness of our cultural heritage. Pako Festa also supports local ethnic community groups in maintaining their traditions and sharing them with the general community (Ballas 1999).

Critical to the Festa is the active involvement – through community representatives on the organizing committee and the Ethnic Communities Council – of the 27 different nationalities that make up Geelong, ranging in size from the 8,000 strong Dutch and 5,000 Croatians to individuals representing the 300 Filipinos and Lithuanians of Geelong. The aim is to include not exclude, to bind rather than factionalise but also to inform and enthuse the younger members of second and third generation migrants about their cultural heritage through its performance and public celebration (Mavros October 2000). The festival also specifically includes and addresses the dominant Anglo community, presenting a range of ethnic as well as indigenous groups through common markers of difference – especially ethnic food, dance, dress and music – and in so doing affirms these practices amongst the now ageing and increasingly Australian-born migrant groups.

Figure 7.1   Battle of the spectacles – Pako and Waterfront

While outsiders tend to be critical of what may be regarded as superficial elements of multicultural identity, expressed in a temporary and non-threatening way within a public space (Watson 1992; Gunew 1996, Ommundsen 1996), the emphasis on food, dance and music is the choice of those groups organising the event and is subject to cross cultural negotiation and deliberate efforts at creating hybrid forms – as world music and dances are explored by those from diverse backgrounds. Such a strategy achieved a real poignancy in 2001 after the September 11th attack on the World Trade Center, as clearly demarcated national and religious groups celebrated their co-existence and the mood of the crowd was a defiant tolerance. This then is a festival that mobilises ethnic difference but does so in a way that is strategic, consciously inclusive, fixed and backward looking to fading traditions but also open to negotiation, change and contestation of an emergent intercultural future.

The organisers of the event are vehement that their aim is financial viability rather than profitability. The 2000 Festa cost $A100,000 to stage, with monies coming from local sponsors, traders and authorities such as the City of Greater Geelong and Geelong-Otway Tourism as well as the state level Arts Victoria and the national multicultural Special Broadcasting Service. However, even though it generates only limited revenue – a survey I conducted in 2000 indicated that each person spent on average only A$23 and the vast majority came from within the region, denying the capacity of the event to generate serious income for the area or revive its ailing economy – the Council still wishes it to move. Thus in 2000 the City Council and local tourism authority exhorted the organisers to capitalise further on the event, suggesting that it should be relocated to the redeveloped waterfront, connected to other tourist events – such as conventions and conferences – and assume a more commercial orientation. Pako Festa would join the New Year Waterfront festival (see Figure 7.1) on the redeveloped Steampacket Place. The quest then was for the Pako Festa as a local community event, to become a slickly packaged Waterfront Major Event as part of the marketing and redevelopment strategies of the city (Author's field notes 1998–2008). Deeply grounded in its particular neighbourhood and the long term traditions of those ethnic communities which make up this area, such exhortations were rejected by the organisers and Pako Festa continues to be run on Pakington Street every February, attracting more and more people each time, as participants and observers.

Having rejected the idea of relocating this event, the city council continued to search for ways to make the Waterfront Precinct a catalyst for further redevelopment and re-imagining. In 1999, this became a major agenda item, not for the authority charged with developing regional tourism, but for a group of city luminaries and key arts bureaucrats, as they decided to bid for a Guggenheim museum for Geelong.

Guggenheim dreaming

In 1998, the story goes, there occurred a dinner party with COGG CEO Geoff Whitbread, National (Melbourne) Arts Gallery Director and Geelong businessman Jim Cousins and former GPAC General Manager Sue Hunt at Mayor Ken Jarvis's house. "The discussion turned to the future of Geelong and what we could do to get the city going in the light of our maturing industry. We were really looking for alternatives to replace the declining manufacturing sector". Tourism and cultural tourism were seen as a start but on their own were not enough. "We recognized that what was needed was a re-imaging of Geelong to become a world city, one that ranks alongside the likes of Edinburgh, Glasgow, Toronto and Bilbao" recalls Jarvis (GBN 2000: 11). To pursue this idea and with real connections into budgets and the State Government, in December 1998, COGG CEO Whitbread, Geelong Mayor Ken Jarvis and State Premier Steve Bracks were invited to meet with Guggenheim Director Thomas Krens in New York. With a cost to ratepayers of A$20,000, they also traveled to Bilbao on the way, to view, be briefed and arrange the traveling exhibition "Bilbao: Transformation of a City" to visit Geelong as a way of informing and enthusing the community on the model. In New York it was proposed that there be a A$1 million "joint" feasibility study – conducted by New York and Victorian experts, but funded by the Geelong bidders – which would demonstrate Geelong's commitment to the project. Krens informed the delegation that "Geelong would need to analyse world-wide trends and come up with a building and a concept that would set new standards in architecture". A realistic cost estimate for a building in Geelong was around A$200-300 million and it was tentatively sited just west of the restored waterfront. As with Bilbao, the Guggenheim Foundation would not contribute to the cost of the building, with funding having to come from local, state and federal governments as well as the private sector. At the time, for Ken Jarvis – "I firmly believe that it's there for us. If we want a Guggenheim enough, we can get it" (GBN 2000).

By December 1999 the City of Greater Geelong had resolved to undertake the feasibility study into the possibility of successfully bidding for a Guggenheim Museum. In the local press and within Council, the project was placed into the context of Geelong's plans for evolving the arts and culture industry, determining what was required for establishing a credible bid, establishing the feasibility of the project, quantifying the economic flow-ons to other industry sectors and seeking inspiration for an emblematic building design (Parfett 2000: 6). Within the Geelong community, opinions divided. For some, the proposed Geelong Guggenheim was much more than great art in a stunning locale. For Peter Hill at least, such projects were about using local culture to turn around the economies of cities that have lost their old manufacturing bases. It was about new jobs in new industries, education and civic excellence. For Hill, writing in the *Geelong Advertiser*: "I'm convinced it will happen somewhere in Australia – Hobart, Newcastle, Fremantle, Cairns, would all be suitable – but I hope it is Geelong". He further recalls how "in the early '80s my home town of Glasgow began its renaissance through culture and the arts. In a little under 10 years it turned itself around from being universally known as "The slum capital of Europe" to winning the accolade in 1990 of European City of Culture. That is another story (having told the story of Mass MoMA), but if Glasgow can do it, so can Geelong" (Hill 2000). Soon after, however, a *Geelong Advertiser* editorial labeled the idea of bidding for a Guggenheim a "dream" with a further editorial noting:

> The fact is Geelong does need to re-invent itself for the future. It cannot expect investors and new employers to come to Geelong rather than elsewhere without good reason…Geelong's economy, given the region's chronic and grossly under-stated unemployment problems, is in serious need of a major boost. The chief problem facing the city, from the perspective of many taxpayers, will be that in

pushing for a Guggenheim it may be tempted to pay less attention to fundamental municipal issues. If city hall wants public support for a Guggenheim it has to ensure it supports those in whose interest it purports to be acting. (GA 2000a: 6).

Unlike the hesitancy of those writing from the provincial city, the arts writer of the Melbourne *Age* was more positive and supportive. Thus in 2000 Robin Usher wrote:

Sleepy Hollow is waking up. Geelong wants to reinvent itself according to a vision based on cultural excellence, international tourism and a lifestyle to attract Melbourne commuters ... The city is consciously trying to rebuild its economy around culture and spectacle, rather than the rust-belt manufacturing industries that have been at its heart for the past 80 years. Skeptics can snigger, but the city's boldest vision has already put it at the forefront of an international field as it seeks to persuade New York's Guggenheim Foundation to establish a museum on its foreshore. (The) Guggenheim Foundation invited the city to make a submission. There is no other formal bid. "This could secure the future for us for the next 100 years" Jarvis says. "But if we let it pass, the city could slip back into the mess it was 15 years ago"... "The Guggenheim would attract a whole new class of intellectual tourism that would build on those already coming to the Great Ocean Road. It would also put Geelong on the world map and allow us to develop Avalon airfield as an international destination (Usher 2000).

Such a bold agenda was being developed in a city which at the time had no coherent or published arts or cultural tourism strategy, no arts officer and had yet to compile its first arts directory (this was launched in 2002)! However, at the same time as Usher was extolling its virtues, serious doubts and real questions were being asked about the feasibility of the bid and of the capacity of Geelong to mount it. Thus on February 25, 2000 Geelong City Council was urged to seek clarification from the Guggenheim Foundation after an *Age* report noted there was "virtually no chance" of securing a Guggenheim Museum, in contrast to the "impression given by the mayor that the Guggenheim Foundation was keen to work with the city towards establishing a museum". One observer quoted a *New York Times* interview with Thomas Krens in which he noted that he was "not looking for new branches". Cr Jarvis said he had always acknowledged the Guggenheim viewed such approaches with some cynicism because they had so many that amounted to nothing (GA 2000b: 3).

Despite such doubts, studies and boosting proceeded apace. The bid itself was seen as a bold and worthwhile thing to do. As the Geelong mayor observed in October 2000:

What we have done is to create the biggest talking point in the Australian art world at the moment. The bid itself is a statement about Geelong – it shows us as positive, bold and forward thinking. In this regard we're already ahead in the 'positive perception' stakes, both within the region and for businesses and people wanting to invest here. That positive perception is crucial in today's business climate. And if we succeed, we will have gained what amounts to a cultural icon, a brand name that will push Geelong onto the world scene (GBN 2000).

Such a view was echoed by Roger Grant, Head of Geelong Otway Tourism who was also a member of the "loose informal Geelong group driving the Guggenheim bid". He expected that such a building – to rival the Sydney Opera House – would have an "astonishing" impact on tourism in the region with strong parallels evident with Bilbao (GBN 2000). Spurred on by key business and civic players in the region, the city council moved to set up a company limited by guarantee – the Geelong Guggenheim Bid Co. Ltd – to progress the project. This separate company was designed to distance the bid from local politics and better attract corporate finance – connecting museums to business in a clear and unabashed way – with the Guggenheim long seen as the organisation which brought business and art together. The new company maintained the key players in the project, those who had an established relationship with the Guggenheim Foundation and also recognised the state significance of the project by including representation by the Premier. The City of Greater Geelong contributed $100,000 to the feasibility study (with additional funds of $500,000 from the Major Projects Program in 2000–01) but also indicated that the next step would require far more resources with the project being of state and national significance requiring those levels of political and financial buy in (GA 13.12.2000).

The bidding company proceeded to secure "Bilbao: Transformation of a City" for Geelong in 2001. Housed in the National Wool Museum – a museum based on the original economic foundations of the region and in a heritage listed building given to the city as part of the 1988 Bicentennial celebrations – the exhibition showed how Bilbao had re-positioned and redeveloped itself around the Guggenheim (Carr 2003). The exhibition presented Bilbao as a paradigm of what Geelong could be if it could replicate Bilbao's strategy for renewal. Indeed it presented the idea of connecting a global museum franchise to major redevelopments of transport and other infrastructure as obvious and attractive to business (Author's field notes 1998–2008). Ken Jarvis, now one of the Foundation Directors, noted that the Bilbao Guggenheim was a "pusher" for economic development, a big bang strategy for Geelong's revitalisation with the starter being the attraction of a global brand to the city which in turn would alter how the town was used and lead to more positive re-branding (Carr 2003). For at least one arts manager, the Guggenheim was seen as worthwhile for Geelong as it would:

• Set off a multiplier effect of expansion linked especially to tourism as the city would no longer just be a gateway to the Great Ocean Road but a destination in itself,

- There would be immediate linkage, networking and opportunities for transference available by being with a major global participant in the economic growth areas evolving from cultural/tourist development.
- Signal Geelong as a culturally aware, progressive city as there would be a transfer/contagion of the connotations associated with art – elite, contemporary – into the city's own image with a "Bilbao effect" of boosting confidence across the city (Carr 2003)

The value of the Guggenheim bid to Geelong then was multifaceted, signaling to the skeptical or indifferent world that this rust bucket regional city had a level of sophistication, attractiveness and boldness that could not only produce a major new gallery but a new image and revitalised economy.

By 2002 the pre-feasibility study by Price Waterhouse Coopers found a major cultural landmark in Geelong would generate up to A$175 million in its first year and attract 5.3 million visitors. Noting that the Geelong waterfront and its carousel had already boosted visitor numbers, the report was also delivered to the Victorian Government which Geelong had asked to help fund a more detailed A$1.5 million feasibility study. If the consultant's study was upbeat, local and state level evaluation was becoming more critical. Thus in a letter to the Geelong Adverstiser in February, local luminary David Henshaw observed:

> If there is talk of the council spending $1 million to $2 million on a feasibility study, I would suggest that the money would be spent more productively for Geelong on our existing art gallery and cultural precinct (Henshaw GA 24.2.2000).

A further feature article noted how the Guggenheim bid had stirred and engaged people from all walks of life allowing locals to focus on some key questions as to whether the city really wanted or understood it, answering these rhetorical questions in the affirmative (Jenning GA 24.2.03).

But as with Bilbao, the decisions were not only to be made locally, though it was clear that local support had waned and that the State government was hesitating at spending even more money on further studies. In connecting to a global museum enterprise, Geelong also became subject to the downs as well as the upside of the Guggenheim's corporate plans. Thus in January 2003 *The Australian* noted "Geelong may abandon its bid for a Guggenheim Museum in favour of a multi-million dollar gallery devoted solely to Aboriginal art" in the wake of fresh financial woes in the New York headquarters of the Guggenheim Foundation. Local doubts on the Geelong bid therefore emerged at the same time as the Guggenheim announced that it would not go ahead with its new US$1.7 billion branch in Manhattan, closed its Las Vegas branch and would cut its staff and operating budget (*The Australian* 2.1.03).

By July 2003 Geelong Council declared the death of "an audacious bid for a cultural icon." The press release continued: "City Hall's interest and money has run out for the ambitious multi-million bid to lure an international museum to Geelong …This council has never unequivocally backed the Guggenheim bid which was backed by the former CEO and a number of people no longer on council". Cr Binnie said the bid was doomed when Krens did not visit during the 2000 Olympics. "Suddenly the bid changed track to a boutique-style museum like a Tate. It's once again veered and now they're talking about an Australian art collection. As far as council is concerned, if there was a vote now it would be knocked back." No money is left after Council spent A$26 million on Skilled Stadium, building a new Olympic pool and upgrading The Arena. The bid "did not stack up" against other community projects and council needed to improve existing cultural assets like Customs House, Osborne House, GPAC and the National Wool Museum. Jim Cousins was unaware of the Council view, and he observed: "It's a loss for Geelong. If that's what they've articulated, we'll make plans to take it elsewhere" (COGG 7.03).

But the city in search of a symbolic saviour did not give up. Even as the Guggenheim bid was being declared dead, civic leaders started to pursue a major convention centre. A COGG report found the region was missing out on tourism dollars through a lack of a suitable exhibition or convention facility. The report proceeded to knock the long-dreamed of Guggenheim on the head in favour of a smaller centre. Council therefore resigned from the Guggenheim Bid Ltd board and withdrew necessary support from the project. Noting that the City had already poured $100,000 into the bid in 2000, the Council also noted an internal report which suggested the estimated A$300 million project costs were a "stumbling block" with a risk assessment highlighting concerns about cost blowouts and future state government support. The report also noted the Guggnheim brand had been battered by collapsed plans for a museum in Brazil and a second New York centre as well as the closing of the Las Vegas branch and cuts in staffing and budgets. The report concluded: "A smaller facility may well be feasible, especially if linked to the convention centre concept". For long term Guggenheim supporter Jim Cousins it was "sad for Geelong that it would not get a Guggenheim" (14.10.2003 GeelongInfo.) but by then there were other agendas emerging. This time for a Cultural Precinct complete with a convention centre! A new vehicle had been found to boost the regional centre, enhance its image and connect the creative arts to its urban and social regeneration. Once more following overseas trends – but in its own way and time – Geelong was now to focus on developing a cultural precinct and knowledge economy as a new take on its claim to being a Cultural Capital.

Building the Cultural Precinct in the Cultural Capital

Geelong had joined other regional cities and metropolitan centres during the 19th century in creating Mechanics Institutes but also, utilizing the considerable wealth generated by the Victorian gold rush, a fine art gallery and collection. It was on this foundation that other cultural institutions were built, in an area near the city centre alongside local government administrative offices and adjacent to a major park. Here then was located City Hall but also the Geelong Gallery (in 1896), the City Library, Heritage Centre and, in 1981 the Geelong Performing Arts Centre. Known in the 1970s as the Civic and Cultural Precinct, these institutions tended to coexist and pursue their own agendas, until being singled out for the most recent phase of Cultural Capital rethinking as a Cultural Precinct in 2007. It was into these various institutions that State and local government support had been lavished with, for example, Jeff Kennett funding the redevelopment of the Art Gallery and Performing Arts Centre in the early 1990s.

Discussion amongst the local arts and welfare community had earlier highlighted the need for youth facilities and it was through the actions of both the arts and youth workers that a bid was made for a youth theatre group and facility. It was Kennett's Liberal government that in 1996 agreed to fund the renovation and conversion of the old central court house building into a young person's theatre. Thus in response to a local submission, the State Government put A$493,000 into the Courthouse to provide cultural services to the 45,000 young people aged between 12–25 in Geelong. These funds provided a new lock up recording studio and rehearsal suite while also adding to the 120 seat theatre, meeting rooms and art room, youth health service and café. As well as supporting youth theatre, the Courthouse complex housed the emergent and soon to be internationally renown Back to Back theatre for the intellectually disabled (News Release 26.5.1999).

Along with these ad hoc developments and the bid for the Guggenheim, there was also efforts within local government to better develop the policy and administrative framework within which such activity was occurring. For some, the challenge was seen as going beyond one local government area, to have Geelong city lead a regional political unit and lobbying organisation. G21 became an organisation which, along with the business-dominated Committee for Geelong, worked with five existing councils to boost the profile and quality of life in the region. To achieve these goals a set of "Pillar Groups" were established to map out priorities and projects and work to effect their realisation. One of the ten groups was concerned with Arts and Cultural Heritage, now recognised as fundamental as Transport and Communications, Life Long Learning and Health and Well Being to the region. I joined this Pillar Group in 2003 and worked within it developing vision statements and priorities for what were called "Lighthouse Projects" to progress the arts and cultural heritage in the G21 region.

Alongside such a regional grouping, the City of Greater Geelong also commissioned Robert Edwards – an earlier director of the National Wool Museum – to develop an arts policy. In 2000 he recommended an accreditation system to enable projects and organisations to be evaluated for funding, support for community based arts organisations and encouraged participation in the arts, especially amongst young people. Another key idea related to the ever present need to attract more cultural tourists to Geelong via a major cultural icon – but here Edwards was clear that it was not to be a Guggenheim but an institution that would be multi-functional with wide appeal. Intriguingly this report on the state of the region's arts was delivered at the same time as the G21 Arts and Cultural Heritage Pillar Group document was released. So in a city that had long lacked official policy and debate on cultural matters, there was now two policy documents vying for public attention and official endorsement, leading to press reports of "City culture wars" (GI 15.8.03). For some within the city Edwards was seen as wedded to the major icon (Guggenheim) rather than a strategy which built on the State government's *Creative Capacity* statement.

Alongside the Edwards document then was another, which had the input from the G21 Pillar Group, called *Creativity* + (2003). The focus of this document, which had grown out of a very broad consultation process with the regional arts community conducted by the G21 Arts and Cultural Pillar Group, was on cultural infrastructure (including options for the Wool Museum and Osborne House), nurturing creativity (via showing local artists on the Council web page), culture for all (through a better strategy for allocating community arts grants and designating Major Events), the cultural economy (by promoting cultural enterprises and/or activities to increase trade, tourism and attract investment, facilitate the development of creative clusters, preferably in precincts identified in the planning scheme, promote Geelong as a film and multi-media-friendly region and quantify and evaluate the economic impact of the arts sector) and cultural leadership (through a Council department, relationships with other departments and work with G21) (Creativity+ 2003: 7). The first comprehensive arts and cultural strategy for the region then, did not pursue the idea of a cultural icon or return to the notion of boosting the waterfront, but rather focused on existing institutions, individuals and organisations to facilitate their development. In short this arts policy, emerging from consultation with the arts community of the region, was about growing extant cultural capital. In this agenda, the place of the Cultural Industries was relatively modest, with the region being presented as but a location for film makers and offering potential for "creative clusters" rather than a pre-existing set of activities. Claims for being a Cultural Capital were thereby subsumed within a broader-based policy agenda for supporting the arts but also an array of other regional development agendas.

The words preceding the strategy are suggestive of the scaled-down nature of the vision where the people of the region are acknowledged as enjoying the creative arts and supporting the major local arts institutions, before arguing that "cultural activities can improve the quality of life for people and assist in tackling social issues such as social exclusion. By bringing people together, providing opportunities to share and interact, increase skills and solve problems, the community's capacity is increased" (Creativity+ 2003). As in Geelong and to some extent Glasgow, the creative arts assume a number of roles here, ranging from the humane to the social and economic. The resulting Council Cultural Strategy – launched in 2004 – lists its rationale for the arts as:

1. Stimulating the creative urge helps us gain an understanding of the many ways we can be human beings.
2. Social benefits give a sense of connection, for creative individuals to make a living and communities to benefit by attracting tourists.
3. Cultural tourism is growing fast with the examples of Leeds, Manchester and Bilbao offered. They have all invested in culture and people have come in vast numbers.
4. By building on our existing arts, cultural and heritage strengths we can create a thriving industry sector; one that is environmentally sustainable, creates jobs and generates attractiveness and an excitement about the city.
5. The benefits of a vibrant cultural sector spills over to other areas of our economy. The transformative power of curiosity and imagining feeds innovation in other sectors – research, IT, construction and design, tourism and hospitality. The creativity generated by cultural activity can be a source of new commercial ideas, exports, patents and industries.

The creative arts in Geelong therefore acquire their value via their humanistic role, their place in community building, economically through the tourism and cultural industries as well as via an innovation economy. It was an agenda and range of uses that the arts had been ascribed across the world.

At the 2004 launch of *Creativity+* and the second edition of the *Arts Directory*, Di Shaw – COGG Manager for Arts and Culture – said that "for the first time, Council was clearly committed to playing a leading and active role in the development and growth of the regional arts industry into the future" (Author's field notes 1998–2008). She foreshadowed a series of forums to shape priorities for action – indicating that as a result of her consultations local artists had a need for assistance with legal issues, marketing and better networking. Local needs were therefore modest and most of these ideas have now come to pass, supporting the growth of local artistic activity. Such actions to assist the localised embodiment of cultural capital, however, continue to sit uneasily alongside institutional efforts to boost the region.

Thus, on the larger scale, the Arts and Cultural Heritage Pillar Group and City Council moved to prioritise as a Lighthouse Project the redevelopment of the city's Cultural Precinct. In 2006 a A$200,000 feasibility study endorsed the idea. To this end the State government gave A$500,000 to develop a joint Master Plan which would include an upgraded GPAC, convention and exhibition centre, a new civic centre, related developments (eg updated gallery, library, hotel) and the possible relocation of the State Government Offices. GPAC, as a major stakeholder in this precinct, formalised its input into this process, arguing that any redeveloped cultural precinct should build on the collective strengths of existing strategies, government initiatives (including the idea of a 'clever quarter' based around the university), create opportunities for private investment to offset public costs and "deliver a precinct solution to replace the current cultural patchwork". (GPAC 2007: 4). The vision of the performing arts centre for this area combines artistic, business, social and economic imperatives which, they argue, would result in "improved liveability, economic growth and a long overdue catch-up in cultural investment appropriate for a major regional city" (GPAC 2007).

For GPAC the aim is to boost attendances within the precinct, especially for locals but also visitors. Their Plan quotes Richard Florida as he asserts that: "Regional cities of the future will thrive by providing an open, accepting environment for cultural and creative people, namely artists, entrepreneurs, scientists and health care professionals". To achieve such an environment for the much sought after creative class, the plan argues that a vibrant and attractive cultural precinct is vital and will assist in changing Geelong's economy from a strong manufacturing to a much more diversified one (GPAC 2007: 4). To achieve this, the plan presents a case for the city library, gallery, Heritage Centre and GPAC to all expand, to share administrative infrastructure, integrate far more and broaden the range of commercial activities around the site. To realise all of this, in May 2008 A\$70 million was allocated within the State Government budget for the further development of Geelong's cultural precinct, with most money (A\$8 million) going to the Courthouse Youth Theatre to add rehearsal space, recording studio and art gallery. The monies are also to fund the expansion of the existing regional art gallery into the current City Hall and to add an additional story to the regional library.

Ideas for Geelong's Cultural Precinct draw heavily on examples from Dundee and Dublin and the work of Simon Roodhouse (Roodhouse 2006) but they also build on the historical accident of Geelong's major visual, literary and performing arts institutions being co-located and immediately adjacent to the city centre. Not unlike Glasgow, the ideal will be realised once the concept has been articulated, political will exerted and funds made available. The precinct is being driven by both the key organisations involved and the City of Greater Geelong as it continues to rethink its image, redevelop its inner urban fabric – now away from the waterfront to other near city areas – and utilise the creative arts, not as the key driver but as a vital component in a broad-ranging strategy for economic and social renewal. Using Richard Florida rather than Bilbao as the model, the quest is no longer for the iconic monument which will kick start a tourist economy, but for a more physically attractive and culturally vibrant city which can attract and keep the creative class who will hopefully populate the expanding service and new manufacturing industries of the city.

Geelong has thereby moved from seeing itself as a Cultural Capital anchored in a refurbished waterfront, iconic gallery, ongoing major events, and a cultural precinct. Rather these are now regarded as components in a complex mix rather than ends in themselves or the sole means to restore economic life and pride in the city. This then becomes the long term and most recent message for places aspiring to be Cultural Capitals, and it was perhaps always the case. However, along the way, what has occurred has been a re-valuing of the creative arts, a connection of the high arts to other art forms and creative endeavor, and a broadening of the arts agenda to being an industry, an economic beacon and vital ingredient

Table 7.1   Economic structure of the City of Greater Geelong, 1991–2006

Economic Sector Census Year	1991		2006	
	No	%	No	%
Extractive –mining, agriculture, forestry and fishing	632	1.1	1,280	1.5
Manufacturing	12,605	22.2	12,422	14.6
Construction	3,507	6.4	7,255	8.5
Retail and Wholesale trade	11,580	20.2	18,232	21.5
Transport	2,240	3.9	3,367	4.0
Communications	887	1.5	1,001	1.2
Finance and Insurance	4,730	8.2	2,021	2.4
Gov't admin and defence	2,288	4.0	3,584	4.2
Property and Business Services	2,707	4.7	7,210	8.5
Education	4,654	8.1	7,195	8.5
Health and Community Services	10,766	18.8	10,179	12.0
Cultural and Recreational Services	688	1.2	1,780	2.1
Personal services	1,062	1.9	3,343	3.9
Accommodation, cafes and restaurants	1,973	3.4	3,824	4.5
Totals (includes sectors not shown)	57,270	100.0	84,976	100.0

Source: G21 Region Community Profile 2006; ABS 1991 Census Expanded Community Profile

in any feasible plan for economic and social regeneration and urban restoration. Here then are the elements which make the arts valuable in new and critical ways, though how each process unfolds is specifically related to the objective, embodied and institutional forms and relationships of cultural capital in any one place as they develop over time.

Geelong as a Sustainable Cultural Capital

In assessing just how sustainable the creative arts are in Geelong it is appropriate to begin with an economic overview of employment in the creative arts and to assess the shift from the manufacturing to a service economy in the region. As Table 7.1 indicates, there has indeed been a major change in the economic foundation of the city as it has moved decisively from an industrial to a service base. However, with such a shift, the place of the Cultural Services has been relatively modest, increasing from a low base to ultimately employ around 2.1% of the workforce.

In 2001 there were 1,731 people employed in "Cultural and Recreational Services", an increase of 66% over the 688 that were employed in 1986. There

**Table 7.2   Some Dimensions of Cultural Capital in Geelong, Victoria
2008**

Embodied Cultural Capital	Objectified Capital	Institutional Capital
Values, training, links of individuals and their groups	Cultural products: music, performance, heritage buildings, films, videos, paintings, writings etc.	Major and minor institutions and policies at local, regional and national level which support cultural activities
771 (448 men and 323 women) who were "Artists and Related Professionals in the 2001 Census 200+ artists who self identified in the Geelong Arts Directory 240 who were registered on the ARC Cultural Industries Data Base Jan Mitchell	Art/Cultural works in the major institutions – Geelong Art Gallery, Regional Library, Historical Records Centre and works in regional and private art galleries . Public art works and records of them, including the Bay Walk Bollards.	Geelong Performing Arts Centre, Geelong Art Gallery, National Wool Museum, Geelong Central Library, Deakin University, Historical Records Centre
Cultural festival participants Publicly present ethnic groups	Major and minor heritage buildings eg Waterfront. Wool stores, Customs House, Arts Precinct, classified by the National Trust or otherwise officially or popularly "valued"	1986 City by the Bay 1990 Steampacket Place G21 Geelong Strategic Plan, G21 Arts and Cultural Heritage Pillar Group City of Greater Geelong Culture Strategy Geelong Otway Tourism Cultural Tourism Strategy Cultural Precinct
Geelong Arts Alliance Art House Collective Geelong Writers Group Arts Newsletter	Individual works or art – paintings, films, videos, writing and performances	The Potato Shed, Courthouse Youth Theatre, Back to Back Theatre
Wathaurong Aboriginal Glass Co-Operative		Local galleries, media businesses, photography studios
Arts entrepreneurs – Jim Cousins, Ken Jarvis	Guggenheim bid	Guggenheim Bid Pty Ltd.

were 771 persons who defined themselves as "Artists and Related Professionals" in 2001. Such employment constituted around 1% of the Geelong regional workforce increasing to 2% by 2006. The largest increases over the 1980s and 1990s occurred for those working in design and illustration, journalism, for authors, and those working in film, TV, radio and as stage directors and media presenters. (ABS Customised tables, 1991, 1996, 2001).

If this is one quantitative assessment of the arts in this region, one emerging from the household Census utilising the ABS definitions, the city council has also been active in tabulating the number and range of artists in the region. Thus in December 2002 the City produced its first *Arts Directory* which itemised 148 practicing artists, illustrators, photographers, musicians, designers, performers, dancers and writers. In addition the Directory noted over 100 organisations, networks, venues and companies connected to the arts industry (Geelong Arts Directory 2002). Significantly, as the Directory relied on self-selection in its compilation, there were no architects, librarians, museum workers or journalists included. Artists in Geelong, therefore, retain the earliest Australia Council definition of their field, with this Directory not including those other activities which comprise, at Federal Government level and in other countries, the cultural or creative industries.

In addition to the readily available quantitative measures of employment and arts organisations, there are other activities and institutions which collectively constitute the Cultural Industries. So for example, over any one year, there would be twenty or thirty major events in Geelong, designed to showcase the city to its various communities and outside tourists. In addition there are well established cultural institutions, smaller organisations and ephemeral networks. These various individuals, collectivities, institutions and their policy contexts can be conceptualised in terms of their embodied, objective and institutional cultural capital, and are represented in Table 7.2.

There are many other individuals and collectivities that can be added to this matrix, as well as a huge number of creative objects. The institutional and social settings through which they circulate and acquire value are all complex stories and the foregoing discussion has focused on five of these – the redevelopment of the Geelong waterfront, the bay walk bollards, the Guggenheim bid, the Pako Festa and plans for a Cultural Precinct.

Some of the key institutions supporting the arts in Geelong – such as the Geelong Performing Arts Centre, the National Wool Museum and the Geelong Art Gallery – have orientations primarily beyond the region and see their roles as bringing the world and its arts to the region, or projecting the culture of the region to the world. In addition they aim to foster through their shows and educational programs, local involvement and learning in the arts. In contrast to such major organisations – or massed forms of institutionalised cultural capital – there are more local gatherings of artists – such as the Geelong Writers Group, The Courthouse Youth Theatre, the Art House Collective and the Geelong Arts Alliance. Operating in very different institutionalised settings compared to the large externally-orientated and funded arts institutions, these are created by and for those working in Geelong. Their primary purpose is one of support – social, economic and political – for those who are writing, painting, sculpting, performing or otherwise making art in the region. In part as a consequence of such different institutional contexts, the value of what is produced and shown within these organisations diverges – with members of the Geelong Writers Group highlighting the semi-private, non-commercial but vital role of the group in ascribing local value to their work (Focus Group – Writers 29.8.04). In contrast, some in the Geelong Arts Alliance are highly skeptical of the major arts organisations in the city and reach beyond these to international venues, publications and for recognition, sale and critical acclaim (Focus Group – Visual Arts 31.7.04). Others include a core group, who run what one artist described as a "tight ship" which generates community-based initiatives and successfully secures grants and commissions (Hartigan 4.5.06). The value generated for active members of the Arts Alliance is therefore far higher – in an economic and profiling sense – though in human and social capital terms, it is similar if not less than those who create community through membership of a writing group. In other words, the value of art in these varied environments is the result of the personal, social, economic as well as political relations in which works are created, circulated and consumed. In these various forms, however, such activity becomes socially and culturally sustaining and through their collective organisational forms, also feed into the political process – either formally or informally – to ensure a relatively high level of political sustainability. The circuits of valuation and the various dimensions of sustainability for the creative arts in Geelong therefore bode well for their ongoing survival and growth.

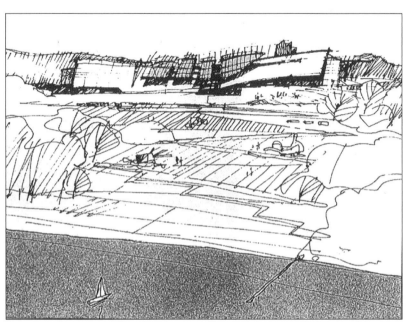

Sketch/plan for Guggenheim, Geelong, Australia

Chapter 8

Cultural Capitals:
Re-valuing the Arts and Re-making
Sustainable City Spaces

Common Context – Local Stories

This book documents a geography of hope. It has described how the creative arts have been activated by individuals, governments and private enterprise to make their communities and cities better places to live and work. While not all examples provide stories of triumph, in general Cultural Capitals have been associated with re-valuing the creative arts and sustainable urban regeneration.

This analysis has occurred within a theoretical framework that focuses on the process of creating value. In this it has isolated embodied, objective and institutional forms of cultural capital as a way of considering the interconnected sites where value is developed, circulated and realised across a range of scales. The cities chosen for examination were all centres of industry which, from the 1970s, encountered a new international division of labour. As their industrial foundations faltered and they shifted painfully towards a service economy, these cities also utilised their creative arts to hasten their social, physical and economic transformation. The case studies have shown that cultural capital is held in significant amounts by local communities, usually as a result of long-term historical development. Such latent cultural capital, present in the built environment, established cultural institutions, the training and work of resident artists may not be fully appreciated by those who live in or visit these localities. But it is on this foundation and with the injection of significant funds, purposeful policy and new definitions of value, that embodied, objective and institutional cultural capital is mobilised and the Cultural Capital emerges.

For any aspiring Cultural Capital then, embodied skills, training and creativity have to be mobilised, valued and objectified into cultural objects which in turn need some sort of institutional location – within an arts policy, an art gallery, in a public space or supported in some other way by an arts organisation. Once mobilised, such capital becomes a constructive force in reshaping cities. The Guggenheim Museum in Bilbao, C.R. Mackintosh and the design industry in Glasgow, performance and heritage in Singapore and the re-imagined waterfront of Geelong have all been associated with creating different forms of cultural capital, in contributing to the symbolic economy of these cities and translating this cultural capital into social and economic forms of capital. While often critically appraised – in terms of Faustian deals between governments, investors and artists which variously corrupt and render the recipients dependent – the case studies have demonstrated that such deals are far better than nothing at all. When given the choice of allowing the collapse of manufacturing to continue, unemployment to go on rising, city buildings to fall further into disrepair, public spaces to be abandoned; or to mobilise private and government investment into supporting artistic productions which can variously reverse these trends, my argument is that the choice is a wise, ethical and sustainable one. Such choices are made within the particular historical trajectories of each place and are nested within different scales of social, economic and political relationships which limit and shape what emerges. They are also made within an array of common contexts – of globalisation, of inter city competition, of post-colonialism and a post-modern symbolic economy.

Chapter 3 therefore described how there were many commonalities between those cities that courted the Cultural Capital label. Thus a heightened movement of capital, migrants and tourists around the world after World War II had generated forces for economic restructuring and differentiated the world into declining industrial and emergent newly industrialising nations. World Cities emerged as the major command and control centres of this new economy while all others competed anew for capital and people in increasingly desperate campaigns for city re-imagining and urban entrepreneurialism. Dealing with abandoned industrial areas and rising unemployment, some cities looked to models offered by Baltimore and Boston in the US – two cities which addressed these traumas through massive state and private investment in waterfront renewal, retail development and creating urban spectacles. In Europe the model was less the festival market place but more the cultural precinct, but both strategies were ultimately about a conscious revisioning of industrial cities as something very different and, for some at least, as centres of the arts or Cultural Capitals. Given discursive clarity by promoters such as Charles Landry and his team at Comedia, the creative city agenda was widely disseminated to other cities, becoming over the 1980s and 1990s the preferred agenda of many.

Associated with the actions of individuals and organisations, such trends appear on the ground in very different ways. The further argument of this book is that the only way to understand where and how cultural capital is mobilised and with what effect, is to look closely at places, as it is a highly localised story; one that will connect across scales and exists within the container of general trends and ideas but still remains particular. Such particularity makes direct copying and generalisation difficult; though it does not preclude emulation, learning and noting common elements in the stories of Cultural Capitals across the world.

Chapter 1 delimited just what constituted a Cultural Capital and where they have been formally sited over the last thirty years – through civic affirmation or official designation – across Western Europe and Canada and to a lesser extent in Asia, the United States, Southern America and Australasia. Chapter 2 addressed the various conceptualisations of this pattern along with related developments in the Cultural Industries, drawing out useful insights from cultural economics, cultural tourism, sociology and cultural geography as a prelude to developing a framework in which to further discuss the various dimensions of Cultural Capitals. Chapter 3 focused on why this was occurring now; discussing necessary preconditions – including economic and spatial restructuring away from manufacturing towards services, the ICT revolution and the emergence of the Cultural Industries, post-modernity and the symbolic economy, the importance of urban entrepreneurialism and inter-city competition and the common context of post-colonialism. But such an overview of context and preconditions also affirmed the necessity of moving beyond the general to localised stories of particular places and people. Examining case studies of Cultural Capitals became the subject of subsequent chapters, with each positioned within one or more of the conceptual frames offered to best explain this development at each location – with Glasgow best interpreted in terms of cultural tourism and the cultural industries, Bilbao by the dynamics associated with post-modernity, Singapore with post-coloniality and Geelong showing how it can and does all come together in the process of emulating other places in the 21st century. As well as describing and explaining these very different Cultural Capitals, each has been assessed in terms of how their arts have been re-valued, how such a process has been associated with a remaking of urban spaces and their social, economic and cultural sustainability.

Re-valuing the Arts

The framework developed in Chapter 2 offered a means by which the process of valuing the arts could be unpacked. It was argued that the value of an art work, an event, a building, a precinct, even a city was very much a socio-cultural creation related to how various elements of cultural capital were embodied, objectified and institutionalised. If Chapter 3 then offered some of the critical contexts and new vehicles by which value was to be attributed from the late 20th century – as a result of economic restructuring towards services, through the symbolic economy and place in a global hierarchy of cities for investment, tourists and migrants – the case study chapters have detailed the ways in which such new values were derived in each place.

Thus in the case of Glasgow, traditions based around the school of design and art collections joined with a sense of distinctiveness to form the foundation for a re-invention of the city's image and a serious bid to be a European City of Culture. Embodied elements cohering around local artists, designers combined with massive art collections and superb heritage buildings via a set of policy frameworks that valued, supported and presented these elements to capture this crown for 1990. While some were sceptical, the very experience of being a City of Culture provided further embodied and institutional supports for the development of the creative arts – especially of performance – but also of the creative industries, particularly design, as well as of cultural tourism in this city. Related developments in retailing and in urban planning meant that the city was indeed re-invented, as the arts were re-valued in economic but also in social terms, forming one basis for improving health and well being in disadvantaged areas.

If the Glasgow experience involved the revaluing of heritage and building on its design history within an EU policy framework, the case of Bilbao involved very different elements. Here a comparable situation of industrial decline, social polarisation and urban decay was met not so much by locally embodied cultural capital, but by importing the internationally validated arts organisation and architects. The approach by the Bilbao government to the Guggenheim Foundation was an exercise in the mobilisation of institutionalised and objectified cultural capital. Thus local policy frames located an iconic art gallery into a co-ordinated program of transport upgrades, tourist development, educational investment and urban redevelopment. Drawing the Guggenheim Foundation to Bilbao allowed the further spread of a cultural brand which in turn lent its institutional value to the city. The resulting objective pile of cultural capital remains one of the great architectural masterpieces of the 20th century and has, within the overall city redevelopment strategy, facilitated a more general re-valuing of the creative arts within Bilbao, while boosting cultural tourism into the region. Here too the new value of the creative arts was to be primarily economic, though the Guggenheim has also been linked to other cultural developments in the city, especially the boosting of regional artists.

In pursuit of "the Guggenheim effect", the quest for one iconic arts institution that would signal a major re-valuing of the arts and trigger a host of related development – in cultural tourism, inward investment and urban renewal – was to be pursued around the world. Here then was a formula that could be readily replicated. However, as the example of Geelong, Australia showed, having a policy objective is not the same as realising it, while valuing the arts purely in this instrumentalist way does not always lead in predictable directions. Thus in the case of Singapore, the building of the Esplanade-Theatres by the Bay complex was part of a broad ranging policy of valuing the creative arts – especially performance and New Asian landscapes – as a foundation not only for cultural tourism but for ensuring the city's ongoing attractiveness to multinational corporations. Valuing the traditional architecture and cultures of ethnic enclaves, however, has not been without embodied challenges, while the resulting objective landscapes raise real questions as to their veracity and authenticity. So too in the case of performance art. While the Esplanade accommodates the western blockbusters – with value ascribed like the Guggenheim through international networks – supports given to theatres and performance spaces as well as arts education across Singapore has generated a lively embodied arts scene. English language theatre and some performance art has thereby been energised and re-valued by local producers and audiences alike, though it has also challenged – through its engagement with issues of homosexuality and politics – the rigid censorship regime of the Singaporean state. There is therefore a tension between official notions of artistic value – once more primarily economic – and others, which are primarily cultural, social and political.

The process of re-valuing the creative arts in Geelong has been a bifurcated one, led on the one hand by a local state desperately trying to re-imagine the city's image and economy and, on the other, by a local arts community struggling for support and recognition. At the institutional level, local and state resources ensured the construction of major arts infrastructure; such as galleries and performance spaces as well as led to a renovated waterfront and new cultural precincts. It was also at this level that the quest for the Guggenheim was launched. At the embodied level of local artists, they have struggled to be heard and taken seriously within this provincial working class town. Thus it was only *after* the quest for a Guggenheim was launched that the city finally attained an arts policy and arts officer as well as an arts directory. Despite the uneven institutional support for the creative arts, however, they nevertheless have emerged from the efforts of individuals such as Jan Mitchell or collectivities like the Courthouse Youth Theatre. Their value is later elevated through official recognition and financial support – as Mitchell's bollards now form the core of the city's urban image and the Courthouse Theatre and Back to Back Theatre the centre of much innovative performance work in the region and internationally. Their value has also been recognised, following Richard Florida, as integral to an overall package which makes Geelong an attractive home and tourist destination, contributing indirectly rather than directly to its economic well being.

The creative arts have therefore been re-valued in all of the case study cities as the core of an economic redevelopment and urban regeneration strategy. However their value always goes beyond the economic to embrace individual quests for expression of self or place, personal or social healing, community building and urban imagining.

The arts in Geelong, as in Bilbao, Glasgow and Singapore have also been central to the remaking of a few, usually inner, urban spaces.

Re-making Urban Spaces

The ways in which each set of cultural capitals have been recognised, mobilised, grown and projected in the case study cities is closely related to the re-making of particular urban spaces. Indeed integral to the Cultural Capital agenda is urban renewal. Again though, as in the case of how each artefact, event or precinct is valued in ways that link embodied with objectified and institutional cultural capital in precise ways, so too their spatial manifestations are specific to each place.

Thus in the case of Geelong, the re-orientation of the Central Activities and retail district of the city towards the bay involved the redesign of its waterfront and it being systematically endowed with public art works. A comparable strategy was adopted by Singapore as it sought to enliven its main river, such that adjacent buildings were restored and oriented towards the water and an array of sculptures telling "the Singapore story" were commissioned to line its banks. They joined notable international works located in the forecourts of major multinational corporations – by the likes of Henry Moore, Salvador Dali and George Ballas – to give the riverwalk a dual sense of connecting to the city's past and representing its internationally oriented future. Such waterfront renewal which integrates urban design with heritage restoration and public art works is now something of a formula, replicated across the globe in innumerable abandoned waterfront areas. While they thereby assume some sameness in both concept and execution, if done well, they can be about capturing the particulars of the place and its waterfront geography – human and physical – through the renovation and public art works. At their best, waterfront renewals are certainly better than ongoing abandonment and, if well designed with a strong connection to their communities, mightily enhancing. As a Mayor of Geelong noted, the redevelopment of the city's waterfront began an ongoing process of urban and economic re-imaging for the city which has seen it ultimately shrug off its "Sleepy hollow" image.

Renovation and re-use of the wool stores along the Geelong bay front is but one element of its re-invention. But it is a pattern replicated in other parts of this city, as the Cultural Precinct is rebuilt around its 19th-century core. The restoration of Chinese shop houses and housing in the selected Indian, Chinese and Malay quarters becomes a further way in which Singapore positions itself as a Renaissance Cultural Capital. In this, heritage restoration is closely tied to cultural tourism as it is too in the case of Bilbao and Glasgow. Thus part of each city's quest to become a Cultural Capital is a systematic re-evaluation and renovation of its industrial or 19th century urban fabric. In the case of Glasgow, this not only involves a massive project of steam cleaning but the re-use of many buildings in Merchant City for bars, restaurants, hotels and design offices and the saving of some Mackintosh buildings destined to be destroyed by motorways! For Bilbao the Old City too has been renovated and, while stimulating the process of gentrification which also sees low income earners displaced from Singaporean shop houses and Glasgow's tenements, the result is at least the maintenance of heritage gems in these cities. Part of being a Cultural Capital then is a process of re-valuing urban heritage and re-using older structures as part of remaking urban space. Whether such an exercise, along with the process or re-valuing the arts in each locality, is sustainable is the subject of the final section.

Sustaining Cultural Capitals

The notion of *sustainability* is fundamental to many discussions of urban and "natural" environments. Central to the sustainability movement is action to ensure that current generations do not use the environment in ways which compromise that available to future generations (Brundtland, 1987; Low, Gleeson and Radovic, 2005). An early and ongoing ecological emphasis of the concept has usefully been extended to human populations, generating notions of social, cultural and economic sustainability. Such a broadening is often associated with the idea of sustainable development whereby economic growth is connected to political engagement, social equity and cultural integrity as well as to ecological balance. This idea connects the ideal of economic development with ecological preservation and socio-political enhancement (Throsby, 2003: 183). A city and its arts agenda can be assessed in these broad terms, such that:

> Economically, growth derived from the arts can be facilitated and ongoing without damaging the physical or social environment while ensuring a wide distribution of benefits;

> Socially, the city is a place of justice and care in which opportunities, services and risks are shared fairly; while action is taken to ameliorate current inequalities and benefit all;

> Culturally a city should ensure the maintenance and expression of its diverse and interconnected social identities, inter and intra generational equity and protection of its built environment (Throsby 2003: 184–185);

> Any Cultural Capital must also arise from and ensure meaningful political participation in decisions that effect people's lives and environments, and;

> Ecologically, a city should function so that the needs of the present will be met without sacrificing the ability of future generations to meet theirs. It should have adequate open space, bio-diversity, clean air and water.

This broad notion of sustainability – with the exception of its biologial dimensions – formed the basis for assessing the efficacy of the case study Cultural Capitals; offering an ethic as well as a framework for their evaluation.

Economic sustainability

In relation to the creation and sustaining of economic value, the shift from manufacturing to services in all four cities accelerated over the 1980s and 1990s and this has been accompanied by larger numbers employed in the arts, Creative Industries and tourism sectors. Such growth has been associated with massive investment – with significant amounts of capital from outside the cities flowing into arts and related infrastructure: theatres, galleries, hotels, shopping centres, airports, public transport and urban renewal projects. Also vital has been the growth in international, regional and national tourists into the four cities. Whether such visitation and employment growth will continue is an open question, but there is little doubt that economic value and some economic sustainability was achieved from 1980 to 2008 as a result of mobilising different forms of cultural capital.

A summary of the relevant data on economic structure and tourism numbers is given in Table 8.1, below. Significantly, while there has been an across the board

Table 8.1   Economic structure and tourist numbers in Bilbao, Glasgow, Singapore and Geelong 1980–2000

Sectors (% emp) City	Manuf 1980s	Manuf. 1990s	Manuf. 2000	Services 1980s	Services 1990s	Services 2000	Tourists 1980s	Tourists 2001
Glasgow	33.8 (1981)	21.1 (1991)	21.0	65.9	77.3	78.0	700,000 (1982) 2.2 mill. (1987)	2.8 mill.
Bilbao	45.5 (1975)	32.0 (1990)	26.9 (1996)	41.7 (1975)	52 (1990)	65.2 (1996)	1.4 mill. (1998)	930,000 850,000 (2003)
Singapore	29.5 (1982)	30.0	30.0	60.0	70.0	70.0	2.82 mill. (1981)	7.5 mill. (2002)
Geelong	22	22.2	13	69	75.9	81.3	229,000 (1991)	311,000 (2001)

Sources: Le Blanc 1984; McNeil 2000; BBC News 2003; Fraser 2005; GOT 2001; Profile of Geelong 2002

shift from manufacturing to services – in terms of employment and contribution to GDP – this sector is incredibly diverse and in each city the numbers of persons actually employed directly by the Cultural Industries is relatively small, numerically and proportionally – averaging around 2%. The direct contribution of these activities to the overall shift to a Service Economy is therefore limited, though in all cases, activities in the creative arts have been firmly connected to re-imagining the respective cities as tourist and investment destinations. As Richard Florida cogently argued some years ago, the economic sustainability of the Cultural Capital agenda has also to be evaluated in terms of how it works as a centre for incoming corporate investment and their executives as well as to tourists (Florida, 2000).

Tourist numbers are therefore instructive and while not solely connected to the rise of the Cultural Capital, are closely associated with it. And here the case of Singapore and Glasgow appear to be by far the most successful in terms of numbers. Singapore's performance on this front is the most impressive and is closely related to its role as an entrepot and airport hub in Asia, while that of Glasgow has been linked to a number of major cultural festivals (1990 in particular) and high profile galleries (such as the opening of the Burrell Collection and the refurbished Kelvingrove Gallery) promoted across Europe. The case of Bilbao is intriguing, as the tourist numbers are closely tied to the profile and success of the Guggenheim Museum. Significantly, after its opening in 1997 tourist numbers shot up over the one million mark (peaking at 1.4 million in 1998). However, subsequent to this year and especially after September 11 and the Madrid bombings, numbers have been falling. In the case of Geelong, always the gateway city within Victoria, tourist numbers have been rising, but not more than the Australian average. The city's campaign to become the City by the Bay with a major tourist profile has stalled somewhat along with its quest for an iconic Guggenheim.

In terms of the numbers actually employed in the Cultural Industries, city level comparisons are plagued by a lack of comparable data, but even with this problem, it is apparent from Table 8.2, that the numbers and proportions are not especially great, though in all cases, this is one of the main objectives of official planning and support for these industries. In short, the economic sustainability of these Cultural Capitals on the back of these industries is questionable, in that direct employment in them is limited. However, the effect of re-imagining these cities as Cultural Capitals, in making them attractive places for the Creative Class to actually live and visit, has to be seen as relatively effective.

Table 8.2   Numbers and proportions employed directly in the Creative Industries – Glasgow*, Bilbao**, Singapore*** and Geelong 2001[#]

Employment in the CIs City	Employment Nos.	Proportion of the Workforce in the CIs
Glasgow	3,297	0.1
Bilbao	3,800	7.2
Singapore	79,000	3.8
Geelong	771	1.0

Sources: * Only includes Film, Radio, TV, Newspapers;**Numbers for employment related to the Guggenheim only while Workforce Proportion related to the "Creative Class" *** Includes Computer Software, Advertising, Publishing; [#]Includes only Artists and Related professionals

Social, cultural and political sustainability

Economic sustainability relates not only to the contribution the Cultural Industries make to employment, to the growth in the service sector and to tourist numbers but also to the ways in which wealth and social benefits are distributed. It is also necessary and appropriate to assess the ways in which the populations of these cities have actively participated in the cultural agenda and how the strategy expresses and supports their cultural diversity. Social, cultural and political sustainability are therefore interconnected, related to the process of re-valuing the arts and will be briefly appraised here for each city.

Glasgow

Glasgow's most impressive edifice related to its claim for Cultural Capital status is the Scottish Exhibition Centre on the Clyde River, known colloquially as

The Armidillo. In addition, there have also been investments in housing the massive Burrell art collection and in the Kelvingrove Galley, both of which have become major draw cards for cultural tourists outside of London. As Chapter 4 described, there have also been concerted efforts to restore the old Merchant City, including buildings by the eminent Arts and Crafts architect and designer Charles Rennie Mackintosh. Part of these efforts focused on one Mackintosh building designed for the Glasgow Herald newspaper and now converted into a design centre – The Lighthouse – and along with other restored buildings and support for the Glasgow School of Art, city planners sought to recapture Glasgow as a centre of design, using this as the centrepiece for marketing the city as "Scotland with Style". Revaluing the cultural capital of the city has therefore built on its industrial heritage buildings and design tradition with particular examples – such as the work of Mackintosh – reassessed and marketed in new terms within an overall tourism policy framework. In addition, the design industries have been built upon the Glasgow School of Art, systematic supports from local and regional governments and a cultural edginess of the city itself.

As with Bilbao there has been some economic success associated with these efforts, registered in tourism numbers and the proportion of the workforce employed in the Service Sector rather than in manufacturing (see Table 8.1). What was noted in Chapter 4, however, is the relatively small numbers employed directly in the sector now most strongly identified with the city – design. However, similar to Bilbao, the improvement in the image of the city associated with its Cultural Capital bid and experience has been real and long-lasting and this in turn has facilitated the attraction of other employers and tourists into the city. Unlike Bilbao these numbers and the ongoing efforts to re-imagine the city – first as a Cultural Capital, then as a City for Architecture and Design, and more recently as the centre for Mackintosh and contemporary Design – along with the existence of an array of major cultural attractions, means that tourist numbers are rising rather than falling. The city, then, appears to be more economically sustainable as a result of its Cultural Capital status.

If the economic dimension of the city is relatively positive, the social and physical dimensions remain problematical. Graphically retold in the People's Palace Museum, the history of the city as a steel and shipbuilding centre is one of long term decline (Author's field notes 2005). As a booming industrial centre, the city was subjected to waves of immigration and poor urban planning in the 19th century and then to major modernist housing developments on its edges in the 1950s and 1960s. As the industry has been rendered redundant so too have the peripheral tower blocks become social and physical scars upon the landscape. While capital, art and social development have been focused on the inner areas, peripheral tower estates along with other black spots – such as the Gorbals – remain indicative of a population beset with high levels of unemployment, ill health, welfare dependency and poor quality housing. Their engagement with a cultural agenda is minimal, though over 1990 and in for example the Gorbals, such engagement did occur at a micro-scale. With ongoing social disadvantage and high levels of poverty however, the social and cultural sustainability of Glasgow's Cultural Capital agenda is therefore questionable.

Bilbao

The most spectacular artefact and one which best symbolises the whole notion of Cultural Capitals is the Frank Gehry designed Museuo del Guggenheim in Bilbao. Built as part of a deliberate international expansion plan by the Director of the New York Guggenheim – Thomas Krens – Bilbao competed with a number of other European cities to "win" the Guggenheim in 1995. The Basque interest was led by the dominant Partido Nacional Vasco (PNV) – a right wing, regionalist party representing business interests but also a political group fired by a spirit of cultural, political and economic autonomy – which was exploring ways in which it could move the region beyond the double bind of deindustrialisation and crippling terrorism (McNeil, 2000: 481). Gehry's design cost Bilbao US$120 million for its construction, US $20million to buy the Guggenheim brand and entitlement to show the Foundation's collection and US $50 million to purchase a local collection (McNeill, 2000: 480).There is also ongoing maintenance and operational costs. Here then is a cultural edifice whose value is readily translated into economic terms, but which also has a cache because of its international status as an architectural icon and branch of a New York-based gallery.

If supported by local business and some political interests, the proposed gallery did not immediately have the endorsement of displaced workers or local artists. Thus in his presentation to the city elders, Gehry had to run the gauntlet of picketing unemployed locals. It was these groups and others who subsequently had to meet much of its cost as public officials diverted 80% of all public arts funding to pay for the Guggenheim (Zulaika, 2001: 12). This raises a question which is echoed across all three cities – namely how much the support for international circuits of cultural capital undermines rather than supports local social, cultural and political sustainability.

Eight years on and opposition to the museum is more muted, perhaps a result of familiarity, pride and an expression of its many dimensions of success – for the museum has undoubtedly boosted tourist numbers and been part of a successful re-imagining of the city. The museum has been successfully integrated into the city's urban fabric, been central to an economic revival based on tourism and the knowledge industries and been one part of a massive program of urban improvement which spans the city, but it has not been able to ameliorate political disquiet and was, initially at least, a drain on other cultural activities across the city. Thus, the cease fire from ETA which portended political peace at the time of its opening has now been abandoned so that sporadic bombings of tourist sites have been occurring again since 2003 (BBC, 2003) raising questions as to its political sustainability.

However in terms of cultural sustainability, the Guggenheim and related re-development has facilitated a broad pattern of cultural sustainability as capital, along with local and international interest, has flowed into other arts venues and been instrumental in the restoration of the old city.Thus the Museum is located in the centre of a cultural district formed by the Museo de Belles Artes, other galleries, the University de Duest and the Old Town Hall, on the Nervion River. A short walk away is the restored old city which is now being reoccupied by residents as well as enjoyed by international tourists (Author's field notes 2005). The institutional forms of cultural capital subsequently intersect with embodied work as the gallery acquires and shows local artists and the city as a whole benefits from related infrastructure investment. But the socialist local government not only pursued cultural icons but upgraded public transport, revitalised derelict industrial sites, invested in education, attracted new industries and restored the Nervion River. In the case of Bilbao, then, there has been some measure of economic, cultural and social sustainability associated with the Guggenheim, though the ongoing separatist violence and the down turn in tourist numbers do not bode well for its ongoing economic and political sustainability.

I would ague, following Wark (1999), that the tapering off of tourist interest in the Guggenheim relates to the very terms of its creation – as a celebrity building designed by a celebrity architect. Connecting to the post-modern urban agenda of spectacle and celebrity means that the need for ongoing renewal and refreshing of the image and reality of the celebrity building is ever present. Once seen and experienced, there is no real need to revisit the site or the city. As a sustainable Cultural Capital, then, Bilbao may have a limited future.

Singapore

The conscious effort by the Singaporean government to re-orient its economy and society towards the Cultural and Creative Industries was foreshadowed in an official investigation in 1989 which recommended significant investment in arts infrastructure. It was from this time that the commitment was made to build the massive Esplanade-Theatres by the Bay complex as a vehicle to attract international acts and therefore tourists from across the region, while also providing an improved cultural climate in which multinational executives could work and locals remain. In addition to this high profile effort to explicitly value western block busters, went measures to restore and revitalise ethnic heritage precincts – of Chinatown, Little India and Kampong Glam – and to clean up and enhance the shores of the Singapore River. Such moves can be read as a somewhat cynical attempt to undo the damage done to heritage buildings and ethnic communities by years of high rise housing development and deliberate social mixing. However, they did involve a revaluing of heritage buildings and precincts that would otherwise had been demolished and a re-imagining of ethnic enclaves as sites of cultural capital. The net effects have been to instil a degree of cultural and social sustainability in a city-state where such dimensions were under severe threat.

Associated with these arts and restoration agendas – which consumed most of the funding and official energies – was another which had the effect of rehousing and supporting the growth of local theatre houses and groups. Thus as well as The Esplanade, the Sub Station and The Necessary Stage were rehoused while other theatre groups were funded and supported over the 1990s. Along with this upgrading of performance infrastructure went a relaxation of the strict censorship regime which had long constrained the sort of theatre that could be performed in Singapore. While remaining a constraint on political satire and engagement with controversial issues – such as ethnic difference, bureaucratic competence and sexuality – the new openness to the creative arts has allowed boundaries to be pushed towards greater free expression and therefore political sustainability.

There remains a tension in Singapore between the post-colonial strategy to ensure the continued rule of the dominant People's Action Party and an economic development agenda which now includes the Cultural Industries. For it has been recognised within Singapore and without, that any serious creative arts agenda has to grow unfettered by official regulation and sanction. Episodes such as the arrest and gaoling of eminent theatre directors and performers – such as Kao Pun Kun in the 1960s – or the banning of performances that include nudity, political satire or gay references in the 1980s and 90s have therefore lessened considerably in Singapore. There has therefore been a recognition of the need to connect the Cultural Industries agenda with artistic freedom. Culturally, then, the creative arts are looking more sustainable in this highly repressive city state as writers, directors and performers negotiate and transgress the strictures that have long stifled the creative arts. In terms of performance art as well as cultural heritage then, there is much to applaud in their cultural and social sustainability which in turn is underpinning their economic sustainability in this most unlikely location.

Geelong

A much smaller provincial city, Geelong has been buffeted by the same globalisation forces which engendered the collapse of ship building in Glasgow and Bilbao and electronics production in Singapore. For Geelong the crisis began in the 1970s and worsened over the next two decades as first its textile and then its car and truck manufacturing industries contracted before a local financial institution's collapse enshrined the label of "rust bucket". The models chosen for emulation ranged from the festival market place of Boston to the Cultural Capital agenda of Glasgow and the Guggenheim of Bilbao. Here then was an Australian city which systematically sought to replicate off shore successes of re-imagining, waterfront redevelopment, the iconic art museum and most recently the cultural precinct. However, as the account in Chapter 7 indicated, not all models can be readily transplanted, nor can all ideals be realised as the city bid for and then had to abandon its quest for a Guggenheim museum. As with the cases of other major developments – such as the Esplanade – Theatres by the Bay in Singapore – once a decision has been taken to become a Cultural Capital, policies are developed, local cultural capital marshalled and the creative arts re-valued. The result in the case of Geelong has been the creation and extension of an array of embodied, objective and institutional forms of cultural capital. Thus the case of the Geelong Performing Arts Centre, established in 1981 as part of an early attempt to render the industrial city more attractive to visitors and locals alike, is of an elite institution that has become expert at outreach activities and central to the redevelopment of an entire Cultural Precinct. Adjacent to it, the Courthouse Youth Theatre, born of local lobbying, housed in a heritage building and financed by significant State inflows of capital, is another space in which innovative and world leading productions are emerging. Along with Jan Mitchell's bay walk bollards, in Geelong there has been the mobilisation of local embodied cultural capital into diverse public settings which in turn have clearly contributed to the re-imagining of this city. The new theatres and public art projects have all occurred within a belatedly developed policy framework. Such developments, along with the bid for the Guggenheim signal a re-valuing of the creative arts in this regional city which is proving economically and socially sustainable. In that such a climate now also supports a broad array of local artists and groups as well as festivals such as the Pako Festa, suggests a firm basis for the cultural sustainability of this city as well.

There are therefore an array of commonalities but also significant differences between the formulation and realisation of cultural capital in each of the case study cities. They are summarised in Table 8.3.

Cultural Capitals as Simulacra

The four examples chosen to explore the Cultural Capital agenda have some remarkable similarities. All have in various ways been tough cities – industrial cities, some with radical socialist pasts, brutal working conditions and more recently, derelict landscapes. They are also variously engaged in shifts towards a service economy dominated by symbolic capital, inter-urban competition, post-colonial politics and re-imagining. In addition they have all consciously developed Cultural Capital agendas and shown a remarkable propensity to copy from each other. Thus Bilbao copied Glasgow, Hong Kong and Singapore, while Singapore modelled itself on Manchester, Glasgow and Melbourne; Glasgow was inspired by Minneapolis, Baltimore and Boston and Geelong by Bilbao, Glasgow, Dundee and Boston. There is therefore a Cultural Capital industry, as the formula for redeveloping old industrial precincts and cities is codified and sold on from one city to the other. In this circulation of models and ideals, a number of international consultants have been critical – including McKinsey and Co, Comedia as well as key individuals such as Charles Landry, Frederico Bianchini and Richard Florida. But the ideal has moved from being the Creative City of Landry – in the 1980s and 90s – to attracting the Creative Class of Richard Florida in the new century.

Having established Comedia in 1978, Charles Landry assembled a team of consultants and personally worked across many countries and cities in his quest to put "creativity" at the centre of contemporary urban life, planning and regeneration. Through investigations, consultancies, public speaking and publications, Landry

Table 8.3   Bilbao-Glasgow-Singapore-Geelong as Cultural Capitals – Similarities and Differences

Commonalities	Divergences/Differences
Role of post-colonial identity making	International or national orientation Singapore – Global Bilbao – Spain, Europe and US Glasgow – England and Europe Geelong – Victoria and Australia
Foundation on "old" economies – 19th century industry (Bilbao, Glasgow, Geelong) or 20th century industrialisation (Singapore)	Levels of artistic freedom Role of surveillance and censorship – Singapore vs Bilbao, Glasgow and Geelong
Moves in the 1970s and 80s away from manufacturing to services	Depth of cultural and arts activity eg Bilbao vs Glasgow, Geelong and Singapore but problems with its engagement
Government policies supporting/driving/ leading cultural development (from the 1980s)	Role of TNCs and capital from outside the city Recency of an arts policy
Waterfront redevelopment	Public art and place narratives
Iconic Buildings/developments	Role of major events/festivals
City as celebrity – urban makeovers/up	Social inclusion vs exclusion
Art as an economic driver/cultural industry revival but also the arts subordinated to economics. Then built on/ignored as emphasis shifts to other knowledge-based industries/cultural industries (IT, design)	Social capital connecting to Cultural capital
Public-private partnerships	
Heritage value – of precincts/old/ethnic identities	Architecture as celebrity – Gehry et al in Bilbao and Geelong vs Singapore/Glasgow
Cultural/event tourism	Connection to (Singapore, Glasgow, Geelong) or a minor support of "real" knowledge-based economic development (Bilbao)

has offered a particular analysis and set of guidelines for the creation of Cultural Capitals. In this role he became a globalising agent, spreading a particular gospel of Creative Cities which he has proselytised from Helsinki to Adelaide, Barcelona to Huddersfield across over 100 cities (see Landry 2000; Landry et al. 1996; Comedia 2003). The approach – as gleaned from publications, web sites and personally attended public lectures in Adelaide and Melbourne over the last twenty years – is to offer inspiration and hope through an optimistic view of what is possible by mobilising human creativity. The pitch is both idealistic and pragmatic as analysis and rhetoric gives way to concrete case studies, suggestions for how to remove barriers, and recommendations for success. The aim is to mobilise creativity – ideas, feelings and abilities to think differently, laterally, synthetically – and ensure that this is then translated into innovation – the economically viable application and realisation of creativity. The successful Creative City then is the one which combines creativity and innovation in a set of physical and social projects which support the arts but also engender the Cultural Industries and the overall social fabric of a city.

It is an incredibly broad agenda – as the urban problems to be solved range from unemployment and derelict areas to crime, lack of child care and poor public transport – but also a highly focused one; in that outcomes, especially economic ones, are essential. As Atkinson and Easthope note (2007), Landry's focus is on bringing creativity into the practice and policies of urban renewal as cities across the Western world face the challenge of globalisation, increased social fragmentation, fear and alienation, growing dissatisfaction with their physical environment and declining sense of locality. It is in this context that the value of the arts becomes infinitely broadened – well beyond individual creativity to embrace art as the vehicle for urban regeneration, economic resuscitation, social renewal and political engagement.

Alongside such strategies go particular views of populations and governance. Thus there is ongoing exhortations for local empowerment, engagement and ownership of the Creative City agenda and its various localised components. But there is also an affirmation of the role of strong leadership, government initiatives and public-private partnerships in the realisation of the agenda as well as the legitimacy of accountability and value for money. As a consultancy company selling the idea of the Creative City, Landry's Comedia and latterly Richard Florida, have a set of socio-economic objectives. In the process of implementing this agenda and satisfying clients – the aspiring Cultural Capitals – the imperative is to get things done, to offer guidance to others that will allow their replication as well as explanations for apparent failures. In all of this, the expert outside consultant has a key role to play. Amidst the ongoing rhetorical commitment to "the feminine" side of planning, then, the pragmatics of offering guidance to cities means a focus on removing obstacles – such as government functionaries, professionals and resistant attitudes – and creating appropriate pre-conditions for success as well as leadership. As *The Creative City* concludes:

> The courage of sticking to your plans in the face of hostility and adversity seems paramount. There is often a need to go against the grain of supposed common sense, conventional wisdom and narrow commercial imperatives (Landry and Bianchini 1995, p. 57).

Local empowerment and the mobilisation of place-based creativity is therefore something that, for Comedia at least, has to be guided, connected to economic outcomes and accountable. Sometimes, perhaps even frequently, political resistance has to be overcome by visionary leaders, who ultimately know best where matters of creativity and culture are concerned. The political sustainability of such an approach I would argue is limited and forms one of the limitations of the Comedia – and many other – approaches to creating Cultural Capitals. Sadly but not unexpectedly this aspect has been present in many examples. Thus, government and offering leadership has been central to the Cultural Capital agendas of Geelong, Singapore, Bilbao and Glasgow. There is therefore a contradiction in these cities at least, between freeing the creative and artistic spirit, pragmatically supporting its realisation and governments offering both leadership and official control agendas.

Thus in all four cities, connecting the locality to international circuits of cultural capital – in the form of eminent architects and in soliciting the international tourist – has created expanding economic but also social value for the arts. But these examples also illustrate the contradictory role of local politics in the process of creating Cultural Capitals – as in Bilbao, Glasgow, Geelong and Singapore local artists and communities were all rendered marginal to state-drive re-development agendas. There are therefore tensions in all of these cities between the economic sustainability of their Cultural Capital agendas and related drives for cultural, social and political sustainability. This is felt most acutely in Singapore, where a dominant one party state invokes strict censorship laws on the one hand but also actively fosters highly innovative theatre and performance on the other. So too in Glasgow, the drive for mainstream galleries and international tourists sits alongside the need to renovate inner city and peripheral housing estates to ensure higher levels of social equity. Cultural and economic sustainability therefore sits uneasily with a lack of social sustainability in this Cultural Capital as the post-Fordist economy collides with the physical and social scars of a decimated modernity. In contrast, Bilbao and to a lesser extent Geelong have engaged their population in the cultural and urban restoration projects which in turn are spilling over into economic sustainability. However, in Bilbao ongoing if marginal claims of political separatism remain and, along with the problems of focusing most energy on the celebrity building, will continue to limit its overall economic sustainability. The future of the Cultural Capital agenda is therefore assured only where it has attained political but also social and cultural sustainability.

References

Adorno, T. (1991a), Culture industry reconsidered, in J.M. Bernstein (ed.) *The Culture Industry: Selected Essays on Mass Culture* (London: Routledge) pp. 85–92.

Adorno, T. (1991b), The schema of mass culture, in J.M. Bernstein (ed.) *The Culture Industry: Selected Essays on Mass Culture* (London: Routledge) pp.53–84.

Alomes, S. and Jones, C. (eds) (1991), *Australian Nationalism: A Documentary History* (Sydney: Harper Collins).

ALP (Australian Labor Party) (2007), *Federal Labor Arts Policy Discussion Paper,* Available online.

Amin, A. (ed.) (1994), *Post-Fordism: A Reader* (Oxford: Blackwell).

Anderson, K. (1988), Cultural hegemony and the race-definition process in Chinatown, Vancouver: 1880–1980, *Environment and Planning D: Society and Space* 6, pp. 127–149.

Anderson, K. (1991), *Vancouver's Chinatown: Racial Discourse in Canada, 1875–1980* (Montreal: McGill-Queen's University Press).

Anderson, K. (1998), "Sites of difference: Beyond a cultural politics of race polarity", in Fincher, R. and Jacobs, J. (eds), 201–225.

Arts for Australia's Sake (1998), Liberal and National Party of Australia Policies for a Coalition Government. *A Stronger Australia.*

Arts 21 (1994), The Victorian Government's Strategy for the Arts into the Twenty First Century (Melbourne: State Government of Victoria).

Arts Victoria (2003), *Creative Capacity+ Arts for all Victorians* (Melbourne: Arts Victoria).

Atkinson, R. (2003), "Introduction: misunderstood saviour or vengeful wrecker? The many meanings and problems of gentrification", *Urban Studies* 40(12): 2343–50.

Atkinson, R. and Easthope, H. (2007), "The consequences of the creative class: The pursuit of creativity strategies in Australian cities', (Adelaide: State of Australian Cities Conference Proceedings), 586–597.

Australian, The (2003), "Aboriginal gallery may edge out Guggenheim" January 2.

Australian Bureau of Statistics (ABS) (1997, 2003), *Cultural Trends in Australia, Overview* No. 4172. (Canberra: AGPS).

Australian Bureau of Statistics (1986, 1991, 1996, 2001), *Census of Population and Housing* (Canberra: Australian Government Publishing Service).

Australian Bureau of Statistics (2001), *Census of Population and Housing; Customised Tables for the City of Greater Geelong* (Canberra: ABS).

Author's field notes (1998–2008), Geelong.

Author's field notes (2000), Singapore.

Author's field notes (2005), Visit to Singapore, Bilbao and Glasgow, August–September.

Azua, Jon (2005), "Guggenheim Bilbao: 'Competitive' strategies for the new culture-economy of spaces', in Guasch and Zulaika (eds).

Ballas, G. (1999), "Pako Festa", *Geelong Advertiser* 23 February.

Baniotopoulou, E. (2001), Art for whose sake? Modern art museums and their role in transforming societies: The case of the Guggenheim, Bilbao, *Journal of Conservation and Museum Studies,* 7. November, 1–7.

Bardham-Quallen, S. (2004), *The Guggenheim Museum* (Farmington Hills, MI: Blackbirch Press).

Barthes, R. (1972), *Mythologies* (London: Cape).

Bartolucci, M. (2000), Undiscovered Bilboa, *Atlantic Monthly* October, 286 (4).

Baudrillard, J. (1981), *For a Critique of the Political Economy of the Sign* (USA: Telos). Translated by Charles Levin.

Baudrillard, J. (1989), *America* (London: Verson).

Bell, D. (1973/1976), *The Coming of Post-Industrial Society* (Harmondsworth: Penguin).

Bell, D. and Jayne, M. (2003), "Assessing the role of design in local and regional economies", *International Journal of Cultural Policy* 9 (3), 265–84.

Bennett, D. (ed.) (1998) *Multicultural States: Rethinking Difference and Identity* (London and New York: Routledge).

Bennett, T. and Carter, D. (eds) (2001), *Culture in Australia. Policies, Publics and Programs* (Cambridge: Cambridge University Press).

Bennett, T., Emmison, M. and Frow, J. (1999), *Accounting for Tastes: Australian Everyday Culture* (Melbourne: Cambridge University Press).

Bernasek, M. (1986), "The Australian manufacturing industry. The challenges for structural change', *Current Affairs Bulletin*, 63, 16–31.

Berry, M. and Huxley, M. (1992), "Big build: Property capital, the state and urban change in Australia', *International Journal of Urban and Regional Research* 16:1, 151–72.

Bhabha, H. (1990), *Nation and Narration* (London: Routledge).

Bianchini, F. (1993), Remaking European cities: The role of cultural policies, in Bianchini, F. and Parkinson, M. (eds), pp. 1–20.

Bianchini, F., and Parkinson, M. (1993) (eds) *Cultural Policy and Urban Regeneration: The West European Experience* (Manchester, Manchester University Press).

BIE (Bureau of Industry Economics) (1985), *The Regional Impact of Structural Change – An Assessment of Regional Policies in Australia* (Canberra: Australian Government Publishing Service).

Bilbao Exposition (2002), *Bilbao: The transformation of a city Exposition Geelong-Melbourne-Australia 2001–2002* Exhibition Booklet.

"Bilbao as a Global City", New Strategic Challenge for 2010, (2002), Metropolitan Bilbao, Bilbao Metropoli http:www.bm30.es/plan/estrategia_uk.html, Accessed 4.8.05.

Birch, D. (1997), "Singapore English drama: An historical overview 1958-1985", in S. Krishnan (ed.).

Birch, D. (2004), "Celebrating the ordinary in Singapore in extraordinary ways: The cultural politics of The Necessary Stage's collaborative theatre", in Kee and Ng (eds) pp. 43–70.

Bondi, L. (1999), "Gender, class and gentrification: enriching the debate", *Environment and Planning D* 17: 261–82.

Borrie, W.D. (1994), *The European Peopling of Australia: A Demographic History 1788–1988* (Canberra: Australian National University).

Booth, P. and Boyle, R. (1993), "See Glasgow, see culture", in Bianchini and Parkinson (eds), 21–47.

Bourdieu, P. (1984), *Distinction* (London: Routledge).

Bourdieu, P. (1994), The field of cultural production, in *The Polity Reader in Cultural Theory* (New York: Polity Press), pp. 50–65.

Boyle, M. (1997), "Civic boosterism in the politics of local economic development: 'institutional positions' and 'strategic orientations' in the consumption of hallmark events", *Environment and Planning A* 29 (11): 1975–97.

Boyle, M. and Hughes, G. (1991), "The politics of representation of the 'real' discourses from te lef on Glasgow's roles as the European City of Culture 1991", *Area* 23, 217–28.

Boyle, M. and Hughes, G. (1994), "The politics of urban entrepreneurialism in Glasgow", *Geoforum* 25 (4), 453–470.

British American Arts Association (1989), Arts and the Changing City: An Agenda for Urban Regeneration (New York: British American Arts Association).

Brooker, P. (1999), *Cultural Theory: A Glossary (*London: Arnold).

Brown, K. (2000), "Tourism trends for the 1990s", http://www.lord.ca/trends_ tourism.htm Accessed 4/6/2001.

Brochure (2005), *Esplanade-Theatre by the Bay* (August).

Brown, K. (2000), "Tourism trends for the 1990s", http://www.lord.ca/trends_ tourism.htm Accessed 4/6/2001.

Brundtland Report (1987), World Commission on Environment and Development, *Our Common Future* (Oxford: Oxford University Press).

Buchanan, I. (1972), *Singapore in Southeast Asia. An Economic and Political Appraisal* (London: G. Bell and Sons Ltd).

Butler, J. (1990), *Gender Trouble: Feminism and the Subversion of Identity* (New York: Routledge).

Butler, R., Hall, C.M. and Jenkins, J. (eds) (1999), *Tourism and recreation in rural areas (*John Wiley and Sons: Chichester).

Bywater, M. (1993), "The market for cultural tourism is Europe", *EIU Travel and Tourism Analyst* 6, 30–46.

Carr, M. (2003), "Banking on the gallery – Geelong's bid for a Guggenheim: Proposing a cultural strategy for economic development', *in Proceedings of The New Wave: Entrepreneurship and the Arts* (Melbourne, Australia: Deakin University), 11 pp.

Castells, M. (1989), *The Informational City* (London: Blackwell).

Castells, M. (1996/2000), *The Rise of the Network Society* (2nd Edition) (Oxford: Blackwell).

Caust, J. (2003), "Putting the 'art' back into arts policy making: how arts policy has been 'captured' by the economists and the marketers", *International Journal of Cultural Policy*, 9 (1), 51–63.

Caves, R. (2000), *Creative Industries – Contracts Between Art and Commerce* (Cambridge: Harvard University Press).

CCC (1999), "Geelong 2010: S Preferred Future", Unpublished report, Geelong.

Centre for Cultural Policy Research (CCPR), University of Glasgow (2004) "Images of the city. Glasgow's changing international appeal", Seminar, January Gilmorehill Centre, University of Glasgow.

Chang, T.C. (1997), "Heritage as a tourism commodity: Traversing the tourist-local divide", *Singapore Journal of Tropical Geography*, 18 (1), 46–68.

Chang, T.C. (1999), "Local uniqueness in the global village: Heritage tourism in Singapore", *Professional Geographer*, 51 (1), 91–103.

Chang, T.C. (2000a), "Renaissance revisited: Singapore as a 'Global City for the Arts'", *International Journal of Urban and Regional Research* 24 (4), 818–831 (1–11).

Chang, T.C. (2000b) "Theming cities, taming places: Insights from Singapore", *Geografiska Annaler* 82B (1), 35–54.

Chang, T.C. (2000c), "Singapore's Little India: A tourist attraction as a contested landscape", *Urban Studies* 37 (2), 343–366.

Chang, T.C. (2005), "Art and soul: Exploring public art in urban Singapore", Manuscript from author.

Chang, T.C., Milne, S., Fallon, D. and Pohlmann, C. (1996), "Urban heritage tourism. The global-local nexus", *Annals of Tourism Research*, 23 (2), 284–305.

Chang, T.C. and Lee, W.K. (2003), "Renaissance city Singapore: A study of arts spaces", *Area* 35 (2), 128–141.

Chow, C. (2005), "Art we there yet?", *The Straits Times*, Inside Track, <http://straitstimes.asial.com.sg/mnt/html/webspesial/in... accessed 3 February, 2006.

Chow, R. (1996), "Where have all the natives gone", in Mongia, P. (ed.).

Choy, L.W. (1994), Chronology of a controversy, <http://www.biotechnics.org/Chronology%20of%2020a%..., accessed 2 March.2006.

Christopherson, Susan and Storper, M. (1989), "The city as studio, the world as a back lot: The impact of vertical disintegration on the location of the motion-picture industry", *Environment and Planning D: Society and Space* 4, 305–20.

CITF (Creative Industries Task Force) (2001), http://www.culture.gov.uk/creative/mapping.html.

City by the Bay Foreshore Tourist Precinct Project (1987), Geelong. Prepared by R.T. Jebb and Associates Pty. Ltd for the Geelong Regional Commission.

City of Greater Geelong (COGG) (1994) *Geelong 2010: A Preferred Future* (Geelong: COGG).

City of Greater Geelong (2000), *Waterfront Geelong: The Future is Here* (Geelong: COGG).

City of Greater Geelong (2003), Press release on the end of the Guggenheim bid.

Cohen, R.B. (1981), "The new international division of labour, multinational corporations and urban hierarchy", in M.Dear and A.J. Scott (eds), 287–315.

Collins, D. (1982), "The 1920s picture palace", in Dermody et al. (eds), 60–75.

Collins, J. (1984), "Immigration and class: the Australian experience", in G. Bottomley and M.de Lepervanche (eds).

Collins, J. (1991), *Migrant Hands in a Distant Land: Australia's Post-War Immigration* (Sydney: Pluto Press).

Collins, R. (1986), *The Basques* (Oxford: Basil Blackwell).

Comedia (2003), Clarity at the cutting edge. http:www.comedia.org.uk/downloads-2.html Accessed 23.10.2003.

Connell, J. and Gibson, C. (2003), *Sound Tracks: Popular Music, Identity and Place* (London: Routledge).

Connell, R. and Irving, T.H. (1980), *Class Structure in Australian History* (Melbourne: Longman Cheshire).

Cooke, P. (ed.) (1989), *Localities: The Changing Face of Urban Britain* (London: Unwin Hyman).

Cosgrove, D. (1989), A terrain of metaphor: cultural geography 1988–89, *Progress in Human Geography* 13, pp. 566–575.

Cosgrove, D. (1990), "…Then we take Berlin: Cultural geography 1989–1990", *Progress in Human Geography*, 14 (4), pp. 560-568.

Craik, J. (1994), "Peripheral pleasures: the peculiarities of post-colonial tourism", *Culture and Policy* 6 (1): 153–182.

Craik, J. (1996), "The potential and limits of cultural policy strategies", *Culture and Policy* 7:1, 177–204.

Craik, J. (2001), "Tourism, culture and national identity", in Bennett and Carter (eds).

Craik, J., McAllister, L. and Davis, G. (2003), 'Paradoxes and contradictions in government approaches to contemporary cultural policy: An Australian perspective', *The International Journal of Cultural Policy* 9:1, 17–33.

Craik, J. (2008), *Revisioning the Arts* http://epress.anu.edu.au/anzsog/revisioning/mobile_devices.tml Accessed 5/3/08.

Creative Nation (1994), Commonwealth Cultural Policy, (Canberra: Australian Government Publishing Service).

Creativity+ (2003), City of Greater Geelong Culture Strategy, August. www.geelongaustralia.com.au.

Crewe, L. (1996), "Material culture: Embedded forms, organisational networks and the local economic development of a fashion quarter", *Regional Studies*, 30 (3), 257–72.

Crewe, L. and Forster, Z. (1993), "Markets, design and local agglomeration: the role of the small independent retailer in the workings of the fashion system", *Environment and Planning D: Society and Space* 11, 213–229.

Crick, M. (1988), "Sun, sex, sights, savings and servility", *Criticism, Heresy and Interpretation* 1: 37–76.

Crumbaugh, J. (2001), An aesthetic of industrial ruins in Bilbao: Daniel Calparsoro's *Leap into the Void* (Salto al vacio) and Frank Gehry's Guggenheim Museum Bilbao, *IJIS* 14 (1), 40–50.

Cuito, A. (2001), *Guggenheim Bilbao* (Madrid: Kliczkowski Publishing).

Cunningham, S. (1992), *Framing Culture. Criticism and Policy in Australia* (North Sydney: Allen and Unwin).

Cultural Ministers Council No. 7 *Employment* National Culture Recreation Statistics Unit, Australian Bureau of Statistics. Canberra: Statistical Advisory Group.

Cunha, D. da (ed.) (2002), *Singapore in the New Millennium. Challenges Facing the City-State* (Singapore: Institute of Southeast Asian Studies).

CURA (1976), *"But I wouldn't want my wife to work here ..." A Study of Migrant Women in Melbourne Industry* (Melbourne: Centre for Urban Research and Action).

Davis, M. (1990), *City of Quartz* (London: Verso).

Davis, M. (1992/95), "Fortress Los Angeles: The militarization of urban space", in Sorkin (ed.).

Dear, M. and Scott, A.J. (1981), (eds) *Urbanization and Planning in Capitalist Society* (London and New York: Methuen).

Debord, G. (1983/1994), *The Society of the Spectacle* (New York: Zone).

De Bruin, A. (1996), From cultural to economic capital: community employment creation in Otara. *Labour, Employment and Work in New Zealand* Proceedings of the 8th Conference, Wellington, pp. 89–96.

De Bruin, A. (1998a), Cultural capital, in P. O'Hara *Encyclopaedia of Political Economy* London and New York: Routledge.

De Bruin, A. (1998b), Towards extending the concept of human capital: A note on cultural capital, *The Journal of Interdisciplinary Economics* 10, pp.59–70.

Department of Culture, Media and Sports (DCMS) (1998) Creative Industries Task Force Report.

Department of Culture, Media and Sports (DCMS) (2000), *Creative Industries Mapping Document* (London: DCMS).

Department of Culture, Media and Sports (DCMS) (2005), www.culture.gov.uk/creative_industries, 2005. Accessed 10.10.2005.

Dermody, S. (1982), "Two remakes: Ideologies of film production 1919–1932" in Dermoday et al. 33–59.

Dermody, S., Docker, J. and Modjeska, D. (eds) (1982), *Nellie Melba, Ginger Meggs and Friends, Essays in Australian Cultural History*, (Malmsbury, Victoria: Kibble Books).

Deutsche, R. (1996), *Evictions. Art and Spatial Politics* (Cambridge/London: MIT Press).

Dicken, P. (2003), *Global Shift: Reshaping the Global Economic Map in the 21st Century* (London: Guildford Press). 4th Edition.

Dovey, K. (2004), *Fluid City: Transforming Melbourne's Urban Waterfront* (Sydney: University of NSW Press).

Duncan, J. and Ley, D. (eds) (1993), *Place/Culture/Representation* (London and New York: Routledge).

Duncan, J. and Duncan, N. (1988), (Re) reading the landscape, *Environment and Planning D: Society and Space* 6, pp. 117–126.

Eco, U. (1986), *Travels in hyper-reality* London: Picador.

Economist.com – Cities Guide (2006), Singapore. http:www.economist.com/cities/findStory.cfm?CIT … Accessed 9.2007.

Economic Survey of Singapore (2002), 2001 Ministry of Trade and Industry, Singapore.

Economic Survey of Singapore (2005), 2004 Ministry of Trade and Industry, Singapore.

EKOS (2003a), *Working Paper 9* Evaluation of Glasgow Business Base, ABI Data – Glasgow Key Sectors.

EKOS (2003b), *Working Paper 10* Evaluation of Glasgow Business Base, ABI Data – Glasgow and Selected Cities Key Sectors.

Elson, D. and Pearson, R. (1981), "Nimble fingers make cheap workers" An analysis of women's employment in third world export manufacturing, *Feminist Review* 7, pp. 81–107.

Ellin, N. (1999), *Postmodern Urbanism* (New York: Princeton University Press).

Euskadi Essencial: A Tour of Euskai Hiria (2005) De Paso Publications.

Evans, G. (2003), "Hard-branding the cultural city – From Prado to Prada", *International Journal of Urban and Regional Research* 27 (2): 417–40.

Experian (2003), *Glasgow economic audit* (Glasgow: Scottish Enterprise Glasgow).

Fensham, R. (1994), "Prime time hyperspace: the Olympic City as spectacle", in Gibson, K. and Watson, S. (eds), pp. 171–185.

Fernandez-Kelly, M.P. (1983), *For we are sold, I am my people: Women and industry in Mexico's Frontier* (Albany: State University of New York Press).

Fincher, R. and Jacobs, R. (eds) (1998), *Cities of Difference* (New York: The Guildford Press).

Fisher, M. and Owen, U. (eds) (1991), *Whose cities? (*London: Penguin).

Flew, T. (1997), "Cultural regulation and cultural policy in the 1990s", *Culture and Policy* 8:1, 171–179.

Florida, R. (2005), *Cities and the Creative Class* (New York: Routledge).

Florida, R. (2003), "Cities and the creative class", *City and Community* 2 (1), pp. 3–21.

Florida, R. (2002), *The Rise of the Creative Class* (New York: Basic Books).

Focus Groups (2004), Geelong. Writers and Visual Artists. Conducted by the author.

For Art's Sake – A Fair Go! (1996), Liberal and National Party Coalition Policy http://www.liberal.org.au/ Accessed 23.6.97.

Forster, Kurt W. (1999), *Frank O. Gehry. Art and Architecture in Discussion* (Senefelderstrabe: Cantz Verlag).

Foucault, M. (1973), *The Birth of the Clinic: An Archaeology of Medical Perception* (New York: Vintage).

Foucault, M. (1977), *Discipline and Punish: The Birth of the Prison* (New York: Vintage Books).

Foucault, M. (1979), *The History of Sexuality: An Introduction* (New York: Pantheon).

Frampton, K. (1980), *Modern Architecture: A Critical History* (London: Thames and Hudson).

Fraser, Andrea (2005), "Isn't this a wonderful place?"(A tour of a tour of the Guggenheim Bilbao), in Guasch and Zulaika (eds).

Fraser, W.H. "Second city of the Empire: 1830s to 1914", http://www. theglasgowstory.com/storyb.php?PHPsE.. Accessed 13.4.06.

Frey, H. (1999), *Designing the City: Towards a More Sustainable Urban Form* (London: E.&F. Spon).

Frey, B.S. and Pommerehre, W.W. (1990), *Muses, Markets and Explorations in the Economics of the Arts* (London: Basil Blackwell).

Friedmann, J. and Wolff, G. (1982), "World city formation: an agenda for research and action", *International Journal of Urban and Regional Research* 6, 292–310.

Friedman, M. (ed.) (1999a), *Architecture and Process. Gehry Talks* (New York: Rizzoli International Publishers).

Friedman, M. (1999), The reluctant master, in Friedman (ed.).

Friel, E. (2004), "'Competitive cities' in the twenty first century", in CCPR.

Froebel, F., Heinrichs, J. and Kreye, O. (1980), *The New International Division of Labour. Structural Unemployment in Industrialised Countries and Industrialisation in Developing Countries* (Cambridge: Cambridge University Press).

Frow, J. (1995), *Cultural Studies and Cultural Value* (Oxford: Clarendon).

Frow, J. (1988), "Economics of value", in Bennett, D. (ed.) *Multicultural Studies: Rethinking Difference and Identity* London and New York: Routledge, pp. 53–68.

Gandhi, L. (1998), *Postcolonial Theory: A Critical Introduction* (St Leonards, NSW: Allen and Unwin).

Garcia, B. (2003), Contemporary issues in cultural policy in Spain, On web, accessed 4.11.05.

Garcia, B. (2005), "Deconstructing the City of Culture: The long-term cultural legacies of Glasgow 1990", *Urban Studies,* 42 (5/6), pp. 841–868.

Garreau, P. (1991), *Edge Cities: Life on the New Frontier* (New York: Doubleday).

Geelong Arts Directory (2002), Geelong, City of Greater Geelong.

GBN Geelong Business News (1997), The Geelong Waterfront.

GA (2000) "Guggenheim support", December 13.

Geelong Info (2003) October 14.

GA (2000a), "Guggenheim dreaming", February 2.

GA Editorial (2000b), "Guggenheim ambitions", *Geelong Advertiser* 25 February.

Geelong Independent (2003), "Culture wars" August 15.

GBN (Geelong Business News) (2000), "Guggenheim Dreaming", 75 October, 10–13.

Geelong Otway Tourism (GOT) (1995), *Cultural Tourism Development Strategy* (Draft) (Geelong: GOT).

Gelder, K. and Jacobs, J.M. (1998), *Uncanny Australia: Sacredness and Identity in a Postcolonial Nation* (Carlton: Melbourne University Press).

Gibbs, A. (1983), *Glasgow: The Making of a City* (London: Croom Helm).

Gibson, K. and Watson, S. (eds) (1994), *Metropolis Now: Planning and the Urban in Contemporary Australia* (Sydney: Pluto Press).

Gibson, C. (2003), Cultures at work: why "culture" matters in research on the "cultural industries", *Social and Cultural Geography* 4 (2), pp. 201–215.

Gibson-Graham, K.J. (1996), *The End of Capitalism as we Knew It: A Feminist Critique of Political Economy* (Cambridge, Mass.: Blackwell Publishers).

Gibson, C., Murphy, P. and Freestone, R. (2002), Employment and socio-spatial relations in Australia's cultural economy, *Australian Geographer* 33 (2), pp. 173–189.

Gibson, L. (2001), *The Uses of Art: Constructing Australian Identities* (St Lucia: University of Queensland Press).

Gilbert-Rolfe, Jeremy with Gehry, Frank (2001), *Frank Gehry: The City and the Music* (London and New York: Routledge).

Glasgow City Council (2006), *Glasgow Cultural Strategy* Executive Summary, Glasgow City Council: Glasgow Accessed 9.1.08.

"Glasgow unveils £1.5m rebranding" (2006), BBC News http:www.news.bbc.co.uk/1/hi/Scotland/3547313/stm (accessed 13.4.2006).

Glass, R. (1964), "Introduction: aspects of change", in Centre for Urban Studies (Ed.) *Aspects of change* (London: MacGibbon and Kee).

Glasson, J., Godfrey, K. and Goodey, B. (1995), *Towards Visitor Impact Management* (Avebury: Aldershot).

Global City 2010. Metropolitan Bilbao (2002), Bilbao as a Global City: New Strategic Challenge for 2010. http:www.bm30.es/plan/estrategia_uk.html.

Goldstone, L. (2003), Cultural statistics, in R. Trowse (ed.) *A Reader in Cultural Economics* (Cheltenham: Edward Elgar), pp. 177–182.

GPAC (2007) Submission to COGG on the Cultural Precinct Unpublished document held by author.

Gregory, D., Martin, R. and Smith, G. (eds) (1994), *Human Geography: Society, Space and Social Science* (Houndmills, Basingstoke: Macmillan).

Gregson, N., Simonsen, K. and Vaiou, D. (2001), "Whose economy for whose culture? Moving beyond oppositional talk in European debate about economy and culture", *Antipode* 33 (4), pp. 616–646.

Groenewegan, P. (1972), "Consumer capitalism", in J. Playford and D. Kirsner (eds).

Guasch, A.M. and Zulaika, J. (eds) (2005), *Learning from the Bilbao Guggenheim* (Reno, Nevada: Center for Basque Studies, University of Nevada).

Guasch, Anna Maria (2005), "Global museum versus local artists: Paradoxes of identity between local and global understanding", in Guasch and Zulaika (eds).

Gunew, S. (1996), "Performing Australian ethnicity", in W. Ommundsen and H. Rowley (eds).

Haacke, H. (2005), "The Guggenheim museum: A business plan", in Guasch and Zulaika (eds).

Harvard Design School (1998), Guggenheim Bilbao Museoa: A Retrospective, Centre for Design Informatics, http://www.cdi.gsd.harvard.edu/ Accessed 12.1.2006.

Hall, P. (1984/1966), *The World Cities* (London: Wedernfeld and Nicholson).

Hall, P. (1997), *Cities in Civilization* (New York: Pantheon Books).

Hall, P. (1998), *Cities in Civilization: Culture, Technology and Urban Order* (London: Weidenfeld and Nicolson).

Hall, P. (2002), Creative cities and economic development, *Urban Studies* 37 April, 1–10.

Hall, S. and Jacques, M. (eds) (1989), *New Times: The Changing Face of Politics in the 1990s* (London: Lawrence and Wishart).

Hall, C.M. and Tucker, H. (2004), *Tourism and Postcolonialism. Contested Discourses, Identities and Representations*, (London, New York: Routledge).

Hall, T. and Hubbard, P. (eds) (1998), *The Entrepreneurial City. Geographies of Politics, Regime and Representation,* (Chichester: John Wiley and Sons).

Hannigan, J. (1998), *Fantasy City. Pleasure and Profit in the Postmodern Metropolis* (London and New York: Routledge).

Hartigan, S. (2006), Interview with the author, Geelong May 4.

Harvey, D. (1989a), *The Condition of Postmodernity* (Oxford: Basil Blackwell).

Harvey, D. (1989b), *The Urban Experience (*Oxford: Blackwell).

Harvey, D. (1994), "Flexible accumulation through urbanization: reflections on 'Post-modernism' in the American city", in A. Amin (ed.) *Post-Fordism. A Reader* (Oxford: Blackwell), pp. 361–386.

Harvey, D. (1996), *Justice, Nature and the Geography of Difference* (Cambridge, Mass.: Blackwell).

Hawkins, G. (1993), *From Nimbin to Mardi Gras: Constructing Community Arts* (St Leonards: Allen and Unwin).

Hawkins, G. and Gibson, K, (1994), "Cultural planning in Australia: policy dreams and economic realities", in Watson, S. and Gibson, K. (eds).

Hauser, S. (2001), "The sterility of Singapore's Chinatown", *De Volkskran* December 29, 2001. Translated by G. Chow. http://www.singapore-window. org.sw02/011229dv.html.

Hebdidge, D. (1989), "New Times. After the masses", *Marxism Today* January, pp. 48–53.

Heiberg, M. (1989), *The Making of the Basque Nation* (Cambridge: Cambridge University Press).

Henderson, J.C. (2004), 'Tourism and heritage in Malaysia and Singapore', in Hall and Tucker (eds).

Heng, R. (2005), 'When queens ruled! A history of gay venues in Singapore', PLURAL, 31 December 2005, http://www.plu.sg/plural/index.php?itemid=32&catid=14, accessed 16 February 2006.

Henshaw, D. (2000), "Think of the cost of Guggenheim", *Geelong Advertiser* 24th February.

Hesmondhalgh, D. (2002), *The Culture Industries* (London: Sage).

Higgott, R. (1984), "Export-oriented industrialisation, the new international division of labour and the corporate state in the Third World: An explanatory essay on conceptual linkage", *Australian Geographical Studies,* 22, 58–71.

Hill, P. (2000), "The Guggenheim story", *Geelong Advertiser* February 2.

Ho, K.C. (1997), "From port city to city-state: Forces shaping Singapore's built environment", in Kim, W.B. et al. pp. 212–233.

Horvath, R. and Gibson, K. (1984), "Abstraction in Marx's method", *Antipode,* 16, 12–25.

Howkins, J. (2001), *The creative economy: How people make money from ideas* London: Allen Lane.

Hudson, R. (1989), "Labor-market changes and new forms of work in old industrial regions: maybe flexible for some but not flexible accumulation", *Environment and Planning D: Society and Space* 7, 5–30.

Hyam, R. (1976), *Britain's Imperial Century 1815–1914. A Study of Empire and Expansion* (London: B.T. Batsford).

IAC (Industries Assistance Commission) (1976), Report into the Performing Arts (Canberra: AGPS).

Ibelings, H. (2003), *Supermodernism: Architecture in the Age of Globalization* (Rotterdam: Nai Publishers).

Igelsias, L. (1998), Bilbao: The Guggenheim effect, UNESCO Courier 51 (9), 3pp. http:www.unesco.org/courier/1998_09/uk/signes/txt1.html Accessed 20 December 2005.

Jackson, P. (1988), "Street life: the politics of Carnival", *Environment and Planning D: Society and Space* 6, 213–227.

Jackson, P. (1989), *Maps of Meaning (*London: Unwin Hyman).

Jackson, R.V. (1977), *Australian Economic Development in the Nineteenth Century* (Canberra: Australian National University Press).

Jacobs, J. M. (1996), *Edge of Empire: Postcolonialism and the City* (London: Routledge).

Jacobs, J. M. (1998), "Aestheticization and the politics of difference in contemporary cities", in R. Fincher and J.M. Jacobs (eds), pp. 252–278.

Jacobs, J. M. (1999), "The labour of cultural geography", in E. Stratford (ed.), pp. 11–24.

Jameson, F. (1984), "The cultural logic of late capitalism", *New Left Review* 146, pp. 53–92.

Jencks, C. (1984/1991), *The Language of Post-Modern Architecture* (London: Academy).

Jenkins, R. (1984), "Divisions over the international division of labour", *Capital and Class* 22, 28–57.

Jennings, G. (2003), "Guggenheim bid", Geelong Advertiser, February 24.

Johanson, K. (2008), "How Australian industry policy shaped cultural policy", *International Journal of Cultural Policy* 14: 2, 139–48.

Johanson K. (forthcoming 2009), "Australian cultural policy" in P. Poirrier (ed.), *La culture comme politique publique: Essais d'histoire comparée De 1945 à nos jours*, Le ministère de la culture, Paris.

Johnson, L. C. (1990), New patriarchal economies in the Australian textile industry. *Antipode* 22 (1), 1–32.

Johnson, L.C. (1991), *The Australian Textile Industry, 1865–1990 – A Feminist Geography* PhD thesis, Monash University, Melbourne, Australia.

Johnson, L.C. (1994a), 'The postmodern Australian city', in Louise C. Johnson (ed.).

Johnson, L.C. (ed.) (1994), *Suburban Dreaming: An Interdisciplinary Approach to Australian Cities* (Geelong: Deakin University Press).

Johnson, L.C. (2000), Placebound. *Australian Feminist Geographies* (Melbourne: Oxford University Press).

Johnson, Louise (2002), "What is the value of the arts?"*Arts and Entreprenuership Conference Proceedings*. CD Rom (Melbourne: Deakin University).

Johnson, L. (2003), "Hybrid spaces and identities: Performing cultural citizenship at Geelong's Pako Festa" in *Proceedings, Institute of Citizenship and Globalisation Conference on Cultural Citizenship*. Deakin University, Burwood, 85–91.

Johnson, L. (2006), "Valuing the arts: theorising and realising cultural capital in an Australian city", *Geographical Research* 44: 3, 296–309.

Juddery, B. (1990), 'Manufacturing', *Australian Business*, October 10, 55–56.

Jupp, J. (ed.) (2001), *The Australian People: An Encyclopedia of the Nation, Its People and Their Origins* (Melbourne: Cambridge University Press).

Kane, K. (n.d.), "Culture, creative industries and local economic development in Glasgow", Scottish Enterprise Glasgow Accessed 8.1.08.

Katsonis, M. (2001), 'Cultural policy in Victoria', Talk to the School of Contemporary Arts, Deakin University, Melbourne. Notes with the author.

Kearns, G and Philo, C. (eds) (1993), *Selling Places: The City as Cultural Capital* (Oxford, Pergamon).

Kee, T.C. and Ng, T. (eds) (2004), *Ask Not: The Necessary Stage in Singapore Theatre* (Singapore: Times Editions).

Khan, S. (2003), "What did culture ever do for us?" *The Observer June 8, 2003* http:arts.guardian.co.uk/cityofculture2008/story/0,,97865,00html Accessed 17.5.2006.

Kinchin, P. (1988), *Glasgow's great exhibitions: 1888, 1901, 1911, 1938, 1988* (Wendleburg, Oxon: White).

King, A.D. (1990), *Urbanism, Colonialism and the World-Economy* (London and New York: Routledge).

Klotz, H. (1988), *The History of Post-Modern Architecture* (Cambridge, Mass.: MIT Press).

Kong, L. (2000a), 'Culture, economy, policy: trends and developments', *Geoforum* 31, 385–390.

Kong, L. (2000b), 'Cultural policy in Singapore: Negotiating economic and socio-cultural agendas', *Geoforum* 31, 409–424.

Kong, L and Yeoh, B. (1994), "Urban conservation in Singapore: A survey of state policies and popular attitudes", *Urban Studies* 31 (2), 22pp.

Krishnan, S. (ed.) (1997a), *9 Lives. 10 Years of Singapore Theatre 1987–1997. Essays commissioned by The Necessary Stage* (Singapore: The Necessary Stage).

Krishnan, S. (1997b), "What art makes possible: remembering Forum Theatre", in Krishnan, S. (ed.).

Kroker, A. and Cook, D. (1986), *The Postmodern Scene: Excremental Culture and Hyper Aesthetics* (New York: St Martin's Press).

Landry, C. (2000), *The Creative City: A Toolkit for Urban Innovators* (London: Comedia/Earthscan).

Landry, C. and Bianchini, F. (1995), *The Creative City* (London: Demos/Comedia).

Landry, C., Greene, L., Matarasso, F. and Bianchini, F. (1996), *The Arts and Regeneration. Urban Renewal Through Cultural Activity* (Stroud: Comedia).

Langenbach, W.R. (2003), Performing the Singapore State 1988–1995, PhD Thesis, Centre for Cultural Research, University of Western Sydney.

Lash, S. and Urry, J. (1987), *The End of Organized Capitalism* (Cambridge: Polity Press).

Laurier, E. (1993), "'Takintosh': Glasgow's supplementary gloss", in Kearns and Philo (eds).

Law, C. (1993), *Urban Tourism: Attracting Visitors to Large Cities* (Mansell: London).

Ley, D. (1983), "Co-operative housing as a moral landscape: Re-examining the post-modern city", in Duncan, J. and Ley, D. (eds), 128–48.

Ley, D. (1993), *The new middle class and the remaking of the central city* (Oxford: OUP).

Ley, D. and Olds, K. (1988), "Landscape as spectacle: World's fairs and the culture of heroic consumption", *Environment and Planning D: Society and Space* 6, 191–212.

The Lighthouse http://wwwthelighthouse.co.uk/page.php? accessed 10.1.08.

Lim, E-B. (2005), "The Mardi-Gras boys of Singapore's English language theatre", *Asian Theatre Journal* 22 (2), 293–309.

Linge, G. J.R. (1975), "The forging of an industrial nation: manufacturing in Australia 1788–1913", in J.M. Powell and M. Williams (eds).

Lingle. C. (1996) *Singapore's Authoritarian Capitalism. Asian Values, Free Market Illusions, and Political Dependency* (Edicions Sirocco, SL: Barcelona).

Lord, G.D. (1999), "The power of cultural tourism" Keynote Presentation Wisconsin Heritage Tourism Conference, Wisconsin Lord Cultural Resources http:www.lord.ca/thepower.htm.

Low, N., Gleeson, B., Green, Ray and Radovic, D. (2005), *The Green City: Sustainable Homes, Sustainable Suburbs.* (Sydney: University of NSW Press).

Luckman, S., Gibson, C., Lea, T. and Brennan-Horley, C. (2007), "Darwin as 'creative tropical city': Just how transferable is creative city thinking?", State of Australian Cities Conference papers, Adelaide, 370–79.

Lyotard, J.F. (1984), *The Post Modern Condition: A Report on Knowledge,* (Manchester: Manchester University Press).

Madden, Christopher (2004), *Making cross-country comparisons of cultural statistics: Problems and solutions.* (Sydney: Australia Council for the Arts).

MacCannell, D. (1973), "Staged authenticity: Arrangements of social space in tourist settings", *American Sociological Review* 79: 589–603.

MacCannell, D. (1976), *The tourist: A new theory of the leisure class* New York: Schocken.

MacDonald, S. (2004), "Badly drawn culture", in CCPR.

MacDonald, S. (2006), "Glasgow design" http:www.seeglasgow.com/media-office/features/architecture/glass, accessed 8.1.08.

Malanga, S. (2004), "The curse of the creative class", *City Journal Winter*, 36–45.

Marshall, P. David (1997), *Celebrity and Power. Fame in Contemporary Culture.* (Minneapolis/London: University of Minnesota Press).

Mavros, J. (2000), Interview with Louise Johnson, January 20.

Marshall, R. (2003), Singapore. Emerging Urbanity.

Marx, K. (1954), *Capital: A Critical Analysis of Capitalist Production, Vol. 1.* (Moscow: Progress Publishers).

Marx, K. (1956), *Capital: A Critical Analysis of Capitalist Production, Vol. 2.* (Moscow: Progress Publishers).

Massey, D. (1984), *Spatial Divisions of Labour. Social Structures and the Geography of Production* (London: MacMillan).

Massey, D. (2005), *For Space* (London: Sage).

Matarasso, F. (1999), *Towards a Local Culture Index: Measuring the Cultural Vitality of Communities.* (Stroud: Comedia).

MacCannell, D. (2005), "The fate of the symbolic in architecture for tourism: Piranesi, Disney, Gehry", in Guasch and Zulaika (eds).

MacLeod, G. (2002), "From urban entrepreneurialism to a 'revanchist city'? On the spatial injustices of Glasgow's renaissance", *Antipode,* 34 (3), pp. 602–624.

Maver, I. "No mean city: 1914 to 1950s", http://www.theglasgowstory.com/storyb. php?PHPsE, accessed 13.4.06a.

Maver, I. 'Modern times: 1950s to the present day', http://www.theglasgowstory. com/storyb.php?PHPsE, accessed 13.4.06b.

McClintock, A. (1992), "The angel of progress: pitfalls of the term 'postcolonialism', *Social Text,* Spring, 1–5.

McKie, R.C.H. (1942), *This was Singapore* (Sydney and London: Angus and Robertson).

McLeay, C. (1997), 'Inventing Australia: A critique of recent cultural policy rhetoric', *Australian Geographical Studies* 35 (1): 40–46.

McDowell, Linda (1994), 'The transformation of cultural geography', in D. Gregory, R. Martin and G. Smith (eds), pp. 146–173.

McGrath, J. 'The rising Burgh: 1560 to 1770s', http://www.theglasgowstory.com/ storyb.php?PHPsE, accessed 13.4.06a.

McGrath, J. 'Beginnings: early times to 1560'. http://www.theglasgowstory.com/ storyb.php?PHPsE, accessed 13.4.06b.

McManus, Phil (2005), *Vortex Cities to Sustainable Cities: Australia's Urban Challenge* Sydney, University of NSW Press.

McNeill, D. (2000), 'McGuggenisation? National identity and globalisation in the Basque country', *Political Geography* 19, 473–494.

Mee, K. (1994), 'Dressing up the suburbs: representations of western Sydney', in K. Gibson and S. Watson (eds) *Metropolis Now. Planning and the Urban in Contemporary Australia* (Sydney: Pluto Press), pp. 60–77.

Merchant City Initiative – Historical development, http://www.glasgowmerchant city.net/history1.html, accessed 4.8.05a.

Middleton, M. (1991), *Cities in Transition: The regeneration of Britain's inner cities* (London: Michael Joseph).

Mies, M. (1986), *Patriarchy and Accumulation on a World Scale. Women in the International Division of Labour* (London: Zed Books).

Mills, C. (1993), "Myths and meanings of gentrification", in J. Duncan and D. Ley (eds), 149–170.

Milne, R.S. and Mauzey, D.K. (1990), *Singapore. The Legacy of Lee Kuan Yew* (Boulder: Westview Press).

Mitchell, J. (2006), Interview with Louise Johnson, Geelong, May 5.

Mitter, S. (1986), *Common Fate. Common Bond. Women in the Global Economy* (London: Pluto).

Mongia, P. (ed.) (1996), *Postcolonial Theory: A Reader* (London: Arnold).

Cultural Capitals

Mooney, G. (2004), "Cultural policy as urban transformation? Critical reflections on Glasgow, European City of Culture 1990", *Local Economy* 19 (4): 327–40.

Mooney, G. and Danson, M. (1997), "Beyond 'Culture City' Glasgow as a dual city" in N. Jewson and S.MacGregor (eds).

Moss, M. "Industrial revolution: 1770s to 1830s", http://www.theglasgowstory. com/storyb.php?PHPsE, accessed 13.4.06.

MITA (2003), *Economic Contributions of Singapore's Creative Industries* (Singapore: Economics Division Ministry of Trade and Industry).

Myerscough, J. (1988), *The Economic Importance of the Arts in Britain.* (London: Policy Studies Institute).

Nash, J. (2000), "Global integration and the commodification of culture", *Ethnology*, 39 (2): 129–31.

Nash, C. (2002), "Cultural geography: Post colonial cultural geographies", *Progress in Human Geography 26 (2)*, 219–230.

Nathan, J.M. (2002), "Reframing modernity: The challenge of remaking Singapore", in D. da Cunha (ed.), pp.187–220.

Newman, P. and Smith, I. (2000), "Cultural production, place and politics on the south bank of the Thames", *International Journal of Urban and Regional Research* 24 (1): 9–24.

News Release (1999), "Court House redevelopment", May 26.

Nicholson, L. (1990), *Feminism and Postmodernism.* (New York: Routledge).

Norton, A. (1996), 'Cultural policy or cultural coercion?' *Culture and Policy* 7 (2): 107–111.

Ockman, J. (2004), "New politics of the spectacle: 'Bilbao' and the global imagination", in, Lasansky, D.M. and McLaren, B. pp. 227–39.

OECD (2002), *Glasgow: Lessons for innovation and implementation* (OECD, Paris).

Visit Glasgow Museums (2004), www.glasgowmuseums.com, accessed 4.8.05.

Offord, B. (2003), *Homosexual Rights as Human Rights: Activism in Indonesia, Singapore and Australia.* (Oxford: Peter Lang).

Ollman, B. (1976), *Alienation: Marx's Conception of Man in Capitalist Societ.* (Cambridge: Cambridge University Press).

Ommundsen, W. and Rowley, H. (1996), *From a Distance: Australian Writers and Cultural Displacement* (Geelong: Deakin University Press).

Pacione, M. (1995), *Glasgow: The socio-spatial development of the city* (John Wiley, Chichester).

Pacione, M. (1990), "A tale of two cities. The migration of the urban crisis in Glasgow" *Cities*, November 304–314.

Parfett, (2000), "Guggenheim: The council plan of attack", *Geelong Advertiser* February 4: 6.

Peck, J. (2005), "Struggling with the creative class", *International Journal of Urban and Regional Research* 29 (4), 740–770.

Peterson, W. (1994), "Sexual minorities on the Singaporean stage", *Australasian Drama Studies* 25, 61–72.

Phillips, A.A. (1958), "The cultural cringe" in S. Alomes and C. Jones (eds).

Piore, M. and Sabel, C. (1984), *The Second Industrial Divide: Possibilities for Prosperity* (New York: Basic Books).

Playford, J. and Kirsner, D. (ed.) (1972), *Australian Capitalism: Towards a Socialist Critique* (Ringwood: Penguin).

Potts, J. (2007), "What's new in the economics of arts and culture?" *Dialogue 26* Academy of the Social Sciences, 8–14.

Powell, J.M. and Williams, M. (eds) (1975), *Australian Space Australian Time* (Melbourne: Oxford University Press).

Prieto, J.G. (2003), *Bilbao* (Leon: Editorial Everest, SA).

Portoghesi, P. (1983), *Postmodernism. The Architecture of the Post-Industrial Society* (New York: Rizzoli).

Poulakidas, G. (2004), *The Guggenheim Museum Bilbao. Transforming a City* (New York: Children's Press).

Power, Dominic (2000), "'Cultural industries' in Sweden: An assessment of their place in the Swedish economy", *Economic Geography* 78 (2), 103–127.

Pratt, A. (2000), The cultural industries: A cross national comparison of employment in Great Britain and Japan, Draft 2. http://www.lse.ak.uk/Depts/ geography/Pratt Publications 1/creative%20inds%20in%20japan.pdf, accessed 21.11.2002.

Prieto, C.S. (nd) "The cultural economics and services in Spain", www.geog. fuuberlin.de/^angeo/home/publikationen/metar39/spain.htm, accessed 9.05.

Profile of Geelong (2002), (Geelong: City of Greater Geelong).

Progress Report (1998), Bilbao www.bm30.es/plan/stat/prs0_uk.html, accessed 12 December 2005.

Radbourne, J. (1993), "Models of arts funding in Australia", *AESTHETEx* 5: 1, 44–57.

Real Instituo Elcan (2004), *Cultural Policy in Spain* (Madrid: Real Instituto Elcan de Estudios Internacionales y Estralagicos).

Reed, P. (1999), *Glasgow. The Forming of a City* (Edinburgh: Edinburgh University Press).

Regionalism Course Team (1985), *Regionalism and Australia* Study Guide B: Origins and Diversity (Geelong: Deakin University Press).

Renaissance City Report (2000), *Culture and the Arts in Renaissance Singapore* Ministry of Information and the Arts (MITA) March (Singapore: National Arts Council) www.nac.gov.sg.

Revitalization Plan for Metropolitan Bilbao (1989), http://www.bm30.es/plan/pri_ uk.html, accessed 23 October 2002.

Rich, D. (1987), *The Industrial Geography of Australia* (North Ryde: Methuen).

Richards, G. (1996a), *Cultural tourism in Europe* CAB International.

Richards, G. (1996b), "Production and consumption of European cultural tourism", *Annals of Tourism Research* 23 (2), 261–283.

Richards, G. (1996c), "The social context of cultural tourism", in G. Richards (ed.) *Cultural tourism in Europe* CAB International, pp. 47–70.

Richards, G. (1996d), "European cultural tourism: trends and future prospects", in G. Richards (ed.) *Cultural tourism in Europe* CAB International, pp. 311–333.

Rodger, J. "Modern time: 1950s to the present day", http:\\www.the glasgow story. com/storyb.php?PHPSE. [Accessed 13.04.06].

Roodhouse S. (2006), *Cultural Quarters: Principles and Practice* (Bristol, UK: Intellect).

Rojek, C. and Urry, J. (eds) (1993), *Touring Cultures: Transformations of Travel and Theory* (London and New York: Routledge).

Rose, D. (2004), "Discourses and experiences of social mix in gentrifying neighbourhoods: a Montreal case study", *Canadian Journal of Urban Research* 13 (2): 278–316.

Rose, M. (1991), *The Post-Modern and the Post-Industrial* (Cambridge: Cambridge University Press).

Rowe, D. and Stevenson, D. (1994), "'Provincial paradise': Urban tourism and city imaging outside the metropolis", *Australian, New Zealand Journal of Sociology* 30 (2): 178–193.

Rowley, K. (1972), "The political economy of Australia since the war", in J. Playford and D. Kirsner (eds).

Rowse, T. (1985), *Arguing the Arts* (Australia: Penguin).

Rowse, T. (2005), *Contesting Assimilation* (Perth, WA: API Network).

Said, E. (1978), *Orientalism* (London: Routledge and Kegan Paul).

Said, E. (1993), *Culture and Imperialism* (London: Chatto and Windus).

Salvado, Francisco J. Romero (1999), *Arriba Espana. Twentieth-Century Spain. Politics and Society in Spain, 1898–1998* (Houndmills, Basingstoke: Palgrave).

Sassen, S. (1991/1992), *The Global City* (Princeton: Princeton University Press).

Sassen, S. (1998), *Globalisation and its Discontents* (New York: The New Press).

Sassen, S. (2000), *Cities in a World Economy* (Thousand Oaks, California: Pine Forge Press).

Sassen, S. (2005), "Global cities: A challenge for urban scholarship", http:www. columbia.edu/cu/21stcentury/issue-2.4/sassen.htm, accessed 24.11.

Sayer, C. (1992) "The city of Glasgow, Scotland – an arts-led revival", *Culture and Policy* 4, pp. 69–73.

Scott, Allan J. (1997), "The cultural economy of cities", *International Journal of Urban and Regional Research* 21 (2), 23–39.

Scott, Allan J, (1999), "The cultural economy: Geography and the creative field", *Media, Culture and Society* 21, 807–817.

Scott, Allan J. (2000), *The Cultural Economy of Cities* (London, Sage).

Scott, Allan J. (2001), "Capitalism, cities, and the production of symbolic forms", *Transactions. Institute of British Geographers, NS* 26, 11–23.

Sedgewick, E.S. (1993), *Tendencies* (Durham: Duke University Press).

Selwyn, T. (1996), *The Tourism Image. Myth and mythmaking in tourism* (John Wiley and Sons: Chichester).

Serle, G. (1973), *From Deserts the Prophets Come. The Creative Spirit in Australia 1788–1972* (Melbourne: Heinemann).

Seo, J-K. (2002), "Re-urbanisation in regenerated areas of Manchester and Glasgow", *Cities* 19 (2), 113–121.

Silverstone, Roger (1997), *Visions of Suburbia* (London and New York: Routledge).

Singapore 73 (1973), (Singapore: Ministry of Culture).

Smith, M. (2003), *Issues in cultural tourism studies* (Routledge: London and New York).

Smith, N. (1979), "Toward a theory of gentrification: a back to the city movement of capital not people", *Journal of the American Planning Assoc.* 45(4): 538–48.

Smith, N. (1996), *The New Urban Frontier: Gentrification and the Revanchist City* (London: Routledge).

Soja, E. W. (1986), "Taking Los Angeles apart: A post-modern geography", *Environment and Planning D: Society and Space* 4: 255–72.

Soja, E. (1989), *Postmodern Geographies: The Reassertion of Space in Critical Social Theory* (London: Verso).

Soja, E. (1996), *Thirdspace: Journeys to Los Angeles and Other Real and Imagined Places* (Cambridge, Mass.: Blackwell).

Sorkin, M. (1992/1995), *Variations on a Theme Park: The New American City and the End of Public Space* (New York: Hill and Wang).

Sorkin, M. (1999), "Frozen light", in M. Friedman (ed.).

Spivak, G. (1993), *Outside in the Teaching Machine*, (New York: Routledge).

Statistics Working Group (SWG) (2002), *Statistics Working Group, No. 7.* Canberra, AGPS.

Statistics Working Group (SWG) (2004), *Statistics Working Group, No. 9.* Canberra, AGPS.

Stevenson, D. (1999), *Art and Organisation. Making Australian Cultural Policy* (Brisbane: University of Queensland Press).

Storper, M. and Walker, R. (1989), *The Capitalist Imperative. Territory, Technology and Industrial Growth* (New York: Basil Blackwell).

Stratford, E. (1999), (ed.) *Australian Cultural Geographies* (Melbourne: Oxford University Press).

Stratford, Elaine (1999), "Australian cultural geographies", in E. Stratford (ed.), pp. 1–10.

2020 Summit (2008) Commonwealth Government of Australia.

Tamney, J.B. (1996), *The Struggle over Singapore's Soul: Western Modernization and Asian Culture* (Berlin/New York: Walter de Gruyter).

Tan, F. (2004), "Singapore theatre", *European Cultural Review* 15. http://www.c3.hu/~eufuzetek/en/eng/15/index.php?mit=tan. Accessed 2 February, 2006.

Taylor, A. (1994), "Profits from the desert? The Adeliaid Festival of the Arts", in Headon, Hooton and Horne (eds). pp. 113–123.

Throsby, D. (2005), *Does Australia Need a Cultural Policy?* (Strawbery Hill: Currency House).

Throsby, David (2003a), "Cultural sustainability", in R. Trowse (ed.) *A Handbook of Cultural Economics* (Cheltenham: Edward Elgar), pp. 183–186.

Throsby, David (2003b), "Cultural capital", in R. Trowse (ed.) *A Handbook of Cultural Economics* (Cheltenham: Edward Elgar), pp.166–169.

Throsby, David (2001), *Economics and Culture* (Cambridge: Cambridge University Press).

Throsby, David (1999), "Cultural capital", *Journal of Cultural Economics* 23 (1), 3–12.

Throsby, D. (1997), *The Economics of Cultural Policy* (North Sydney: Policy and Planning Division of the Australia Council).

Throsby, David (1986), *Occupational and Employment Characteristics of Artists* (North Sydney: Policy and Planning Division of the Australia Council).

Throsby, Charles David and O'Shea, Margaret (1980), *The regional impact of the Mildura Arts Centre* (North Ryde: Macquarie University, School of Economics and Financial Studies).

Throsby, Charles David and Withers, Glen (1979), *The Economics of the Performing Arts* (Melbourne: Edward Arnold Australia).

Throsby, Charles David and Withers, Glen (1984), *What Price Culture?* (North Sydney: Policy and Planning Division of the Australia Council).

Throsby, Charles David and Thompson, Beverley (1994), *But What Do You Do For a Living? A New Economic Study of Australian Artists* (Strawberry Hills, Sydney: Australia Council).

Tibbetts, M. (n.d), "'Art as competitive advantage': The Creative Industries Cluster Initiative in Scotland" Scottish Enterprise Online.

Trowse, R. (ed.) (2003), *A Handbook of Cultural Economics* (Cheltenham: Edward Elgar).

Trowse, Ruth (1997a), Introduction, in R. Trowse (ed.) *Cultural Economics: The Arts, The Heritage and The Media Industries* (Cheltenham, UK: Elgar Reference Collection), pp. 1–14.

Trowse, Ruth (ed.) (1997b), *Cultural Economics: The Arts, The Heritage and The Media Industries* (Cheltenham, UK: Elgar Reference Collection).

Turner, L. and Ash, J. (1975), *The Golden Hordes* (London: Constable).

UNESCO (2000a), *Culture, Trade and Globalisation: Questions and Answers* (Paris: UNESCO Publishing).

UNESCO (2000b), *International flows of selected cultural goods, 1980–1998, Executive Summary* UNESCO Institute of Statistics (Paris, UNESCO Culture Sector).

UNESCO (2000c) *World Culture Report* (Paris: UNESCO) www.unesco.org/culture/worldreport/html_eng/contents.shtml, accessed 25.10.05.

Urry, J. (1990), *The Tourist Gaze: Leisure and Travel in Contemporary Societies* (London: Sage).

Urry, J. (2000), "The 'consumption' of tourism", *Sociology* 24 (1): 23–35.

Usher, R. (2000/01), "Reinventing a city: Bilbao reborn", *Time Europe* 156 (25) p. 68.

Usher, R. (2000), "Just the spot for a Guggenheim", *The Age* February 4.

Viar, J. (2005), "The Guggenheim Bilbao, Partner in the arts: A view form the Fine Arts Museum of Bilbao", in Guasch and Zulaika (eds).

Ward, Stephen V. (1998), "Place marketing: A historical comparison of Britain and North America" in Hall, T. and Hubbard, P. (eds) *The Entrepreneurial City.*

Wark, McK. (1999), *Celebrities, Culture and Cyberspace* (Sydney: Pluto Press).

Waterfront Geelong Concept Plan (1994), (Geelong, Victoria: City of Greater Geelong).

Waterfront Geelong: The Future is Here (2000), (Geelong, Victoria: City of Greater Geelong).

Watson, S. (1992), "Contested spaces: Cross cultural issues in planning", *Culture and Policy* 4, 19–33.

Watson, Sophie (1991), "Gilding the smokestacks: the new symbolic representation of de-industrialised regions", *Environment and Planning: Society and Space* 9: 59–70.

Webster, A. (1998), *Gentleman Capitalists. British Imperialism in South East Asia 1770-1890* (London: Tauris Academic Studies).

Wee, C.J.W.-L. (2002), "National identity, the arts and the global city", in da Cunha (ed.).

Weedon, Chris (1987), *Feminist Theory and Poststructuralist Theory* (Oxford: Basil Blackwell).

Wikipedia (2006), "History of Singapore", http://en.wikipedia.org/wili/History of modern Singapore, accessed 16 February 2006.

Williams, C.C. (1997), *Consumer Services and Economic Development* (Routledge, London and New York).

Williams, Raymond (1983), *Keywords* (London: Flamingo).

Wilson, E. (1991), *The Sphinx in the City. Urban Life, the Control of Disorder and Women* (London: Virago).

Wiseman, J. (1998), *Global Nation? Australia and the Politics of Globalisation* (Cambridge: Cambridge University Press).

Wishart, R. (1991), "Fashioning the future: Glasgow" in M. Fisher and U. Owen (eds), 43–53.

www.thelighthouse.co.uk, accessed 5.2.08.

www.geohive.com.global/geo.php?xml=cc_sect. Accessed 8.12.05.

www.gorbalslive.org.uk, accessed 10.12.06.

www.comedia.org.uk/themes-3_1htm, accessed 12.9.04.

www.culture.gov.uk/creative_industries, accessed 4.11.05.

www.mica.gov.sg/MTI%20Creative%Industries.pdf (2003) *Economic Contribution of Singapore's Creative Industries*(Singapore: Creative Industries Strategy Group, Ministry of Information, Communication and the Arts), accessed 9.11.05.

www.realinstitutoelcano.org/documentos/110/IN040428.pdf   (20042)   Cultural
   Policy in Spain (real Instituto Elcano de Estudios Internacionales y Estrategicos),
   accessed 9.11.05).
Yeo, R. (1994), "Theatre and censorship in Singapore", *Australasian Drama
   Studies* 25 (October), 49–60.
Yeoh, B.S.A. (2005), "The global cultural city? Spatial Imagineering and politics
   in the (multi) cultural marketplaces of South-East Asia", *Urban Studies* 42
   (5/6), 945–958.
Yeoh, B.S.A. and Kong, L. (1994), 'Reading landscape meanings: State constructions
   and lived experiences in Singapore's Chinatown', *Habitat International* 18: 4,
   17–35.
Yeoh, B.S. and Huang, S. (1996), "The conservation-redevelopment dilemma in
   Singapore", *Cities* 13: 6, 411–422.
Zukin, S. (1991), *Landscapes of power: From Detroit to Disney World* (Berkeley:
   University of California Press.
Zukin, Sharon (1995), *The Culture of Cities* (London, Blackwell).
Zulaika, J.U. (2001), "Tough beauty: Bilbao as ruin, architecture and allegory", in
   J.R. Resina (ed.).
Zulaika, J. (2005), "Desiring Bilbao: The Krensificaiton of the museum and its
   discontents", in Guasch and Zulaika (eds).

Index

ABC (Australian Broadcasting Company/
    Commission) 198, 200, 206, 208
    Adorno, Theodore 44–5, 47
Aboriginal 42
Adelaide 13, 76, 78, 208, 209, 249
Advertising 16, 17, 19, 21, 46, 49, 76,
    108, 115
Africa 33, 77, 125
Agglomeration 16, 28
Amsterdam 12, 73, 74, 85
Anderson, Kay 39, 42, 53
Annapolis Royal (Nova Scotia, Ca) 13
Antiques 16
Anthropology 24
Antwerp 13
Architecture 16, 17, 19, 68, 75, 108, 115,
    116, 238
Art House Collective (Geelong, Australia)
    213, 230
Arts industry 16
Arts 21 (Policy, Victoria, Australia) 210
Asia 33, 63, 77, 87, 125, 158, 161, 193,
    199, 236, 242
Aswan 6
Athens 6, 12, 85
Auckland 52–3
Austin 48
Australasia 21, 23, 58, 59, 77, 87, 236
Australia 5, 9, 13, 15, 18–19, 29, 43,
    44, 47, 48, 49, 55, 59, 61, 62, 75,
    76, 77, 87, 125, 171, 179, 187,
    193–231
Australia Council for the Arts/Australia
    Council 18, 200, 201, 203, 204,
    206, 230
Avignon 13

Baltimore 13, 65, 101, 127, 144–5, 212,
    236, 248
Bangkok 73, 163

Barcelona 13, 17, 112, 115, 126, 249
Basques 18, 125–7,133–36, 139–140,
    145–6, 245
Baudrillard, Jean 68–69, 147
Beijing 6, 12
Belfast 13
Bell, Daniel 63
Bergen 13
Berlin 6, 85, 129, 131
Bhabha, Homi 188
Bianchini, Frederico 17, 76, 248
Bilbao 3, 5, 13, 14, 16, 53, 55, 58,
    60, 63, 65, 66,69, 78–80,
    123–152,155,162,165, 181, 183,
    193,194, 214, 218–219, 221, 226,
    227, 235, 236, 238, 239, 240, 242,
    244, 245–46, 247, 248, 251
Birmingham 13, 88
Bologna 6, 12
Bonaventure Hotel 64–5, 66
Bondi, Elizabeth 40
Boston 4, 34, 48, 63, 75, 101, 212, 236,
    247, 248
Bourdieu, Pierre 23, 24, 25, 30, 35–37, 38,
    49, 51–53, 104, 105
Boyle. Mark 95, 102, 104, 105
Brasilia 12
Brazil 223
Brisbane 4, 63, 76, 202, 206, 209
Britain 15, 19, 43, 49, 59, 67, 75,
    125–6,159,161–2,194, 207
British Empire 85, 87, 89, 92, 125,
    125–6,155–161,198
Broadcasting 15, 17, 46
Bruges 13
Brussels 13, 138
Buchanan, Ian 163. 167
Buenos Aires 6, 73
Burgess, Ernest 40

Burrell, William (Collection) 87, 96, 97, 100, 242, 244
Butler, Elizabeth 68, 69

Cairo 6
Canada 9, 15, 20, 75, 236
Canberra 20, 209
Canmore (Alberta, Ca) 13
Caraquet (New Brunswick, Ca) 13
Castlemilk 91, 92
Caves, Richard 17, 26–9
Celebrity 5, 27, 123, 143, 147–9
Censorship 156, 170, 183–8, 198, 247, 251
Chang, Michael 185
Chang, T.C. 74, 171–6, 180
Chicago 48, 115, 182
Chillida, Eduado 140
China 9, 157–9, 161, 183, 195
Chinatown 39, 42, 156, 164, 165, 166–74, 246
Chinese 159–60, 186, 188, 197, 240
Citizen's Theatre 105, 106, 118
City by the Bay plan (Geelong, Australia) 211, 212, 229
Class 28, 36, 37, 40, 41, 50–1, 58, 72, 76, 103, 117, 119, 161
Clyde River 86, 87, 98, 100, 107, 117, 243
Colonial(ism) 33, 42, 53, 56, 58, 76, 155, 157, 161
Comedia 56, 76, 236, 248–51
Computer software (including games) 8, 9, 14, 15, 16, 19, 28, 115
Cool Britannia 15, 111
Copenhagen 12
Copyright 8, 26, 28, 70
Cork 13
Courthouse Youth Theatre (Geelong, Australia) 224, 227, 229, 230, 239, 248
Cousins, Jim 218, 223, 229
Cracow 13
Crafts 15, 16, 49
Craik, Jennifer 33, 206
Creative Class 6, 41, 44, 47, 48–9, 56, 62, 103, 143, 186, 227, 243

Creative Industry/ies -11, 13, 14, 16, 17, 19, 20–21, 23, 26, 31, 62, 86, 100, 107, 108, 113–9, 237, 241
Creative Nation 18, 202, 206–7
Creativity + 225–6
Crewe, Louise 44
Crowsnest Pass (Alberta, Ca) 13
Cullen, Gordon 97–99
Cultural Economics 23, 24, 25–31, 46, 49, 53, 236
Cultural Geography 24, 25, 38–44, 53, 237
Cultural Goods 8–9, 13–14
Cultural Industry(ies) 8, 12, 14, 15, 18–19, 23, 24, 25–31, 47, 56, 58, 62, 63, 64–7, 92, 103, 107, 108, 110, 119, 143, 150, 156, 179, 189, 204, 225, 236, 237, 243, 247, 250
Cultural Precinct 193, 212, 222, 223–8, 230, 236, 240, 247
Cultural Studies 24, 28, 47
Cultural tourism/t 24, 32–38, 53, 72, 86, 94, 96, 110, 115, 116, 119, 124, 139,149, 151,166, 206, 207, 215–8, 226, 236–7, 238
Culture 5, 6, 8
Cunningham, Stuart 202
Curitiba 13
Cuzco 13

Damer, Sean 102–3
Darwin 44
Davis, Mike 64, 151
DCMS (British) Department of Culture, Media and Sport 15–16
De Brun, Anne 50, 52–3
Debord, Guy 65
Deindustrialisation 56, 79
Denmark 89
Design 14, 15, 16, 17, 19, 21, 48, 53, 62, 68, 76, 93, 109, 110–117, 120, 213, 226, 235, 237, 240, 244
Disney Corporation/Disnefied/ificaiton 45, 145, 148
Disorganised capitalism 70
Distinction 36
Donnelly, Michael 103
Drumchapel 91, 92, 105
Drumheller (Alberta, Ca) 13

Dublin 212, 227
Duetsche, Rosalind 6
Dundee 114, 212, 227, 248
Easterhouse 91, 92, 105
East India Company 158
Economics 23, 25, 32
Edge Cities 59
Edinburgh 6, 87, 95, 101, 105, 108, 114, 119,195, 218
Elizabethan Theatre Trust 200
Embodied (cultural capital) 25, 30, 51–4, 80, 104, 108, 123, 142, 152, 229, 230, 235, 238, 247, 248
England 35, 77, 102, 109, 125, 163
ETA (Euzkadi Ta Askatasuna Basque Nation and Liberty) 134–5, 245
Esplanade Theatres by the Bay 66, 79, 153 (Pictured), 156, 179,181–3,188, 238, 246, 247
Europe 17, 21, 23, 33, 34, 37, 40, 47, 58, 63, 76, 78, 85, 86, 89,102, 109, 115,123, 125, 126, 127, 135, 155, 161,193, 199, 203, 213, 236
European Union 6, 9, 62, 79, 85, 101, 107, 110, 114, 124,127, 135, 138, 141, 150, 155, 195, 238
Exhibitions/Expositions 17, 88, 100, 118, 139

Fashion 16, 17, 49, 70
Feminism 40, 57, 68
Fernie (BC Canada) 13
Festival(s) 4, 12, 23, 34, 38, 39, 41, 42, 97, 100, 116, 137, 145, 182,189, 208, 209, 210, 215–18, 242
Film 8, 14, 16, 26, 27, 28, 31, 38, 46, 48, 64, 65, 68, 70, 96, 116, 117, 193,197, 201, 206, 210, 211, 225, 229
Fifth Passage Gallery (Singapore) 185–6
Flexible accumulation 70
Flexible specialization 63, 70
Florence 6, 12, 85
Florida, Richard 3, 41, 48–9, 53, 56, 62, 119, 184,186, 194, 209, 227, 239, 242, 248–50
Foucault, Michel 68, 69
Forum Theatre 187–8

France 9, 77, 135
Frankfurt 73, 74
Friedman, John 72, 73–4, 75
Friel, Eddie 97, 115
Froebel, Heinrichs and Kreye 59
Frow, John 52
Furniture 17

Gallery/ies 12, 15, 16, 24, 34, 38, 93, 94, 96, 101, 104, 106, 109, 139, 189, 193, 196, 200, 208, 210, 222, 224, 227, 230, 241, 246
Gandhi, Leila 157, 188
Garcia, Beatrice 118
Gay and Bohemian Index 48, 119
Gays 38, 48, 176, 184–187, 247
Geelong 3, 5, 11, 13, 15, 53, 54, 55, 58, 60, 63, 69, 78–80,131, 140, 155, 162,165, 191 (Pictured), 193, 194, 196, 197, 204, 211–231, 235, 239, 240, 242, 247–48, 251
Geelong Arts Alliance 230–1
Gehry, Frank 27, 66, 123, 129, 132–33,140, 143–151, 245
Genova 13
Gentrification 39–42, 108, 117, 143, 174, 175, 240
Germany 9, 60, 77, 89
Gibson, Chris 44
Gibson-Graham, Katherine 56
Gilbert-Rolfe, Jeremy 149
Gimenez, Carmen 129
Glasgow 5, 11, 13, 14, 34, 39, 53, 55, 58, 60, 63, 69, 77, 78–80, 85–120, 123, 125, 126, 127,133, 135, 138, 151,155,162, 164, 165,181, 193,194, 212, 214, 218, 219, 225, 227, 235, 237–8, 239, 240, 242, 243–245, 247, 248, 251
Glasgow Action 97–98
Glasgow Boys 87
Glasgow East Area Renewal Program (GEAR) 94–5
Glasgow School of Art 98, 110, 115, 116, 119, 244
Glasgow Green 105, 112
Glasgow Style 93, 94, 110, 119–20
Glass, Ruth 40

Global City of the Arts (Singapore) 179, 180, 184, 186
Globalisation 56, 59, 60, 71–75, 79, 124, 137, 155,193, 208, 236, 247
Global City/ies 74, 143
Goldstone, Leo 9
Gorbals 90, 91, 93, 95, 102, 105, 112, 118, 165, 244
Govan 105, 116, 165
GPAC (Geelong Performing Arts Centre, Australia) 211, 223, 226–7, 229, 230, 248
Graz 13
Guggenheim:
    Bilbao -5, 17, 27, 39, 53, 65, 66, 121 (Pictured),123–152, 180, 235, 242, 245–6, 247
    Geelong 3, 55, 193, 212, 218–223, 233 (Pictured), 239, 243, 247
    New York 5, 27, 128, 223, 245
        Foundation 3, 79, 123, 124, 128–131, 141, 151, 155, 219, 220, 221, 222, 238,
        Effect 238

Habitus 36
Hall, Peter 73, 74–5
Hannigan, John 65–6
Harvey, David 34, 35, 36, 38, 39, 40, 43, 51, 60, 65, 71, 75, 101, 144–5 147, 151, 203
Hawkins, Gaye 201–2
Heiberg, Marianne 179/133
Heidelberg School 242/196, 243/197
Helsinki 4, 12, 249
Heritage 5, 17, 24, 33, 34, 38, 39, 45, 53, 93, 94, 109, 110, 112, 116, 155, 156, 157, 161, 166, 169, 170–79, 189, 193, 208, 213, 224, 225, 227, 235, 240, 246
Hesmondhalgh, David 46–7, 59
Hey on Wye 13
Hobart 20, 195, 219
Holland 89
Hong Kong 6, 9, 46, 73,163, 179, 181, 184, 248
Housing Development Board (HDB, Singapore) 164, 165, 175

Howard, John -207
Human Geography 24
Hum drum activities/workers 17, 27
Hybrid (isation/ised) 33

Image(ining) cities/regions/precincts 34, 39, 109, 111, 115, 117, 119, 123, 151, 214, 222, 236
Imperialism 78, 124–6,157,193
India 46, 77, 125, 157,158
Indian 159–160, 188, 240
Inter-urban competition 71–5, 78
Indonesia 77, 161, 162
Information Economy 62, 210
Institutional cultural capital 25, 51–4, 80, 93, 101, 105, 108, 118, 123, 142, 152, 229, 230, 235, 238, 247
Intellectual Property (IP) 17, 26, 28, 31, 46
Italy (ian) 35
Ireland 9, 60, 77

Jackson, Peter 41–2
Jacobs, Jane 42–3, 53, 156
Jameson, Frederic 43, 64, 151
Japan 9, 60, 89, 161, 163, 207
Jarvis, Ken 218–9, 220, 221, 229
Jencks, Charles 66, 144
Jewellery 15, 17, 176

Kampong Glam 156, 159, 164, 166, 170, 177–9, 246
Keating, Paul 18, 206–7
Kelly, Michael 96
Kelowna (BC) 13
Kelvingrove 88, 116, 244
Kennett, Jeff 209, 210, 212, 215, 224
Knowledge economy/industries 47, 71, 62–3, 75, 211
Kong, Lily 174, 175
Korea, Republic of 9, 176
Krens, Thomas 128–130, 140, 218–220, 223, 245
Krishnan, Sanjay 187–8
Kun, Kuo Pao 188, 247
Kyoto 6

Lally, Pat 105

Landry, Charles 3, 56, 76,166, 194, 209, 236, 248–50
Lee Kuan Yew 161, 162–3, 179
Las Vegas 129, 131, 222, 223
Latin America 46, 125, 155
Leisure 8, 32, 116, 180, 211
Ley, David 40, 41
Libraries 14, 15, 16, 17, 93, 108, 116, 208, 210, 227
Lighthouse, The 111–3, 119, 244
Lijang 13
Lille 13
Lim, Madeline –186
Literature/ Literary arts 8, 16, 19, 21
Little India 156, 164,165, 166, 169,174–7, 246
Liverpool 100, 101
London 4, 6, 12, 16, 40, 41, 67, 70, 73, 74, 95, 109, 114, 126, 159, 181, 182, 195
Los Angeles 4, 6, 12, 28, 64–66, 70, 73, 74, 132, 133, 148, 149
Luxembourg 13
Lyotard, Francois 68–9

MacCannell, Dean 33, 135, 144
Mackintosh, Charles Rennie 68, 86, 88, 94,100, 106, 110–116, 235, 244
Madrid 12, 73, 126, 134, 136, 138, 141, 242
Malaysia/Malaya 9, 77, 87, 158–63
Malay(s) 158–160, 188, 240
Manchester 13, 127, 135, 138, 212, 226, 248
Marshall, David 147
Marx, K. 49–50
Massachusetts Museum of Modern Art (MassMoMA) 45, 128, 132, 219
Massey, Doreen 10, 12, 57
McDonald sisters 88, 118
McKinsey and Co. 97, 248
McLellan Galleries 87
Mecca 6
Mechanics Institutes 195–6, 223
Media 26, 31, 46, 62, 68, 207, 225, 229
Melbourne 6, 13, 20, 42, 77, 78,181, 182,195,196,197, 209, 210, 211, 212, 213, 215, 220, 248, 249

Merchant City 94, 97–8, 110, 116, 118, 240
Mexico 9, 60
Mexico City 73, 74
Miami 73
Milan 6
Miles Better campaign (Glasgow) 79, 96
Mills, C.A. 39
Milwaukee 13
Minneapolis 97, 101, 248
MITA (Ministry of Information, Technology and the Arts [Singapore]) 20
Mitchell Library 88
Mitchell, Jan 213–4, 215, 248
Modern/modernity 23, 34, 93, 251
Moines 13
Montreal 6
Mooney, Gerry 104
Morris, Meaghan 147
Mumbai 6
Museo de Belles Artes (Bilbao, Spain) 133, 141, 246
Museum(s) 14, 16, 17, 24, 30, 34, 38, 101, 104, 108, 116, 138, 139, 150, 189, 208, 210, 212, 224, 225, 247
Music 8, 9, 14, 16, 17, 18, 46, 48, 68,116, 207, 216, 217
Myerscough, John 15, 97, 104, 106, 179

Nash, Catherine 78
Nash, June 33
National Arts Council (Singapore) 173, 179,186
Neo-classical economics 25–29
Neo-liberal(ism) –25, 47, 56, 59, 60, 76–7, 104, 119, 204, 209
Nervion River (Bilbao, Spain) 123, 137, 139, 246
Netherlands/Holland 77, 89
New Asian Landscapes 170–9, 238
New International Division of Labour (NIDL) 56, 57, 58, 59–60, 79, 126–8, 135, 162, 235
New Times 70
New York 3, 4, 6, 12, 45, 47, 73, 74, 96, 123, 128, 129, 130, 133, 140, 148,181, 182,187, 219, 269/223

Newcastle 11, 13, 195,199, 212, 219
Ng, Josef 186, 187
Night club 15
North America 21, 23, 33, 40, 58, 63, 86,
    125, 187,193,195, 201, 212, 213

Objectified cultural capital 25, 51–54, 80,
    93, 101, 105, 108, 118, 123, 142,
    152, 229, 230, 235, 238, 247
Ockman, Joan 124, 148
OECD 10, 12, 62, 107, 119
Olympics 17
Orientalism 157, 169
Oteiza, Jorge 140
Othering 24, 32–33, 157
Owen Sound (Ontario, Ca) 13

Pacific Islanders 52–3
Pacione, Michael 91, 95
Page and Park 112
Pako Festa 215–8, 230
Palmer, Bob 105
PAP (People's Action Party, Singapore)
    156, 161–2, 189, 247
Paris 4, 6, 12, 35, 73, 74, 85
People's Palace 88, 103, 117, 244
Performing arts/ performance 4, 5, 12, 16,
    17, 18, 21, 27, 41, 45, 49, 62, 109,
    155, 179–189, 193, 208, 216, 224,
    226, 247
Photography 8, 14
Piore and Sabel 63
Pittsburgh 127
Place making 24
Pollock 91, 92
Popayan 6,
Porto 13
    Portugal 77
Post-colonial/ism 5, 33, 41, 43, 57, 58,
    77–79,155–189, 202–3, 236, 237
Post-Fordist/ism 56, 57, 58–59, 65, 70,
    143,149–151, 251
Post-modern/ity 5, 23, 24, 34, 41, 43,
    56, 57, 58, 63–71, 72, 78, 123,
    124,143–4, 155, 236, 237
Post-structuralism 38, 156
Post-tourist 72
Potts, Jason 25

Poulakidas, George 148
Powell River (BC, Ca) 13
Power, Dominic 17
Prague 13
Pratt, Andrew 16–17
Print media/newspapers 16
Public art 24, 44, 117, 155, 213–4, 240,
    248
Public goods 26, 203, 204, 207
Publishing 14, 19, 21, 26, 46, 48

Race 39, 42
Radio 8, 9, 16, 48, 62, 108, 115, 197–198,
    202, 204, 229
Raffles, Stamford 158–9, 164
Red Clydeside 89, 90, 93, 95
Red Dear 13
Reed, Peter 97
Regina (Saskatchewan, Ca) 13
Re-imagining the/a city 96, 101, 107, 109,
    110–111, 118, 132, 214, 218, 243,
    244, 245, 246, 247, 248
Renaissance City (Singapore) 173, 179,
    180, 183
Restructuring 4, 57, 58, 85, 88, 101, 127,
    208, 236
Reykjavik 13
Richards, Greg 36–7, 38, 49, 53
Rio de Janeiro 131
    Rose, Damaris 40
Riviere-du-loup (Quebec Ca.) 13
Rome 6
Roodhouse, Simon 34, 227
Rotterdam 13
Rowse, Tim 200

Said, Edward 157
Saint-Jean-Port-Joli (Quebec, Ca) 12
Salamanca 13
Salzburg 128
San Francisco 48
Santiago 13
Santiago de Compostela 13
Sao Paulo 73, 74
Sassen, Saskia 72, 73–4, 75
Sauer, Carl 38
Scotland 77, 87, 91, 107, 114, 119, 125,
    187

Scott, Allan 28, 44, 69–70
Sen, Ong Keng –185
Serra, Richard 132, 133, 140
Seoul 73, 74
Service Industry/ Sector Economy 19, 36,
    40, 58, 61–2, 85, 92, 99, 119, 123,
    149, 160, 228, 235, 242, 243
Seville 6, 125, 129
Shanghai 12, 73
Sharma, Haresh 187
Shenzen 13
Ship building 87, 89, 91, 107, 126, 127, 138
Simulacrum 5, 69, 248–51
Singapore 4, 5, 9, 12, 13, 14, 20–21, 27,
    39, 48, 49, 53, 55, 58, 60, 61, 62,
    63, 73, 74, 75, 77, 78–80, 155–190,
    193, 209, 214, 235, 238, 239, 240,
    242, 246–47
Slum clearance 90–91, 94, 164–6
Smith, Michael 72
Smith, Neil 40
Sociology 23, 24, 44–49
Socio-spatial polarisation 90, 92
Soja, Edward 43, 64
Sorkin, Michael 65, 151
South America 87, 236
Spain 5, 9, 13, 17–18, 19, 49, 59, 61, 62,
    75, 77,123–52, 187
Spectacle 5, 33, 41, 44, 60, 64, 65–6, 123,
    143,144–9, 152, 213
Special Broadcasting Service (SBS
    Australia) 204, 208, 218
Spence, Sir Basil 91
Sport 8, 15, 116
St Petersburg 131
Stockholm 12, 17
Stoke-on-Trent 100
Substation, The (Singapore) 187, 247
Sustainable/ility 7, 24, 25, 57, 81, 94, 109,
    111, 116, 118–120, 124, 130, 137,
    143, 150, 151–52, 179, 183, 193,
    228–31, 240–48
Sweden 17, 19, 89
Switzerland 9
Sydney 11, 19–20, 39, 41, 42–3, 73, 74,
    75, 77, 195,196, 210,197, 209, 212
Symbolic economy 45–6, 57, 63–71, 78,
    101, 115, 155, 180,193, 235–6

Taipai 73
Tamney, J.B. 180
Tan, Alvin 187
Television/TV 8, 9, 16, 28, 31, 46, 62,
    96,108, 115, 201–2, 204, 207, 210,
    229
Thatcher, Margaret 97, 104
The Necessary Stage 156, 247
Theatre(s) 15, 16, 34, 101, 104, 116, 126,
    189, 196, 200, 241, 247, 248, 251
Theatreworks 185
Theme parks 64
Thessalonika 13
Throsby, David 23, 29–31, 49, 50, 53
Thunder Bay (Ontario) 13
Timorous Beasties 117
Tokyo 73, 74
Tong, Goh Chok 226/180, 230/184
Toronto 12, 40, 132, 217, 218
Tourist(m) 14, 16, 19, 32, 56, 71–2, 78,
    96, 101, 108, 109, 136, 138, 150,
    163, 169, 180, 206, 208, 212, 217,
    236, 241, 242, 243
Tourism Studies 23, 24, 25, 32, 49
Tourist gaze 24, 35, 37, 156
Trowse, Ruth 26–8

UNESCO 6, 8, 9, 10, 31
United Kingdom (UK) 5, 9, 13, 15–17,
    47, 59, 60, 61, 62, 64, 91, 108,
    115,155, 199
United States of America (USA) 9, 12, 13,
    14, 46, 47, 59, 61, 62, 64, 75, 77,
    87, 101, 115, 123, 125, 129, 132,
    179,197, 236
Urry, John 35, 36, 38
Usher, Robin 220

Value 3, 5, 6, 8, 21, 23, 25, 28, 30, 31, 33,
    50–53, 63, 82, 93, 114, 115, 116,
    155, 156, 176–9, 183,189, 195,
    202, 204–5, 207, 210, 214, 222,
    226–231, 235–239
Vancouver 12, 39, 40, 41, 75, 171,
    220/174
Venice 131
Viar, Javier 141

Visual arts 8, 9, 14, 17, 18, 26, 62, 116,
          117

Wark, Mackenzie 147
Washington DC 48
Waterfront redevelopment 35, 54, 55, 193,
          208, 209, 211, 212–15, 218, 227,
          235, 236, 240, 247
Watson, Sophie 39
Weimer 12
Welfare good 23
West Indies 86
Williams, C.C. 104, 107
Williams, Raymond 5
Wisconsin 34
Wilson, Elizabeth 67–8

Wishart, Ruth 104
Wollongong 13, 199
Women/Females 34, 37, 38, 40, 41, 60,
          67–8, 87, 90, 91,163
Workers City 101, 102–6
World/Global Cities 12, 56, 57, 72–5, 149,
          193, 217, 236

Xian 13

Yeoh, Brenda 174, 177–8
Yew, Lee Kuan 207–08/161–2,179

Zukin, Sharon 6, 36, 38, 45–6, 47
Zulaika, Joseba 126, 130, 145–7
Zurich 73, 74